This is the first English-language collection of essays on modern German history with a generational theme. Responding to a recent shift in social historical writing away from an exclusive focus on class towards an interest in other 'imagined communities' of ethnicity, gender and generation, it addresses, first, the extraordinary power and persistence of a German tradition of youthful rebellion extending from the *Sturm und Drang* in the eighteenth century to the student revolts of 1968. At the same time it analyses the impact of the dramatic ruptures and discontinuities in modern German history on the formation and interaction of successive historical cohorts. Using a variety of different approaches, including literary and oral history, the collection pays particular attention to the way generational identities interacted with those of class and gender. The book adds to our understanding of generations, the balance between continuity and discontinuity in modern German history, the generational roots of National Socialism and the Hitler Youth generation's impact on East and West German society.

GENERATIONS IN CONFLICT

GENERATIONS
IN CONFLICT

*Youth revolt and generation formation
in Germany 1770–1968*

EDITED BY

MARK ROSEMAN

University of Keele

CAMBRIDGE
UNIVERSITY PRESS

Published by the Press Syndicate of the University of Cambridge
The Pitt Building, Trumpington Street, Cambridge CB1 1RP
40 West 20th Street, New York, NY 10011–4211, USA
10 Stamford Road, Oakleigh, Melbourne 3166, Australia

First published 1995

Printed in Great Britain at the University Press, Cambridge

A catalogue record for this book is available from the British Library

Library of Congress cataloguing in publication data
Generations in conflict: youth revolt and generation formation in Germany, 1770–1968
/ edited by Mark Roseman
p.   cm.
Includes rev., papers from a Germany History Society Conference
'The Generation Game' held at the University of Keele in April 1991 – Pref.
ISBN 0 521 44183 8
1. Youth movement – Germany – History.
2. Youth – Germany – Attitudes – History.
3. Student movement – Germany – History.
4. Socialism and youth – Germany – History.   I. Roseman, Mark.
HN.19.G4   1995
943'.00825 – dc20   94-21000   CIP

ISBN 0 521 44183 8 hardback

CE

Contents

About the contributors

Richard Bessel, born 1948, is Senior Lecturer in History at the Open University. He is the author of *Germany after the First World War* and *Political violence and the rise of Nazism* and editor of *Life in the Third Reich*. He is also co-editor of the journal *German History*.

Jacob Borut, born 1956, is based at the Yad Vashem Institute in Jerusalem. He is the author of several chapters and articles on the Jewish communities of nineteenth- and twentieth-century Germany and an editor of the Institute's *Pinkas Hakehillot Germania*.

Michael Buddrus, born 1957, grew up in the GDR and worked at the University of Rostock and the Akademie der Wissenschaften, Berlin, before transferring to the University of Siegen after the fall of the Berlin wall. He is now attached to the Außenstelle Potsdam of the Institut für Zeitgeschichte. He is the author of *Zur Geschichte der Hitlerjugend 1922–1933*, and *Die Organisation 'Dienst für Deutschland'. Arbeitsdienst und Militarisierung in der DDR* and co-author of *Deutsche Jugend 1933–1945. Eine Dokumentation*.

Heinz Bude, born 1954, is a writer living in Berlin and a member of the Hamburg Institut für Sozialforschung. His books include *Deutsche Karrieren. Lebenskonstruktionen sozialer Aufsteiger aus der Flak-helfer-Generation*; *Bilanz der Nachfolge. Die Bundesrepublik und der Nationalsozialismus*; and *Im Glanz der Bilder. Der Sammler Peter Ludwig*. He co-edited *Radikalisierte Aufklärung. Studentenbewegung und Soziologie in Berlin 1965 bis 1970*.

Rainer Elkar, born 1945, is a Lecturer in Social and Economic History at the University of Siegen and Academic Director of the Institute for European Regional Research. He has published numerous books and articles on the history of the early modern period and in particular on the history of crafts, educational history and regional history. He is co-editor of the *Jahrbuch für Regionalgeschichte*.

Elizabeth Harvey, born 1957, is Lecturer in History at the University of Liverpool. She is the author of *Youth welfare and social democracy in Weimar Germany: the work of Walter Friedländer* and *Youth and the welfare state in Weimar Germany*.

Peter Lambert, born 1956, is lecturer in Modern European History at the University of Wales, Aberystwyth. He has published widely on German historiography and questions of German identity and is currently engaged in writing a study of the politics of German historians since 1914.

Alexander von Plato, born 1942, is director of the Institut für Geschichte und Biographie at the Fernuniversität, Hagen. He is the author of *'Der Verlierer geht nicht leer aus'. Betriebsräte geben zu Protokoll*, and co-author (with W. Meinecke) of *Alte Heimat, Neue Zeit* and (with R. Eckhart) of *Wendezeiten-Zeitenwende. Zu 'Entnazifizierung' und 'Entstalinisierung'*. He is co-editor of *'Wir kriegen jetzt andere Zeiten'. Auf der Suche nach der Erfahrung des Volkes in nachfaschistischen Ländern* and an editor of the journal *BIOS. Zeitschrift für Biographenforschung*.

Dagmar Reese, born 1952, is a historical sociologist based in Berlin and currently engaged in the *Förderprogram Frauenforschung des Senates Berlins*. She is the author of *'Straff, aber nicht stramm – Herb, aber nicht derb'. Zur Vergesellschaftung der Mädchen im Bund Deutscher Mädel im sozialkulturellen Vergleich zweier Milieus* and co-author of *Rationale Beziehungen? Geschlechterverhältnisse im Rationalisierungsprozeß*.

Jürgen Reulecke, born 1940, is Professor of Modern and Contemporary History at the University of Siegen. He is the author of numerous studies on the history of social policy, social reform, the labour and youth movements.

Mark Roseman, born 1958, is Senior Lecturer in History at the University of Keele. He is the author of *Recasting the Ruhr: manpower, economic recovery and labour relations in the German mining industry 1945–1958* and *Neither punitive nor powerless: Western Europe and the division of Germany*.

Cornelie Usborne, born 1942, is Senior Lecturer in History at the Roehampton Institute, London and is currently Wellcome Research Fellow. She is the author of *The politics of the body in Weimar Germany*.

Joachim Whaley, born 1954, is a fellow of Gonville and Caius, Cambridge. He is the author of *Religious toleration and social change in Hamburg 1525–1819* and editor of *Mirrors of mortality: studies in the social history of death*.

Acknowledgements

The origins of this collection date back to a German History Society Conference 'The Generation Game' which I organised at the University of Keele in April 1991. That conference would not have been possible without the very generous assistance of the Goethe Institute Manchester, and its then director, Dr Murjahn. Thanks for financial assistance are due also to the British Academy, the Committee of the German History Society under its then chairman Richard Evans and the History Department at Keele. I would like to thank all those who took part in the conference, either as discussants or from the floor, for making it such a stimulating event.

Since then, all the papers have been very substantially revised and a number of new contributions added. I am very grateful to CUP's (anonymous) readers for their helpful and constructive comments and to our editor, Richard Fisher, for his patience and support.

This is in no sense of the word a *Festschrift*, but because I and so many of the contributors either knew him well personally as a friend or colleague or benefited from his many important publications on youth policy, youth resistance and more widely on German social history, this collection is affectionately dedicated to the memory of Detlev Peukert.

Abbreviations

AfS	*Archiv für Sozialgeschichte*
ADLV-Zeitung	*Deutsche Lehrerinnenzeitung*
ALD	Archive of the Landesoberbergamt, Dortmund
BAK	Federal Archive, Koblenz
BBA	Archive of the German Mining Museum, Bochum
BDF	Federation of German Women's Associations
BDM	*Bund deutscher Mädel* (League of German Girls)
BfM	*Bund für Mutterschutz*
DGBA	Archive of German Trade Union Federation, Düsseldorf
DJ	*Deutsches Jungvolk*
FDJ	*Freie Deutsche Jugend*
GDST	Archive of the Gesamtverband des deutschen Steinkohlenbergbaus, Essen
HJ	*Hitler-Jugend* (Hitler Youth)
HSTAD	Hauptstaatsarchiv Düsseldorf
HZ	*Historische Zeitschrift*
GG	*Geschichte und Gesellschaft*
IfGA/ZPA	Institut für Geschichte der Arbeiterbewegung. Zentrales Parteiarchiv, Berlin
IVB	Industrieverband Bergbau (Miners' Union)
IGB	Industriegewerkschaft Bergbau (Miners' Union)
IGBEA	Archive of the Mining Union, Bochum
JA	Jugendarchiv beim Institut für zeitgeschichtliche Jugendforschung, Berlin
JRM	*Jungstreiter-Rundbrief der Mädels*
JSH	*Journal of the History of Sexuality*
KPD	Communist party
LAS	Schleswig-Holsteinisches Landesarchiv in Schleswig

NSDAP	*Nationalsozialistische Deutsche Arbeiterpartei* (Nazi party)
ObaD	Oberbergamt Dortmund
SBZ	Soviet Zone of Occupation
SED	Socialist Unity party
SPD	Social Democratic party
SMAD	Soviet Military Administration of Germany
VfSW	*Vierteljahresschrift für Sozial- und Wirtschaftsgeschichte*
WWA	Westfälisches Wirtschaftsarchiv
ZdKW	*Zahlen der Kohlenwirtschaft*

CHAPTER I

Introduction: generation conflict and German history 1770–1968

Mark Roseman

I

Why adopt a generational perspective on modern German history? One obvious reason is the striking persistence of youthful rebellion in Germany. From the 1770s onwards, German society found its values and norms subjected to recurrent and intense challenge by rebellious youth, initially by the young writers of the *Sturm und Drang* in the late eighteenth century, then by the youthful enthusiasts of the Young Germany movement in the 1830s and 1840s, later by the thousands of youngsters who climbed the Hohe Meißner mountain, turning their backs on Wilhelmine Germany. In the post-1918 era youthful separatism reached its zenith, with almost half of all German youth organised in some group or other. The Weimar Republic's short life was punctuated by the regular spectacle of youngsters taking to the streets and its demise was heralded by young protesters in brown shirts, carrying their torchlit zealotry through the length and breadth of Germany. And more recently, few voices of the international youth movement in the 1960s attained the self-confident, iconoclastic authority of a Rudi Dutschke or rejected the system with quite such uncompromising ruthlessness as did an Ulrike Meinhof.

A second reason is that few other nations have experienced such a succession of dramatic breaks in their historical narrative. Germany emerged as a nation only in 1871, industrialising at breakneck pace to become one of the world's leading powers by the end of the century. Then in 1914 came an increasingly total war, followed after four years by defeat, upheaval, the violent overthrow of the old regime and the creation of Germany's first democracy. Less than

I am indebted to John Gaffney, Liz Harvey, Joan Roseman, Cornelie Usborne, David Vincent and Joachim Whaley for their many comments and advice.

fourteen years after the signing of the Weimar Constitution,
Germany experienced a new and even more radical change with the
creation of the 'Third Reich'. A dozen years further on, and the
Fatherland suffered a more total defeat than has ever been endured
by an advanced industrial nation. After the interregnum of the
occupation, Germany again found itself flung headlong on a new
course, or rather two new courses. The West had a second try at
democracy and experienced the dramatic social and economic
transformation wrought by the economic miracle; the East under-
went a new set of radical social and political changes under the
banner of Real Existing Socialism. The result of each of these
ruptures was that successive generations grew up under social and
political conditions that differed markedly, sometimes fundamentally, from those of their predecessors. Few other national histories offer such obvious potential for dividing one cohort from
another and rendering them unable to communicate across the gulf
between their respective socialisations and experiences.

Juxtaposing these two facts – the tradition of youthful revolt and
the recurrence of discontinuities – makes clear that German history
offers fascinating ground on which to analyse generational identities
and generation conflict. But it also presents something of a paradox.
The long line of youthful rebellions, often apparently so similar in
form and style, would suggest that some sustained ideology or
inherited cultural pattern had inclined successive generations to rise
up against their parents. But looking at such turning points as 1918,
1933 or 1945 the dominant impression is of changes in nation and
society so abrupt as to divide one generation from the next. A
culturally and socially inherited tradition of youthful rebellion,
then, or a history of discontinuities, of cohorts unable to communicate with each other? In attempting to answer this question the
present volume aims to identify not only why generation conflict
takes place but also its relationship to the wider patterns of modern
German history.

Within those wider patterns the problem of National Socialism of
course commands the historian's particular attention. Here, too, the
generational theme is an important one. A number of scholars have
seen the National Socialist movement as essentially a generational
rebellion. Some have identified a long tradition of over-confident
youthful recklessness, nationalism and intolerance leading from
Sturm und Drang to *Sturmabteilung* and Dachau. Others have empha-

sised the transformative experiences of total war and defeat and have traced National Socialism's origins to the specific cohort mentality of the generations forged by trench warfare and the home front. Thus here again the notion of a long tradition of youthful rebellion vies with an emphasis on rupture and discontinuity. In taking up these issues this collection aims to shed new light on the generational roots and impact of National Socialism.

II

It is a surprising fact that this is the first English-language collection on German history to adopt a generational theme. Why have historians been so slow to take up the issue? In the case of British scholars, it is partly because they have had so little first hand experience of real generational revolt. Elsewhere, interest in generations was often the result of historians being confronted by some example of youthful rebellion in their own days.[1] This was evident in Germany in the 1920s, when an increasingly organised and noisy youth inspired Karl Mannheim to produce the first fully articulated historical theory of generations.[2] And it was again the case in the 1970s when, in the aftermath of the student revolts, historians in Germany and the USA were galvanised into looking for earlier incarnations of generational conflict.[3] In Britain, youthful rebellion has been so muted and unpolitical that the issue has had great difficulty forcing its way into the academic consciousness at all, even among British historians of countries such as Germany, where the tradition of youthful revolt was so much better established.[4]

In any case, generations have always seemed rather flimsy craft compared with the sturdy steamships of social class. Social historians, generally adopting a materialist approach, have tended to

[1] Alan B. Spitzer, 'The historical problems of generations', *American Historical Review*, vol. 78 (1973), p. 1353.
[2] Karl Mannheim, 'Das Problem der Generationen', *Kölner Vierteljahreshefte für Soziologie*, vol. 7 (1928), pp. 157–180 and pp. 309–350.
[3] Philip Abrams, '*Rites de Passage*: the conflict of generations in industrial society', *Journal of Contemporary History*, vol. 5 (1970), 1, p. 175; see also the introduction to D. Dowe, *Jugendprotest und Generationenkonflikte in Europa im 20. Jahrhundert. Deutschland, England, Frankreich und Italien im Vergleich* (Bonn 1986).
[4] On the other hand, because a subpolitical proletarian youthful 'deviancy' was so marked in Britain, British *sociologists* have long taken an active interest in the subject. Their work, in particular that of the Centre for Contemporary Cultural Studies in Birmingham, has been highly influential in Germany. Cf. Stuart Hall and Tony Jefferson, *Resistance through rituals: youth subcultures in post-war Britain* (London 1976).

assume that social groupings attain real identity and force only if they share some clearly defined material interest. Since it was not clear that there was any enduring material interest that could unite one generation and divide it from another, it was hard to see much significance in generational divisions. And certainly the hold which class conflict held on the collective imagination of capitalist societies from the mid-nineteenth century until well into the post-1945 era seemed to bear out the view that the only conflict worth talking about was that between the owners of the means of production and those who possessed nothing but their labour.

Over the last few years, however, historians have begun to concern themselves more intensively with groupings, collectives and boundaries other than social class. In part this is because the end of the cold war and the collapse of Soviet Communism has robbed Marxist-influenced academic discourse of some of its political bite (rather oddly so, since the survival of the sclerotic regime in the Kremlin was surely never the proof of the quality of Marx's analysis). But the international events of the late 1980s in fact served only to reinforce an intellectual shift that was already underway. The influence of Michel Foucault, Jacques Donzelot and other French critical theorists has been one important ingredient in this process.[5] Foucault's work, in particular, has increased historians' awareness of the power inherent in establishing the language and categories used to describe society. Against this general background, recent interest in nations and nationalism has revealed how powerfully an imagined common identity, in this case ethnic or national identity, can shape collective behaviour. The result has been a new sense of the degree to which class, as a perceived and felt entity, as a way of defining common interest and common purpose, shares with other types of social grouping the status of an 'imagined community'.[6]

The corollary of these various insights has been a new interest in the way modern societies classify and categorise themselves along lines of ethnicity, race, religion, gender and, most relevant for our purposes, generation. In the context of German history, a small but growing number of scholars over the last ten years have begun not

[5] See e.g. Michel Foucault, *Discipline and punish: the birth of the prison* (New York 1977), and see the discussion of Foucault's influence and also that of Norbert Elias in Detlev Peukert, *Grenzen der Sozialdisziplinierung. Aufstieg und Krise der deutschen Jugendfürsorge 1878–1932* (Cologne 1986), pp. 18ff.; Jacques Donzelot, *The policing of families* (London 1980).

[6] The term was coined by Benedict Anderson, *Imagined communities: reflections on the origins and spread of nationalism* (London 1983).

only to take issues of youth and generation more seriously but also to adopt new questions and approaches. Whereas the older German studies, for example, often tended to focus on the organisational level of the youth movement and rather take for granted the movement's claim to speak for the younger generation as a whole, newer work has cast its net wider, to include the wider social and ideological realities and limits to generational identities. Historians have also begun to consider the process by which the German state defined and refined the generational categories, at the 'social disciplining' of young people and at youthful resistance to such social engineering. These new questions and approaches inform many of the contributions to the present volume.

What are generations? The starting-point for any analysis must be that 'generation' is, first and foremost, a word aspiring to catch social phenomena in its net rather than a clear-cut social reality for which we happen to have coined a term. Like most labels for social groupings it leads a double life as a term in common parlance and an instrument of historical and social analysis. Perhaps more than most it has been used with very varying meanings and very different levels of precision. Moreover, because historically generations have been much less the subject of theory than has social class, the historian of generations cannot have recourse to the same well-rehearsed set of understandings. At one level, therefore to ask 'What is a generation?' would be to miss the point. There is no single phenomenon.

Even so, we can at least sketch out some of the concept's boundaries and parameters. At its least ambitious, though perhaps most widely applicable level, it can be used to describe any age-defined subgroup within a given wider population which has some recognisable and distinct characteristic. This is the approach taken here by Jacob Borut's analysis of the Jewish community at the end of the nineteenth century. Borut begins with the observation that the 1880s and 1890s saw the Jewish community become far more assertive, self-confident and anti-assimilationist. His biographical analysis of contemporary Jewish activists reveals that the advocates of the new approach were considerably younger than the defenders of the old cautious line. He argues persuasively that the age split revealed different mentalities between those socialised before and after Jewish emancipation. The former continued to regard their religious freedom as a luxury and tended to keep their heads down; the

latter took their religious freedoms for granted and asserted community interests more aggressively.

It is clear that these two 'generations' are very much secondary
phenomena. Though there are, as Borut argues, parallels with
developments in the wider community, the generations as described
exist only within the confines of one religious subgrouping and are
constituted simply by the fact that on a given issue – in this case how
best to pursue the community's corporate interest – the experiences
of younger and older activists led them in different directions. The
great value of Borut's approach lies thus not in defining a clear-cut
social grouping but in introducing a model of delayed causation.
The historian's natural inclination, confronted with a political
change, is to seek some contemporaneous or directly preceding
cause. Borut reminds us that the cause may lie some thirty to forty
years earlier, in some decisive change from the experience of the
outgoing to that of the incoming cohorts. Whilst a small number of
other historians of Germany have adopted similar methodologies,
Volker Berghahn and Detlev Peukert being notable examples,[7]
there is scope for a great deal more work to be done on these lines.

Since the nineteenth century, a number of sociologists and to a
lesser extent historians have tried to use generations as a more
ambitious category, whereby society as a whole is divided up into a
number of generations. Discounting some early theories which followed a genealogical model according to which the next generation
would emerge almost mechanically every fifteen to twenty years or
so, most models of generations fall into one of two categories.[8]
Sociologists have tended to conceptualise generations as distinct
phases in the life-cycle, for example, 'childhood', 'youth',
'adulthood' and 'old age'. Conflict takes place between young and
old, for instance, or youth and adults, along lines determined by the
roles and situation characteristic of each life phase. In contrast to the
genealogical model, individuals move from one generational grouping to the next as they age their way through the life-cycle. For
society as a whole, the demarcation lines between the generations
will remain relatively fixed, evolving only as a result of the relatively

---

[7] Volker R. Berghahn, *The Americanisation of German industry* (Leamington Spa 1986); Detlev
Peukert, *The Weimar Republic: the crisis of classical modernity* (London 1991).
[8] See Irmtraud Götz von Olenhusen, *Jugendreich, Gottesreich, Deutsches Reich. Junge Generation,
Religion und Politik 1928–1933* (Cologne 1987), pp. 14–18; Ortega y Gasset, *The modern theme*
(London 1931).

long-term processes of change which affect social definitions of the
life-cycle.

Sociologies of youth, old age and so on offer many insights but
usually fall short of providing direct models for the kind of generational phenomena in which historians are interested. For one
thing, there is the bewildering diversity of explanations – psychoanalytical,[9] structural–functionalist,[10] phenomenological[11] and so
on – as to how and why particular life-phases take on specific
characters.[12] For another, there is the problem that sociologists often
seek to explain enduring universal features of modern society,
whereas the historian is interested in the nationally specific or the
points where conflicts or rebellion come to a head. Often, too,
life-phase models are static, lacking the dimension of change. And
they tend to be more efficient at explaining the common characteristics of *individual* behaviour on the part of the members of each
life-phase than why at some points a collective consciousness or
group identity emerges.

Historians have therefore tended to conceptualise generations in a
second way, namely as historical cohorts. Here generations are
defined by key experiences; the demarcation lines etched into the
societal age pyramid are the dates on which formative experiences
take place. According to this view, the individual's steady progress
through the life-cycle has no impact on his or her generational
identity. That individual remains always on one or other side of a
particular historical generational divide. For society as a whole, the
generational divide between any two cohorts steadily ages as the
years pass following the defining event or experience. At some point,
the older generation will disappear altogether. The most comprehensive and sophisticated model of historical cohorts is still that
evolved by Karl Mannheim during the 1920s.[13] His definition
introduced a number of powerful distinctions, most notably between
the cohort characterised by common experiences and characteristics
(what Marx would have called a generation in itself) and the self-
conscious cohort that attained a real self-conscious identity. Many of

9 Erik Erikson, *Childhood and society* (Harmondsworth 1965).
10 E.g. S. N. Eisenstadt, *From generation to generation: age groups and social structure* (New York
   1966).
11 E.g. Helmut Schelsky, *Die skeptische Generation* (Düsseldorf 1963, special edition).
12 See also Hartmut M. Griese, *Sozialwissenschaftliche Jugendtheorien. Eine Einführung* (Weinheim, Basel 1982).
13 Mannheim, 'Problem der Generationen'.

the essays in this volume explicitly or implicitly benefit from his analysis.

There remains, however, no common agreement as to the point at which the decisive experience of a particular cohort takes place; Mannheim assumed it is during adolescence; others, such as Glen H. Elder, have argued that a cohort may share certain early childhood experiences and that these can be decisive.[14] Some analysts, indeed, challenge the notion of a formative set of experiences altogether and adopt a cumulative experiential model.[15] Apart from such uncertainty, the chief problem with cohort models is that – unless one is arguing that there are persistent discontinuities of a consistent kind – it is not obvious that they explain why in a particular culture there should be marked, frequent and powerful recurrence of generation conflict. And a cohort model alone will not explain why it is so often the life-phase group *youth* which is at the centre of generational conflict.

The choice between the life-phase or cohort model of generation conflict is closely linked to the question posed at the beginning of this chapter about continuity or discontinuity in German history. If the persistence of generational conflict is essentially about a tradition, and about inherited patterns of behaviour, then it may well be that the enduring character of particular life-phase groups (or perhaps of the relationship between them) is the decisive factor in defining identities and provoking conflict. On the other hand, if *discontinuities* are decisive, this suggests that conflict arises because of the contrasts between the formative experiences of the cohorts involved. Or perhaps the choice is a false one, belying a more complex interaction between cultural continuity and cohort specificities. Continuity or discontinuity, life-phase groups or cohorts? In introducing the other contributions to this volume, the remaining part of this chapter seeks to answer these questions.

---

[14] Glen H. Elder and Avsholm Caspi, 'Persönliche Entwicklung und sozialer Wandel. Die Entstehung der Lebensverlaufsforschung', in Karl Ulrich Mayer (ed.), *Lebensverläufe und sozialer Wandel* (special issue of *Kölner Zeitschrift für Soziologie und Sozialpsychologie*) vol. 31 (1990), pp. 22–57.

[15] See for example M. Jennings, M. Kent and R. Jansen, 'Die Jugendlichen in der Bundesrepublik', *Politische Vierteljahresschrift*, vol. 17 (1976), pp. 317–343; Kendall J. Baker and Russell J. Dalton, *Germany transformed: political culture and the new politics* (Cambridge 1981), pp. 45–50. Jacob Borut's essay implicitly treats the age-range between the 20s and mid-30s as the period in which decisive political experiences are garnered.

III

Joachim Whaley's essay immediately challenges many of the schematic distinctions we have just made. Whaley describes how the poets and dramatists of eighteenth-century Germany manufactured an image of youth which was to exert extraordinary influence on German culture until well into the twentieth century.[16] Using three celebrated works of the late eighteenth and early nineteenth centuries as examples, Whaley shows how, despite the coming and going of a succession of literary modes, German writers from the *Sturm und Drang* onwards continually returned to the theme of youth as a spiritual force somehow outside adult society, enjoying a special mission of redemption. This idea of youthful redemption went hand in hand with the idea that natural or spiritual forces needed to assert themselves against the purely rational or material. Youth's mission was thus conceptualised primarily as an aesthetic one, bringing pure aesthetics into a world of philistinism and materialism, yet, as Whaley shows, this was an argument that could take political overtones. It was also one that might be linked to the nationalist cause.

As subsequent essays demonstrate, the power of this myth and the recurrent belief that youth somehow stood outside society, representing an aesthetically pure and more moral alternative capable of redeeming contemporary society from its current ills, was an important and distinctive feature of German development. Society's perception of youth, and indeed youth's perception of itself, was rarely just of a particular generation. It was always permeated by a sense of mission and alternative possibility. What is distinctive about 'generation conflict' in Germany, then, is as much the way a particular generation, youth, became a cultural label, a projection or repository, as the actual conflict or differences between real social groupings.

This interaction between literary ideal and social identities is the subject matter of Rainer Elkar's account of the Young Germany movement in the pre-1848 era. Using an outstanding array of sources, Elkar shows how the intellectual world of a small group of

---

16 There is a sizeable German literature on the youth myth. See Thomas Koebner, Rolf-Peter Janz and Frank Trommler (eds.), '*Mit uns zieht die neue Zeit*'. *Der Mythos Jugend* (Frankfurt 1985); Hans Heinrich Muchow, *Jugend und Zeitgeist. Morphologie der Kulturpubertät* (Reinbek 1962); Walter Rüegg (ed.), *Kulturkritik und Jugendkult* (Frankfurt 1974).

literati and intellectual friendship clubs in the third quarter of the
eighteenth century spread to university and *Gymnasium* culture. The
cult of youth, its linkage to a particular language of moral and
aesthetic redemption, thus graduated from a few intellectual circles
to become the common language for generations of students in the
early nineteenth century. Then, during the 1830s and early 1840s,
Elkar (as, indeed, the authorities at the time) detects a further shift.
Out of this widely disseminated literary culture, Young Germany
became something more – an expression of identity among young
Germans. This new sense of broad group identity was coupled with
a growing self-confidence and an increasingly political consciousness. The imagined community 'Young Germany' and the reality of
many young Germans thus moved closer together.

At first sight, what is happening here is the literary manufacture
of a generation. Yet as Whaley and Elkar show, this is far from the
whole story. In the first place, it is clear that fantasising about youth
was triggered partly by changes in everyday social definitions of how
youth, as a phase in the life-cycle, was to be lived. In fact, Whaley
echoes John Gillis in arguing that it was in the second half of the
eighteenth century that youth in a modern sense emerged at all.[17] It
was only then that social, cultural and legal norms began to define
the age-span of youth more narrowly and uniformly.[18] As well as
becoming better defined, the life-phase youth (initially only among
the more affluent bourgeoisie) was becoming increasingly associated
with, in Rainer Elkar's words, a 'moratorium', a period of 'time
out', when individuals with most of the biological and intellectual
capacities of adulthood were nevertheless free of the responsibilities
of adulthood and were not, or not fully, integrated into working life.
In two senses this moratorium was crucial to understanding the
evolution of a myth of youthful redemption. First, it helped trigger
the fantasies about youth. Youth was not yet fully integrated into
society, and was therefore seen as capable of transcending social
particularity. It was free from labour and therefore attractively free

---

[17] John R. Gillis, *Youth and history: tradition and change in European age relations, 1770 to the present*
(New York, London 1981, 2nd edn.), pp. 38ff.
[18] Even if there was, perhaps, more of a sense of maturation and thus more of a conception of
'adolescence' in pre-industrial times than Gillis has acknowledged. See Michael Mitterauer, 'Gesindedienst und Jugendphase im europäischen Vergleich', *GG*, vol. 11 (1985), 2,
pp. 177–204.

from the constraints of the material world.[19] Second, as Elkar shows, it was the concentration of youth at educational institutions that was the organisational prerequisite for the dissemination of the culture of Young Germany. For the ideology of Young Germany, the societies and brotherhoods of the *Gymnasien* and universities performed the same functions as working-men's associations were later to perform for the emergence of socialist culture.

In addition, as Whaley reminds us, youth's position was also changing as a result of the evolution of the modern family. The family (again, initially among urban, prosperous groups) was evolving into a domain of private relationships, away from the unit of economic activity it had once been. Even if it is unclear that this change really led (as some historians have claimed) to more 'affective' relationships,[20] it does seem that the increasingly private character of the bourgeois family brought a new willingness to challenge the authority of the father of the household. Youthful rebellion in the private domain, then, was a widely shared experience which added resonance to the literary evocations of the *Sturm und Drang*.

Youth impelled itself into the contemporary imagination also because it was a rapidly growing group. The ratio of the age group 15–29 to the 30 and over group reached 2:3 in the late eighteenth century and almost 3:4 in England by the 1840s. In Germany, as elsewhere in late eighteenth- and early nineteenth-century Europe, educational and employment opportunities for young middle-class youth often failed to keep up with this growth, a fact which helped give successive waves of educated youth a sense of collective grievance against established society. When they managed to find suitable employment Goethe's contemporaries lost a lot of their animus. Indeed, right up to 1968, the periodical mismatch between 'baby-boom' generations and the opportunities open to them was to be a key factor in stoking the atmosphere of generation conflict.

The changing definition of youth and the demographic shifts which we have identified as providing some of the foundations for the production of youthful ideology were characteristic of most European countries. They cannot explain the particular resonance enjoyed in Germany by the notion of youthful redemption, its

---

[19] See also Frank Trommler, 'Mission ohne Ziel. Über den Kult der Jugend in modernen Deutschland', in Koebner *et al.*, *Der Mythos Jugend*, pp. 14–49, here p. 24.

[20] See Lawrence Stone, *Family, sex and marriage in England 1500–1800* (London 1977).

ability to inspire a movement of the breadth of Young Germany, or its particular moral and aesthetic character.

If we cast off the distorting lenses created by the terms in which it described itself, Young Germany seems as much a class movement as an expression of generation conflict. The emergence of its ideology was closely linked to the formation of the *Bildungsbürgertum* – that mixture of state officials, academics, clergy and professionals that had begun to leave its mark on eighteenth-century Germany. It was from this emergent social group that the young manufacturers of the notion of youthful redemption came. The experience of the *Sturm und Drang* cohort was, as Whaley observes, not just that of a 'baby-boom' generation but in many ways that of a non-aristocratic class in a society in which the nobles and princes still held the key to advancement. Many young intellectuals had to take transitional employment as house tutors for the aristocracy (and might be condemned to a life of such activity) – which forced them to adapt to this milieu and at the same time reminded them of their relatively underprivileged position.[21] In the context of such unworthy dependence on aristocratic whim, it was natural for the young bourgeois to seek to define their worth and value in spiritual, aesthetic terms. Surely, the heroic, aesthetic moral character of 'youthful redemption' is in fact an unstated (perhaps unconscious) plea for society to shift its values and recognise the true value of those whom it still regarded as second best? Young Germany, then, was about the frustration of those not nobly born. At the same time, the whole ideology of youth was permeated by the caution of a class which, as Knigge put it, lived off the crumbs that fell from rich men's tables.[22] For the literary cult of youth seldom actually defended the notion of outright rebellion. Youth was presented as the hope of the future but was rarely called upon to slay the father. Here, too, the *Bildungsbürgerliche* origins of the movement were evident.

The reality, then, as Wolfgang Hardtwig has observed,[23] was a dynamic interaction between emergent class and generational identities. On the one hand, the cult of youth was in many respects

---

[21] H. Gerth, *Bürgerliche Intelligenz zum 1800. Zur Soziologie des deutschen Frühliberalismus* (Göttingen 1976, 2nd edn.), pp. 51–60.

[22] Cited in James J. Sheehan, *German history 1770–1866* (Oxford 1989), p. 217.

[23] Wolfgang Hardtwig, 'Krise der Universität, studentische Reformbewegung (1750–1819) und die Sozialisation der jugendlichen deutschen Bildungsschicht. Aufriß eines Forschungsproblems', *GG*, vol. 11 (1985), 2, pp. 155–176.

the projection on to youth of the hopes and frustrations o‚
Bildungsbürgertum.[24] But as Young Germany gained its own identity,
it acted as the dynamic propagator of bourgeois values and, indeed,
helped influence the actual content of those values.

One reason why the image of united youth was so evocative for
Germany's young bourgeoisie was undoubtedly the weakness of
another imagined community: the German nation. Eighteenth- and
early nineteenth-century Germany lay segmented, a patchwork of
particularities rendered seemingly impotent by its fragmentation.
'Adult society', established society, was indelibly divided by the
border-lines of principalities. But youth, Young Germany, was a
fluid group not yet cast into the fixed moulds of particular interests.
It stood outside, not just in the sense of potentially rejecting some of
the norms of what was becoming bourgeois society, but also in the
sense that it was seen as being not yet particular, but transcendent.
The vision of youth and the vision of united nationhood were to
remain closely linked throughout the nineteenth and twentieth
centuries.[25] The projection 'youth', in other words, remained so
strong in Germany partly because the projection 'nation' was so
fragile.

There is one more ingredient, perhaps the most important of all,
that explains why the idea of youth rebellion enjoyed such powerful
symbolic status in the German cultural tradition: the fact that
family and state were experienced (consciously or unconsciously) as
part of the same patriarchal order. This might seem odd, since the
modern family's defining characteristic was that its inner relationships were *divorced* from the wider organisation of society and
economy. Yet, if in legal, economic and social terms family and
society were separating into private and public spheres, it is clear
that at the psychological and metaphorical level the authority and
stability of the family and the authority and stability of state and
society were not experienced so distinctly.

What gave this psychological 'mapping' its logic and its particular
subversive power was the fact that the German states and German
society were so imbued by a patriarchal *Obrigkeit*. It was an obvious
step for youngsters rebelling against the father figure in their own

---

24 Andreas Flitner, *Die Politische Erziehung in Deutschland. Geschichte und Probleme 1750–1880*
(Tübingen 1957), has shown that the history of youth is full of such adult projections.
25 A connection of course made explicit by the volunteers against Napoleon and the Jena
Burschenschaft in 1815. Sheehan, *German history*, pp. 405ff.

family to see in their rebellion a wider significance, a political quality, aimed against authority as a whole. Similarly, many members of the educated middle class, critical of the existing political system, saw youthful rebellion against the father as a powerful metaphor of the force for political change. Conversely, for those seeking to uphold the existing order, youthful rebellion, even 'semirebellion' seemed particularly threatening precisely because it attacked – in real or metaphorical terms – fatherly authority at both the immediate family level and at the level of the state.

Another facet to this projection of father–son relationships on to the wider social order was the perception, which can be found in the eighteenth century and was increasingly common in the nineteenth, that the patriarchy was losing its virility and that a new vigour and potency was required. That is to say, because the power of the state was so closely associated with patriarchy and manly, martial qualities, challenges to that power as a result of domestic social change, or of competition from the powerful Napoleonic and British empires abroad, or simply because the emergence of modern, urban civilisation seemed to undermine the assumptions and values upon which the old monarchies rested, were experienced as challenges to the virility of the patriarch. It was natural, then, to look to young men for new blood and vigour, an image, as Whaley points out, that occurs in the work of both Schiller and Hölderlin.

The revolution of 1848, while providing a minority of students with their most glorious moment, also showed Young Germany's limitations. The movement's political goals were ill defined, often playing second fiddle to a wider call for aesthetic renewal. It was partly for this reason that student involvement at the barricades was, as Elkar argues, very limited. The restricted character of student activism was also a sign that young members of the educated middle classes showed little solidarity with their contemporaries among the journeymen and young workers. Young Germany was rarely more than a subsection of the young, male, educated, middle class.

Youth was in reality anything but universal. It is clear that the sense of group identity and cohesion which helped shape Young Germany was in fact created and reinforced as much by the daily experience of class differences as by generational divisions. As Elkar argues, the journeymen, too, had something of a 'youth' culture in that their own career structure created a well-defined phase between childhood dependency and the 'adulthood' of ⌣ employment as independent master craftsmen. They, too, had their rituals and pattern of informal or formal association. Yet when contemporaries spoke of youth, they rarely if ever meant the young journeymen. The ironic fact is, then, that the notion of a universal youth was being sustained and carried by a youth movement whose sense of identity rested on its very particularity. In this respect, too, Young Germany exemplified the class from which it sprang. For, if 1848 revealed anything, it was the particular interests lurking beneath the bourgeoisie's language of universality.

IV

It was not until the last quarter of the nineteenth century that a challenging youth culture re-emerged. Few writers have done more to research and explain this phenomenon than the historian Jürgen Reulecke, and in the present volume he describes four facets of the emergence of a new preoccupation with youth during the late Bismarckian and Wilhelmine eras. The first was the emergence of a set of public initiatives, designed to improve youth welfare and influence youthful behaviour. Initially the preserve of the church and voluntary middle-class organisations, such initiatives reached a new intensity after 1910 when for the first time the state came to play a major role in 'youth saving', as Derek Linton has called it.[26] This intensive public and state concern with youth was sustained and extended in Weimar and reached its highest intensity in the Third Reich and subsequently in the GDR.

Secondly, Reulecke notes a powerful resurgence and modification of the German youth myth. Bourgeois reformers of a variety of different stamps saw in youth the possibility of a more healthy society, or the test-bed for projects of social transformation. As Reulecke notes, 'youthfulness' or 'youth' became once again popular labels, denoting a particular kind of life-style or a particular kind of society – an intellectual shorthand for an alternative, more healthy way of living. At the same time a more negative version of the same myth was to be found, with dark dangers conjured up if youth were to be led astray.

---

[26] Derek Linton, *'Who has the youth has the future': the campaign to save young workers in imperial Germany 1870–1914* (Cambridge 1991).

Third and fourthly, the period saw the emergence of new forms of youthful expression. On the one hand, there were the first signs of a separate proletarian youth culture. Young workers began to enjoy limited leisure time and prosperity and to demonstrate greater self-confidence and independence from their elders. Youthful participation in strike activity grew rapidly. On the other hand, there was the emergence of a limited but influential alternative youth culture among young educated middle-class males, the famous *Wandervogel*. The high point of the movement was reached in 1913 with the great meeting of 'Free German Youth' on the Hohe Meißner near Kassel. Though the youth movement was then to disintegrate into several factions, its influence grew steadily and in Weimar most youth groups were in some way or other affected by the style of the *Wandervogel* and their successors, the post-war *Bünde*.

What explains this simultaneous explosion of interest in, and visible, challenging activity by, young people? As in the earlier period, the new public preoccupation with youth was not invented out of thin air, but arose against the backdrop of changes in the hard social reality of youth experience. Once again, demographic factors helped put the relations between older and younger generations back on to the agenda. The 1870s had seen the beginning of a new spurt in population growth – producing a new surplus of teenagers in the 1890s. Young people were thus highly visible. Secondly, again as in the late eighteenth century, important changes were taking place in the everyday definition of youth as a life phase. Towards the end of the nineteenth century, the well-off began to have smaller families and to devote themselves more intensively to their offspring's upbringing. Improvements in transport and urbanisation meant that many more youngsters were able to travel on a daily basis from home to school, sometimes to university, and thus to stay at home for a longer period of their lives. As a result, as John Gillis and other authors have noted, this was the period in which 'adolescence' was being discovered, and an increasing distinction was made between the dependence of the teens and the independence of the mid- to late 20s.[27] These developments in turn help to explain the new conception, apparent in the social

---

[27] See Gillis, *Youth and history*, pp. 95–131 and Donzelot, *Policing of families*.

policy Reulecke describes, of youth as a dependent life-phase requiring intensive nurturing and protection from negative social influences.

In the Wilhelmine period, just as in the *Vormärz*, these demographic and social changes were the backdrop to a process of 'imagining' a youthful identity into being – a process which, just as in the *Vormärz*, was also shaped by the influence of patriarchal structures, by the nature of the German bourgeoisie and by fears about the fragility of national unity. We will return to these parallels in a moment. But even a cursory glance makes clear the crucial difference between the two epochs: youth's loss of autonomy. In the earlier period, the adult bourgeoisie's role, though crucial, had been rather passive. It had provided the soundboard against which youthful writing and protest had resonated, and as the early Young Germans had become older Germans, they had acted as key transmitters of the values of Young Germany, helping to perpetuate and extend the movement. But in the 1890s it was the adult world which laid down the agenda. The protest culture of the *Wandervogel* was very largely anticipated by critical spirits in the adult generation and the youngsters' anti-urban protest was the product of a more general unease. Even where the adults were ostensibly reacting to new youthful behaviour, it is the size and character of the adult reaction rather than youth's challenge to the adult world, which is often striking.[28] It is extraordinary, for example, how much attention the initially tiny *Wandervogel* groups were able to attract; and as Derek Linton has argued, the state's concern with proletarian youth was out of all proportion to the threat posed by young workers to the public order.[29] The declarations of 'autonomy' on the part of the youth movement, and the much vaunted slogan 'youth is led by youth' were, we might say, voiced so vehemently precisely because the reality was so different. Even the youth movements themselves were increasingly run by state, churches or other organisations.

One of the reasons for this loss of autonomy lay in the changing definition of youth itself. The age range which society so labelled started younger, and the period of close dependence on one's parents, as we have seen, continued for longer. Another factor was more general – the expansion of state social policy and of 'Foucauld-

28 See also Trommler, 'Mission ohne Ziel'.
29 Linton, *'Who has the youth has the future'*, pp. 219ff.

ian' struggles by burgeoning medical and pedagogical elites to expand their influence. From the 1880s onwards, Germany, Scandinavia and Britain saw public bodies assume increasing social responsibilities and a growing official involvement in social engineering. So it was understandable that a sizeable and growing population group, such as the young, and particularly one which was being redefined by the new structures of family life as increasingly dependent, should attract a growing amount of official policy.

Neither of these factors, of course, explains the intensity with which such efforts were made in Germany, nor why myths about youth should again become so important in German society. Here again, Reulecke is very suggestive, outlining a whole range of cultural, social and psychological factors, many of which we have already encountered in the earlier pieces. Once again, youth figured as a projection of hopes for national unity amidst fears about the fragility of the nation. Now, however, the fears were centred far more on social conflict than on regional particularism. The existing political system did not seem able to integrate the working class, a fact which led the bourgeoisie to feel increasingly powerless. Utopian fantasies about youth and social renewal could avert the gaze of troubled bourgeois from the painful reality of massive social inequality and growing working-class protest. That was why the behaviour of *working-class* youth played such a role in triggering official policy. Young workers' protests contained a cultural menace precisely because they collided with the notion of youth as a group capable of transcending inner divisions.

Beyond this general fear of social conflict, the character of the youth myth, and, in turn, of the new middle-class youthful protest movements, was strongly influenced by the particular situation of the *Bildungsbürgertum*. As Klaus Vondung has argued, the closing decade of the nineteenth century was a period in which the *Bildungsbürgertum* felt increasingly apprehensive, not just about the threat from the left, but about its loss of influence in general.[30] The emphasis on aesthetic and moral renewal, which had once served to distinguish the educated middle class's special qualities from the aristocracy, now functioned as an escape from the threat of disempowerment in mass industrial society. Here again, the image of

---

[30] Klaus Vondung (ed.), *Das wilhelminische Bildungsbürgertum. Zur Sozialgeschichte seiner Ideen* (Göttingen 1976).

working-class youngsters struck a special chord. The sight of this group of young men, wantonly and conspicuously spending surplus (though hardly over-generous) wages on themselves, aroused middle-class anxieties about the effects of a materialist age, and collided head on with the image of youth as spiritual alternative to a corrupt society.[31]

One source of preoccupation with youth that Germany shared with many other European countries at this time was a feeling that urban living was sapping the strength and health of modern man. Under the influence of social Darwinism there was growing concern that civilisation was interfering with the workings of the law of survival of the fittest. This encouraged throughout Europe a preoccupation with young people's health and military capacity. In Germany, social-Darwinist fears were reinforced by anxieties about a national loss of manliness and virility.[32] Sometimes youth itself was seen in danger of emasculation, leading to calls for youth fitness programmes and the like. But equally characteristically youth was extolled as the agent which could restore the nation's virility.

Once again we see authority in family and state experienced as part of the same patriarchal order. By the end of the nineteenth century, the sense that the nation had lost its way and that the vigour and authority of its leadership was being undermined had become so strong that it spilled over into the private domain, bringing the institution of the family into question. Here too, it is Jürgen Reulecke who has done so much of the pioneering work in this area. As he reminds us, many writers and, increasingly, many sections of the youth movement saw the family as part of the process whereby the warrior male was weakened and feminised. As a result there were attempts to take youth out of the family's reach, into the world of the *Männerbund*,[33] a bond of males modelled on the medieval orders. This was a development that became particularly

---

[31] See Eve Rosenhaft, 'Restoring moral order on the home front: compulsory savings plans for young workers in Germany 1916–19', in Frans Coetzee and Marilyn Shevin-Coetzee (eds.), *Authority, identity and the social history of the Great War* (Oxford and Providence forthcoming).

[32] Something recently expertly explored by Nicolaus Sombart, *Die deutschen Männer und ihre Feinde. Carl Schmitt – ein deutsches Schicksal zwischen Männerbund und Matriarchatsmythos* (Munich 1991).

[33] A term one would translate as 'male order' were it not for the unfortunate association with 'catalogue'! See Jürgen Reulecke, 'Männerbund versus Familie. Bürgerliche Jugendbewegung und Familie in Deutschland im ersten Drittel des 20. Jahrhunderts', in Koebner et al., *Der Mythos Jugend*, pp. 199–223.

apparent after World War 1, when a new kind of youth movement emerged, the *Bünde*.

In all sorts of ways, then, youthful protest, and the promise apparently held out by youth, were the products of an increasingly anxious adult bourgeois world. To that extent 'generational conflict' was very much a secondary phenomenon, the product of class anxieties. And yet the preoccupation with youth, precisely because it combined anxieties about class society, materialism and the loss of male virility, lay at the most profound level of the Wilhelmine educated middle-class psyche.

V

Until the First World War, generation conflict was conceptualised by contemporaries as a confrontation between something called 'youth' and established society. But in Weimar, as our contributors show, generations began to be seen rather differently. Now, the generations which dominated public attention were perceived far more as historical cohorts, as groups defined by having gone through a particular crucial experience. Most famously, there was the 'front generation', a group contemporaries saw as having been forged by the experience in the trenches. And there was the New Woman, a different kind of young woman, the product of the new challenges and opportunities which war had brought to German society and of the break up of older institutions and certainties. (Indeed, as we will see below,[34] the fact that young *women* now seemed to form an active part of the younger generation was one of the strongest arguments for believing that a new historical cohort had emerged.) Even when contemporaries talked about youth as such, rather than using new generational labels, they often stressed the specific experiences that had ostensibly made post-war youth quite different from its predecessors. Mannheim's work on generations raised this contemporary awareness of cohort differences to the highest degree of theoretical sophistication.

In terms of our original model, perhaps it is at this point that the discontinuity thesis begins to hold water. Yet in a wide-ranging survey of the reality of wartime experience, Richard Bessel shows

---

[34] On the relationship between gender and generation in twentieth-century German history see below, pp. 36ff.

that the notion of the front generation was largely imaginary. To define a cohort on the basis of its experience at the front ignored not only the large proportion of the population that *did not* get called up (not least the female part of the population), but also the enormously varied nature of the military experience itself. Active service in the trenches was the fate of only a small minority of servicemen. And after the war, there was every indication that wartime service did not produce one particular identity or set of attitudes or beliefs.

Similarly, as Dagmar Reese and Elizabeth Harvey indicate, the New Woman was only one kind of female type that emerged after the war. The 'vamp' or good-time girl seems a million miles away from the provincial young lady described by Reese's respondent. In any case, as Cornelie Usborne shows, the image of the New Woman was actually an agglomeration of a number of different impressions and observations, not least the discovery by middle-class social reformers of working-class women's behaviour. Though the behaviour was probably not new at all, the discovery helped foster the notion of a New Woman.

Closer examination reveals, then, that here were new generational 'myths', and that these myths incorporated many of the features, or responded to many of the anxieties, which we have seen defining the youth myth in the nineteenth century. This is particularly clear in the case of the front generation. The image of the front generation was, indeed, only a modest evolution of the older youth myth, particularly since the youth myth itself had been instrumentalised by some writers in 1914 to link the notion of youthful renaissance to the military cause.[35] Like the youth myth, the front generation was seen as standing somewhat outside society and transcending class divisions. Both groupings were seen as a virile uncorrupted body of men, united by camaraderie, demanding a more moral, less material society. The difference was that the character of the front generation was seen as deriving from the experience of the trenches rather than immanent qualities of youth. The front generation was thus less a sign that wartime experience had produced a distinct cohort of men – as the notion itself suggested – than of the fact that the impact of war and defeat on society as a whole had caused the imagining of generations to be couched in new terms.

[35] Trommler, 'Mission ohne Ziel', pp. 18, 23.

Bessel's argument here thus in some respects bears out the conclusion of Robert Wohl's *The Generation of 1914*, namely that the notion
of the wartime generation was more a literary and intellectual
invention than the product of a genuinely shared and decisive set of
cohort-forming experiences.[36] And yet, as Hans Mommsen has
observed of Wohl's study,[37] generation conflict in Weimar was
clearly a far more pervasive and powerful phenomenon than this
would suggest. Getting on for half of Weimar's young people were
organised in some youth group or other and many of these groups
bore at least some hallmarks of a common youth culture. Youth was
increasingly perceived (and increasingly perceived itself) as a separate entity at odds with Weimar society.

Sometimes, this youthful challenge was conceptualised by contemporaries as coming from a broad age-range including those of
the 'front generation', i.e. extending from the adolescents of the
post-war period up to those who had fought in the war and returned
to Weimar society in their early to mid-20s. But often the real sense
of change and conflict focused on the younger elements, those in
their teens to early 20s.[38] Was it possible, then, that, even if the
'front generation' was a myth, wartime and post-war experience had
forged a distinctive cohort out of those too young to have served at
the front? Both Reulecke and Usborne provide some persuasive
reasons for believing that a distinct youthful cohort did grow up on
the home front. In many households the fathers were called up and
thus wartime youth grew up freed from parental authority – and this
in a society with a traditionally very powerful authoritarian paternal presence. The result was to give youngsters new licence to
self-expression and independence and to reinforce a challenge to
established conventions (not least in sexual morality) that was
already implicit in the more emancipatory variants of bourgeois
reform proposals in the pre-World War 1 period. As the authority of
the state itself crumbled and fell, the sense of challenge at home and
in wider society reinforced each other.

The rift between the generations was then exacerbated after the

---

[36] Robert Wohl, *The generation of 1914* (London 1980).
[37] Hans Mommsen, 'Generationskonflikt und Jugendrevolte in der Weimarer Republik', in
Koebner *et al.*, *Der Mythos Jugend*, p. 50.
[38] Larry Eugene Jones acknowledges this distinction in his essay, 'German Liberalism and the
alienation of the younger generation in the Weimar Republic', in Konrad J. Jarausch and
Larry Eugene Jones (eds.), *In search of a Liberal Germany: studies in the history of German
Liberalism from 1789 to the present* (Oxford 1989), pp. 287–321.

war by the interaction between demographic and economic factors in a way we have seen in earlier periods. Whilst those who had served at the front were reintegrated into the economy, their younger counterparts often found it hard to gain apprenticeships. Even when they did, earnings were low and such youngsters were much more likely than more experienced workers to be rendered jobless by rationalisation. For educated middle-class youngsters, too, times were hard. Particularly after 1925 the universities were hopelessly over-filled and the income of students often under the minimum living standard.[39] Students suffered from an acute shortage of housing and faced a drastic deterioration of employment chances even before the impact of the slump. Many young bourgeois men found themselves forced to take on manual work.[40]

To this extent, then, a combination of war and demographic factors *did* provide the social basis for a distinctive cohort experience, dividing the generations. But in reality it is already clear that the distinction between generations as cohorts and generations as life-phase groups is misleading. A lot of what makes the young generation in Weimar seem to adults and feel to itself like a separate cohort was in fact the result of perceptions, patterns of behaviour and official policies that had their roots in the Kaiserreich. The war would not have created the impression of a moral gulf between young and old, for example, were it not for the well-established propensity in German culture to see challenges to patriarchal authority in the family as somehow linked to assaults on the strength and virility of the wider patriarchal order in state and nation. Family battles thus took on an immediate moral and political significance. At the same time, the fragility and then the collapse of the wider political order in 1918 made the adult world hypersensitive to any changes in family relations between parents and children – a hypersensitivity which is abundantly clear in Usborne's account of the New Woman. The war thus clearly did help to strengthen the degree to which parents and youngsters felt estranged from each other and separate in their identities. It enhanced the cultural resonance and moral import of their ten-

---

[39] Michael Stephen Steinberg, *Sabers and brown shirts: the German students' path to National Socialism 1918–1935* (Chicago 1977).
[40] Elisabeth Domansky and Ulrich Heinemann, 'Jugend als Generationserfahrung. Das Beispiel der Weimarer Republik', *Sozialwiss. Informationen für Unterricht und Studium*, vol. 13 (1984), 2, p. 17.

sions. But the process was in many ways an intensification of a pre-existing pattern.

Even without the shock and divisive effects of wartime experience and defeat, there is ample evidence that just as the narrow youth cult in the late eighteenth century had begun to gain its own dynamic, to disseminate its values through the structures and sub-culture of school and university, so the ideas and ethos of the *Wandervogel* would be disseminated through school and youth group. This was all the more so because in the last years of the Kaiserreich and in Weimar so much of the youth movement's 'work' was – sometimes rather paradoxically – being done for it by the adult world and the state.

In the first place, the state helped to create an increasingly separate and homogeneous youth by disseminating and enforcing the new conception of adolescence. Through regulations which prevented the Socialists from developing their own political youth, through a welter of pedagogical, social and criminal legislation defining and imposing a definition of youth across the classes, the state created an institutional ring fence around adolescence and was able to bring new groups – notably the children of the skilled working class – into the category.[41] Secondly, though the state's main aim was to create a loyal and patriotic youth, it found itself compelled to adopt approaches to which young people had been proven to respond; particularly in Weimar we find a whole range of adult-sponsored youth organisations thus disseminating the Free Youth Movement's own values such as the emphases on community and youth's independence, the principle 'youth is led by youth', and the escape from urban life. Thirdly, this tendency to propagate Free Youth Movement values was reinforced by the fact that state and voluntary associations were partially 'captured' by bourgeois reformers who shared many of the ideals and fantasies that had helped give rise to the *Wandervogel*. Pedagogues, youth group workers and many other figures ensured that the state, in effect, did the youth movement's work for it.[42]

In sum, inherited patterns of youthful activity and new cohort experiences fused together. Sometimes, as in the adoption of the

---

[41] Detlev Peukert, *Jugend zwischen Krieg und Krise. Lebenswelten von Arbeiterjungen in der Weimarer Republik* (Cologne 1987), pp. 306–307.

[42] Elizabeth Harvey, *Youth welfare and social democracy in Weimar Germany: the work of Walter Friedländer* (New Alyth, Perthshire 1987).

language of the 'front generation' by those too young have served, a new language was simply grafted on to older ideas and practices. Sometimes, the impact of war and defeat gave a fundamental new direction to youth activity or, as in the evolution of the *Bünde*, reinforced changes that were already underway when the war started. In the end, however, the distinction between inherited practice and new experiences became increasingly irrelevant. Even if it was incorrect to imagine that a new cohort had been carved out by the transformative experiences of war and defeat, the cumulative processes we have described produced a younger generation that looked different and increasingly saw itself as new and distinct. The youth cohort had, in some senses at least, been imagined into being.

As Elizabeth Harvey demonstrates, Weimar's political crisis reinforced youth's sense of separate identity and unity (though later it also glaringly exposed its limitations). Even more than in earlier periods, the fantasy that youth might redeem the nation gained in attractiveness in response to what many saw as Germany's desperate, divided and beleaguered condition at home and abroad. Many of those adult dreamers who turned to youth for salvation did so because they saw the Weimar political system from its very inception as dishonourable or based on party politics, and thus congenitally incapable of uniting and restoring the nation. And many of those young people who defiantly waved the banner of autonomous youth did so in a spirit of rejection of the existing political order.

This leads on to the question of how far youthful protest allied itself with, or led on to, National Socialism. This is one area of the history of generation conflict in Germany on which a great deal has already been written.[43] Many commentators have noted the relative youth of the Nazi party. In 1920/21 the average age of the party's founder members was 33; after the party's refounding in spring 1925 the second guard was even younger, averaging only 29. Nazi members and voters were young in relation both to the age structure of the electorate as a whole and to the following of other parties. The only other party that could match them was the Communist party (KPD).[44]

---

[43] The best introductions in the English language are the works by Peter Stachura. See his *Nazi youth in the Weimar Republic* (Santa Barbara 1975); *The German youth movement 1900–1945: an interpretative documentary history* (London 1981).

[44] Michael Kater, 'Generationskonflikt als Entwicklungsfaktor in der NS-Bewegung vor 1933', *GG*, vol. 11 (1985), 2, pp. 229–234.

A number of analysts have interpreted this as showing a generational link between wartime experience and a Nazi mentality. Some believe the front experience lent itself to later Nazi support,[45] and certainly many Nazi leaders publicly presented themselves and the party in this light. Others emphasise the home front experiences of those too young to have fought in the war.[46] And some, such as Michael Kater, have tried to synthesise the two, drawing on both the deprivation of the home front and the shock of combat to explain a broad youth response to Nazi politics.[47]

We have already learned to be sceptical about the idea of a decisive new set of generational experiences 1914–1918, particularly in relation to a supposed front generation. By the early 1930s, as Richard Bessel argues, members of the front generation were to be found in all the major political parties. On the other hand, it is possible that the war did offer experiences to a significant *sub*cohort; in other words that there were sufficient men who learned cohort-specific lessons from the front experience to constitute a generational effect even if, as Bessel proves, the generation as a whole cannot be reduced to any one-dimensional political model. We cannot pursue this in any further depth here. But the limitation of this experiential approach is obvious: it cannot provide a sustained explanation for the continued Nazi appeal to youth. By 1933 many of the teenagers and 20–year-olds who flocked to the Nazi party were far too young to have been in the front generation; quite a number were too young even to have retained the sort of home front experience described by Peter Loewenberg.

The other kind of explanation has been to see a link between the tradition of youth movement and youthful protest and the development of Nazi politics. Fritz Stern and Walter Laqueur have been in the vanguard of those who observe from the Wilhelmine era onwards a steady shift in the youth movement and youth culture towards aggressive *völkisch* nationalism, facilitated not least by a negative feedback cycle of teachers inculcating nationalism into youngsters who then became more nationalist than their teachers.[48] But as other historians have pointed out, a strong facet of the youth

45 Sigmund Neumann took this view; see Spitzer, 'Historical problems', pp. 1362–1363.
46 Peter Loewenberg, 'The psychohistorical origins of the Nazi youth cohort', in Peter Loewenberg, *Decoding the past* (New York 1983).
47 Kater, 'Generationskonflikt'.
48 See Walter Z. Laqueur, *Young Germany: a history of the German youth movement* (New Brunswick 1984, 2nd edn.), pp. 7, 42ff.

movement before 1914 was what Hans Blüher called 'a protest of youth against the stifling of the spirit'.[49] Jürgen Reulecke and Hans Mommsen have been at the forefront of these emphasising the emancipatory elements of the youth movement – the challenge to confidence in material progress and the *häßliche Konventionen* of bourgeois life, the rejection of militarism and authoritarianism, and the call, at the Hohe Meißner, for the autonomy of youth.[50]

Certainly, the bourgeois youth movement did become somewhat more nationalist in the years before and during the war. The Weimar era saw further changes in the free youth movement which prefigured some elements of National Socialism. The model of the *Wandervogel* was replaced by the *Bund*. There was a greater emphasis on discipline, uniforms and hierarchy, and on sacrificing the individual for the communal good. The emergence of the *Männerbünde* also signified, as we have seen, a rejection of the family and a search for a different, more virile, more comradely order. The new *Bünde* were often strongly nationalist in sentiment, some virulently so. As Peter Lambert reminds us, there was also a strong racist and nationalist movement among the students. Yet Bessel and Harvey make clear just how diverse in political terms were the wishes of the various different elements of both the front generation and their younger counterparts. There was no united 'youth vote'. And elsewhere other authors, among them Hans Mommsen, have noted the fact that a great many leading figures in even the more nationalist elements of the Weimar youth movement remained distant from the National Socialists both before and after 1933.[51]

What comes out particularly strongly from the work by Whaley, Elkar, Reulecke and Harvey is that the most consistent feature of the bourgeois youth movements' view of themselves and their role was that it was naively unpolitical, indeed, often anti-political and certainly anti-party. Youth was seen, and saw itself, as the alternative to the dirty, divided material world of party politics. The shabbier Weimar politics looked, the more the youth movement clung to the idea of representing an alternative. True, for a brief moment in 1918 there had been the fantasy that such an aesthetic

---

[49] Mosse, *Crisis of German ideology*, p. 172; Ulrich Herrmann, 'Der "Jüngling" und der "Jugendliche". Männliche Jugend im Spiegel polarisierender Wahrnehmungsmuster an der Wende vom 19. zum 20. Jahrhundert in Deutschland', *GG*, vol. 11 (1985), 2, pp. 205–216.

[50] Reulecke, 'Männerbund', p. 204; Mommsen, 'Generationskonflikt'.

[51] Mommsen, 'Generationskonflikt'.

alternative could be directly brought into politics, but the youth movement soon withdrew to its stance of political non-involvement.[52] Indeed, as we have seen, the very appeal of youth as a projection lay in its ability to provide an escape from the political problems of the day.

The dilemma for young people in Weimar, as Elizabeth Harvey demonstrates so convincingly, was that after 1928 the growing social and economic crisis challenged the political abstinence of organised youth and left young people feeling obliged to make a stand. But precisely because the youth ideology they shared was so anti-political, the result of this new commitment was not uniform support for any political party. Beyond their aversion to party politics, there was no common platform. Indeed, there was a laughable irony in the fact that the youth movement was united in its notion of a united youth standing above politics, and yet fractured beyond belief into myriad colourful youth fraternities – far more divided than the world of adult politics.

There was thus no direct road from the youth movement to National Socialism. Many of the analyses which have tried to explain why the Nazis gained so much youth support have in fact confused two separate issues, namely why it is that some people vote for radical and activist parties and others do not, and why it is that in some epochs and not others, radical, activist politics are more successful. It seems to be the case – for reasons that have little to do with any peculiar set of epochal circumstances – that whenever an activist or violent style of politics emerges, it is more likely to be attractive to younger men. They have generally more energy, ambition and frustration than experience, ties and scepticism. The fact that the Nazi movement was largely composed of the young, then, should not in itself surprise us; it does *not* prove that the movement's emergence was caused by a set of experiences peculiar to the young. It merely confirms that, given a set of factors propitious to the rise of a violent paramilitary politics, it was most likely to be the young who responded.

Even so, it *is* clear that the Nazis benefited in a number of ways from the myths and traditions surrounding bourgeois youth. In the first place, the youth movement's anti-political stance in the pre-

[52] Willibald Karl, *Jugend, Gesellschaft und Politik im Zeitraum des Ersten Weltkrieges* (Munich 1973).

ceding era had meant, as Larry Eugene Jones has shown recently, that the traditional parties had been unable to build up a firm clientele of younger supporters.[53] So that when, at the end of the 1920s, the growing crisis impelled many youngsters to enter politics, the situation was fluid and the Nazis were able to win considerable young support. Secondly, it is clear that the Nazis were able to deploy to good effect the well-established imagery of youthful redemption. The Nazis depicted themselves as the youthful 'nation', transcending old divisions of class and particularity and ready to replace the moribund political system with a kind of anti-political politics. Their own youth movement, though small, enjoyed success even before 1933 by drawing on many facets of the *bündisch* traditions.[54] The *Frontkämpfer* image, too, was a ready-made model of generation conflict which the Nazis made particularly their own. These images not only helped secure the Nazis a sizeable following among the younger generations, but also had appeal for older groups as well. The youth myth, after all, was no preserve of the young.

Like Jacob Borut's essay, Peter Lambert's account of Weimar's most effective guild, the historians' *Zunft*, provides a valuable reminder that there are many dimensions to generation change and conflict that lie outside the story of youthful rebellion and youthful myth. Not least of the essay's virtues is that it reminds us that generation conflict is not just something which historians observe but something in which they participate. And, whereas Borut's community activists were eventually triumphant, Lambert's essay shows how a combination of institutional self-confidence and control of patronage and recruitment disarmed any challenge on the part of younger, more liberal, scholars to the orthodoxies of Prusso-German historicism. The lesson may be that generational revolt within institutional settings can be successful only when the older generation has lost confidence in its own values.

---

[53] Jones, 'German liberalism and the alienation of the younger generation'.
[54] See on this also Michael Kater, 'Bürgerliche Jugendbewegung und Hitlerjugend in Deutschland von 1926 bis 1939', *AfS*, vol. 17 (1977), pp. 127–174.

VI

Even after they came to office, the Nazis continued to draw on previous traditions both of youth policy and of organised youth activity. Like the authorities in Wilhelmine and Weimar Germany, they sought to use youth organisations to integrate youth and harness it to the social and political order. And like the fears of previous eras, the Nazis' anxieties about the nation's health led to intense concern with young people's physical condition. The new regime was willing also to use those symbols and practices of the free youth movement which had proved their worth in enthusing and mobilising the young.

Yet the new regime in many ways fundamentally altered the relationships between youth, state and society. In part this was, as Dagmar Reese explains, simply because the new state was so much more active and brooked no obstructions. Even when it was disseminating practices and values that differed little from those of the old youth movement, the point was that these values were now being extended to the furthest corner of the country. Where earlier regimes had half-heartedly tried to draw proletarian youth into the net of the bourgeois youth movement, the Nazis now forcibly broke down any elements of a youthful proletarian subculture and drew the young working class into the Hitler Youth. The Hitler Youth's efforts in this direction were complemented by an active programme of deproletarianising youngsters through teaching them a trade.[55]

The Nazis' policy was in any case not just a more active version of the 'youth saving' of earlier times. Above all, the Nazis jettisoned the earlier notion of shielding youth from the demands of adult society. In the first place, they were not interested in depoliticising youth. Of course, even in the past the idea of keeping youngsters out of politics had never stopped the authorities from trying to instill patriotism and nationalism. But now the promulgation of Nazi racist and nationalist values was pursued at every level of youth activity. Moreover, the nurturing aspect of adolescence was replaced by a wild activism and an increasing emphasis on combat and competition. Whereas older policy makers had hoped to achieve the goal of a healthy nation by a controlled mixture of sport and rest, the new

---

[55] John Gillingham, 'The deproletarianisation of German society: vocational training in the Third Reich', *Journal of Social History*, vol. 19 (1986), pp. 423–432.

movement demanded performance, struggle, victors and losers from every minute of the young person's day. Tendentially, therefore, the Nazis were actually destroying the distinct character of the youthful life-phase. The notion of adolescence as a moratorium, as a pro-tected sphere of nurture and careful integration into society, was being replaced by the idea of importing the competitive struggle of the adult world into young people's everyday lives.

What was the impact of Nazi policy on generational conflict and generational identity? First, the totalitarian nature of the Nazi regime ensured not only that a far larger part of youth was reached by the new movement, but also that organised youth lost its independence. Whereas in Weimar Germany state efforts had para-doxically helped to produce an increasingly autonomous youth movement there could be no question of this in Nazi Germany. Initially, it is true, the Nazis used the idea of youthful rebellion to attract youngsters to the Hitler Youth. Not a few Hitler Youth members were able to exploit their position to oppose parents or teachers. But generation conflict in general was, if not eliminated, then sharply disciplined and suppressed.[56] In Hitler Youth publi-cations from 1934–35, for example, there was repeated criticism of 'youthful opposition'.[57] The more control over the population in general was consolidated, the less the regime had an interest in keeping generation conflict alive.

All this should not be taken to mean that youth was quiescent. On the contrary, as von Plato and Reese remind us, the Nazis mastered, at least for a while, the trick of robbing the youth movement of its independence whilst still profiting from its elan. They achieved the synthesis of Free German Youth movement and state incorporation which earlier youth administrators had hoped for but failed to implement. It was generational mobilisation without generational conflict. The model of the youthful rebel was 'reconfigured' – both in Nazi ideology and in the self-perception of the youngsters them-selves – into the image of the youthful vanguard not at odds with the rest of society but rather helping to create the society of the future. Over time, it is true, the growing rigidity of state control under-mined the movement's dynamism. By the end of the 1930s the

[56] On what remained see Detlev Peukert, *Die Edelweißpiraten. Protestbewegungen jugendlicher Arbeiter im Dritten Reich* (Cologne 1980).
[57] Arno Klönne, *Jugend im Dritten Reich* (Cologne 1982), p. 87.

enthusiasm of young people and their consciousness of being a generation apart were beginning to be eroded. Yet these tendencies were then only beginning to emerge and for much of the period the Nazis really did succeed in harnessing youthful verve and energy to their cause.

One of the innovative features of the work by von Plato, Reese and Buddrus both in this volume and elsewhere is that they are less concerned with changes during the Third Reich than with the legacy of Nazi Germany for the post-war era. What, then, was the longer-term impact of Nazi experience on the formation of the post-war generations?

It is a striking fact that whilst our contributors on Weimar Germany are at pains to relativise the notion of a new cohort formed in the crucible of war, our analysts of the transition from the Third Reich to the post-World War 2 era are unanimous in seeing the Hitler Youth generation as forming a new cohort, indeed, of being the generation which in Dagmar Reese's words like no other accords to Karl Mannheim's definition. For one thing, it had been exposed far more than any previous cohort to a homogeneous socialisation: differences of class, gender, region and religion had lost their decisive influence on the character of youth experience. For another, its socialisation differed markedly from that of its predecessors or successors: uniquely, this cohort was exposed to the full force of Nazi ideology without possessing the experience of previous political epochs to relativise what it was being told. As Reese and von Plato show in their different ways, the experience of the young broke through the social boundaries of their parents; provincial girls were dragged out of the conventional restrictions of the young lady, and working-class boys thrust into a classless world of social interaction and social advancement.

Of course, with an eye to Richard Bessel's methodology, it would clearly be wrong to claim that the Third Reich and the war offered totally uniform experiences. Even if older social distinctions were being eroded, the war was surely creating distinctions that were new and equally real – between being bombed out or having an intact home, between staying at home and being evacuated, between families that became fatherless and those that remained intact, between town and country and so on. But what, from the evidence of the essays here, really cemented the Hitler Youth cohort's subject-

ive consciousness of being a separate generation was the collision of
their socialisation with the experience of defeat and its aftermath. It
is the particular psychological position of the Hitler Youth generation *after defeat* that gives it such a distinct profile.

What our contributors identify is the Hitler Youth generation's
overwhelming experience of disorientation, not only because of the
destruction and defeat into which Germany had been led by the
beloved *Führer*, but also because after the war the adult establishment began so quickly to disown the past. Older Germans buried
their unease at their own complicity in exaggerated calls for the need
to pardon and rescue the young.[58] Members of the Hitler Youth now
found themselves in the peculiar position of being treated by the
adult generation as having been the true convinced Nazis. At the
same time, they resentfully noted the pressures on them to deny all
the positive facets of their past experience. Small wonder, then, that
the Hitler Youth generation felt so adrift and so isolated.

Probably the most powerful impression that emerges from
Michael Buddrus's analysis, based on newly released archival material, of post-war youth policy in East Germany is an almost total
communication gap between young people and their political
leaders. The latter were not only considerably older, but had a
completely different set of experiences in the Third Reich and the
war. Many had spent the Nazi era in exile or suffering persecution –
a fact which applied to a considerable section of the returning
political class in the Western zones as well. Probably never in
Germany history has there been such a discrepancy between the
experience of two cohorts as between the former Hitler Youth and its
new political masters, and, particularly in the East, there has probably never been such inability to understand where the other side
was coming from. As Buddrus shows, the GDR leadership's attempts
at communication with the young were thus doomed from the start.

'Why are young women silent?' asked a headline in 1946. The same
question, a year or two later, could be asked about young men as
well. There is at first sight a great irony in the fact that the Hitler
Youth generation, the best-defined and most homogeneous in
German history, is also one of the most silent. Generation conflict in

[58] See for instance Mark Roseman, 'The organic society and the "Massenmenschen":
integrating young labour in the Ruhr mines, 1945–1958', *German History*, vol. 8 (1990), 2,
p. 176.

the post-war era was muted not only in the Soviet Zone, where official repression soon muffled any nascent attempts at youthful autonomy, but also, as my own contribution argues, in Western Germany. And yet, when we look at the issue more closely, the reasons for this silence confirm our understanding of the mechanisms that had operated in earlier periods, making it clear that the degree of generational conflict in a particular period often stood or stands in only a distant relationship to the degree to which successive cohorts have been shaped by distinct experiences.

A vital ingredient missing in the post-1945 era was the belief in a myth of youthful redemption. The Nazis had contaminated the old myths, or at the very least made them too hot to handle. A whole cultural tradition of thinking about the *Volk* had either been destroyed or gone into very deep freeze. In other words, what was lacking was the cultural projection or fantasy that could give a youthful voice its social role. This was most evident amongst members of the Hitler Youth themselves who, as Alexander von Plato and I note, had learned to distrust all such myths and fantasies intensely. Buddrus demonstrates persuasively that it was the East German leadership's failure to understand this new *Nüchternheit* that constituted one of the most important aspects of the communication gap between young and old.

Apart from the destruction of older myths, another decisive feature of the war and immediate post-war period was its impact on family life. The enormous losses on the battlefield and in the bombing raids, the destruction of housing, the evacuations, the flight and expulsions from the East and other forces meant that no period of modern history has seen such fundamental disruption of the primary structures of family and private life; nor have family ties ever been so crucial to survival as in the post-war era. For the Hitler Youth generation and perhaps even more for those born during the 1930s, the family was, as Helmut Schelsky discovered, at once so threatened and yet so important as to preclude what had become the characteristic struggle of the adolescent against adult society.[59] When in earlier periods young people had challenged parental authority or had rejected the family in search of a new masculinity,

---

[59] Dieter Wirth, 'Die Familie in der Nachkriegszeit. Desorganisation oder Stabilität?', in Josef Becker, Theo Stammen and Peter Waklmann (eds.), *Vorgeschichte der BRD. Zwischen Kapitulation und Grundgesetz* (Munich 1979), pp. 203–204; H. Schelsky, *Wandlungen der deutschen Familie in der Gegenwart* (Stuttgart 1981, 5th edn.).

we now see that their confidence to do this had rested on the fact that the basic structures and rhythms of private existence had remained relatively stable and intact. This no longer applied after the Second World War.

Another vital element of the post-war situation was the lack of political alternatives. The Hitler Youth may well have felt themselves betrayed by their elders and have bitterly rejected the older generation's volte face after the war and its attempt to 'save the young'. They may well have resented the way they were being asked to deny all the positive facets of their experience and reject the past. And yet, as I try to argue in my analysis of relations between the generations in the Ruhr workforce, the problem in protesting about all this was that there was so little political alternative. The Allies' power (and thus the proxy power of the German elites the Allies appointed or allowed to come forward) made rejection of the new political settlement difficult. Then there was, as Dagmar Reese emphasises, the uneasy knowledge for the ex-Hitler Youth members of their own complicity in a regime which, it was beginning to emerge, had been fundamentally more barbaric than they had allowed themselves to believe. And in connection with this, the young were offered a carrot for renouncing their former experiences: the youth amnesty absolving them of complicity. In both post-war Germanies, as von Plato and Buddrus show, there was a sort of secret pact between the elders at the political helm and the Hitler Youth generation. In return for the amnesty, the latter agreed to stay silent and not rock the boat.

The silence of the ex-Hitler Youth did not, however, mean that the specific experience of this cohort played no role in influencing its behaviour or shaping its contribution to post-war society. Perhaps the most striking element of Alexander von Plato's essay is his argument that under the surface both East and West Germany shared a common experience: that of the Hitler Youth generation becoming the *Wirtschaftswunder* generation. Drawing on his own extensive oral history work in both West and East Germany (the latter, almost uniquely, *before* the wall came down), von Plato argues that the Nazis had created a disciplined, adaptable and mobilised generation with, in political and psychological terms, 'no place to go' in the post-war period. Rejecting political involvement, the members of this generation threw themselves after 1949 into new safe, 'apolitical' areas of social and economic activity. In these spheres they demonstrated the effort and energy they had learned in the 1930s, drawing on the secondary values of their Nazi socialisation whilst jettisoning the more overtly political elements that had no relevance in the post-war period. As von Plato and I emphasise, both systems provided ample opportunities for individuals to prosper. In the East, growth was admittedly slower, but the enormous migrations westwards created for those left behind great opportunities for upward mobility that lasted into the 1960s and created out of the Hitler Youth generation a cohort that was closely identified with the system. This identification lasted until the economic problems of the late 1970s and beyond.

The Hitler Youth generation thus provides a vital and somewhat macabre link between the Nazi years and the stability of the two post-war German societies. Macabre, because the implication seems to be that the Nazi socialisation had provided an effective foundation for the smooth functioning of post-war societies – even for the smooth functioning of West German democracy. However, as the 1960s revolts were to reveal, this silent reorientation bore significant psychological and cultural costs.

VII

Until the late nineteenth century, the story of generational conflict was primarily a male one. Indeed, the young were frequently referred to as *Jünglinge*, an exclusively male term. It was only in the 1920s that the gender-neutral *Jugendliche* entered common parlance, a sign of the way the concept of youth was being redefined in Wilhelmine Germany and particularly Weimar.[60] As Usborne, Reese and Harvey demonstrate in different ways, the Weimar era saw young women beginning to emulate their male counterparts and break free from the traditional constraints on their social behaviour. There were, for example, the New Women, the youngsters entering new occupations or abandoning in their social and sexual behaviour the conventional modesty and celibacy expected of the unmarried woman – their behaviour a sign that the loosening of family authority during World War 1 had affected young women as much as men. There were also the educated middle-class girls who entered the youth movement. The latter group did not so much

---

[60] Herrmann, 'Der "Jüngling" und der "Jugendliche"'.

challenge norms of sexual behaviour as break free from the domestic sphere, engaging in the same sorts of group evenings, hikes and camps as their male counterparts.

Thus generational patterns of behaviour begin to cross the gender divide and this strengthened the perception in Weimar of young people as a cohort apart. Elizabeth Harvey's piece provides eloquent testimony of the way in which members of the Protestant girls' youth movement found themselves drawn into the same kind of political involvement as their male counterparts, particularly in the closing years of Weimar. As Dagmar Reese makes clear, girls' socialisation during the Nazi era, and their psychological situation in 1945, showed many parallels to the experience of their male counterparts. Girls were indisputably part of the Hitler Youth generation.

In an essay which combines a wide-ranging theoretical perspective with empirical research, Dagmar Reese sees an analogy between the triumph of bourgeois individualism at the beginning of the nineteenth century and the emergence of a new female subjectivity at the beginning of the twentieth. For our purposes, this invites us to see another, more particularly generational parallel. In the early nineteenth century, Young Germany can be seen as part of the assertion of bourgeois culture.[61] It was a movement that grew out of and acted as vanguard for the assertion of the values and influence of the *Bildungsbürgertum*. In a similar fashion, it was under the aegis of the youth movement at the beginning of the twentieth century that middle-class German women first broke through many of the social and cultural barriers previously delimiting female development.

Yet the female emancipation that took place was very constrained and partial and did not readily convert to an enduring liberation of the adult woman. It is possible that one might, here too, see some parallel with the fate of Young Germany after 1848 – its loss of elan in a Germany where feudal elements continued to enjoy control of political power. In reality, however, the parallel should be replaced by a contrast: the very patriarchal myths and anxieties which had helped give Young Germany such prominence and cultural power limited young women's ability to achieve real equality with their male counterparts or to carry through the experiences of youth into their adult lives.

---

[61] Cf. Hardtwig, 'Krise der Universität', p. 176.

This is demonstrated most acutely by Cornelie Usborne's essay. As the New Woman discovered, participating in the same behaviour as her male counterparts produced an entirely different level of reaction from the adult world. In fact, young women, like young working-class men, found that they attained a symbolic negative significance for the contemporary world, with adult public opinion particularly sensitive to their transgressions. Just as young male workers in the late nineteenth century inflamed the adult world because of the collision between bourgeois fantasies about a classless and anti-material youth and the reality of young workers unabashedly defending their class interests or acting as happy-go-lucky consumers, so the assertiveness of the New Woman thrived on and shocked a society in which the patriarchy had been emasculated by war, defeat and the removal of the living patriarch himself, the Kaiser. Indeed, the New Woman dealt adult bourgeois sensibility a double blow by threatening not only conventional gender demarcations, but class distinctions of sexual and social behaviour as well.

The very aggressive reaction to New Woman derived, as Usborne argues, not just from the collision between injured masculinity and assertive young women. The metaphor of the national family had since the 1880s become increasingly racial-biological in its articulation. The old image of youth providing new vigour to replace a weakening patriarchy had come to be seen in increasingly eugenic terms. In this conception (if that term may be excused), women had a special role to play as custodians of healthy offspring. This pro-natalism further circumscribed the range of possible roles for women and thus the New Woman's promiscuity – with all its implications of sex without reproduction and of risks of sexual disease and sterility – aroused special fears about the health of the nation. Indeed, the New Woman existed as much in the nightmares of the pro-natalists as in reality. Insofar as young women really *did* engage in new kinds of sexual behaviour, they had to reckon with forceful social disapproval and with a powerful political backlash, articulated not least by the National Socialists.

In a different way, young women in the bourgeois youth movements, too, had to contend with the values of a culture that was, as we have seen, increasingly inspired by the desire to refound the vigour and potency of the Reich. The separatist masculine order of the *Bündische* youth was not welcoming to young women. Girls could, it is true, form their own youth groups without brooking the sort of concerted disapproval engendered by the New Woman, but only as long as they effectively renounced their sexuality and became 'youngsters' rather than women. The not very feminine activities of hiking and camping were tolerated precisely as long as it was understood that this should have no implication for the role of adult women.

Even in Weimar's hostile ambience of injured and hypersensitive male pride, it is possible that more middle-class girls might have gone on from their youthful activism to embrace the more openly emancipatory politics of the pre-First World War feminists had it not been for the fact that the political process itself was seen as so discredited. As Usborne shows, older feminists could rouse no enthusiasm among the younger generation for 'conventional' feminist politics. The more the younger generation absorbed the condemnation of party politics, the less attractive became the notion of asserting their interests as women in the political sphere.

Many members of the girl's movement not only abjured feminist politics but also accepted at least some of the conservative and eugenic views on women's role. As Harvey has shown, the Protestant girls' movements were trying to conceptualise a specifically feminine contribution to society. And yet at the same time, as Usborne demonstrates so powerfully, many found themselves alienated from the bourgeois family. Girls who had grown up with an absent father during the war often found it hard to accept the returning warrior's insistence on restoring his authority in the family. Many girls felt the continued patriarchal style of their fathers to be out of synch with Weimar's more liberal climate. In addition, as we have seen, the bourgeois family was being discredited for its role in domesticating and unmanning German (male) youth. For all these reasons, social surveys revealed the massive alienation of Weimar's girls from their own families.

Thus young woman's generational breakthrough in Weimar was in many respects also a sort of dead end, offering women individually and collectively no new adult role and instead signifying a gender confusion rather than a redefinition of identity. This disorientation crisis, as Dagmar Reese shows, was magnified dramatically for the members of the Hitler Youth generation. On the one hand, they emerged from the Third Reich with a welter of new experiences behind them. The *Bund deutscher Mädel* (BDM) and the demands of war had catapulted many girls into responsibilities and

experiences denied previous generations. But on the other hand this
same generation found itself after the war confronted with a powerful tide of opinion to restore the sanctity of the family which had no
place for new roles for women. Moreover, for the same reasons as
their male counterparts, young women saw no safe or politically and
psychologically acceptable way in which to hold on, at least overtly,
to the positive facets of their Hitler Youth experience. The post-war
labour market offered few women much opportunity to develop
their skills. And thus the BDM girls 'remained silent'.

   In reality, then, there was no straightforward dynamic transmission process between youthful revolt and female emancipation
on the lines of the nineteenth-century interaction between Young
Germany and bourgeoisie. The new life-styles of young women in
Weimar and the Third Reich may have contributed to the changing
self-perceptions of their successors in the 1960s and beyond, but the
transmission process was both delayed and indirect.

VIII

Perhaps more than any other youth rebellion in modern German
history, the 1968 revolt raises a question about continuity and
discontinuity in German history. In style, there seemed to be more
than a shade of earlier youthful rebellions.[62] It was not so very long
before that aggressive self-confident students had turned on their
professors, a parallel that had even Jürgen Habermas warning of the
dangers of a left-wing fascism. On the other hand, the values being
propagated by the 1968 generation seemed more characteristic of
the Western liberal tradition than of earlier German protest movements. True, anti-materialist and anti-urban themes abounded, but
the attitudes to politics, to liberty and to the nation bore few signs of
earlier youth movements. Indeed, as Heinz Bude points out, the
1968 revolution was credited with making West Germany's defini-
tive break with the values of the past – of representing the cultural
and psychological consummation of the formal political westernisation that had taken place in the years after 1945. So how far, then,
was 1968 specifically German in character? How far did it mark
continuity or discontinuity? Or, to return to the poles with which

[62] On the many parallels see Hermann Glaser, 'Mythen des Jugend-Stils. Impressionen und
   Assoziationen', in Hermann Glaser (ed.), *Jugend-Stil. Stil der Jugend. Thesen und Aspekte*
   (Munich 1971), pp. 7–25.

our argument began, was generation conflict the product of the collision of two cohorts with very different socialisation and experiences? Or did it signal the revival or the inheritance of certain 'conventions' or cultural patterns of youthful behaviour and relations between youth and the adult world?

In the 1960s as in earlier periods we see a literary-cultural force playing a crucial role in shaping generational identity. In the case of the 1960s, it was the youthful protest culture emanating from the USA in music, film and literature. That culture conveyed a sense of youthful innocence ranged against the stultifying narrowness of consumerist capitalism and the manipulative abuse of power by American imperialism. There was thus a new set of 'youth myths' which helped to shape the identity of the new cohort. The existence of this ideology not only helped a protesting community 'imagine' itself into being, but also transformed its impact. Instead of a few thousand students taking to the streets, adult society felt itself confronted by a concerted generation. Both participants and observers were misled, for example, into thinking that the revolts crossed class barriers when in fact, unlike the youth movement in Weimar, the protests of the 1960s were restricted much more narrowly to academic youth. With time, however, this barrier was crossed (not least through the medium of commercial pop culture) as the values and self-identity of the protest generation reached out to a much wider cross-section of youth.

What were the domestic realities which gave this ideology relevance and resonance? Once again demographic changes provided a clear-cut collective material grievance: the experience of a baby-boom generation in a world unprepared to receive it. The creaking educational system was – as in other Western countries – wholly unprepared for the mass influx of qualified young school leavers. It was the universities which most lamentably failed to adapt to the new demand, and this is one reason why the locus of generational conflict shifted back up the age-range to the student generation, in contrast to the younger and socially broader youth movement of Weimar.

On top of these demographic pressures, there were undoubtedly major differences in the patterns of socialisation of younger and older generations, differences that give some plausibility to the view that here were two discrete cohorts at odds with each other. This was in part simply the result of accelerating social and economic change. The youngsters of the 1960s, for instance, had spent their later childhood and teens in a period of economic growth and prosperity almost unparalleled in human history. Most would only dimly remember the economics of the pre-currency reform period and would (until 1967) never have consciously experienced a recession. As elsewhere in the West, this youthful experience of post-war affluence, uninhibited by the older generations' memories of shortage and crisis encouraged, as Ronald Inglehart has noted, the espousal of a new set of 'post-material' values.[63] A crucial prerequisite, then, for the ideologies of liberation and anti-materialism that suffused the new youth identity was the absence of the economic tribulations which had shaped the outlook of the parental generation.

Other distinctive features of the 1968 generation's experience, however, were, as Heinz Bude argues, far more directly related to the ruptures in German history than to international trends. Above all, a great many members of this generation were burdened and troubled by a characteristic set of wartime and post-war family experiences. Their reaction was all the more explosive because of the way in which these experiences were entangled with and symbolised Germany's wider problems in dealing with its past. Once again, it was the perceived overlap between family and national experience that gave generational rebellion its symbolic and emotional force.

In the first place, the taboos of German public life reached into and affected the everyday level of private family interchange. So many parents, be it as functionaries in the regime, as former supporters of the National Socialists, as soldiers on the Eastern Front, or whatever, had some facet of their past which they were unhappy to talk about openly. To grow up in post-war families was to grow up in strained silences. Secondly, the enormous demands on the family posed by wartime and the immediate post-war period often placed a massive burden on the children. The parents were often irrevocably divided by their very different experiences on home and battle front, and yet forced together by the exigencies of survival in defeated Germany. The differences were buried in a struggle to survive – and the children often found themselves the repository for their parents' frustrations and secret fears and wishes. Bude's persuasive image

[63] Ronald Inglehart, *The silent revolution: changing values and changing political styles among Western publics* (Princeton 1977).

here of an unbearable family burden rests not just on the evocative
symbol of Baselitz's erection but also on the testimony of numerous
oral history accounts and autobiographies, and of sociological
surveys conducted in the immediate post-war years.[64] The failure to
deal with the political legacy of the past, and the taboos on so many
political issues, thus had their analogue in the emotional burdening
of the children by the parents' inability to communicate. It was the
attempt to throw off this double bind that gave the 1968 generation
such animus and identity.

So far, the cohort model – emphasising the different values of the
generations – would seem to fit the 1968 experience. And yet, as
Heinz Bude argues, there was, as in earlier periods, considerable
intergenerational collusion. Above all a substantial element of the
adult world was itself waiting for change and felt as burdened by the
stifling silence about the past and its mortgage on the future as did
members of the younger generation. As Bude reminds us, a growing
number of observers had been warning of the rigidity of German
society, its failure to deal with its past and, specifically, of the
incapacity of the educational system to create the society of tomor-
row. Social change was, in Bude's words, simply waiting for a group
to carry it out and youth came to be perceived as the agent to break
through the taboos and create a more open climate. In other words,
the generational revolt was once again a product of an interrelation-
ship between the adult and youthful worlds. It was the expression of
a shared syndrome and set of aspirations on the part of young and
adult members of the educated bourgeoisie as much as it was the
product of different cohort experiences.

How far did 1968 fit into a longer German tradition? At a meta-
historical level, using concepts such as 'cohort experience', 'demographic pressures', 'interaction between ideology and experience',
'perceived parallels between family and national experience', 'intergenerational collusion' there are clearly considerable parallels
between the forces at work in the late 1960s and the causes of earlier
explosions of generation conflict. Indeed, there is good reason to
believe that at least some of the mechanisms we have uncovered lie

---

[64] See Heinz Bude, *Deutsche Karrieren. Lebenskonstruktionen sozialer Aufsteiger aus der Flakhelfer-Generation* (Frankfurt 1987); Heinz Bude, *Bilanz der Nachfolge. Die Bundesrepublik und der Nationalsozialismus* (Frankfurt 1992); Gerhard Baumert, *Deutsche Familien nach dem Kriege* (Darmstadt 1954), p. 251.

behind generation conflict in other countries and societies too. But
below the level of these broad mechanisms, it is clear that there are
also striking differences between pre-war generation conflict and
1968. Almost all the features of the older notion of Young Germany
had disappeared. There was now a far clearer emphasis on individual liberty, for example. There were perhaps still some vague
echoes of earlier notions of aesthetic and moral redemption, but the
new movement did not incorporate the image of healing the divisions in the nation. On the contrary, many of its representatives
sought to mobilise the working class and promote revolution. There
was now no rejection of politics. In all these values, young Germans
differed little in their broad ideological framework from their
counterparts abroad. Like their foreign counterparts, too, they were
avowedly anti-patriotic. Of the *völkisch*-nationalist strain in earlier
youth movements, not a trace. On the part of the older generation,
too, there was no romantic conception of youth as the saviour of
society or the embodiment of national unity.

The older romantic conception had disappeared not just because
the Nazis had discredited it but also because the 'red threat' was so
much lower on the bourgeoisie's agenda. Bourgeois youth protest no
longer represented an intellectual escape route for a bourgeoisie
paralysed by fear of socialism. On the contrary, a lot of the more
radical spirits within the youth movement wanted to 'reinvent' class
conflict and increase working-class consciousness of the contradictions inherent in capitalist society. The fact that they so lamentably failed to do so reaffirmed the older generation's perception that
the working class had now become much more integrated into the
existing order.

In addition, fears about German patriarchy were no longer relevant. On the one hand, the biological perception of the nation was,
if not dead, then forced into the backwaters of political vocabulary.
So that whilst there may have been (as after the First World War) a
widespread problem for young men that the father had come back
defeated and demoralised from the war, in other words a destruction
of the patriarch,[65] this experience had no wider political meaning in
a society in which the whole vocabulary of national greatness and
national potency had been fundamentally discredited. On the other,

---

[65] See Gerhard Baumert, *Jugend der Nachkriegszeit. Lebensverhältnisse und Reaktionsweisen* (Darmstadt 1952).

there was no great need for a youthful rebellion against the stern father. Instead, as Shelsky's surveys discovered, even by the 1950s styles of parenting had already become far less authoritarian than in the past. There was thus no longer the problem, as in Weimar, of the authoritarian family cut adrift in a more liberal society.

Thus, with his emphasis on the 'Germanness' of the German experience of 1968, Heinz Bude might on the surface seem to have hit the wrong note. Clearly, 1968 *was* 'German' in the sense that the roots were as much autochthonous as they were bred in the new youth ideology emanating from the USA, and in the sense that those roots grew out of peculiarities of the German experience as much as or more than they were nurtured by conditions (such as the baby boom or general affluence) which internationally had helped breed youth protest and post-material politics. But it was not German in the sense of marking a clear continuity with earlier forms of generation protest. Though the broader mechanisms are congruous, the direct experiences involved were very much new to the post-1945 era.

But what Bude has uncovered is the essential paradox of 1968: unlike earlier generation conflicts it was articulated in language which had little to do with its origins. In the past, the forms and language of the youth movement had revealed the psychological and social context from which it sprang.[66] Now, however, the vocabulary of Marx and Woodstock almost completely concealed the post-war family dramas which had helped give the generation such animus. It was a curious fact that although the 1968 generation wanted to break through the taboos and the silences it was not prepared to acknowledge its own vulnerability or to confront fully its own relationship with the past.

In that sense, our assessment of the impact of 1968 is ambiguous. On the other hand, no other generational revolt in German history could claim such 'success' as the 1968 revolt. None could claim to have made such enduring changes to the political culture of the nation and none would be seen in retrospect as having played such an integral role in the nation's political development. This was perhaps testament, above all else, to the more realistic mission which the adult world had delegated to the young. The job of shaking up

---

[66] The adoption of the 'front generation' label by those too young to have fought in the First World War perhaps offers some parallel to the 'mis-identification' of the 1968 generation.

society and breaking its taboos was an eminently attainable one. It
required of the young no more than they were capable of. What
distinguished the generation revolt of 1968 from earlier incarnations, then, was the new realism of the adult bourgeois world.
The *Bildungsbürgerliche* escapism which had so shaped the German
youth myth until 1945 had disappeared. On the other hand, the
'success' as Bude notes, looks more ambiguous. Edgar Reitz's *Zweite
Heimat* reminded us recently that the *'68er* created a new kind of
taboo, in many cases burying his or her own relationship with the
family and the past under a new language of radical confrontation.
Perhaps that is why so many former strident left-wing members of
the 1968 generation are now striking oddly nationalistic poses in the
post-1989 world. They cleared the air for West German culture; but
perhaps, until now, at the cost of losing sight of their own identity.

CHAPTER 2

The ideal of youth in late eighteenth-century Germany

Joachim Whaley

At the beginning of the second act of Schiller's *Don Carlos*, the young prince begs his father Philipp II to entrust him with at least some of the affairs of state. Faced with his father's refusal, on the grounds that he is too young and inexperienced, Carlos exclaims 'Twenty-three years old, and I've done nothing to achieve immortality!'[1] By the standards of the late twentieth century, one might think a young man of 23 who is impatient, even despairing, at the thought that he has done nothing to secure immortality rather unrealistic. Yet in 1787 when the play appeared such a sentiment would not have seemed extraordinary. For the last decades of the eighteenth century saw the explosion of a veritable cult of youth. Schiller himself and a number of others had in fact achieved immortality by the time they reached their early 20s. Of course they were not typical. Yet they gave expression to an ideal of youth which had a significant impact at the time. They also established the basis of a long-term tradition.

Schiller and his contemporaries represented the first dramatic modern manifestation of youth rebellion and conflict between generations. To analyse the preconditions of this phenomenon and to try to define its character is to confront some of the most intractable of all historical problems. For the tension and conflict between generations was rooted in the core of the development of both the modern family and modern society as a whole.

The birth of the modern family presents us with something of a paradox: no sooner was it born than it was faced with dissension and dislocation. Edward Shorter, Lawrence Stone and many others have argued that its evolution was accompanied and reinforced by the freer expression of love and affection, as well as the development of strong, and more purely emotional, bonds between members of a

---

[1] F. Schiller, *Sämtliche Werke* (5 vols, Munich 1981), vol. II, p. 49.

small, nuclear family unit.² Its emergence was also characterised by
the appearance of conflicts and internal ruptures. The emancipation
of individuals from the extended family unit ultimately distanced
them from the authority of the ruling patriarch. The most spectacu-
lar manifestation of this new freedom was the rebellion of the young
against paternal authority.

The development of the family mirrored that of society as a whole.
To an extent, indeed, the family was itself the product of social
change. From the early eighteenth century onwards the highly
stratified society of estates gradually began to give way to a class
society. Here, too, the theme was liberation. With regard to the
eighteenth century, historians speak of the emancipation of the
middle classes from princely or aristocratic society.³ And again,
emancipation was accompanied by conflict. The most obvious conflicts were those of interest and class, social conflicts in the classic
sense. But, often cutting across these, we also find the social equivalent of the internal conflict within the family: the rebellion of youth
against social and political authority.

The emergence of modern youth of course affected all of Europe;
we need only mention the impact of Rousseau in France or the role
of Wordsworth in England. But, in Germany, the ideal or cult of
youth assumed a far greater cultural and political significance for
the longer term. At the same time the history of this ideal reveals
something far more complex than a simple challenge to parental or
patriarchal authority.

From the late eighteenth century the ideal of youth in Germany
was linked to a particular set of ideas or uncertainties about modern
society. In the *Sturm und Drang*, as will be shown below, this started
with anxiety about the relationship between modernity and nature.
In subsequent generations these anxieties became entwined with
political issues. The desire to translate natural relationships into
political structures was accompanied by passionate hopes in a
society where it seemed perennially that the creation of the true
national state was imminent.

Thus the German youth movements of the late nineteenth and
twentieth centuries owed more than just a vague spiritual debt to

² E. Shorter, *The making of the modern family* (London 1976); Lawrence Stone, *Family, sex and
marriage in England 1500–1800* (London 1977).
³ H.-U. Wehler, *Deutsche Gesellschaftsgeschichte*. Vol. 1: *1700–1815* (Munich 1987), pp. 124–217.

the young rebels of the eighteenth century.[4] They inherited a similar uncertainty about the national political structures of German society and a similar response to them: the notion that contemporary society had gone disastrously wrong and that the true Germany might only be reached by a path which in the first instance led, not back, but forward to nature.

This chapter has three aims. First, it will outline some of the factors which contributed to the emergence of the first self-consciously youthful rebels in the 1770s. Secondly, it will examine three relatively well-known texts by Goethe, Schiller and Hölderlin to illustrate the evolution of an essentially literary cult of youth in relation to the contemporary social and political development of German society. In conclusion it will comment on the role of youth groups in the early nineteenth century, their politicisation and engagement in the national cause.

I

One point should be stressed from the start. In discussing 'youth' in the eighteenth century we are primarily concerned with a small minority in social terms. The youthful rebels of the period after 1770 were essentially middle class in origin. They were educated and they articulated their rebellion above all through the medium of literature. The most significant group in this context is that of the *Sturm und Drang* in the 1770s. No later group ever attained the prominence in the public eye enjoyed by Goethe and his early associates. But numerous groups followed, some literary, but many simply consisting of informal associations of students. The *Sturm und Drang* set the tone and the style of youthful rebellion. Its social composition also remained typical until well into the nineteenth century. There can be no question, in other words, of a mass movement.[5]

There were in broad terms three preconditions for the emergence

[4] Walter Z. Laqueur, *Young Germany: a history of the German youth movement* (New Brunswick 1984, 2nd edn.), *passim*; M. Gerhard, 'Das Zielbild "hoher Jugend". Ein Leitgedanke von Winckelmann bis George', *Jahrbuch des Freien Deutschen Hochstifts* (Tübingen 1971), pp. 448–455.

[5] See the contribution by Rainer Elkar in this volume. See also John R. Gillis, *Youth and history: tradition and change in European age relations, 1770 to the present* (New York, London 1981, 2nd edn.), pp. 37–93; Hans Heinrich Muchow, *Jugend und Zeitgeist. Morphologie der Kulturpubertät* (Reinbek 1962), *passim*; Walter Rüegg (ed.), *Kulturkritik und Jugendkult* (Frankfurt 1974).

of this movement: demographic change, intellectual change and political events.

The first factor was demographic pressure and social change. The population of the German territories, which had declined in many areas after the Thirty Years' War, began to grow again.[6] Consolidation and gradual increases in certain areas before 1740 was followed by quite dramatic growth thereafter. Overall the population increased from about 13 million in 1700 to roughly 25 million in 1800. In some areas the population increased by up to 100 per cent between 1740 and 1800 alone and in regions such as Silesia and Pomerania the rate of growth after 1750 exceeded that quoted for England and Wales at the same time.

This rate of increase was to escalate even more dramatically in the period 1800–50 when the disjuncture between population growth and economic development was to have even more dramatic consequences. Indeed, the exploration of the social, cultural and political implications of the rejuvenation of the age structure of the population of Western Europe under the impact of rapidly accelerating population growth remains one of the great challenges for historians. But the first effects were already evident in the later decades of the eighteenth century. Worsening conditions in both urban and rural areas contributed to a rise in unrest and general lawlessness in the 1780s and 1790s. And while the increases were most marked at the lower end of the social scale, the impact on the middling classes was also significant.[7]

There is evidence, for example, that the number of those seeking to qualify at universities increased markedly. The large number of universities in Germany (compared even with France and Spain) and the lack of any entry requirements made higher education quite easily available. The existence of elaborate systems of government studentships and of student hostels in many areas further encouraged expansion. Even without a studentship a young man might, like Anton Reiser, pay his own way by eking out an existence as a private tutor on the side.[8] Despite the lack of precise figures it seems clear that the growth in student numbers was increasingly perceived

---

[6] Wehler, *Gesellschaftsgeschichte*, pp. 67–70.

[7] *Ibid.*, pp. 170–176, 193–201; H. Brunschwig, *Enlightenment and Romanticism in eighteenth-century Prussia*, transl. F. Jellinek (Chicago 1974), pp. 101–118.

[8] A. La Vopa, *Grace, talent, and merit: poor students, clerical careers, and professional ideology in eighteenth-century Germany* (Cambridge 1988), pp. 97–133.

as a problem: so much so that by the 1780s attempts were being made to restrict the intake by introducing examination entry requirements.[9]

Equally significant was the fact that many graduates found themselves in a hopeless situation. Traditionally, a university degree had been the passport to a government or ecclesiastical post. In the late eighteenth century this ceased to be the case. Quite simply, the system was over-producing academically qualified young men. For many the fate of the private tutor, or *Hofmeister*, awaited: a degrading existence filled with humiliation and frustration, poorly paid and almost totally lacking in prestige.[10] Henri Brunschwig wrote of a massive unemployment crisis among young intellectuals around 1800, which he saw as one of the underlying explanations for the emergence of literary romanticism in Prussia.[11]

For the talented minority, and indeed for many who tried and failed, the only hope of escape lay in writing. Both Goethe and Herder, for example, saw writing as a way of advertising their talents and securing employment at a princely court. And both of them succeeded. Many more did not, particularly after the first generation of rebels had established themselves both as professionals and as arbiters of literary and philosophical orthodoxy.[12]

Young writers, both those who succeeded and those who failed, were part of one of the most significant social developments in Germany in the eighteenth century: the emergence of a new *Bürgertum*. It incorporated elements of the old urban middling groups but it could also embrace members of the aristocracy. Above all else it embodied a new sense of moral identity which increasingly made education the main criterion of *Bürgerlichkeit*.[13]

It was largely from the more modest bourgeois elements within this group that the first literary rebels emerged. By virtue of their

---

[9] Brunschwig, *Enlightenment*, pp. 119–146; H. Gerth, *Bürgerliche Intelligenz um 1800. Zur Soziologie des deutschen Frühliberalismus* (Göttingen 1976, 2nd edn.), p. 49 *et passim*.
[10] Gerth, *Intelligenz*, p. 49; La Vopa, *Grace, talent, and merit*, pp. 111–133.
[11] Brunschwig, *Enlightenment*, pp. 147–163.
[12] V. Žmegač (ed.), *Geschichte der deutschen Literatur vom 18. Jahrhundert bis zur Gegenwart*. Vol. 1: *1700–1848* (2 vols, Königstein/Ts. 1978), vol. 1, Part 1, pp. 194–200; H. Kiesel and P. Münch, *Gesellschaft und Literatur im 18. Jahrhundert. Voraussetzungen und Entstehung des literarischen Marktes in Deutschland* (Munich 1977), pp. 77–103.
[13] W. Martens, 'Bürgerlichkeit in der frühen Aufklärung', in F. Kopitzsch (ed.), *Aufklärung, Absolutismus und Bürgertum in Deutschland*, Nymphenburger Texte zur Wissenschaft, vol. XXIV (Munich 1976), pp. 347–63; W. Martens, *Die Botschaft der Tugend. Die Aufklärung im Spiegel der moralischen Wochenschriften* (Stuttgart 1968).

education, they no longer belonged to the old society of the estates. Yet lack of job opportunities meant that they could find no niche in the new world of the *gebildete Stände* either. They were in a sense excluded from the new society before it was properly born.[14] It is hardly surprising therefore that the central message of many young critics was that the new society was in many ways more perniciously evil and corrupt than the old, so that from the *Sturm und Drang* onwards even the Middle Ages came to be regarded as a golden age by comparison.[15]

This points logically to the second important precondition for the emergence of youth rebellion after 1750, namely intellectual change. The *Aufklärung* developed in Germany from the 1720s.[16] Like the Enlightenment in Europe generally, it was characterised by rigorous rationalism, but more than in most European countries it sought to operate within the existing institutional framework of state and church. The *Aufklärer* were not dissident revolutionaries. They aspired to improve existing institutions not to abolish them. Authority, whether secular or ecclesiastical, was not challenged *per se*, but only when it was exercised in an unreasonable manner.

Aufklärung provided the wider ideological context of *Bürgerlichkeit*. And only insofar as enlightened ideas were rejected by authority did enlightened groups represent a potential opposition. By about 1770, in fact, *Aufklärung* had come to represent a kind of governing orthodoxy in many German states, particularly in the Protestant areas. If the *Aufklärer* felt themselves to be outsiders in the 1740s and 1750s, this was no longer so by about 1770. The devastation caused by the Seven Years' War necessitated wide-ranging reconstruction and reform programmes as rulers sought to rebuild their territories and to restore their tax revenues.[17] The *Aufklärer* had joined the establishment, by invitation of the princes.

---

[14] Gerth, *Intelligenz*, pp. 47–48.

[15] Žmegač, *Geschichte*, pp. 207–208. See also S. Brough, *The Goths and the concept of the gothic in Germany from 1500 to 1750* (Frankfurt, Bern, New York 1985), *passim*; K. von See, *Deutsche Germanen-Ideologie. Vom Humanismus bis zur Gegenwart* (Königstein/Ts. 1973), pp. 34–43.

[16] J. Whaley, 'The Protestant Enlightenment in Germany', in R. Porter and M. Teich (eds.), *The Enlightenment in national context* (Cambridge 1981), pp. 106–117; J. Whaley, 'Rediscovering the *Aufklärung*', *German Life and Letters*, NS vol. 24 (1981), pp. 183–195.

[17] H. Liebel, 'Der aufgeklärte Absolutismus und die Gesellschaftskrise in Deutschland im 18. Jahrhundert', in W. Hubatsch (ed.), *Absolutismus*, Wege der Forschung, vol. CCXIV (Darmstadt 1973), pp. 488–544; Brunschwig, *Enlightenment*, pp. 101–178; F. Venturi, 'La première crise de l'ancien régime (1768–1776)', *Etudes sur le XVIIIe siècle*, vol. 7 (1980),

The *Sturm und Drang* was critical of the *Aufklärung* and took a different view of man; taught by Rousseau and drawing on indigenous German Protestant mysticism through Hamann, they insisted that man was more than just a reasonable machine. They criticised the *Aufklärung* for having ignored the creative, spiritual and mystical dimensions which alone gave human existence ultimate meaning. By implication, a preoccupation with practical and useful reform, however praiseworthy, failed to answer the real needs of human society and could never lead it to the highest goals.[18]

The *Sturm und Drang* thus represented a radical extension of the *Aufklärung* and a bridge to later movements such as classicism. It was a phase which a small but ultimately influential group of writers passed through on the road to the evolution of a radically new aesthetic vision: that of a harmonious, balanced and refined society dedicated not to the mundane business of providing material goods but to the higher cause of the pursuit of beauty; the qualitative rather than the quantitative. The themes of *Sturm und Drang*, which will be discussed below, fed easily and rapidly into the more constructive and more enduring framework of classicism. What Josef Chytry has called 'the quest for the aesthetic state' in German thought was soon captivated by the supposed example of the ancient world and preoccupied with the possibility of recapturing its spirit.[19]

Demographic pressures and the evolution of enlightenment thinking exercised a cumulative effect in the long term. The dynamic challenge to youth was, however, provided by political events. In *Dichtung und Wahrheit* Goethe described how the triumph of Prussia in the Seven Years' War (by virtue of Frederick the Great's survival rather than by virtue of his victory) had an electrifying effect on young people in many parts of Germany. The war created the first patriotic generation.[20] Its end inaugurated the great enlightened reconstruction programme and that in turn both raised hopes and stimulated demands for further and more radical changes. In the next decade the American War of Independence enthralled many German observers and soon afterwards the political debate in

pp. 9–24; R. Vierhaus, *Deutschland im Zeitalter des Absolutismus*, of *Deutsche Geschichte*, vol. VI ed. J. Leuschner (Göttingen 1978), pp. 186–189.
[18] *Ibid.*, pp. 200–213; A. Huyssen, *Drama des Sturm und Drang. Kommentar zu einer Epoche* (Munich 1980), pp. 44–84.
[19] J. Chytry, *The aesthetic state: a quest in modern German thought* (Berkeley, Los Angeles, London 1989), esp. pp. 1–218.
[20] Vierhaus, *Deutschland*, pp. 186–189.

Germany was stimulated further by news of the Batavian movement
in the Netherlands.[21] Then in 1789 the French Revolution transformed the politics not only of France but of the whole Western
world. The impact on Germany was complex. Initially the news of
the Revolution inspired many, if not most German intellectuals.
Few went so far as the Mainz radicals in wishing to set up a German
republic immediately, but most thought they saw the dawn of a new
era in which it would be possible to assist in the birth of a new
society. After 1789, the future ceased to be distant.

Hopes were, however, confounded by reality. In France emancipation in the first instance generated the Terror and then led
inexorably to dictatorship and the frustration of many of the heady
ideals of 1789. In Germany the debate about the implications of the
Revolution was overtaken by events: the invasion of the French
revolutionary armies, the dissolution of the Holy Roman Empire
and the Napoleonic reorganisation of Germany, which was then
itself reorganised in 1815.[22]

The ever increasing pace and ever more dramatic scale of change
in Germany after the 1760s is of crucial importance to an understanding of the sharpness of the sense of generation in this period. As
many contemporaries realised, the result of the changes, of the
dramatic discontinuity of history as it appeared, was to create a
series of age groups, each with its own experiences, which lived side
by side without really knowing each other.[23] Above all, however,
the promises of new beginnings and new worlds reinforced the
morale of those who believed they would be instrumental in forging
the new beginning and who believed they would inherit the new
worlds. In other words the position of the young was strong because
they knew, or at least passionately hoped, that they had a crucial
role to play in what many saw as a new springtime of mankind.
Many espoused the dream of a new and natural society, to which

[21] R. Vierhaus, 'Politisches Bewußtsein in Deutschland vor 1789', *Der Staat*, vol. 6 (1967), pp.
175–196; J. Schlumbohm, *Freiheit. Die Anfänge der bürgerlichen Emanzipationsbewegung in
Deutschland im Spiegel ihres Leitwortes* (Düsseldorf 1975); Wehler, *Gesellschaftsgeschichte*, pp.
345–352; H. Dippel, *Germany and the American Revolution, 1770–1800* (Chapel Hill 1977).
[22] G. P. Gooch, *Germany and the French Revolution* (London 1920); T. C. W. Blanning, *The
French Revolution in Germany: occupation and resistance in the Rhineland 1792–1802* (Oxford 1983),
esp. pp. 18–82, 317–336; G. Ueding, *Klassik und Romantik. Deutsche Literatur im Zeitalter der
Französischen Revolution 1789–1815*, Hansers Sozialgeschichte der deutschen Literatur, vol.
IV (Munich 1987), pp. 19–62; Žmegač, *Geschichte*, pp. 331–348.
[23] See the comments in J. Reulecke, 'Jugendprotest. Ein Kennzeichen des 20. Jahrhunderts?',
in Dieter Dowe (ed.), *Jugendprotest und Generationenkonflikte in Europa im 20. Jahrhundert.
Deutschland, England, Frankreich und Italien im Vergleich* (Bonn 1986), pp. 1–11.

they alone, as young people as yet uncontaminated by the poison of traditional attitudes, held the key.

Rapid change implied fragmentation and increasing divisions between age groups. Yet there was an underlying continuity of ideals amongst the educated young in successive decades in this period. This went beyond a perennial assertion of the promise of youth. It extended to attitudes to society and politics, to religion and art. In successive decades those attitudes were, however, expressed in different aesthetic modes, and this accounts for the fact that many scholars have ignored the continuity of what one might call the tradition of 'young' literature in Germany. It was a tradition which rested not only on the emergence of youthful authors but on their espousal of certain ideals of youth and of the role of youth in society.

II

These ideals were first formulated in the 1770s by the *Sturm und Drang* group. It included Goethe and Herder, Lenz, Klinger and others. They were all born between 1740 and 1752. None of them were noblemen; some were of extremely humble origin. All studied at university, largely theology and law. They were ambitious, eager to make a mark and to achieve a secure position in a princely government by means of their writing. This in itself significantly limited their revolutionary zeal.[24]

Insofar as the movement had a philosophy it was provided by Herder in his *Journal meiner Reise* of 1769, his *Auch eine Philosophie der Geschichte* of 1774 and various essays, notably his contributions to the symposium *Von deutscher Art und Kunst* of 1773. In these writings, and those of Goethe in the same period, we find an ambivalent mixture of rebelliousness tempered by a longing to belong.

Attempts to see the *Sturm und Drang* writers as forerunners of the Jacobins are not convincing. In the first place the major concerns of these writers were aesthetic rather than political. Only insofar as they discussed the wider social context of art did they engage in a very generalised form of *Kulturkritik* or *Gesellschaftskritik*. But in the first instance the contribution they wished to make was to art rather than to politics.[25]

They believed that *Aufklärung* had failed. Far from liberating

---

[24] Žmegač, *Geschichte*, pp. 194–200; A. Huyssen, *Drama des Sturm und Drang. Kommentar zu einer Epoche* (Munich 1980), pp. 44–47.
[25] Huyssen, *Drama*, pp. 30–37.

man, enlightened rationalism had subjected him to an even more pernicious tyranny. For rationalism had deprived man of his soul. It had even deprived religion of all meaning. Rationalism was calculating, mechanical, characterised by what Herder described as 'a paper culture' in which the head was divorced from the heart. Society had become alienated from nature. The emancipation of the *Bürgertum* had elevated greed for profit alongside despotism as the dominating force in modern society.[26] The age predicted by Goethe's Götz von Berlichingen (the play was published in 1773) had arrived: 'the age of fraud' in which 'the worthless . . . will govern with cunning' and fatally ensnare those with truly noble spirits.[27]

In broad terms, the political stance which emerged was both anti-absolutist and anti-capitalist. Opposition to rationalism implied opposition to centralism. And it was in this context that the Middle Ages, which allegedly embodied the tradition of *alte deutsche Freiheit*, came to be seen as the benevolent antithesis of the centralised bureaucratic state of the eighteenth century.[28]

If fragmentation and alienation was the diagnosis, the logical cure was harmony and wholeness. This meant the creation of a natural society. Man's alienation could only be overcome if head and heart were once more united.

For these young writers the starting point was a new view of art. Inspired by Edward Young's *Conjectures on original composition* of 1759 they came to believe that through self-knowledge and self-esteem even modern man was capable of cultivating genius. The artist must reject sterile rules and forms based on French models. He must also free himself from Lessing's belief that literature, in particular drama, must have a public, morally educative function. He must be inspired by Prometheus, who isolated himself from the world in order to do great deeds for mankind. He must be guided by Shakespeare who in his writings had apparently solved the paradox of individual freedom in the global order.[29]

It was not merely a question of substituting one model for

[26] Žmegač, *Geschichte*, pp. 207–208.
[27] Quoted by R. Grimminger (ed.), *Deutsche Aufklärung bis zur Französischen Revolution 1680–1789*, Hansers Sozialgeschichte der deutschen Literatur, vol. III (Munich 1980), p. 481; Žmegač, *Geschichte*, pp. 216–218.
[28] For the following see: Žmegač, *Geschichte*, pp. 200–209; Huyssen, *Drama*, pp. 20–30; Grimminger, *Deutsche Aufklärung*, pp. 57–69.
[29] J. Schmidt, *Die Geschichte des Genie-Gedankens in der deutschen Literatur, Philosophie und Politik 1750–1945* (2 vols, Darmstadt 1988), vol. I, pp. 120–149, 158–178, 254–268; Grimminger, *Deutsche Aufklärung*, pp. 327–340.

another: Shakespeare instead of Racine. For the free and natural rhythm of Shakespeare's language reflected the fact that it represented true poetry. On the basis of historical investigation, Herder concluded that poetry was not the product of a high degree of civilisation but the original form of human communication: poetry preceded prose. He concluded, however, that it was still possible for such true poetry to be written. The poet could by virtue of his imagination and command of language communicate with nature, with the true character of humanity.[30]

True poetry was therefore also most likely to be demotic poetry. This has led some to claim that *Sturm und Drang* writers were therefore democrats. Insofar as their poetic theory was fundamentally anti-court in tendency, this was undoubtedly true. But their identification with the people was strictly circumscribed. Herder was, for example, emphatic in asserting 'The *Volk* is not the rabble on the streets; the rabble does not sing and versify but habitually shouts and brutalises.' The *Volk* was indeed the antithesis of the court, of 'polished' society. It represented, however, not the people but the idealised 'nation', the true Germans. Democracy was the ideal but it was not to be a democracy of the rabble.[31]

The definition of the poet and his relationship with the people and hence with society also implied a series of political attitudes. There is no such thing as a political theory of the *Sturm und Drang*. An often savagely expressed hatred of tyrants, even though it landed Christian Daniel Schubarth in prison for ten years, did not add up to a coherent political philosophy. On the other hand we can find numerous hints about the kind of society which was thought most conducive to the emergence and efflorescence of genius. Again, Herder's vision was the most explicit. He praised the patriarchal society of biblical times, the 'organic' communities of the early civilisations. They were organised like large families (the most natural of all human units). There were no divisions according to mental or manual labour, or according to class or estate. They enabled people to live as 'whole' human beings. The highest form of natural society, according to Herder, was the Athenian democracy. It had evolved naturally out of the pre-statist communities of the Homeric period. It represented a society where literacy and philo-

---

[30] Schmidt, *Genie-Gedankens*, pp. 120–149.
[31] Žmegač, *Geschichte*, pp. 209–212; Huyssen, *Drama*, pp. 30–37; Grimminger, *Deutsche Aufklärung*, pp. 334–340.

sophical culture were natural dimensions of the life of the Athenian *Bürgertum*.[32]

Two important points emerge from this brief survey of the social and political implications of *Sturm und Drang* poetics. First, criticism of contemporary society did not mean the rejection of all authority. Indeed, patriarchal authority in the natural family is one of the principles idealised by Herder and others. What was criticised was the perversion of authority, in both state and church, by rationalism and materialism. Thus the democratic freedom of Athens was not to be equated with anarchic liberty or emancipation from all authority. The prime function of freedom in this system was to guarantee the liberty of creativity and cultural expression.

Secondly, it is significant that even in this emphatically pre-classical phase, writers such as Herder singled out Athens as a model. Here was a society which emerged in the 'youth' of humanity, a society which managed to retain a youthful spontaneity which it employed in the pursuit of the highest goal of man, namely art. Unlike Rousseau, these German writers did not idealise the state of nature. On the contrary, they looked forward to the creation of a sophisticated, cultured society similar to that which had once existed in Greece.

The ideas of the *Sturm und Drang* had considerable radical potential: in politics, they could embrace radical democratic notions; in religion, orthodox Christianity could be replaced by something more accurately described as paganism. Yet for all the outrage of their heresies, the *Sturm und Drang* writers clung to other notions, such as patriarchalism, which were hardly radical or emancipatory. For this reason it is inaccurate to see the movement narrowly in terms of a generational conflict. As Bengt Algot Sørensen has shown, the drama of the 1770s rarely depicts straightforward rebellions of sons against fathers: more common, for example, was conflict among brothers, at the root of which often lay opposing ideals of the family. The drama of the *Sturm und Drang*, like much of the writing of the group generally, is the drama of semi-rebellion. Protest was accompanied by a deep desire to belong – to a true family, to a 'natural' society – to be at the centre of the world.[33]

[32] Chytry, *Aesthetic state*, pp. 47–54; Žmegač, *Geschichte*, pp. 207–212.
[33] B. A. Sørensen, *Herrschaft und Zärtlichkeit. Der Patriarchalismus und das Drama im 18. Jahrhundert* (Munich 1984); R. Quabius, *Generationsverhältnisse im Sturm und Drang* (Cologne, Vienna 1976).

The *Sturm und Drang* was a relatively short-lived movement. Yet its elevation to the German literary pantheon has served to obscure the real historical continuity and evolution of many of its ideals in subsequent decades. Through several literary phases and momentous historical changes in the era of the French Revolution the concept of youth acquired an important political dimension. Indeed by about 1810 the natural utopia had, for many, assumed a more clearly defined ideal form; namely, the community of the nation. The growing link between the ideal of youth and the concept of the nation in the period after 1770 forms a central theme of the analysis which follows below.

III

The evolution of this ideal during the last decades of the eighteenth century can best be illustrated with reference to three literary works: Goethe's *Werther* (1774), Schiller's *Die Räuber* (1781) and Hölderlin's *Hyperion* (1797–79). They belong to different decades and span different literary periods, too. They are not conventionally linked together by literary scholars. They do, however, document the development of the ideal of youth in relation to the social and political context in Germany between the *Sturm und Drang* and the Wars of Liberation. They illuminate the politicisation of that ideal and its increasing focus on the potential of the nation.

Goethe's *Die Leiden des jungen Werther* was the most outstanding literary work of the *Sturm und Drang* generation. The outrage which it provoked in many quarters was testimony to its radical rejection of established convention.[34] Werther's suicide and the fact that the book contained no hint of any disapproval of his action scandalised traditional churchmen and older enlightened critics alike. Werther's failure to find any comfort at all in Christianity, his identification of himself with Christ without the humility to recognise the salvation that Christ's sacrifice brought for all men, was both outrageously sacrilegious and subversive of all order, both secular and religious. At the same time, however, Werther's rebellion was ultimately futile

---

[34] K. Scherpe, *Werther und Wertherwirkung. Zum Syndrom bürgerlicher Gesellschaftsauffassung im 18. Jahrhundert* (Bad Homburg, Berlin, Zurich 1970), pp. 11–107. One of the best guides to this text is the illuminating commentary by E. Trunz in J. W. von Goethe, *Werke. Hamburger Ausgabe*, ed. E. Trunz (14 vols, Munich, 1981, 10th edn.), vol. vi, pp. 517–605. See also M. Swales, *Goethe: the sorrows of young Werther* (Cambridge 1987).

and self-destructive: it had no earthly objective. Once it becomes
clear that his love for Lotte will not be reciprocated, Werther has no
reason to live. His is a narrowly personal world; it revolves exclusively around his own emotions. Altruism, or any wider sense of social
or political motivation, is alien to his nature.

Criticism of society does none the less play a part in Werther's
letters.[35] He pours scorn on the rules which conventionally govern
art, as they do civil society in general. He delights in discovering the
natural simplicity of the poor and the uneducated and proclaims the
nobility of the patriarchal family of old.[36] In his conversations with
Albert, Lotte's betrothed, Werther repeatedly returns to the theme
of the aridity of rationalism, the suffocating effects of 'civilised'
restraint.[37] Yet for all Werther's identification of his own situation
with that of the simple folk he describes in his letters, he is ultimately
concerned with solely his own plight. In his first conversation with
Albert, he compares the intolerable situation of an unrequited lover
with that of a people languishing under a cruel tyranny: rebellion
was both inevitable and just.[38] But in Book 2 the wider concern
disappears. Werther can only experience nature as love. When love
is denied, death is the only way out.

Goethe's novel incorporates most of the central themes of the
Sturm und Drang. More than most literary works of the movement it
also emphasises the ultimate futility of the position of the young.
Werther offers no comfort and for this reason Goethe later disowned
him.[39] Werther *was* ultimately dangerous because he was nihilistic.
But for this reason, the novel was all the more effective in establishing an image of youth: a young man in self-imposed isolation
from society, whose pursuit of nature leads him literally over the
edge of the world.

Werther in many ways reflected the political vacuum and stag-
nation of the period in which it was written. Schiller's *Die Räuber* of
1781 reflects the beginnings of a political movement, of debate, of
anticipation of a new world order. At the same time its hero, Karl
Moor, not only moves in a wider social and political framework but
is guided by philosophical principles which elevated and 'idealised',

[35] G. Lukács, *Goethe and his age*, transl. R. Anchor (London 1968), pp. 35–49; Swales, *Werther*,
pp. 49–58.
[36] Goethe, *Werke*, vol. VI, pp. 9–10.   [37] For example, *ibid.*, pp. 45–50.
[38] *Ibid.*, pp. 46–48.
[39] See the documentation printed in *ibid.*, pp. 534–541; Scherpe, *Werther und Wertherwirkung*,
pp. 105–107.

in the philosophical sense, the vision of nature which Werther had experienced in almost purely sensual terms. The second edition of the play (1782) was provided – not however, it seems, by Schiller himself – with a frontispiece depicting a lion over the motto 'In Tirannos'. Yet there are limits to the political radicalism expressed in it, and it culminates not in the triumph of justice or the vindication of noble youth, but in the remorse and repentance of the rebel.[40]

IV

Die Räuber is the story of an ageing and ailing father and two sons: Karl, the elder, a wayward absentee at the start of the play, and Franz, the younger son at home, deeply resentful of his brother's absence. The father is both head of the family and ruling prince. His illness and his inability to see the evil perpetrated by his younger son therefore leads to the breakdown not only of the family but also, by implication, of government. The emphasis throughout is on the failure of the father, the breakdown of just authority. The family before its breakdown is presented as an idyll to which a return is desired but impossible.[41]

The breakdown of authority, its terminal crisis, is precipitated by the younger son, Franz. He is not only younger, but also less well endowed in other ways. He is ugly, mean-minded and deeply resentful of the disadvantages nature has inflicted on him – and determined to use his intelligence and cunning to overcome them. Reason, in other words, is to be employed to promote envy, greed and base ambition. What he wants is power and in order to achieve it he must remove both his father and his elder brother Karl.

When it becomes known that the wayward Karl is to write to his father begging forgiveness and announcing his intention to return to the bosom of his family, Franz seizes his opportunity. Franz suppresses the letter and, by telling the most outrageous tales of Karl's reputation as a licentious bandit, induces the father to allow him to write to Karl disowning him. The father is therefore tricked into disowning and disinheriting his favourite and elder son and heir.

[40] T. J. Reed, *Schiller* (Oxford 1991), pp. 17–24; Grimminger, *Deutsche Aufklärung*, pp. 491–492; Žmegač, *Geschichte*, pp. 247–249.
[41] Schiller, *Sämtliche Werke*, 1, p. 610. See also Sørensen, *Herrschaft und Zärtlichkeit*, pp. 161–176.

Franz hopes to inherit not only Karl's position in the family, but also the territory and Karl's beloved Amalia. This initial act of treachery sets in motion a complex, and often rather absurd and improbable series of events: Franz's repeated unsuccessful attempts to seduce Amalia; the apparent death, but in fact only imprisonment, of the father; the rumoured death of Karl and then his eventual return; the liberation of the father; the exposure and suicide of Franz. The significance of the subsequent death of the father, murder of Amalia by Karl and self-sacrifice of Karl becomes clear in the context of the story of Karl Moor himself.

Karl is the splendid antithesis of his younger brother. Handsome and strong, his freedom and nobility of spirit are underlined by the enduring love of Amalia and of his father, despite all Franz's intrigues and efforts to blacken the heir's name and reputation. His first appearance in the play, about to be declared leader of a band of robbers in an inn on the Saxon border, is an outburst of angry and unrestrained rebellion. He declares his disgust for this 'ink blot century', 'the limp age of eunuchs'; he denounces all book learning and the evil and injustice wrought by the application of rational calculation to human affairs. Nature has been corrupted, freedom suppressed by the oppressive rule of law.[42]

Yet it soon becomes clear that Karl is neither a common bandit nor a real social revolutionary. Some critics have seized upon his declaration that an army of men like him would transform Germany into a republic that would make Rome and Sparta look like convents by comparison. They have taken this as the first declaration of a republic on the German stage.[43] But they overlook the fact that a republic is really the last thing that Karl wants. He soon dissociates himself from the revolutionary vision of Spiegelberg, his competitor for leadership of the robbers. Indeed, Moor's order to exercise restraint, his ban on reckless marauding and violence later prompts an attempt by Spiegelberg to depose him.

What Karl Moor really yearns for is justice in the old order of things: a return to his rightful place in the idyll of the family and hence in the community at large. Increasingly, he is filled with remorse by his past rebellion and lawlessness. That very rebellion, however, renders his return to society impossible. When he attempts

---

[42] Schiller, *Sämtliche Werke*, I, pp. 502–505.
[43] *Ibid.*, p. 504. See also Reed, *Schiller*, pp. 17–24; W. Große, *Friedrich Schiller. Die Räuber* (Frankfurt, Berlin, Munich 1986), pp. 94–101.

to break away from the robbers to reclaim Amalia after the death of both brother and father, the robbers hold him to his oath of loyalty to them. The only way out is for him to murder Amalia and to recognise that his situation is impossible. Law cannot be restored by lawlessness. His rebellion, far from saving the world, has very nearly destroyed it. Only his own self-sacrifice can begin to make amends for the disruption of order and harmony. He resolves to deliver himself into the hands of a poor man with eleven children who will be able to claim the reward on his own head. His self-sacrifice in the face of failure is ultimately his sole contribution to the establishment of social justice. Moor cannot change the world but merely hope to improve the lot of one poor man within it.[44]

It is tempting to interpret Karl Moor's fate as yet another abject capitulation to the oppressive political and social regime in Germany. There is, however, more to it than that. Certainly, Moor admits defeat. But in doing so he makes a clear choice and a statement. The kind of rebellion he tried represented the wrong kind of revolution. Indeed, he implies that the only kind of revolution currently on offer, social and political upheaval, cannot bring about a natural and just world in which love and beauty will hold sway. Violence can only lead to the purely mechanical reversal of the status quo. It cannot elevate either man or society.

v

This kind of premonition before 1789 became more intense as a diagnosis based on experience during the 1790s. At the same time the ideal and mission of youth assumed a clearer definition in the form which ultimately influenced Stefan George and elements of the early twentieth-century youth movement. Nowhere is this more clearly demonstrated than in Hölderlin's novel *Hyperion* (1797).

Hölderlin (aged 19 in 1789) was typical of those German intellectuals who greeted the news of the French Revolution with almost boundless hope.[45] He had strong republican sympathies and applauded the Mainz Republic in 1792. The failure of a German revolution affected him deeply and preoccupied him continuously

[44] Schiller, *Sämtliche Werke*, I, pp. 612–618.
[45] P. Gaskill, 'Hölderlin and revolution', *Forum for Modern Language Studies*, vol. 12 (1976), pp. 118–136; Chytry, *Aesthetic state*, pp. 123–131; Žmegač, *Geschichte*, pp. 77–86.

over the next few years. The result of his reflections is set out in *Hyperion*.[46]

In a series of letters to a friend named Bellarmin ('the beautiful German'), Hyperion reflects on his life and on the recent collapse both of love and revolution. The revolution in question is the abortive uprising of the Greeks, abetted by Russia, against the Turks in 1770. The parallel between Greeks and Germans is clear, with the Russians playing the role of France and the Turks representing the repressive regime in Germany.[47] One central question underlies the whole novel: what can a revolutionary hope to achieve? Hyperion, as Josef Chytry puts it, 'plays out the reality of the young German intellectual of the French revolutionary period who is obsessed with the proximity of liberation'.[48]

Hyperion begins his narrative in a state of dejection. He has become a hermit. Having failed to change the world, he lives alone, at one with nature and by virtue of that in harmony with the gods. Yet the very process of narrating his story enables him to develop a deeper understanding of his experience. The present at the end of the novel is divided from the present at its start by the rejuvenating process of reliving the success and failure of the past. In writing, Hyperion rediscovers the mission of the poet and reaches the point where harmony once more seems possible in a world of dissonance.[49]

Hyperion's story is one of friendship and love. His early years had been guided by a sage and teacher, Adamas. His first friendship as an independent young man is with a fiery youth named Alabanda: an idealist and a revolutionary, never more so than when he denounced the evils of his age. Alabanda shows the young Hyperion that there are some who do want to change the world, that not all have forgotten the ideal society that once was in ancient Greece. In the euphoric state of what Hyperion calls the 'honeymoon' of their friendship, they vie with each other to produce ever more radical visions of the future. Yet even at this stage Hyperion has doubts. He believes, for example, that Alabanda has too great a faith in the power of the state. And he despairs that man will ever release himself from his chains.[50]

[46] P. Gaskill, *Hölderlin's Hyperion* (Durham 1984), esp. pp. 32–49; Ueding, *Klassik und Romantik*, pp. 452–460; D. Constantine, *Hölderlin* (Oxford 1988), pp. 83–104.
[47] Gaskill, *Hyperion*, pp. 34–35. [48] Chytry, *Aesthetic state*, pp. 128–129.
[49] Gaskill, *Hyperion*, pp. 13–26.
[50] F. Hölderlin, *Sämtliche Werke und Briefe* (2 vols, Munich 1970), vol. I, p. 607.

Pessimism in world affairs is matched by optimism in the affairs of the heart. Hyperion's meeting with Diotima introduces him to love and to the real possibility of a world of beauty. Diotima will have nothing of politics. Her ideal is a world 'like a domestic home, where each adapts to the other without thinking and where each lives for the other out of happiness and joy simply because that is the way that our hearts dictate'.[51] In his love for Diotima Hyperion imagines that he has at last begun to recapture some of the qualities of the ancient world. He longs for these qualities, currently restricted within the confines of his relationship with Diotima, to form the basis once more of a new world order.

Inspired by Diotima, Hyperion elaborates the historical-political theory of his 'more beautiful world'.[52] The model is that of ancient Athens, whose society developed out of man's gradual awareness of others outside himself. Man's divinity endowed him with beauty. Beauty in turn spawned art, which enabled man to rejuvenate himself, and religion, which enabled man to see his own beauty outside himself in the shape of gods he himself has created. The *Geistesschönheit* (spiritual beauty) of the Athenians enabled them to evolve a free society; it gave substance to their state. They developed freedom, unlike the arbitrary tyranny of the North. Their philosophy was founded upon poetry, and they saw that at the end of philosophy all contradictions were once more resolved in poetry. Unlike the cold, rational and reasoning North, the Athenians placed man at the heart of nature; nature was the priestess and man was her god.

Hyperion's sense of a higher mission, reinforced by Diotima's conviction that he will be the 'educator of our people',[53] is, however, diverted by Alabanda's plea that he join the uprising of the Greeks. Hyperion tears himself away from Diotima and throws himself into the rebel cause as an associate of Alabanda's mysterious League of Nemesis. In the fighting, he finds a practical vocation; he believes he really is assisting at the birth of a new world.[54]

The uprising turns out to be an unmitigated disaster. During its short and catastrophic course Hyperion also loses all respect for his fellow revolutionaries: the *Volk* of whom he had expected so much has succumbed to murder and pillage. Hyperion realises that he was

---

[51] *Ibid.*, p. 634.   [52] *Ibid.*, pp. 655–665.   [53]*Ibid.*, p. 668.
[54] *Ibid.*, pp. 685ff., 707–708, 722–726.

deluded in trying to found his Elysium with the aid of a band of robbers.[55] To crown his misfortunes he receives the news of Diotima's death. He has lost everything: the attempt to change the world has failed, and in making the attempt Hyperion forfeits his philosophical muse as well as his love.

Many critics have argued that the upshot of all this is disillusionment and despair. This is not, however, obvious. In a brief self-imposed exile Hyperion travels to Germany where he finds a depressing scene: a land of barbarians, made worse by 'diligence and learning and even by religion'. The Germans are a divided people: craftsmen, thinkers, priests and lords but no human beings; a selfish, materialist and philistine people who transform creative young men into mere shadows within years. Hyperion cannot wait to leave this unlovely land of the spiritually dead and finds solace and inspiration once more in nature.[56]

'Nächstens mehr' (more anon) the novel ends. No third volume ever appeared. But the ending underlines the fact that Hyperion has found a way forward. In nature he has found again the holy source, with the implication that the source can still give life in the future as it did in the past. Harmony will emerge from dissonance: 'The dissonances of the world are like the quarrels of lovers. There is reconciliation in the midst of every argument and all divisions are finally once more healed.'[57] There is still hope; the 'more beautiful world' is still before us; the 'springtime of the peoples' will blossom. The role of the poet is to instruct by means of interpreting the world: he is a seer, a medium between nature and man.

What is striking about *Hyperion* is the similarity of its themes to those of the *Sturm und Drang* critique of modern society in the 1770s. There is the same scorn for mere reason, the rejection of crass materialism and greed, the conviction that the key to the future lay in nature. Above all there is a similar scepticism about whether revolution involving violent social and political upheaval can bring about a better society. And finally, the role of the poet is still central, though it has moved closer to the inner life of the nation: as Diotima declared to Hyperion, that epitome of noble youth, 'You will become the educator of our people.'[58]

[55] *Ibid.*, p. 699.   [56] *Ibid.*, pp. 737–743.   [57] *Ibid.*, p. 744.   [58] *Ibid.*, p. 668.

VI

The continuity of the ideal of youth and the development of its relationship with the concept of the nation is all the more striking for the fact that it ran through a succession of aesthetic modes: from *Sturm und Drang* through classicism to the rejection of classicism and beginnings of romanticism proper in the 1790s; from Rousseauian rebellion against rationalism in the 1770s to philosophical idealism in the 1790s. In each phase it was new young writers who translated the ideal of youth into the new idiom. The emphasis was on the aesthetic realm, but the relationship with the political world became increasingly close. The two spheres finally became inseparable, indeed virtually indistinguishable, after 1789.

The French Revolution promised precisely the kind of new beginning many had yearned for. What happened in France rapidly proved to be an false dawn, but that did little to dampen the hopes of the believers. The fact that the French had failed did not mean that others would not succeed. Hölderlin, for example, partially turned away from the Greek ideal and in the years after writing his novel found a new commitment to Germany. He did not reject Greece outright. However, he now sought a synthesis of Greek and 'national' elements in order to foster the development of a Grecian-style society in Germany.[59]

Hölderlin's odyssey was by no means the end of the road. The ideal of youthful genius and its mission in the world was developed by subsequent generations, too. However, Hölderlin's arrival at a commitment to the nation provides a suitable point at which to conclude with some remarks about the implications this analysis of the *Sturm und Drang* and its successors for both the Wars of Liberation and for the youth movements of the twentieth century.

In the light of the evolution of the ideal of youth from the 1770s onwards, it becomes easier to understand many of the aspects of the involvement of young intellectuals in the rebellion against Napoleon. This is not to argue that their engagement was in any way materially relevant to Napoleon's defeat: they were insignificant beside the Russian, Austrian and Prussian armies, and their ideals were ignored at the Congress of Vienna. They were, however,

---

[59] Ueding, *Klassik und Romantik*, pp. 690–718; Chytry, *Aesthetic state*, pp. 148–177. See also A. Beck, *Hölderlin's Weg zu Deutschland* (Stuttgart 1982), *passim*.

important in generating a myth of a German national uprising, of a Nordic Christian rebellion against the irreligious French. It was a rebellion of the soul against the rationalist revolution and its pernicious fruit. It was, in other words, a conflict in which the mission of German *Kultur* was to transcend the chaos and anarchy of the age in order to establish a natural society with what Hölderlin called *Geistesschönheit* as its foundation.[60]

These ideals did not emerge in a vacuum after 1800. They were not merely the product of an overwrought romantic reaction to French rule in Germany. They were the product of several decades of aesthetic rebellion with socio-political implications. And they show, too, that there was more to romanticism than the futile and self-destructive quest for the blue flower. There was also, as there had been in the *Sturm und Drang*, a serious agenda for the salvation of civilisation.[61]

The material presented above also provides a broad context for understanding some aspects of the twentieth-century German youth movements. It is surely significant that Hölderlin was read and studied intensively for the first time after about 1900 and that in the 1920s and 1930s literary scholars became seriously preoccupied for the first time with the problem of generations in cultural history and hence with the writers of the period after 1750.[62]

It is thus hardly surprising to find a broad similarity of views, too. Walter Laqueur wrote of the modern youth movement that 'it was a basically unpolitical form of opposition to a civilisation that had little to offer the young generation, a protest against the lack of vitality, warmth, emotions, and ideals in society'.[63]

That is in effect to say that over a century later educated young Germans were still suffering from and protesting against the ills first diagnosed by their predecessors in the second half of the eighteenth century.

---

[60] James J. Sheehan, *German History 1770–1866* (Oxford 1989), pp. 371–388; Wehler, *Sozialgeschichte*, pp. 506–530; Muchow, *Jugend und Zeitgeist*, pp. 113–141; O. W. Johnston, *Der deutsche Nationalmythos. Ursprung eines politischen Programms* (Stuttgart 1990), *passim*.

[61] See, for example, the stimulating comments in C. Wolf, 'Der Schatten eines Traumes. Karoline von Günderrode – ein Entwurf', in C. Wolf, *Lesen und Schreiben. Neue Sammlung* (Darmstadt, Neuwied, 1980), pp. 225–283. An account of what one might call 'applied' Romanticism can be found in T. Ziolkowski, *German Romanticism and its institutions* (Princeton 1990).

[62] Zmegac, *Geschichte*, p. 77; Reulecke, 'Jugendprotest', *passim*; W. Schachner, *Das Generationsproblem in der Geistesgeschichte. Mit einem Exkurs über den Hainbund*, Gießener Beiträge zur deutschen Philologie, vol. xlix (Gießen 1937).

[63] Laqueur, *Young Germany*, pp. vi–vii.

CHAPTER 3

Young Germans and Young Germany: some remarks on the history of German youth in the late eighteenth and in the first half of the nineteenth century

Rainer S. Elkar

It was in the 1830s and 1840s that 'youth' first surfaced as a political slogan in Germany, in the form of the Young Germany movement.[1] But what did the 'Young' in Young Germany really mean? Was it just a political programme and rallying cry, around which clustered a variety of democratic goals? Or was it, in fact, a description of the age of those involved, a sign that the youth of Germany was on the march? That many young Germans of the time were influenced by the ideas of Young Germany is not in doubt;[2] not a few suffered police repression as a result. But did Young Germany really embody the will of a whole generation of young people? What *were* the links between young Germans and Young Germany?

Another way of approaching the phenomenon is comparative. Young Germany was by no means unique on the European scene. In 1831 Giuseppe Mazzini founded the Young Italy movement in Marseille. Three years later in Switzerland, it joined up with Young Poland and Young Germany to form Young Europe. Unaffiliated to this federation there was also a Young France. In Ireland, the Catholic-intellectual Young Ireland proved that the political rally-

---

The following essay is a revised version of R. S. Elkar, 'Von der Aufklärung zur Revolution. Über die Transformationsprozesse in der Jugendkultur des Vormärz', in H. Reinalter (ed.), *Die demokratischen Bewegungen in Mitteleuropa von der Spätaufklärung bis zur Revolution 1848/9* (Innsbruck 1988), pp. 211–230. Translated by Mark Roseman.

[1] R. S. Elkar, *Junges Deutschland in polemischem Zeitalter. Das schleswig-holsteinische Bildungsbürgertum in der ersten Hälfte des 19. Jahrhunderts. Zur Bildungsrekrutierung und politischen Sozialisation* (Düsseldorf 1979).

[2] There is now a sizeable historical literature on eighteenth- and nineteenth-century bourgeois socialisation. For full references, see Elkar, 'Aufklärung zur Revolution'. See also R. S. Elkar, 'Historische Sozialisationsforschung und Regionalgeschichte. Umrisse, Methoden, Zwischenergebnisse', in F. Kopitzsch (ed.), *Erziehungs- und Bildungsgeschichte Schleswig-Holsteins von der Aufklärung bis zum Kaisserreich* (Neumünster 1981), pp. 15–59; Christa Berg (ed.), *Handbuch der deutschen Bildungsgeschichte*. Vol. III: *1800–1870: von der Neuordnung Deutschlands bis zur Gründung des Deutschen Reiches* (Munich 1987).

ing cry of youth could be fused with a denominational-nationalist movement. All these 'young' of Europe were being swept along in a current that would eventually lead them to the revolutionary events of 1848. That was what they had in common. But what were the distinguishing features of Young Germany? Was it inspired by a small and socially uniform avant-garde of intellectuals? Or was it a broad political movement bridging the barriers of social class?

For the secret political police[3] in the German states, this question posed itself with particular urgency. On the one hand, they tended to see in the revolutionary spirit of the 1830s and 1840s the efforts of a small conspiratorial clique of refugees, intellectuals and literary figures. Yet at the same time many secret reports voiced the fear that Young Germany might extend its influence and touch off a real 'material revolution' amongst the 'popular masses'. What they really meant was that journeymen might become involved. The journeymen formed an unstable potential source of agitation not only on German soil[4] but also from neighbouring countries with strong democratic or republican influence.[5] After an abortive assault on the Frankfurt police headquarters, fears about the journeymen were revived by the festival of craftsmen at Steinhölzli near Bern on 27 July 1834.[6] The authorities were particularly worried about the potential threat posed by the 'young generation' – a name adopted by one of the democratically oriented journals of the time.[7] But was it just the pious hope of a few intellectuals or were the police fears justified?

The present essay analyses in four stages the origins and impact of youth culture in Germany between the end of the eighteenth

---

[3] K. Glossy, *Literarische Geheimberichte aus dem Vormärz* (Vienna 1912) (reprinted Hildesheim 1975).

[4] H. J. Ruckhäberle (ed.), *Bildung und Organisation in den deutschen Handwerksgesellen- und Arbeitervereinen in der Schweiz* (Tübingen 1983); R. S. Elkar, 'Die Mühsal der Walz. Selbstzeugnisse wandernder Handwerksgesellen als Quellen für die Sozial- und Bildungsgeschichte des Handwerks im 19. Jahrhundert', in Ungarische Akademie der Wissenschaft (ed.), *II. Internationales Handwerksgeschichtliches Symposium* (Veszprém 1983), vol. I, pp. 293–313; R. S. Elkar, 'Umrisse einer Geschichte der Gesellenwanderungen im Übergang von der frühen Neuzeit zur Neuzeit', in R. S. Elkar (ed.), *Deutsches Handwerk im Spätmittelalter und Früher Neuzeit. Sozialkunde - Volkskunde - Literaturgeschichte* (Göttingen 1983), pp. 85–116.

[5] W. Schieder, *Anfänge der deutschen Arbeiterbewegung. Die Auslandsvereine im Jahrzent nach der Julirevolution von 1830* (Stuttgart 1963); J. Grandjonc, 'La France et les émigrés allemands expulsés de Suisse (1834–1836)', *Cahiers d'histoire* (1968), pp. 401–422.

[6] Glossy, *Literarische Geheimberichte*, pp. xxxiii–l.

[7] A survey of the entire German-language press to be found outside Germany is given in J. Grandjonc, 'Deutsche Emigrationspresse in Europa während des Vormärz 1830–1848', in *Heinrich Heine und die Zeitgenossen. Geschichtliche und literarische Befunde* (1979), pp. 229–323.

century and the revolution of 1848. First, it looks at how, starting in the 1770s, the word 'young' came to be used by young Germans not just to describe their age but as a label defining their identity. Against this background, the chapter moves on to analyse how far and why Young German literature was able, in the years leading up to the revolution of 1848, to create a sense of political mission amongst the young. Thirdly, the analysis moves outside the social boundaries of the academically educated middle classes. How strong were the links and tensions between academic youth, on the one hand, and youngsters from craft and working-class backgrounds, on the other? Finally, and leading on from this, the essay considers the rifts which opened up within the younger generation during the 1830s and 1840s, and which ushered in a far-reaching process of dissociation.

I

Young Germany emerged from an eighteenth-century tradition of the *Freundschaftsbünde*, circles of friends sharing ideas, feelings and experiences. Though the immediate contact dissolved when their members reached adulthood and pursued different careers, the circles often continued in a different form, with letters replacing personal conversations. Frequently, the letters would be read out amongst the remaining members of the circle, and some found a wider audience in the journals of the time, a number of which reserved a regular section for such correspondence.[8]

Several circles were to attain great significance in German literary history. One of the earliest was founded in Halle, whilst the most famous was the *Göttinger Hain*.[9] The friendships were sustained not only by discussion and correspondence, but also by the students' albums (*Stammbücher*) which recorded important events in public

---

[8] See R. Brockmeyer, 'Geschichte des deutschen Briefes von Gottsched bis zum Sturm und Drang' (doctoral thesis, Münster 1959) and the older standard work, G. Steinhausen, *Geschichte des deutschen Briefes. Zur Kulturgeschichte des deutschen Volkes* (2 vols, Berlin 1889–1891, reprinted Dublin and Zurich 1968); Alexandru Dutu, Edgar Hösch and Norbert Oellers (eds.), *Brief und Briefwechsel in Mittel- und Osteuropa im 18. und 19. Jahrhundert* (Essen 1989). On the press, see M. Lindemann, *Geschichte der deutschen Presse*. Vol. I: *Deutsche Presse bis 1815* (West Berlin 1969).

[9] A. Kelletat (ed.), *Der Göttinger Hain* (Stuttgart 1967), pp. 405ff.

and private life.[10] Rituals of friendship like the exchange of albums
bound the groups together, creating an intimate public space,[11]
separate from the rest of society. The Göttinger Hain also maintained its own group journal, the *Bundesjournal*. Here minutes were
kept of the meetings, and the texts which had been read out or sent
in were commented on and corrected. The best works were then
entered into the *Bundesbuch*. In 1774, the year when most of the
Hain's members joined, the honorary chairman, Heinrich Christian
Boie, was already 30 and thus no longer a youngster. Otherwise,
with the exception of Gottlieb Friedrich Ernst Schönborn (born
1737), all the others were aged between 18 and 28, most of them
having been born in the 1750s or late 1740s.[12]

Boie grew up in Meldorf (Schleswig-Holstein). At the *Gelehrtenschule* there the senior boys kept a *Primaner* album from 1767
onwards, and the three volumes of this album, 1767–1812, 1816–
1874 and 1875–1913 provide a rare glimpse into the intellectual
history of school pupils from the enlightenment to the Kaiserreich.[13] Because of the school's peculiar position as an 'academic
Gymnasium', the pupils were strongly influenced by student traditions and in this case by the centuries old tradition of student
albums. In their album, the Meldorf pupils recorded poems and
sayings, either made up by themselves or copied from their
favourite literature. The first volume reveals that the students read
above all Gellert, Haller, Hölty, Klopstock, Schiller and Wie-
land.[14] Boie himself did not go to the Meldorf school and instead
attended one in Flensburg.[15] Nevertheless he constituted an important link between the *Göttinger Hain* and those *Freundschaftsbünde*
north of the Elbe who were influenced by its ideas. From 1781 he
worked in his home town of Meldorf as a senior *Land* official and

---

[10] On albums generally, see G. Angermann, *Stammbücher und Poesiealben als Spiegel ihrer Zeit nach Quellen des 18.-20.Jahrhunderts aus Minden-Ravensberg* (Münster 1971); W. Blankenberg and F. Lommetsch, *Studenten-Stammbücher 1790–1840* (Kassel 1969).
[11] E.Mannheim, *Die Träger der öffentlichen Meinung. Studien zur Soziologie der Öffentlichkeit* (Brünn, Prague, Leipzig, Vienna 1933).
[12] A good overview of the biographies of the *Hain* members can be found in Kelletat, *Göttinger Hain*, pp. 375–396.
[13] School archive of the Gelehrtenschule Meldorf in Holstein.
[14] F.Kopitzsch (ed.), *Aufklärung, Absolutismus und Bürgertum in Deutschland* (Munich 1976), p. 82; F. Kopitzsch, *Grundzüge einer Sozialgeschichte der Aufklärung in Hamburg und Altona* (2 vols, Hamburg 1982).
[15] On Boie see J. Behrens, 'Boie, Heinrich Christian', in O. Klose and E. Rudolph (eds.), *Schleswig-Holsteinisches Biographisches Lexikon* (Neumünster 1971), vol. II, pp. 70–72.

thus provided a personal link for the Meldorf pupils to the *Hainbund* members they so admired.

Hölty and Klopstock, the poets of the *Hain*, continued to be widely read by young people right up to the 1830s. So, too, did the two Stolbergs.[16] What attracted educated youth to them was not only their very sentimental pietism[17] but also the way they fused an emotional friendship cult with reverence for youth, nature and patriotism. There were, true enough, many voices critical of the *Göttinger Hain*, but such public criticism of the *Hainbündler* served only to strengthen the appeal of *Hain* sentiments and style to their generation, and to the generation that followed them. The literary circles seemed to capture a youthful mood and so criticism of them by outsiders confirmed young people's feeling of being a generation apart.

II

The *Göttinger Hain*'s mixture of love of nature, cult of friendship, pietism and patriotism exerted a powerful influence north of the Elbe right up to the 1830s. And as we uncover the evidence for this, we also discern the contours of a 'pupil culture'[18] which was to provide the framework for the later reception of the Young Germany movement. This culture was manifest above all in three areas. First there were the public graduation ceremonies, at which senior pupils graduating from the school gave farewell speeches. In small and medium-sized towns without a university, these ceremonies were an important feature of civic life and acted as a sort of rite of initiation into civic society. The pupils were well versed in public speaking since rhetoric was taught not just as part of German but also as a component of their Latin and Greek lessons.[19] There were, though, limits to the degree which students were able to express their own ideas and personality at the ceremonies: with family, staff and local dignitaries before them they had to match a number of different expectations.[20] For their family members, the ceremony was after all

---

[16] *Primaneralbum*, vol. II, School archive Meldorf, and the curricula in the annual reports.
[17] G. Kaiser, *Pietismus und Patriotismus im literarischen Deutschland. Ein Beitrag zum Problem der Säkularisation* (Wiesbaden 1961).
[18] On the concept of a *Schülerkultur* see Elkar, *Junges Deutschland*, pp. 227–231.
[19] G. Schaub, *Georg Büchner und die Schulrhetorik. Untersuchungen und Quellen zu seinen Schülerarbeiten* (Bern, Frankfurt 1975).
[20] An evocative description of a graduation ceremony can be found in T. Storm, 'Der Amtschirurgus - Heimkehr', in T. Storm, *Sämtliche Werke*, edited by P. Goldammer (Berlin, Weimar 1972), vol. IV, pp. 385–400.

mainly the public demonstration of a family success and one which had a much more direct personal meaning than studying in a distant university town. Even so, something of the pupils' own persuasions comes through.

A second element of this student culture, and one which offered greater opportunities for self-expression, were the albums. True, in Meldorf, the teacher had the right to inspect the pupils' work. Nevertheless this does not seem to have led to any restrictions. The things the students wrote and recorded in the album corresponded very much to the books they were reading – something we can check not only by reference to the official curriculum, but also because in the *Gymnasium* library in Husum the volumes still contain the borrowing marks from this period.

Finally, in the nineteenth century there was an abundance of pupils' clubs and associations. Here, too, Schleswig-Holstein offers a number of examples. In 1828 an 'association for academic study' was founded at the Christianeum Gymnasium in the town of Altona, near Hamburg, at that time under Danish rule.[21] It was modelled on a similar association that had been founded in 1817 at the Johanneum Gymnasium, situated near Hamburg.[22] At other schools, too, pupils created similar bodies.[23]

It is evident that these clubs and associations had less in common with student corporations than with the style of the *Hainbund*. In Altona and Ratzeburg the pupils held speeches and submitted written texts. The minutes of the meetings and the reviews of the texts can be found in the archive of the Christianeum, almost completely preserved. The Altona association also had its own library, one of whose first acquisitions was the complete works of Klopstock. Even in the 1830s we can still see the influence of the *Göttinger Hain* north of the Elbe. The members of the association read essays such as 'What thoughts and feelings are awakened in a young man of sensitivity and spirit by the early autumn?' or 'What thoughts are prompted by the worthy contemplation of nature?' The 'virtues of a sociable life' were praised, and topics such as 'happiness', 'humanity', 'freedom' and 'religion' were frequently

---

[21] N. Hansen, *100 Jahre Altonaer Wissenschaftlicher Primaner Verein Klio* (Altona no date [1928]).
[22] H. Schröder (ed.), *200 Jahre Christianeum zu Altona 1738–1938* (Hamburg 1938); *Festschrift 450 Jahre Gelehrtenschule des Johanneums zu Hamburg* (Hamburg 1979).
[23] Elkar, *Junges Deutschland*, p. 229.

discussed in a manner which drew on the sensibility of the *Hainbund* and the ideas and logic of the Enlightenment.

For the period between 1818 and 1847 we can observe the choice of reading of Husum pupils. The book most often borrowed was Johannes Daniel Falck's *Taschenbuch für Freunde des Scherzes und der Satire* (Pocket book for lovers of jokes and satire).[24] Of the poets of the *Hain*, the most popular were those with some sort of connection with Germany north of the Elbe. Friedrich Leopold von Stolberg, for example, moved to Eutin in 1781,[25] while Heinrich Wilhelm von Gerstenberg hailed from Tondern, which then belonged to Schleswig (though it is now part of Denmark),[26] and Friedrich Cramer taught from 1775 onwards as professor at the Christianeum.[27] Klopstock, Bürger and Hölty were also on the pupils' reading lists.[28]

The proximity of the *Hainbund* and its patriotic tone also stimulated an enthusiasm for national independence. This was, after all, a time when the duchies of Schleswig and Holstein were beginning to detach themselves from the culture of the Danish state and to develop a German cultural identity. The emergence of a new political consciousness amongst educated youngsters is visible at a graduation ceremony which took place in March 1822 at the Altona Christianeum. Some of the speeches followed the usual lines, but the fourth in particular betrayed the sentiment of the Hainbund with a title 'On the inner sensations which separation and farewell awaken in a person of feeling'.[29] Heinrich Brinckmann then created a stir with his account, delivered in Latin, of 'Reasons ... for our most heartfelt wish that the Greeks succeed in their struggle for liberation from their burdensome unchristian yoke'. The Greek war of liberation was then in its second year, following Alexandros Ipsilantis' move into Moldau and the Greek uprising. At the time Brinckmann delivered his speech, the first national assembly at Epidauros was just two months old, Byron had not yet left for Greece, and yet here was a pupil dwelling in public on this politically controversial issue.

---

[24] The book appeared in several editions - Leipzig 1789, Weimar 1802 and 1803.
[25] See Kelletat, *Göttinger Hain*, pp. 390–392.
[26] W.Kließ, *Sturm und Drang. Gerstenberg, Lenz, Klinger, Leisewitz, Wagner, Maler Müller* (Velber 1966).
[27] R. Erhardt-Lucht, *Die Ideen der Französischen Revolution* (Neumünster 1969), pp. 112–128.
[28] On the impact of the *Hainbund* in Schleswig-Holstein, see also O. Klose and C. Degn, *Die Herzogtümer im Gesamtstaat 1721–1830* (Neumünster 1960), pp. 170–173.
[29] *Schulprogramm Altona 1822/1823* (in the archive of the Christianeum).

The excited mood in the auditorium was then skilfully exploited by the final speaker, Ludolf Wienbarg, who in 'German verse' described 'the benign influence of nature on the refinement of the uneducated person'. His words moved the female members of the audience to tears. If Brinckmann's speech was the more obviously political, Wienbarg's pathos was equally infused by a political-aesthetic mission. In the *Gymnasium* it was traditionally the classical languages which were seen as the real medium of poetry. With his German verses Wienbarg challenged this tradition. Thus the students revealed a mixture of Philhellenism,[30] sentimentality and national pathos. These values marked out the space in which the political socialisation of a young generation took place.

Eleven years later in the summer semester of 1833, Ludolf Wienbarg, by now a young *Privatdozent*, delivered the lecture 'On aesthetics' to an over-full lecture theatre at Kiel University. A year later his remarks appeared in print with the title *Campaigns in aesthetics*, and with the inscription 'To you, young Germany, and not to the old I dedicate these lectures'.[31] The police and censorship officials went quickly to work and in 1835 Wienbarg's *Campaigns* was banned.[32]

Because like-minded writers such as Heinrich Heine, Theodor Mundt, Robert Prutz (himself a great fan of the *Hainbund*'s writing), and not least Wilhelm Marr, who published one of the first monographs on Young Germany,[33] were all going into print around the same time or soon after, it was generally assumed that the dedication to 'Young Germany' in Wienbarg's book was, in fact, directed to a secret society. Whether or not such an organised body existed, it *is* clear that a Young German consciousness was beginning to emerge. There was a group of like-minded young people to whom Wienbarg particularly appealed, above all the academically educated who

---

[30] On Philhellenism as a political-literary movement, see C. M. Woodhouse, *The Philhellenes* (London 1969).
[31] L. Wienbarg, *Aesthetische Feldzüge. Dem jungen Deutschland gewidmet* (Hamburg 1834), reprinted, edited and with an introduction by W. Dietze (Berlin, Weimar 1964). On Wienbarg, see D. Lohmeier, 'Wienbarg, Christian Ludolf', in Klose and Rudolph, *Lexikon*, vol. II, pp. 246–248 (with a list of works and further references).
[32] A list of the banned texts in Prussia in 1834 can be found in Glossy, *Literarische Geheimberichte*, pp. 22–23, secret report from Mainz, December 1834.
[33] R. E. Prutz, *Der Göttinger Dichterbund. Zur Geschichte der deutschen Literatur* (Leipzig 1841, reprinted Bern 1971; W. Marr, *Das junge Deutschland in der Schweiz. Ein Beitrag zur Geschichte der geheimen Verbindungen unserer Tage* (Leipzig 1846), reprinted with an appendix 'Anarchie oder Autorität' (Glashütten/Ts. 1976).

had been exposed to similar socialisation processes as Wienbarg himself. They understood the finer points of Wienbarg's argument, sharing his view that a new era required a new type of politics and a new aesthetic. The close connection between politics and aesthetics in the thinking of this generation was very clear; in this respect at least there was little to distinguish the 'old' young Germans of the nineteenth century from the 'new' young Germans of the twentieth.

The emergence of this new mood did not escape the secret informants of the political police:[34]

> What could have been predicated has indeed taken place! The official steps which had to be taken against Young Germany have engaged the interest of the more educated classes of our inhabitants. They debate the direction taken by Young Germany and in order to understand it properly seek to buy the books by the movement. It is good that the books are so expensive that many are put off from buying them.

It was evident that censorship alone could no longer suppress the movement. The police informant hoped that the worst might yet be prevented by an 'improved education for our youth'. The real threat to youth was that they might be led astray by the 'panegyricists' and their 'dangerous sentiments'. However, the chances of a healthy 'German national education system' being created were small because 'the teachers of our youth – and this applies to the teachers at state schools in our free city (i.e. Frankfurt am Main) – are, almost to a man, intoxicated by political liberalism'.

Young Germany had thus reached the younger generation, not just the students but also school pupils. Censorship had if anything increased the attractiveness of its literature. Often it did not require the enthusiasm of the teacher for the ideas of the movement to spread. Like Wienbarg himself,[35] many pupils were secret users of lending libraries, a practice at which their teachers often looked askance. One example will suffice to show how the ideas of Young Germany spread through the schools. In October 1837 Theodor Mommsen, who was to become the celebrated classical historian and winner of the Nobel prize for literature, joined the 'association for academic study' at the Christianeum in Altona. His maiden

---

[34] Glossy, *Literarische Geheimberichte*, secret report from 2 December 1835, pp. 42ff.
[35] See Wienbarg's autobiographical notes in F. G. Kühne, *Portraits und Silhouetten* (Hanover 1843), vol. II, p. 180; see also R. S. Elkar, '"Junges Deutschland" und Gelehrte Schule. Einige unbekannte Dokumente zur Biographie Ludolph Wienbargs', in *Christianeum*, vol. 30 (1975), pp. 12–18.

speech was on the topic 'an introduction to the writings of young Germany'. He enthralled his hearers with deliberations on a 'general emancipation' which would encompass politics, religion and literature. He saw this as the goal of such writers as Wienbarg, Laube, Mundt and Gutzkow and was critical of other writers who restricted their aims to a purely political process of emancipation. Sketching out the way politics and literature must develop in the future, he argued:[36]

It is clear that the mood of the times is favourable for the young literature or, more precisely, that this literature is an expression of the mood of the times. Young Germany can thus not be restricted to the few names already mentioned. All over Germany there are undoubtedly numerous as yet unknown supporters of the new teaching. And there are even more who do not yet know themselves that they are its supporters, people who perhaps have not even read anything from the movement. Because that is what we mean by the 'mood of the times': the same changes taking place independently in many minds, because the same causes are at work. It is true that the process can express itself in different forms. But even if it is still only a few who throw themselves fully behind the demand for general emancipation, with each new particular question of emancipation that arises more and more liberal voices can be heard. Liberalism, no longer restricted to the political sphere, gains more and more spiritual ground and spreads itself further and further in the minds of the people. In Berlin, people with hearts and minds attuned to the modern age come together. Often they gather round – this, too, a sign of cultural progress – outstanding women (Rahel Varnhagen, Charlotte Stieglitz). And finally we ourselves, we who wish to call ourselves liberal, are we young Germans or not? If you have recognised that the holy spirit is in young Germany, then do not deny it.

With more precision than some of the Young German writers themselves the pupil Theodor Mommsen had shown how a literary movement could draw from and reinforce the *Zeitgeist*. In later life, in the fourth book of his *History of Rome*, Mommsen argued that there was a direct connection between 'economic conditions', the 'social conditions' which developed from them and the resulting effects on 'civilisation'.[37] Some of this later insight was already evident in Mommsen's portrayal of Young Germany as an emanation of the mood of the times.

---

[36] Quoted from A. Wachholtz, 'Aus Theodor Mommsens Schulzeit', in *Festschrift der 48. Versammlung deutscher Philologen und Schulmänner in Hamburg, dargebracht vom Lehrerkollegium des Königlichen Christianeums zu Altona* (Altona 1905), p. 33.

[37] T. Mommsen, *Römische Geschichte, Band 3, Viertes Buch: Die Revolution* (Munich, dtv edition 1976), p. 414 (corresponds to II, p. 401).

Above all, Young German literature drew on, and in turn strengthened, two tendencies in German youth culture. On the one hand the watchword 'young' had become a powerful symbol, a synonym for being liberal, free-thinking, emancipated, non-reactionary. The secret reports from the movement's opponents confirmed, though hardly with approval, that the notion of 'youth' had become indelibly imbued with such political associations. On the other hand, young people had gained a sense of identity and a generational mission which was to impel them to political action in 1848.[38] This political consciousness was new and marked a fundamental difference between Young Germany and *Hainbund*. Young Germany was no longer just about discussing one another's writings and refining one's sensibility. Instead, emerging out of the literary and cultural movements of the late eighteenth century,[39] youth had come to be seen as the key hope for political change. Trust in the experience of age was being displaced by faith in the energy and purity of youth. What was evident here was part of a long-term, fundamental paradigm shift affecting political life in Germany, a shift which reached its consummation in the *Jugendstil* and young German culture of the early twentieth century and whose influence can be felt up to the present day.[40]

It is obvious that the youth culture described here has been very much an intellectual-academic one. To what extent did the young of the 'working classes'[41] participate in this culture? How far was there an emergent unified young generation?

The university disciplinary records list countless disputes and fights between students and journeymen, between students and soldiers, night watchmen or police and between students and 'philistines', as the remaining citizens were called in student parlance. What interests us amongst all this blood-letting are the tensions that existed within the same age group – between the students and the

---

[38] R. S. Elkar, 'Schüler des Christianeums in Vormärz und Revolution', *Christianeum*, vol. 28 (1973), pp. 25–28.

[39] See also Joachim Whaley's chapter in this collection.

[40] H. Mommsen, 'Die Rolle des "Jungen Deutschland" in der deutschen Arbeiterbewegung nach 1914', in L. Niethammer (eds.), *'Die Menschen machen ihre Geschichte nicht aus freien Stücken, aber sie machen sie selbst.' Einladung zu einer Geschichte des Volkes in NRW* (Berlin, Bonn 1984), pp. 123–126.

[41] 'Working classes' is used here not as a narrow or overly precise category but to group together all those who shared roughly the same position in the production process – the 'workers', 'journeymen' or 'wage-earners' – and thus to contrast them with members of the academic and economic bourgeoisie.

young inhabitants of the town. And when we look closely at the
records, we discover not only the enormous social gulf that existed
between students and their non-academic contemporaries, but also
that the emerging enlightened culture of the academic youth was far
from being what it seemed. The young future members of the
academically educated middle classes continued, in fact, to be
influenced by centuries-old feudal traditions and privileges and,
indeed, to insist on those privileges. The calls for a glorious new age
of emancipation and democracy were, it turns out, made by students
and grammar-school pupils who were seldom ready to abandon
their own social position and distinctions.

In student argot, the students themselves were the *Burschen* or
lads, and the journeymen were known as the *Knoten* or knots, a
nickname derived from the gnarled handles of the journeymen's
walking sticks. Apart from accompanying the journeymen on their
long and weary travels, the sticks could also be used as a crude
weapon of defence against the students' daggers and even sometimes
to attack the young academics. One witness of such encounters was
the student Georg Büchner,[42] a young poet later to die in 1837 at the
age of only 23, here writing in Gießen during May 1834:[43]

I have little time for the goings-on of the students. Yesterday they received
a beating from the philistines. The students called for aid – 'lads, to the
street!' But none save the members of two fraternities came, and they had
to call in the university judge in order to save themselves from the young
cobblers and tailors. The judge was drunk and insulted the townsfolk. I
wonder he didn't get a beating himself. The most amusing aspect of it is
that the journeymen, being of a liberal persuasion, set about the loyalist
fraternities. The whole affair is supposed to recur this evening; there are
mutterings that the students may quit the town. I hope the students get
beaten again. We support the townsfolk and remain in the town.

Such disputes were no peculiarity of Gießen. Erlangen, for
example, was witness to riotous incidents between students and
craftsmen in 1744, 1751, 1774 and 1819. What often provoked the
'philistines' and 'knots' was the students' arrogant manner. The
students would, for example, sharpen their blades on the cobbles,

[42] H. L. Arnold (ed.), *Georg Büchner I–III* (Bonn 1975, 2nd edn.); T. M. Mayer (ed.), *Georg Büchner. Leben, Werk, Zeit. Ausstellung zum 150. Jahrestag des 'Hessischen Landboten'* (Marburg 1985).
[43] G. Büchner, *Sämtliche Werke*, edited by W. E. Lehmann (Hamburg, Munich 1971–72), vol. II, p. 429.

when the journeymen were forbidden by law from carrying swords.[44] Büchner's reference to the university judge reminds us that the universities exercised their own jurisdiction, independent of the normal courts. This was a perennial source of complaint from soldiers and citizens. The universities, for their part, jealously defended their legal privilege. For example, when a Danish government official suggested that Kiel University's rights of self-jurisdiction should be reduced,[45] the consistory (a body akin to the senate of a British university) vigorously opposed the suggestion that the normal authorities were competent to adjudicate on student matters.[46] Its stance documented not just professorial sympathy for the temperament and antics of academic youth, but the pride and sense of distinction on the part of representatives of the 'educated orders'. The professors in the consistory wanted to ensure that misdemeanours and offences committed by their own kind should be pursued according to the honour code of their own social order.

Of all the conflicts between town and gown, it is the *Knotenrevolution* in Mainz in 1790 which has been accorded the greatest significance by historians. Here, the conflicts between craftsmen and students were so intense that troops had to be called in from Hessen-Darmstadt and Nassau-Usingia.[47] In a country whose national history has been so short of revolutions, it is easy to see why German historians have seen in this an event of real significance. The craftsmen, for example, bore with them the *tricolore* of the French Revolution when they marched on the university buildings. Could this not be seen as the bourgeoisie imposing the symbol of *Liberté, égalité, fraternité* on the Bastille of an academic aristocracy? Whatever its significance, it should be borne in mind that – as in Erlangen and later in Kiel – the Mainz uprising was part of a long chain of disputes reaching back into the eighteenth century.[48] In 1732 students wounded a servant. In 1752 conflict with the police led to excesses, the students again demanding to be treated under

[44] E. G. Deuerlein, *Geschichte der Universität Erlangen* (Erlangen 1927).
[45] Schleswig-Holsteinisches Landesarchiv in Schleswig (LAS) 47, no. 167, Letter from Jensen to the academic consistory, 30 March 1836.
[46] LAS 47, 167, Letter from the academic consistory to curator Jensen, 13 July 1836.
[47] H. Mathy, 'Studien und Quellen zur Gerichtsbarkeit an der Universität Mainz', in *Festschrift Johannes Bärmann*, vol. 1 (Wiesbaden 1966), pp. 116–160; H. Kersting, 'Die Mainzer Zeitung unter Leitung von Johannes Weitzel' (doctoral thesis, Mainz 1953); K. G. Faber, 'Görres, Weitzel und die Revolution', in *HZ*, vol. 194 (1962), pp. 37–61.
[48] The following episodes are listed in Mathy, 'Studien und Quellen', pp. 158ff.

special jurisdiction. In 1761 law students attacked a goldsmith during the night. In 1768 several students tried to free a journeyman from police custody. In 1779 students were involved in a battle with the police. In 1782 there were disturbances between students and craftsmen. In 1785 a student of the philosophical faculty injured a policeman who tried to apprehend him during nocturnal disturbances. In 1786 a theology student injured a sentry. In 1787 students assaulted two girls from the town. In 1791 a pro-rector reported a student to the cathedral chapter for 'incitement'. In 1792 students attacked a royal coachman. All these incidents took place in Mainz. In Kiel, resisting the police was one of the commonest misdemeanours. There were twenty such cases in one year alone.[49]

When looked at together these many individual incidents reveal certain clear patterns. Above all, the confrontations revolved around two main issues: money and honour. Non-payment of rent, debts and restaurant and public-house bills joined embezzlement as frequent subjects of legal dispute between students and the citizens of the town. Evidently the flight into university jurisprudence in such cases remained so common that the Leipzig law professor Friedrich Stein demanded in his 1891 handbook of academic jurisdiction 'that the civil law for the protection of property and person must form an inviolable boundary' to the 'freedom of academic life'.[50] As far as invoking the legal protection of the person is concerned, it was the daughters of the townsfolk (unless they came from academic backgrounds themselves) who most frequently found themselves the unwilling target of the students' attentions. Girls were physically abused, sometimes dangerously so; journeymen found their partners being abducted from the dance floor with insults and abuse. When we read in a recent publication that to satisfy their 'love-starved hearts' the students had to 'make do' with 'the daughters of the people', what we learn from the subtext of this patronising portrayal of the relationship between the two sides is that it was as much about power as about love. The students could impose their will and demonstrate their power more easily over those of lower social standing.[51]

The frequent confrontations with police, troops or town guard

[49] LAS 47, no. 746, Untersuchungen wegen nächtlicher Ruhestörungen 1847–1849.
[50] F. Stein, *Die akademische Gerichtsbarkeit in Deutschland* (Leipzig 1891), p. 113.
[51] H. König, *Burschen, Knoten und Philister. Erlanger Studentenleben von 1743 bis 1983* (Nuremberg 1983), p. 15.

were sought by the students as ritual tests of courage. It is true that in the student honour code, the *Komment*, such representatives of authority were not capable of giving satisfaction. They were, however, armed and this made conflict with them seem more honourable than with unarmed townsfolk. The attempt by students to free themselves from 'dishonourable', i.e. non-academic police, custody, and the ensuing triumphal processions to the university chancellor were public demonstrations of social honour. In students' eyes the world was divided into those who were allowed to carry weapons and those who were not – and the latter group included the citizens of the town.

Against this background, it is hard to see in the Mainz events anything very unusual, and certainly not the class warfare waged by the exploited against their exploiters. For one thing, the wrath of journeymen and guilds was directed against a socially hetero-geneous group of professors, canons of the cathedral chapter and students, a group which certainly had little to do with the exploitation of the working class. Nor can the carrying of the *tricolore* by the craftsmen be seen as the clear expression of a social-political confrontation. Indeed, it was odd that the craftsmen should regard the colours as a protest against the university at all. If there were sympathisers for the French Revolution in Mainz, they were undoubtedly to be found within the enlightened-reformed university, and the wider academically educated middle classes.[52] The order of the *Illuminati* enjoyed a following amongst academics, students and civil servants. Amongst the professors there were some avant-garde spirits,[53] whilst shortly before the arrival of the French some students, including the later Jacobin of Mainz, Friedrich Lehne, tried to form a reading circle. Thus it was a symbol of doubtful force which was carried to the university buildings. In historical perspective, the *tricolore* could hardly be seen as constituting a political barricade between the two sides.

Instead, the background to the events seems to lie very much in the conventional ritualised conflicts between students and craftsmen. The craftsmen were primarily interested in revenge for the

[52] K. Fuchs, 'Anmerkungen zu einer zeitgenössischen Kommentierung der Mainzer Universitätsreform von 1784', in H. Weber (ed.), *Tradition und Gegenwart. Studien und Quellen zur Geschichte der Universität Mainz mit besonderer Berücksichtigung der Philosophischen Fakultät.* Vol. 1; *Aus der Zeit der kurfürstlichen Universität* (Wiesbaden 1977), pp. 167–181.
[53] H. Mathy, 'Das Mainzer Geistesleben am Vorabend der Französischen Revolution', in Weber, *Tradition*, p. 158. See also J. Rachold (ed.), *Die Illuminaten. Quellen und Texte zur Aufklärungsideologie des Illuminatenordens (1776–1785)* (Berlin 1984).

perennial student assaults on their property and above all on their sense of social status and honour[54] — be it as journeymen or as citizens. It is noteworthy that the Mainz 'revolution' forged new alliances between master craftsmen and journeymen. Normally the two sides were divided by their conflicting interests as employer and employee. Yet here their shared interests as 'citizens' brought them together against the academic community.

How was the conflict to be resolved? The craftsmen were not campaigning for a new social order. What they wanted was to establish the clear rule of law. This, too, shows that the revolutionary flag was being carried not as a symbol of revolution but as a gesture of defiance. The university was quick to try and appease the guilds, promising to punish a number of students held in custody. But this was not enough — not yet. Further disturbances ensued and now it was the university's turn to feel that its rights had been violated, after several students were badly injured by police and troops. In the end punishments were handed out on both sides. But the students were tried within the 'academic forum', by their own social equals and away from the public courts. Not so the craftsmen. The distinction between the social orders was thus preserved. For all the new rhetoric of liberal-minded youth, then, it is apparent just how far youth cultures continued to be defined and shaped by the 'old social order'.

III

During the second half of the eighteenth century and the first half of the nineteenth there was thus no unified youth culture. Journeymen and students may have belonged to the same age group[55] but immense social barriers divided them. It was thus scarcely conceivable that a united youth could really be the harbinger of a new social order. The notion of a united youth remained the utopian dream of the academically educated middle classes — themselves in reality shaped, far more than they wished to admit, by feudal privileges and attitudes.

[54] A. Grießinger, *Das symbolische Kapital der Ehre. Streikbewegungen und kollektives Bewußtsein deutscher Handwerksgesellen im 18. Jahrhundert* (Frankfurt, Berlin, Vienna 1981).

[55] On the age of the craftsmen, see R. S. Elkar, 'Wandernde Gesellen in und aus Oberdeutschland. Quantitative Studien zur Sozialgeschichte des Handwerks vom 17. bis zum 19. Jahrhundert', in U. Engelhardt (ed.), *Handwerker in der Industrialiserung. Lage, Kultur und Politik vom späten 18. bis ins frühe 20. Jahrhundert* (Stuttgart 1984), p. 270.

Apart from the two sides' sense of status and honour, what divided them was the very different structures of their everyday lives. The young academics were unique in the degree to which they enjoyed a free 'moratorium'[56] between childhood and adult working life. During this interlude they enjoyed a great deal of personal freedom, time and space to shape their future lives. This applied, incidentally, to the offspring of poorer families who managed to reach university. For, if they had managed to surmount the huge financial obstacles to getting to and through the *Gymnasium*, grants were usually available to get through university. But the number managing to reach university from poorer backgrounds was very small. Moreover, there was a surplus of university graduates in the early nineteenth century and this led to a further cutback on university recruitment from outside the families of the academically educated middle classes.[57]

The journeymen faced a much harder situation than their more academic counterparts. As apprentices they not only had far less free time but did not even enjoy the full use of their earnings. Part of them had to be given to their parents and part saved for the years as journeymen. Very few could live on what they earned on the road. There was thus no moratorium free from economic pressures. Yet it would be wrong to say that, in contrast with middle- and upper-class youngsters, they did not enjoy a 'youth'.[58] True, they did not have the same freedom, but they did enjoy work-free time which they, too, could use to create their own culture.[59] And the culture that emerged was a distinct, plebeian/proletarian one. Thus, here too, we see why liberal-bourgeois views found it hard to make inroads into the youth culture of journeymen and young workers.

There were, of course, instances of genuine unity amongst youth. Georg Büchner's views for example, were characterised by a rigor-

---

[56] H. H. Muchow, *Sexualreife und Sozialstruktur der Jugend* (Reinbek 1959); H. H. Muchow, *Jugend und Zeitgeist. Morphologie der Kulturpubertät* (Reinbek 1962).

[57] H. Titze, 'Überfüllungskrisen in akademischen Karrieren. Eine Zyklustheorie', in *Zeitschrift für Philosophie*, vol. 267 (1981), pp. 187–226; R. S. Elkar, 'Elitenbildung oder Massenuniversität. Zu Problemen der Bildungsrekrutierung im 19. Jahrhundert', in S. Hoyer and W. Fläschendräger (ed.), *Die Geschichte der Universitäten und ihre Erforschung* (Leipzig 1984), pp. 108–131; see also Joachim Whaley's chapter in this volume.

[58] U. Herrmann, 'Was heißt "Jugend"? Jugendkonzeptionen in der deutschen Sozialgeschichte', *Der Bürger im Staat*, vol. 32 (1982), p. 26.

[59] J. Reulecke and W. Weber (eds.), *Fabrik-Familie-Feierabend. Beiträge zur Sozialgeschichte des Alltags im Industriezeitalter* (Wuppertal 1978); G. Huck (ed.), *Sozialgeschichte der Freizeit. Untersuchungen zum Wandel der Alltagskultur in Deutschland* (Wuppertal 1980).

ous egalitarianism which extended to the social and economic spheres as well as the political.[60] They were not the norm in the political movements of the 1830s and 1840s, but they were not quite as exceptional as historians have often assumed.[61] In 1834 Büchner threw himself into bringing radical (i.e. democratic-republican) academics and craftsmen together for political action. Gießen was a good place to initiate such a campaign. A few years earlier Paul Follen, Christian Bansa and Professor Vogt had instituted a reading circle there which became 'the only semi-legal meeting place for academics and craftsmen'. Büchner had been in contact with this group in 1832. He then founded in Gießen and in his home town of Darmstadt a 'Society of human rights'. The society attracted both students and craftsmen, though the former were in the majority. The participants discussed political questions of the day – amongst them topics such as 'liberalism', 'popular agitation', 'revolution' and 'communal property'. At the behest of two Swiss students they discussed whether to establish links to the craftsmen's associations which had been set up in Switzerland in autumn 1833 and to the Swiss Young Germany movement, in existence since spring 1834.[62] It is no accident that it was students who made this proposal. In Switzerland as in Germany members of the academically educated middle classes and writers played a leading role in shaping political ideas. 'Proletarianised intellectuals' like August Becher and Wilhelm Marr exerted a major influence on the ideas of the emergent workers' and journeymen's associations.[63]

Yet the contacts between students and craftsmen remained limited and, not only that, were the product of a relatively short-lived transitional phase that reached its high point in the 1830s and was already in decline in the 1840s. During the 1830s, critical bourgeois intellectuals did indeed play a key role in the emergence of a working-class political movement.[64] During this early phase, there was considerable scope for bourgeois and labour figures to join together in agitation for liberal rights and freedoms. Soon, however, the bourgeois advisers proved increasingly dispensable, particularly

[60] Büchner, *Sämtliche Werke*, p. 422.
[61] R. Görisch and T. M. Mayer (eds.), *Untersuchungsberichte zur republikanischen Bewegung in Hessen 1831–1834* (Frankfurt 1982); H. J. Ruckhäberle, *Flugschriftenliteratur im historischen Umkreis Georg Büchners* (Kronberg/Ts. 1975).
[62] T. M. Mayer, 'Georg Büchner. Eine kurze Chronik zu Leben und Werk', in Arnold, *Georg Büchner*, pp. 357–425, here above all pp. 378ff.
[63] Ruckhäberle, *Bildung*, pp. 16ff.   [64] Schieder, *Anfänge*, pp. 90ff.

as the workers' education movement took shape, and the craftsmen's and workers' associations attained a new independence.[65] Spurned by the labour associations, radical students found the main arena for their political activism in the democratic clubs. They were often to be found on the executives of these associations, alongside representatives of the left Liberal bourgeoisie.[66] They focused their energies increasingly on establishing an egalitarian legal order. In the university context, for example, radical students could be found in the 1840s supporting the movement for the removal of a separate university jurisdiction.[67] It was a sign of their isolation from the labour movement that very few were involved in attempts to create *social* equality, particularly as many lacked any understanding of the economic preconditions for such an idea. It is worth noting that the students were nonetheless not completely cut off from the popular movement of the 1848 revolt. Students provided substantial contingents, sometimes whole units, to the Free Corps of Vienna, Budapest and Schleswig-Holstein.[68] Student protest was not always limited to the pen.[69]

In general, though, the 1840s saw a broadening rift between the two youth cultures and the bodies which gave political expression to their political views. One reason for this was undoubtedly the growing divergence between the interests of the bourgeoisie as a whole, on the one hand, and the craft community, on the other. The youth 'subcultures'[70] were then carried along with their respective social group. Whereas journeymen's protest had in the past shown little correlation with general economic trends, from the 1820s economic crisis was increasingly to lie behind their collective behaviour.[71]

The structural crisis in the crafts trades left the journeymen

---

[65] Ruckhäberle, *Bildung*, pp. 9ff.
[66] R. Weber, 'Die Beziehungen zwischen sozialer Struktur und politischer Ideologie in der Revolution von 1848/9', *Zeitschrift für Geschichtswissenschaft*, vol. 13 (1965), pp. 1187–1193.
[67] H. Thielbeer, *Universität und Politik in der deutschen Revolution von 1848* (Bonn 1983), pp. 195ff.
[68] E. Schwalm, *Volksbewaffnung 1848–1850 in Schleswig-Holstein. Vorarbeiten zu einer Psychologie und Soziologie der Schleswig-Holsteinischen Erhebung* (Neumünster 1961), pp. 282–295. Intellectuals and students made up 22.47 per cent of 1126 Free Corps members in Schleswig-Holstein.
[69] Thielbeer, *Universität*, p. 120.
[70] Critical notes on the concept of subculture can be found in Herrmann, 'Was heißt "Jugend"?'. See also John Clarke *et al.*, *Jugendkultur und Widerstand* (Frankfurt 1979).
[71] A. Grießinger, 'Handwerkerstreiks in Deutschland während des 18. Jahrhunderts. Begriff - Organisationsformen - Ursachenkonstellationen', in Engelhardt, *Handwerker*, pp. 407–434.

feeling increasingly isolated. The conflict of interest between master craftsmen and journeymen on corporate and economic questions continued undiminished. As is well known, the 1848–49 revolution saw the master craftsmen in the Frankfurt parliament and the craftsmen's assemblies not only simultaneously advocating political Liberalism and economic protectionism, but also regularly at odds with, and certainly never working together with, the journeymen.[72] In addition, different craft sectors fared very differently from one another and could rarely be counted on to make common cause. As a result the youth culture of the journeymen within the 'working class' became increasingly isolated and autonomous.

The contrast between their prospects and those of the young aspirants to the academically educated middle classes was striking. The latter could in general look forward to a rosy future. The growing career opportunities for the educated bourgeoisie offered ample prospects for considerable prosperity and social status, though at the price of abandoning any radical-democratic dreams of younger years. For the journeymen no comparable prospects existed. The established craftsmen, caught in the crisis themselves, were in no position to offer great opportunities to the young.

Should we see the increasingly desperate situation of the journeymen as providing the decisive impetus to the emergence of working-class politics? Did the 'cradle of the labour movement' lie in the craftsman's workshop?[73] Certainly, many of those involved in shaping the new proletarian youth culture were still familiar with the old protest forms and patterns of association of the journeymen. Indeed, the traditional modes of journeymen's protest continued to surface right up to the 1848 revolution. The Erlangen riots provide one example. Another example was the still common practice of 'strolling out' in protest against unemployment. In other words, though the traditional certainties of the craftsman's life were disappearing, many journeymen understandably stuck to the patterns of behaviour and protest which had belonged to their socialisation.

[72] J. Bergmann, 'Das Handwerk in der Revolutionen von 1848. Zum Zusammenhang von materieller Lage und Revolutionsverhalten der Handwerker 1848/1849', in Engelhardt, *Handwerker*, pp. 320–346; M. Simon, *Handwerk in Krise und Umbruch. Wirtschaftliche Forderungen und sozialpolitische Vorstellungen der Handwerksmeister im Revolutionsjahr 1848/9* (Cologne, Vienna 1983).

[73] W. Kaschuba, 'Vom Gesellenkampf zum sozialen Protest. Zur Erfahrungs- und Konfliktdisposition von Gesellen-Arbeitern in den Vormärz- und Revolutionsjahren', in U. Engelhardt, *Handwerker*, p. 406.

Partly because of this, no direct line can be drawn from journey-men's associations to the new labour movement. When a new type of political culture and ideology emerged in the associations of the working class, it was frequently not representatives of the dying trades that provided the leadership in these associations. The pro-letarian movement was forged often by workers in trades with a relatively recent tradition or with a high educational standard, for example the cigar-makers or printers. What emerges, then, was a fusion of old and new. Together, journeymen with the experiences of solidarity and conflict provided by their years on the road, journey-men forced to take on factory work, and factory workers without a craft background forged a new political culture, and one associated with patterns of economic, social and cultural life that differed substantially from the once stable world of journeyman and master craftsman.

Against this background, there was no longer any possibility that academic bourgeois youth might act as the catalyst for the creation of a single youth culture linked by common assumptions and a sense of youth's common identity. The youth culture of students and *Gymnasiasten* lost any function outside the narrow social confines of the bourgeoisie. Of course, the rituals of the young academic con-tinued to exist; the honour code or *Komment* continued to exert an influence on the pattern of student life. But the student culture not only lost any appeal outside the university or *Gymnasium* walls, it also lost the cutting edge of protest. After the revolution, the young ceased to challenge the older generation with the values of emanci-pation and reform. Instead, they simply accepted the career pattern held out to them by their elders.

v

We are bound to ask whether the school pupils, students and journeymen looked at here really provide a cross-section of German youth in the period 1780–1850. Clearly, these groups were all urban and male. Girls have hardly been mentioned, except as victims of male assaults, nor has there been any word on the sizeable propor-tion of young people employed in agriculture. It might seem arbi-trary to exclude such groups, and certainly historians have often shown a blind spot where non-urban, non-male youth was con-cerned and have ignored the quite favourable sources available on young women and young agricultural workers. The point of excluding these groups in the present essay, however, is that young urban males were what *contemporaries* meant when they used the term 'youth'. In fact, it was doubtful if they included even the journeyman within the category.

The notion of youth developed from an image of school pupils and students; it thus incorporated the values, rules, traditions and expectations of the academic bourgeoisie.[74] German historians of youth and education have identified a linguistic distinction between the *Jüngling*, which corresponded to the specific, narrow conception of youth just outlined, and the *Jugendliche*, meaning youth in a broader, less normative sense.[75] The *Jüngling* was born in the eighteenth century. From the 1780s and 1790s until the Napoleonic wars it was the goal of the studying *Jünglinge* 'to provide the state with honest and serviceable men'.[76] It was a generation committed to reform and one which asserted youth's right to shape its own future.[77] Their children were the *Jünglinge* who saw themselves as Germany's political avant-garde and called for democratic revolution. A heady brew of adolescence, liberal education and political engagement produced in this latter generation the attitudes and values of Young Germany. But then, in the years of political reaction after the failed revolution, the brew lost its potency. Above all, the political engagement disappeared. True, the notion of the *Jüngling* survived into the period of the second German empire, but it had lost the 'nasty' whiff of the avant-garde.[78] In the Kaiserreich, the notion of the *Jüngling* was extended to include the '*Jüngling* from the people', who as an apprentice or journeyman sought to increase his knowledge and skills and to win the respect of his parents and supervisors at work. The many Christian *Jünglings* associations and official state agencies hoped to use this notion to create a stable and satisfied class of craftsmen and *Jüngling* thus became a term linked to

---

[74] T. von Trotha, 'Zur Entstehung von Jugend', *Kölner Zeitschrift für Soziologie und Sozialpsychologie*, vol. 34 (1982), pp. 254–277.

[75] W. Hornstein, *Vom 'jungen Herrn' zum 'hoffnungsvollen Jüngling'. Wandlungen des Jugendlebens im 18.Jahrhundert* (Heidelberg 1965); W. Hornstein, *Jugend in ihrer Zeit. Geschichte und Lebensformen des jungen Menschen in der europäischen Welt* (Hamburg 1966). Hornstein's work has been critically analysed in L. Roth, *Die Erfindung des Jugendlichen* (Munich 1983).

[76] W. Hardtwig, 'Sozialverhalten und Wertwandel der jugendlichen Bildungsschicht im Übergang zur bürgerlichen Gesellschaft (17.-19.Jahrhundert)', *VfSW*, vol. 73 (1986), p. 329.

[77] W. Hardtwig, 'Krise der Universität', p. 176.

[78] U. Herrmann, 'Der "Jüngling" und der "Jugendliche"'.

attempts to preserve the status quo. It was ironic that it was only in the hands of the conservative authorities of the Kaiserreich that the notion of the *Jüngling* should be allowed to bridge the classes. In the pre-revolutionary period, when the notion of 'youth' had ostensibly stood for a broad emancipatory movement, the reality of the *Jüngling* had, in fact, been far more socially circumscribed. Apart from some individual contacts, the German youth movement never attained a broad and enduring political impetus, spanning the barriers of class and status. The youth culture of protest always remained restricted to the educated middle and upper class, both in terms of the social origins of the participants, and in terms of the way those involved consciously or subconsciously conceptualised 'youth'. This limitation was true of the years of Young Germany and it remained true of the 1960s – indeed, was even truer of the latter than of the former.

CHAPTER 4

The battle for the young: mobilising young people in Wilhelmine Germany

Jürgen Reulecke

Over the last few years, historians of twentieth-century Germany have increasingly recognised the importance of generational group-ings and divisions in influencing both intellectual climate and poli-tical attitudes and conflict. Particularly in the period between the end of the nineteenth century and the Nazi era, tension and conflict between 'youth' (however defined) and the established generations came to be as decisive as divisions along socio-economic class lines in shaping Germany's political development.

Though the roots of these generational tensions can undoubtedly be traced further back, it was in the Wilhelmine era that they emerged strongly for the first time. In public debate about the way society saw itself, for example, the concepts of 'youth' and 'young generation' played a central role. At the same time large numbers of youth organisations, some autonomous, some affiliated to other movements, came into being in these years. There was also a marked increase in educational and social research concerned with young people.[1] Great efforts were made by state and church to win the hearts and minds of the young and integrate them into established society.[2] In short, there was an explosion of concern with, and

[1] On the history of youth in the nineteenth and twentieth centuries, see John R. Gillis, *Youth and history: tradition and change in European age relations, 1770 to the present* (New York, London 1981, 2nd edn.); Michael Mitterauer, *Sozialgeschichte der Jugend* (Frankfurt 1986). On the 'invention' of youth at the turn of the century see Lutz Roth, *Die Erfindung des Jugendlichen* (Munich 1983) and Peter Dudek, *Jugend als Objekt der Wissenschaften. Geschichte der Jugend-forschung in Deutschland und Österreich 1890–1933* (Opladen 1990).
[2] On these efforts see Thomas Nipperdey, 'Jugend und Politik um 1900', in Thomas Nipper-dey, *Gesellschaft, Kultur, Theorie* (Göttingen 1976), pp. 338–359 and Klaus Saul, 'Der Kampf um die Jugend zwischen Volksschule und Kaserne', *Militärgeschichtliche Mitteil-ungen*, vol. 6 (1971), pp. 97–125. See also Jürgen Reulecke, 'Bürgerliche Sozialreformer und Arbeiterjugend im Kaiserreich', *AfS*, vol. 22 (1982), pp. 299–329; Detlev Peukert, *Grenzen der Sozialdisziplinierung. Aufstieg und Krise der deutschen Jugendfürsorge 1878–1932* (Cologne 1986) and especially Derek Linton, *'Who has the youth has the future': the campaign to save young workers in Imperial Germany 1870–1914* (Cambridge 1991).

awareness of, youth that was arguably far more extreme than in other industrialised Western nations.

The aim of the present essay is first, to outline the diverse and often contradictory forms in which these new tensions between youth and adult society emerged and developed in Wilhelmine Germany. At the same time, it analyses *why* the whole question of youth should have assumed such importance, and attempts to place the Wilhelminian preoccupation with youth in the broader context of a growing feeling of insecurity on the part of the German bourgeoisie. Finally, it will consider briefly the legacy of Wilhelminian generation conflict for the Weimar republic and the Third Reich.[3]

I

It is important to note at the outset that the typically German forms of youth movement and youth welfare which arose around 1900 were just part of a broad and varied spectrum of bourgeois attempts at renewal and reform. During the nineteenth century the bourgeoisie had provided some important initiatives towards modernisation, but parts of the bourgeoisie, especially of the educated middle class, were still very much in the grip of pre-modern value systems and consequently found it very difficult to adapt to the new circumstances.[4] Towards the end of the century, therefore, these groups felt seriously threatened on all sides; first by the enormous progress which was taking place in the technical and economic sphere, and secondly by the deteriorating social and political situation which could well undermine their comfortable existence and traditional status.

The reactions were many and varied. On the one hand there were all kinds of proposals and calls for reform. On the other there was escapism of all sorts, in particular a predilection for myths and cults. The growing insecurity about status also expressed itself in

---

[3] This essay has not looked at female youth because of the lack of research in this area. See above all Derek S. Linton, 'Between school and marriage, workshop and household: young working women as a social problem in late imperial Germany', *European History Quarterly*, vol. 18 (1988), 4, pp. 387–408. There have been a growing number of publications on girls in the bourgeois youth movement. See for example the essays in the *Jahrbuch des Archivs der deutschen Jugendbewegung*, vol. 15 (1984/85); Marion E. P. de Ras, *Körper, Eros und weibliche Kultur. Mädchen im Wandervogel und in der bündischen Jugend 1900–1933* (Pfaffenweiler 1988); Irmgard Klönne, *Ich spring in diesem Ringe. Mädchen und Frauen in der deutschen Jugendbewegung* (Pfaffenweiler 1990).

[4] See also the essays in Klaus Vondung (ed.), *Das wilhelminische Bildungsbürgertum. Zur Sozialgeschichte seiner Ideen* (Göttingen 1976).

aggressive attitudes directed both outwards and inwards and in a
tendency towards pathos and grand gestures. One further result was
a new interest in theories about society, culture and all aspects of
civilisation; these became subject of much study and critical
appraisal. In this connection youth was discovered as a social force
with a twofold significance: young people could be the starting point
for a fundamental recovery and revival in the spiritual, social and
national-traditional (*völkisch*) life of the country; but many members
of the middle classes feared that youth could also represent a serious
danger to society. If left to their own devices young people could be
misled by radical demagogues, especially by the Socialists, and
might be unwilling to accept the heritage of their fathers.

Many middle-class observers feared that the temptations and
softening effects of modern civilisation were damaging to young
people. A life of comfort, they believed, would undermine basic
middle-class virtues, jeopardise the manly discipline of the army and
thus render the country unable to defend itself. Young people from
the fast growing lower-class areas of the big cities were regarded as
being a particular problem: in terms of politics, morality and health
they were considered to be both at risk themselves and a danger to
others.[5]

Apart from the bourgeoisie's general anxiety about contemporary
social conditions, it is worth noting that another reason for the
growing interest in youth was the simple statistical fact that the
years around 1900 (until about 1910) saw the highest birth rates
that there have ever been in Germany. While the birth rate
remained high, infant mortality was also being reduced thanks to
advances in medical science. Coupled with this there was the
increased social security of a flourishing modern industrial state and
the development of a state welfare system at public expense.[6] All this
led to a continuous growth in population size, which later gave an
impetus for the slogan 'people without space' (*Volk ohne Raum*). And
finally a word should be said about economic conditions: the real
value of wages was rising, and people were starting to have more free
time from work.[7]

[5] See Klaus Tenfelde, 'Großstadtjugend in Deutschland vor 1914', *VfSW*, vol. 69 (1982),
pp. 182–218.
[6] See Gerhard A. Ritter, *Der Sozialstaat. Entstehung und Entwicklung im internationalen Vergleich*
(Munich 1989).
[7] See Jürgen Reulecke, 'Vom blauen Montag zum Arbeiterurlaub', *AfS*, vol. 16 (1976),
pp. 205–248.

Against this general background, official concern with youth was motivated above all by two considerations. The first was one of health policy and the problem of fitness for military service. In the eyes of contemporary observers, industrialisation and city life were leading to a dangerous decline in the number of healthy recruits. Such was the leading opinion expressed in 1909 in the first volume of the *Zeitschrift für Jugendwohlfahrt* (Magazine for Youth Welfare).[8] It went on to explain that the foundations for this military capability were laid in earliest childhood, for example by mothers breast-feeding their children. Its investigations claimed to show that children who had not been breast-fed were less healthy; indeed that at the age of 20 they were 50 per cent less fit for military service than children who had been breast-fed. Children now came to be seen not so much as God-given new life, but rather as material to be shaped along prescribed lines. The growing concern with youth in the decade before World War I was thus not only a symptom of a general unease about the direction which modern civilisation was taking, but also reflected a new attitude towards society's right and duty to engage in social and racial engineering. This new approach to youth at the beginning of the century was not a purely German phenomenon, and it is no coincidence that the famous book *The Century of the Child* by the Swedish educationalist Ellen Key was published in 1902.

In addition to other considerations, healthy children saved the state a lot of money; they were the basis of a productive and efficient workforce. It is difficult, though, to isolate any one set of motives. There was a general tendency – which was particularly pronounced in Germany – for practical economic and political objectives to merge with social-Darwinist ideas such as the theory that in the struggle for survival between the nations only a fit and healthy nation would have an assured future.

Thus concern for better health was one reason for the attention given to children and young people. A further initiative in this area, incidentally, was the very active movement promoting sport and outdoor activities such as hiking. Alongside this campaign for

---

[8] F. Hentig, 'Jugendfürsorge und Staatsinteresse', *Zeitschrift für Jugendwohlfahrt*, vol. 1 (1909), p. 4.

improved health there was, however, a second challenge arising from the young generation around 1900. Youth seemed to be a source of political danger and one which if care were not taken could threaten the whole structure of society. Working-class youth was behaving in an ever more rebellious fashion and since 1889 had been taking an increasing part in strike activity. However, the youth of the upper middle class were also giving cause for concern. They were seen as being in danger of rejecting the values, norms and attitudes of their parents. Religion, authority, homeland (*Heimat*) and fatherland, profession and family – all these elements of the basis of society seemed to be under threat. Even in the middle and upper classes of Wilhelmine society the moral fibre of the nation was being threatened by the vices of young people: pub life, useless passion for sport, the temptations of the big cities and other assorted forms of youthful dissipation.

Even before the turn of the century there had been an upsurge of youth organisations, the majority of them linked to the churches or concerned with social reform. But after 1910 a full-scale 'battle for youth' began with the motto 'he who wins the youth wins the future'. Now there was increasing involvement by political groups, political parties and the state, all of whom directed their attention to youth work, setting up youth clubs, cadet corps and youth groups with recreational, sporting or cultural activities. By 1908 some 750,000 young males or about one in five of the 14 to 20 age group were organised in groups of this sort. The semi-official *Jungdeutschlandbund* (Young Germany League) acted as an umbrella organisation for the majority of these initiatives and was well on the way to becoming a fully state-run youth system when World War 1 broke out.

It is worth noting at this stage that by no means all youth organisations belonged to this category of official groups created to influence youthful behaviour. Indeed, one of the reasons why the adult establishment became so concerned to win over German youth was the existence of 'free', i.e. autonomous, youth-led movements, movements which in turn had grown out of a reaction against adult attempts to force young people into conformity.

All the efforts at encouraging a healthy and politically integrated youth formed only one part of the Wilhelmine interest in the younger generation. Equally characteristic of the period was the growing tendency among sections of Germany's middle and upper middle classes to engage in what became a veritable cult of youth.[9] 'Youthfulness' or 'youth' became popular labels, applied to all kinds of proposals. Indeed, 'youth' came to represent a vision of society in its own right. Instead of denoting merely a biological phase between childhood and adulthood (or between 'primary school and barracks'), it came to encapsulate a life-style independent of age. Youth was thus the code-word for a renaissance, for the forging of a new, more healthy world.

To a certain extent, official nationalism was able to draw on this spirit, and to use it as an integrating force. In speeches and in many other symbolic ways, Wilhelm II was presented as the young emperor at the head of a young nation, ready to provide the inspiration for the creation of the more healthy world of the future.[10] Increasingly, however, official nationalism was unable to paper over the splits and cracks in the imperial fabric. Instead, the notion of youth became enlisted in the service of a diverse and increasingly frenzied range of bourgeois movements and initiatives. On the one hand, there were social reform movements and experiments with new life-styles, some advocating complete withdrawal from industrial society. At the other end of the spectrum there were doctrines of salvation involving aggressive nationalism, anti-semitism and racism. Thus, from about 1895, we find a diverse range of middle-class thinkers creating a cult of youth. Some were literary figures, some were *Kulturkritiker* (culture critics) interested in theories of civilisation and culture, others were *Lebensreformer* (life reformers) exploring new life-styles.[11] One example of the youth-cult ideology can be found in the famous quotation from Arthur Moeller van den Bruck in 1904: 'The nation needs a change of blood, an uprising of the sons against the fathers, the replacement of old age by youth.'[12]

Behind this attack on the fathers lay a feeling of uncertainty about the role of the middle-class family. The ideal had been a life of privacy in the sheltered family circle, with the absolute authority of the father and a rigid division of roles. But doubts were beginning to

---

[9] On the youth cult see Walter Rüegg (ed.), *Kulturkritik und Jugendkult* (Frankfurt 1974); Thomas Koebner, Rolf-Peter Janz and Frank Trommler (eds.), *'Mit uns zieht die neue Zeit'. Der Mythos Jugend* (Frankfurt 1985); Barbara Stambolis, 'Der Mythos der jungen Generation' (doctoral thesis, Bochum 1982). See also Joachim Whaley's essay in this volume.

[10] See Thomas A. Kohut, *Wilhelm II and the Germans: a study in leadership* (Oxford 1991).

[11] See Wolfgang R. Krabbe, *Gesellschaftsveränderung durch Lebensreform* (Göttingen 1974); Edeltraud Klueting (ed.), *Antimodernismus und Reform* (Darmstadt 1991).

[12] Arthur Moeller van den Bruck, *Die Deutschen*, vol. 1 (Minden 1904), p. 142.

spread, and this ideal was now being questioned. There was increasing support for a new kind of social group, one claimed to be more appropriate for a forward-looking generation: the *Männerbund*. The term *Männerbund* came from the book by the sociologist and ethnologist Heinrich Schurtz *Altersklassen und Männerbünde* (Age groups and men's alliances)[13] – another book which appeared in the productive year of 1902. Here the heroic men's alliance is presented as a noble ideal and contrasted with the soft family life, where the female influence dominated and where men were turned into weaklings.

Although these were, at least to start with, extreme views, the traditional view of masculinity was in fact changing substantially at this time. The ideal of what was considered manly or masculine was being extended by two factors: first by an ethos of war, combat and heroism; and secondly by homo-eroticism. Thus the cult of youth was frequently linked to an espousal of manly camaraderie and an attack on the bourgeois family. This male-orientated ideology was, in turn, enormously influential on the young men of the day. For young men growing up in the period 1900–10 it was above all the heroes of Karl May books who disseminated such values. From the middle of the 1890s onwards these adventure stories flooded the market for children's books and were enormously popular; their influence on young people's thinking should not be underestimated. They are set in a world of clear-cut black and white distinctions, and the main character is young, manly, noble in character and German. With or without the help of some noble savage the hero fights for order, humanity and the victory of good over evil – and is invariably successful. Boundless patriotism, love of nature and pseudo-Christian religious feelings form the underlying themes of the stories. The effects of the books on the young readers was to make them identify with the heroes, yearn for far away places and long for manly adventure. There are, incidentally, many auto-biographies which document the lasting effect Karl May's books had on the thinking and attitudes of those young men who read them. May's novels also reveal the utopian, unpolitical way in which youth was being idolised. What the bourgeois reformers were

[13] Heinrich Schurtz, *Altersklassen und Männerbünde* (Berlin 1902). For this and the following section see Jürgen Reulecke, 'Männerbund versus the family: middle-class youth movements and the family in Germany in the period of the First World War', in Richard Wall and Jay Winter (eds.), *The upheaval of war: family, work and welfare in Europe 1914–1918* (Cambridge 1989), pp. 439–452.

asking was how the individual could remain pure and noble in an evil and confusing world, or – transported to national level – how a nation could hold on to its soul in spite of modern civilisation and technology. The answer was always apolitical, involving solutions far removed from the corrupting, oppressive everyday world. Often the answer was found in man-made paradises, in exciting distant lands or in imaginative utopias. Sometimes, however, it was to be found deep within the heart of the individual (see for example the *Jugendstil*, the paintings of Fidus, the escapism to Monte Verita, and the founding of *Landkommunen*, country communes).[14] There was a wholesale rejection of political commitment, as can be seen, for example in the often cited quotation from Goethe 'a political song is a bad song' (*ein politisch Lied – ein garstig Lied*). There was no place for the day to day political struggle, for laborious efforts to achieve small political reforms. Reform of society was reduced to reform of the individual. This is shown by the splendid one-sidedness of the message from the Hoher Meißner in 1913, a message which was later to become the gospel of the bourgeois youth movement.

IV

As we have seen, attempts by middle-class circles to provide pastoral care for young people and to supervise their welfare had been increasing since about 1890. They did not, however, remain unchallenged. There was a pull in the other direction in the form of the *Wandervogel* movement.[15] Composed mainly of students and older school pupils, this movement started in Berlin and Hamburg, rapidly gaining popularity in other cities and beyond. The impetus for the movement came from a number of sources: first from the new trends already mentioned in art, literature and contemporary social criticism; also from the cult of youth which was currently being promoted by middle-aged writers, and finally from a neo-romantic view of nature as an antidote to the cold rationality of city life. Parallel to this movement and to some extent merging with it, some of the younger educationalists were trying to develop a new youth

[14] See e.g. Janos Frecot, Johann Friedrich Geist and Diethart Kerbs, *Fidus 1868–1948* (Munich 1972); Ulrich Linse, *Zurück o Mensch zur Mutter Erde. Landkommunen in Deutschland 1890–1933* (Munich 1983); Jost Hermand, *Grüne Utopien in Deutschland* (Frankfurt 1991).
[15] See amongst many other studies Walter Z. Laqueur, *Young Germany: a history of the German youth movement* (New Brunswick 1984, 2nd edn.).

culture which was intended to spread outwards from experimental 'free school communities'. The traditional adult forms of conduct and way of life were rejected in these circles. New ideas and forms of behaviour were introduced in many areas of life: new ways of people relating to each other, new ways of dressing, travelling, singing and dancing. New forms of artistic activity were explored and new styles of behaviour in public adopted. Though in statistical terms only a small proportion of the total youth population was involved, the movement became increasingly popular and slowly influenced the style in other groups of young people, too.

Before splintering into a lot of individual groups and subgroups, this 'alternative' youth movement reached its high point at a meeting on 12 October 1913 on the Hoher Meißner, a mountain near Kassel. In the famous words of this occasion these *Freideutsche* (free Germans) committed themselves to a life based on 'self-determination, personal responsibility and inner truthfulness' – the *Meißnerformel* (formula of the Meißner).[16] Of course social action, political activity and political allegiance were not ruled out by these precepts, but they were not part of the programme and they belonged in the realm of individual conscience.

The aims of the *Freideutsche* (free Germans) of the Hoher Meißner were greeted with some enthusiasm by a number of people from the fields of literature and philosophy, and by various critical commentators and writers with reforming ideas, especially those advocating personal life reform. On the other hand, conservative-minded adult groups and many authorities viewed the *Freideutsche* and the *Wandervogel* with great suspicion because of their demands for youth autonomy. The authorities preferred to support instead the associations for organised youth welfare which were spreading at the same time. These organisations were in the process of developing out of previously existing groups: on the one hand out of Christian boys' and girls' clubs; on the other out of the youth sections of the *Volkswohlvereine* (people's welfare groups), from cadet corps and from patriotic militia groups. In 1911 the *Jungdeutschlandbund* (Young German League) was formed, incorporating most of these organisations and also the Scout movement, which had began to attract followers in Germany in about 1908. Supervised by an old

[16] See the document collection Winfried Mogge and Jürgen Reulecke (eds.), *Hoher Meißner 1913. Der Erste Freideutsche Jugendtag in Dokumenten, Deutungen und Bildern* (Cologne 1988).

field marshal, the *Jungdeutschlandbund* acted as an umbrella organisation and by 1914 had reached the size of almost 750,000 members.

Thus we see here two opposing tendencies which continued to operate in modified form after World War 1: on the one hand organised youth welfare organisations and activities linked to national or ideological aims (called *Jugendpflege* or youth saving); on the other hand a free youth movement claiming autonomy for the young generation. The former aimed to produce loyal citizens and conformist members of society; young people were to become accustomed to industrious habits, conscientious behaviour, unquestioning obedience and loyal devotion to duty. The latter called for a complete cultural-spiritual renewal and the creation of a 'new mankind'. Common to both of them was the belief that young people should be educated towards their goals in a sheltered environment safe from the pressures of everyday life. The political and social conflicts of the times should be kept at bay as far as possible; i.e. any form of party politics and pressure had to be kept away from the young people 'between primary school and barracks', so that they could first gain maturity. One of the most famous slogans of the free youth movement was, for instance, *rein bleiben und reif werden* (remain pure and become mature).[17]

From 1904 onwards, there was also a third strand to youth activity. Alongside the contrasting forces of organised middle-class youth welfare and the free youth movement, there was also the labour youth movement. Its adult leaders shared many of the same ideas about sheltered development.[18] True, they believed that young people should be brought up ready to fight for a better future and decent living conditions; but their main emphasis was on improved general education, social activities and carefree youthful life, free from day to day political pressure. The young workers themselves, though, took a somewhat different view from their adult leaders. In accordance with the Youth Internationale, which had been established in 1907,[19] they demanded that young people should enjoy self-determination and should take part in the current

---

[17] Quotation from Walter Flex, *Der Wanderer zwischen beiden Welten* (1917, 1st edn.).
[18] For this and the following remarks see Erich Eberts, *Arbeiterjugend 1904–1945. Sozialistische Erziehungsgemeinschaft. Politische Organisation* (Frankfurt 1980).
[19] Richard Schüller, *Geschichte der kommunistischen Jugendinternationale*. Vol. 1: *Von den Anfängen der proletarischen Jugendbewegung bis zur Gründung der KJI* (Berlin 1929).

political struggle. This led to a disagreement in the German social democratic movement summed up in an over-simplified form in the phrase 'politics or education'. External events played a part in ending the argument: a law was passed in 1908 regulating the activities of clubs and societies (*Reichsvereinsgesetz*) and this made it illegal for young people to be members of societies with political aims. Labour youth work now concentrated on providing a greatly increased number of educational programmes and disseminating carefully chosen information about social and political issues in so-called 'youth committees'. This work was often hindered by police intervention but it continued none the less.

V

With the outbreak of World War I a new phase in German history of youth began. As we have seen, most youth-centred initiatives in the peace-time empire aimed at strengthening and refining what were seen as young people's desirable qualities and at controlling and redirecting all those forms of youthful strength which might destabilise the system – for example their sexuality, their aggressiveness and their spontaneity. But the ideal of a sheltered environment could no longer be maintained in the war. Fathers and teachers were often away in the war, and many children in the 10 to 14 age group had to work now to support the family. Young labour was used extensively in firms working for the war effort. Youth had to be part of the *Heimatfront* (home front) and so gained access to public life. It was given a new sphere of activity, especially in industrial production, and in many cases carried out the functions of adults.

Thus youth experienced a new freedom of action, and with most of the fathers away was no longer subject to strict family discipline. Young people overthrew previous taboos and flouted the rules of respectable behaviour. Young people's behaviour was perceived by the public, and particularly by the bureaucracy and the military authorities, as a sign of a growing *Verwahrlosung* (degeneracy). Many adults called for stricter state supervision. There were attempts to combat the development with emergency laws: stricter curfews were imposed, assemblies of young people were broken up by the police, measures were introduced making it compulsory to save money (*Zwangssparerlässe*) and finally plans were drawn up to conscript young people into an army cadet force (*Reichsjugendwehrgesetz*). However, these attempts to tame the younger generation were not sufficient to halt the inner erosion of the home front. It was almost impossible to enforce the regulations, and even the 'threat of the front' was ineffective because the young people who took part in hunger riots, strikes and looting in the second half of the war were not old enough for the army. After the infamous *Steckrubenwinter* (turnip winter) the situation on the home front became ever more intolerable and the basic necessities of life ever more difficult to obtain. Many young people (not only from the lower classes) became increasingly radicalised and politicised. The phrase 'class struggle of youth' came into use to describe the situation.[20]

Many young people from the generation born in and after 1902 (i.e. the cohort not sent to the front, conscription extending only as far as the birth-years 1900–01) reacted with bitterness to the hardships they were suffering and condensed their frustration into the phrase 'the war is our parents'.[21] Increasingly they saw through the war propaganda as empty words and distanced themselves from the values and virtues demanded by the state. However, too much can be made of this generation gap and it was not nearly as clear cut as some interpreters have suggested. As well as youth activities which crossed class boundaries, there were also strong bonds of loyalty which crossed age boundaries, particularly in families which were struggling to survive. Within the younger generation itself there were also growing tensions, for example between different political leanings, between younger and older elements and between the newly confident girls and the boys who still jealously guarded their dominance. Particularly in the middle-class youth movement, i.e. in the groups of the *Wandervogel* and the *Freideutsche*, these tensions led to serious disagreements.[22]

There was no doubt, however, that a new self-confidence now characterised the younger generation. Thrown into adult life, or at least aspects of it, by the wartime conditions, young people grew up

---

[20] See Elisabeth Domansky, 'Politische Dimensionen von Jugendprotest und Generationen-konflikt in der Zwischenkriegszeit in Deutschland', in Dowe, *Jugendprotest und Generationen-konflikt*, pp. 364ff.; see also Gudrun Fiedler, *Jugend im Krieg. Bürgerliche Jugendbewegung, Erster Weltkrieg und sozialer Wandel 1914–1923* (Cologne 1989); Ute Daniel, *Arbeiterfrauen in der Kriegsgesellschaft. Beruf, Familie und Politik im Ersten Weltkrieg* (Göttingen 1989), esp. pp. 151ff.

[21] Quoted from Ernst Glaeser, *Jahrgang 1902* (reprinted Kronberg 1978).

[22] See above all Fiedler, *Jugend im Krieg*.

at an early age, while the adult generation itself seemed to produce nothing but failure. The result was that people in virtually all youth associations started to think that they were the saving force for the nation and held the key to the future; they thus adopted the ideas of the youth cult of the pre-war years. 'Collectively, youth now laid claim to becoming the norm for the entire society rather than remaining a segregated sphere' (E. Domansky).[23]

However, once the war had ended, this optimistic self-assessment rapidly turned out to be a delusion. There was very little scope in the post-war years for the development of such avant-garde ideas. Admittedly some tentative first steps were taken towards finding alternative ways of life, for instance in a short-lived *Landkommunen-bewegung* (country communes movement) and similar experiments,[24] but these were not of major importance.

The young generation that had stayed at home in the war had already had its share of deprivation and hardship but after the war there was the further depressing experience of coming into contact with the soldiers returning from the front. Often there was an age difference of only a few years between them. The young soldiers had first gone to the war in high spirits, later perhaps with less enthusiasm but driven by a sense of duty. But as the war dragged on this was replaced by disillusion, disgust and a deadening of mind and spirit. Adrift and uprooted, these youths had nothing to hold on to except the camaraderie of front line soldiers – a particular kind of *Männerbund*. This community spirit of the trenches, later much glorified, often gave the young soldiers the only emotional security they had. After the war many of them found it difficult or impossible to cope with the bleak everyday life of the post-war years, often with the additional burden of physical injury or psychological damage. They formed the nucleus of the new 20- to 40-year-old middle generation in the Weimar republic. Cheated out of their youth, unsettled by the turmoil of the post-war years and often dissatisfied with the government of the Weimar republic they were eager to find new purpose and direction – and followers in the younger generation.[25] It is significant that almost all the leaders of the Nazi movement came from this 'front generation'.

[23] See Domansky, 'Politische Dimensionen', p. 364.
[24] See Linse, *Landkommunen*; also S. Linse, *Barfüßige Propheten. Erlöser der zwanziger Jahre* (Berlin 1983).
[25] On the analysis of this cohort from a psycho-historical perspective see Peter Loewenberg, 'The psychohistorical origins of the Nazi youth cohort', in Peter Loewenberg, *Decoding the past* (New York 1983). See also Richard Bessel's contribution in this volume.

CHAPTER 5

Jewish politics and generational change in Wilhelmine Germany

Jacob Borut

Until the 1890s German Jews' behaviour in the intolerant social climate of the Kaiserreich was guided by the principle that 'step-children must behave twice as well'.[1] The style of their public activities was cautious and reserved. The early 1890s, however, saw a profound change. Now the Jewish community became much more open, self-assertive, sometimes even belligerent. The contention here is that these changes were closely connected with the entrance into the field of Jewish politics of a new generation, with a distinct set of formative generational experiences.

The aim of this essay is to describe the nature of German Jewry's public activities before the 1890s, examine the changes that then took place, and finally establish and explain the connections between those changes and the age and generational experiences of the various groups of activists that had initiated them.

I

Since their emancipation in 1871 (1869 in the North German Confederation) the Jews of Wilhelmine Germany had theoretically been equal before the law, but in practice continued to be subject to a variety of forms of discrimination.[2] Their position within German society can best be illustrated by a little story that appeared in some

This is a revised version of my paper at the 1991 German History conference 'The Generation Game'. I would like to thank Professor Moshe Zimmermann and the Koebner Centre of German History in the Hebrew University of Jerusalem, for their assistance towards my participation.
[1] See, for example, Martin Mendelssohn, *Die Pflicht der Selbstverteidigung* (Berlin 1894), p. 22.
[2] See Wenda Kampmann, *Deutsche und Juden. Studien zur Geschichte des deutschen Judentums* (Heidelberg 1963); Eva Reichmann, *Flucht in den Hass* (Frankfurt 1965); Reinhard Ruerup, 'Judenemanzipation und bürgerliche Gesellschaft in Deutschland', in E. Schulin (ed.), *Gedenkschrift Martin Goehring. Studien zur europäischen Geschichte* (Wiesbaden 1968), pp. 174–199; Peter Pulzer, *Jews and the German State* (Oxford 1992).

Jewish newspapers in 1891. The story began with a report in the
Berlin daily *Berliner Boersen-Courier* to the effect that the officers of the
Prussian Second Guards regiment, stationed in Berlin, had spent a
quiet evening with their wives in a Jewish kosher hotel, having been
taken there by the regimental doctor, himself a Jew. On learning
about the report, the officers of that regiment had immediately
prosecuted the editor and reporter for libel. (In fact, it was the state
prosecution that filed the suit on behalf of the officers.) During the
trial, the *Berliner Boersen-Courier* admitted that the story was false, but
claimed that it constituted no offence against the officers involved.
The court, however, ruled otherwise. It stated that the role of a
Prussian officer included not only military, but also social obligations, one of which was to restrict social intercourse to places of
'good' society. By writing that the officers had dined in a kosher
hotel, stated the court, the paper had created the impression that
they visited a place frequented by members of the Jewish population, which was not what was expected from Prussian officers, and
therefore the paper had indeed insulted them.

Before turning to the sentence, it should be noted that a few
months before the Berlin trial, Theodor Fritsch, a famous anti-
semitic agitator, had been sentenced in Leipzig for an article which
had maligned a local Jewish merchant, to a fine of 30 marks. (The
fine was later increased to 80 marks on appeal.) In the Berlin trial,
by contrast, the editor of the *Berliner Boersen-Courier* was fined 300
marks, and the reporter of the story an additional 200.[3]

Social inferiority, and *de facto* legal inferiority, were constant. But
the ways German Jews responded to it were not. Historians of
Jewish responses to anti-semitism agree that the early 1890s in some
respects marked a watershed in German Jewish history. The key
turning point has usually been seen as the founding in 1893 of a
large Jewish national organisation, the *Centralverein Deutscher Staats-
buerger jüdischen Glaubens* (henceforth CV).[4]

Most historians see this organisation as marking a shift from a
passive, sometimes even submissive political attitude to a self-

[3] *Der Israelit*, vol. 32 (1891), 44, 4 June, p. 817; *Allgemeine Zeitung des Judentums*, vol. 55 (1891),
22, 29 May, *Gemeindebote*, p. 2; and see p. 4 for the report on Fritsch's fine. For the
Fritsch trial itself see *Allgemeine Zeitung des Judentums*, vol. 55 (1891), 8, 19 February,
Gemeindebote, p. 2; and see there other cases in which he was sentenced to higher fines.
[4] An annotated bibliography about the CV is to be found in Arnold Paucker, 'Die Abwehr
des Antisemitismus in den Jahren 1893–1933', in Herbert A. Strauss and Norbert Kampe
(eds.), *Antisemitismus von der Judenfeindschaft zum Holocaust* (Bonn 1984), pp. 164–171.

conscious Jewish activism.[5] Before 1893 the Jews avoided taking a public stand against anti-semitism. They preferred to keep silent, believing that with the inevitable progress of society the problem would disappear by itself. In the meantime, a Jew should not stand up in public defending his Jewish interests, because that would only add credence to anti-semitic charges that Jews were a separate group that had not integrated into German society. The CV's leaders, by contrast, were convinced that Jews could and should combat anti-semitism publicly, 'Im Lichte der Öffentlichkeit',[6] and should not be afraid of identifying themselves openly as Jews who were protecting their interests.

My own research has established that the changes in what can be termed 'Jewish politics' in this period were on a much wider scale,[7] affecting not only the reaction, or rather non-reaction towards anti-semitism, but also the wider field of Jewish public activity. (Jewish public activity here means public activity performed by leaders of institutions, organisations and legal bodies that were acknowledged as representing German Jews, especially the Jewish communities, the *Cultus* or *Synagogengemeinden*; in other words, what sociologists like to call Jewish group action.)

An examination of that Jewish public activity up to the 1890s shows it to have several persistent characteristics, reflecting an enduring collective mentality. Those were, first, apprehension and hostility towards constituting specific Jewish organisations. Before the modern era, there had been in each Jewish community a thriving network of Jewish organisations, which had constituted an almost autonomous Jewish subculture within the surrounding society, taking care of the whole spectrum of human needs from

---

[5] Ismar Schorsch, *Jewish reactions to German antisemitism 1870–1914* (Columbia University Press 1972); Jehuda Reinharz, *Fatherland or promised land* (Ann Arbor 1975); Marjorie Lamberti, *Jewish activism in imperial Germany* (New Haven 1978); Sanford Ragins, *Jewish responses to antisemitism in Germany 1870–1914* (Cincinnati 1980).

[6] This important slogan of the CV was already emphasised in its first *Aufrufe* (see *Allgemeine Zeitung des Judenthums*, vol. 57 (1893), 21, 26 May, *Gemeindebote*, p. 1; *Aufruf* in the Central Archives for the History of the Jewish People, Jerusalem, TD24, esp. p. 6), and constantly repeated in its publications, described as the main characteristic of the CV's activity in comparison with earlier defence efforts. See also Wilhelm Levinger, 'Abwehr des Antisemitismus', *Juedisches Lexikon* (Berlin 1927), vol. I, p. 66, and Ragins, *Jewish responses*, p. 87.

[7] The following information is based upon my doctoral dissertation, ' "A new spirit among our brethren in Ashkenaz": German Jewry in the face of economic, social and political change in the Reich at the end of the 19th century' (Hebrew University, Jerusalem 1991).

cradle to grave.[8] As Jewish society had modernised and opened up
to the outer world, this organisational network had largely disappeared. What remained were mainly organisations devoted to
specific religious needs, or welfare societies. The latter were looked
upon favourably by local authorities, since, by providing for the
Jewish poor, they took some of the load off the official welfare
institutions. Such religious and welfare associations aside, there was
great opposition within Jewish circles to the creation of new Jewish
groups. When in 1882 some Jewish students in the Berlin university
formed a group dedicated to the study of Jewish history, the most
severe attacks came – as two of the group's founders wrote in their
memoirs – not from anti-semites, but from Jews who believed that
one should 'conceal everything that had even the tiniest connection
with the name "Jewish"'.[9]

A second key characteristic was the tendency to keep activities out
of the public limelight. Jewish activities were not kept secret, but
Jewish leaders did avoid publicity, even when it might have helped
their organisation, for example in fund raising. Reports of their
activities were sent only to Jewish newspapers and not to the
German general press, even though it was common knowledge that
the former had a very limited readership. Thirdly, there was the
tendency to keep contact with political authorities down to a
minimum. Jewish organisations concentrated on practical, inner
Jewish matters, such as philanthropic or spiritual activities. Their
leaders avoided setting up organisational targets that would bring
them in contact with political authorities, such as defending Jewish
interests, fearing that this might appear to be demonstrating an
unwillingness to integrate.

Finally, when contact with the authorities was unavoidable, any
conflict was evaded and any friction that occurred was hidden from
public knowledge. This happened, for example, when the Jews
helped the masses of Jewish immigrants fleeing from Russia through
the Prussian border. Jewish organisations involved soon found out
that Prussian border guards and officials were treating immigrants
unfairly. They chose to deal with that problem by appealing to

[8] 'Hevrah, Havurah', *Encyclopaedia Judaica*, vol. VIII (Jerusalem 1971), cols. 440–442; David
Sorkin, *The transformation of German Jewry, 1780–1840* (New York 1987), pp. 113–114.
[9] Julius Cohen (ed.), *Geschichte des akademischen Vereins für jüdische Geschichte und Literatur. Zum
25. Stiftungsfeste* (Berlin 1908), p. 4; J. Levy, *Geschichte des akademischen Vereins für jüdische
Geschichte und Literatur in Berlin im Gründungsjahre 1882–1883* (Berlin 1913), pp. 8–9.

friendly, liberal-minded officials in Berlin, carefully avoiding any confrontation with the local authorities involved, and keeping the matter quiet.

These characteristics of Jewish public activity reflect a kind of unspoken mentality that was also revealed by the Jewish non-reaction against anti-semitism. It can be summed up by stating that German Jews were worried about their public image as a minority in an intolerant society which suspected them of being a non-assimilating, self-centred group. They therefore avoided any organised and public defence of Jewish interests, including combating anti-semitism, and chose to leave such subjects to the authorities or to friendly Christians, or to the inevitable progress of history which, they believed, would erase all remaining prejudices.

The 1890s witnessed a dramatic change in Jewish mentality and public behaviour as, in response to a new wave of anti-semitism,[10] the former mode of operation was heavily criticised and challenged from within. A famous pamphlet, entitled *Schutzjuden oder Staatsbürger?*, accused the Jewish leadership of behaving like the Jews of the Middle Ages, depending on patrons for protection, instead of acting as proud citizens. From all across the Reich came calls for the Jews to stand up for their own rights, and not to rely on others.

What followed was the development of a new style of Jewish politics which can be described as an open and public stand of the Jews for their own rights and needs, and even more than that: Jews started to build a new and unique semi-culture of their own. By that I mean not a complete subculture, but a set of organisations in several walks of life, aimed specifically at Jews – something that had been anathema only a few years before.

II

The period we are discussing was one of great changes in German political culture. Traditional *Honoratiorenpolitik* was in decline and German politics was turning into what Hans Rosenberg has called a

---

[10] See Peter Massing, *Rehearsal for destruction* (New York 1949), chapters 5–7; Peter Pulzer, *The rise of political antisemitism in Germany and Austria* (New York 1964), chapters 12–13; Werner Jochmann, 'Struktur und Funktion des Antisemitismus', in Werner Mosse and Arnold Paucker (eds.), *Juden in Wilhelminischen Deutschland* (Tübingen 1976), pp. 436–460; Werner Jochmann, 'Struktur und Funktion des Deutschen Antisemitismus 1878–1914', in Strauss and Kampe, *Antisemitismus*, pp. 120–135; Richard Levy, *The downfall of the anti-semitic political parties in imperial Germany* (New Haven 1975), chapters 3–7.

'political mass market'.[11] Industrialisation and concomitant changes such as substantial internal migration, urbanisation, increasing levels of education, a revolution in communications and so on led to the lower strata becoming increasingly politically conscious. German politics came to resemble mass politics.

The character and origin of the political developments of the 1890s have been the subject of major historiographical controversy. Many German historians, most notably Hans-Ulrich Wehler,[12] have seen German politics up to the First and, indeed, the Second World War as being controlled by the established elites, particularly the *Junkers* and their allies among the heavy industrialists. These elites effectively blocked the rising bourgeoisie as well as the masses of proletarians from gaining political influence. What appears as an age of mass politics, they argue, was just a successful 'manipulation from above', a distraction of the masses from the real issues of power-sharing by diverting attention either to patriotic slogans or to immediate economic needs. As is well known, this view has since been challenged by a group of British historians,[13] for whom the 1890s were a period of fundamental change in German politics. In this latter view, the political elites had to adapt themselves to pressures coming from below and to restructure their whole mode of operation. Parties that failed to do so (above all the Liberal parties), were punished by losing heavily at the polls and suffering a major loss in their political influence.[14]

In the view of the present author the politics of the 1890s were indeed new politics, and not a manipulation. Furthermore, the new Jewish politics which evolved in this period manifested and

---

[11] Hans Rosenberg, *Grosse Depression und Bismarckzeit* (Berlin 1967), pp. 120–121.
[12] See his books *Bismarck und der Imperialismus* (Cologne, Berlin 1969), and *Das Deutsche Kaiserreich 1871–1918* (Göttingen 1983, 5th edn.). But see his article 'Zur Funktion und Struktur der nationalen Kampfverbaende im Kaiserreich', in Werner Konze, Gottfried Schramm and Klaus Zernack (eds.), *Modernisierung und Nationale Gesellschaft im Ausgehenden 18. und im 19. Jahrhundert* (Berlin 1979), pp. 113–124.
[13] The leading exponents of this view are David Blackbourn, Richard Evans and Geoff Eley. For a short summary of their historiographical position see Richard Evans's introduction in *Society and politics in Wilhelmine Germany* (New York 1978), pp. 11–39.
[14] On the controversy see Wolfgang Mock, '"Manipulation von Oben" oder Rekrutierung an der Basis? Einige neuere Ansaetze in der englischen Historiographie zur Geschichte des deutschen Kaiserreichs', *HZ*, vol. 232 (1981), 2, pp. 258–375; Theodor S. Hamerow, 'Guilt, redemption and writing German history', *American Historical Review*, vol. 88 (1983), 1, pp. 68–71; Roger Fletcher, 'Social historians and Wilhelmine politics: manipulation from above or self-mobilization from below?', *Australian Journal of Politics and History*, vol. 32 (1986), 1, pp. 86–104.

responded within the Jewish realm to wider German developments. The political changes undergone by German Jewry were not the result of a conspiracy on the part of either German or Jewish elites, and thus provide an example of new politics that had indeed evolved from the grass roots and were not imposed from above.

The politics of the 1890s had several important characteristics, which clearly differentiate them from the traditional *Honoratioren-politik*. In the first place there was the massive use of political propaganda. This is especially evident in the new style of election campaign. Where once elections had been quiet and honourable ceremonies, they now turned into noisy affairs with candidates touring their constituencies, holding mass rallies and distributing large numbers of leaflets and brochures. But even when elections were not being held, the new politics were characterised by the continuous use of mass propaganda. In fact, the ability to exploit such techniques efficiently became a prerequisite for political success.[15]

Following the effective use of mass propaganda by anti-semitic parties in Hessen and Saxony, there were increasing calls in the Jewish press for Jews to adopt the new agitation methods to defend themselves. It was explicitly argued that this style of agitation was characteristic of the new times and thus essential to influence the public mind. Consequently, Jewish individuals and groups embarked on an open fight against anti-semitism, exploiting new mass propaganda techniques such as distributing leaflets and brochures, holding mass rallies, or visiting anti-semitic rallies in order to counter the main speaker.

A second feature of the new era was the development of an extra-parliamentary political system. The 1890s witnessed the development of strong pressure and interest groups, some of which managed to gain dominant positions in German politics.[16] The question as to why this took place has been one of the main issues in the historiographical controversy mentioned above. German historians argued that the dominant elites used interest organisations such as the *Bund der Landwirte* and patriotic pressure groups such as

---

[15] See especially David Blackbourn, 'The politics of demagogy in Wilhelmine Germany', *Past and Present*, vol. 113 (1986), pp. 152–184.

[16] On some of those groups see Hans-Jürgen Puhle, *Agrarische Interessenpolitik und Preußischer Konservatismus im Wilhelminischen Reich 1893–1914* (Bonn, Bad Godesberg, 1975); Geoff Eley, *Reshaping the German right* (New Haven 1980); Roger Chickering, *We men who feel most German: a cultural study of the Pan-German League, 1886–1914* (Boston 1984).

the *Flottenverein* as a way of manipulating the masses. Through such mass organisations the elites hoped to preserve loyalty to the regime and enlist support against opposition from the left. British historians, especially Eley, claimed that the patriotic pressure groups expressed the true feelings of activists from the grass roots (or at least the middle rank), and in fact often came into conflict with the government, in its various ranks, which was seen as being insufficiently nationalistic.

We mentioned earlier the important Jewish organisation founded in 1893, the CV. This group is treated by modern historians as a defence organisation, aimed at fighting anti-semitism. It was indeed founded for that purpose, but a close examination of its early history shows that its leadership did very little to fight anti-semitic propaganda. What really preoccupied the group was the task of becoming what Eugen Fuchs, its most important ideologue, called 'a Jewish interest group in an age of interest groups'.[17] Fuchs expressed openly the view that the Jews had to defend their interests in relation to the German authorities. And the way to influence the authorities was not through reason, but by pressure, based upon masses of supporters. Therefore, the main target of the CV in those years was to enlist mass Jewish support, and at the same time to represent and defend German Jews against acts of injustice by government officials. A close examination of the operational methods adopted by the CV reveals a striking similarity to those employed by the larger German interest groups, including the use of the developing mass media, enlisting the help of friendly parliamentarians to bring pressure upon government officials, and unleashing a wide mobilisation campaign, targeted at all classes and groups within the specific population sector close to the organisation, aimed at reinforcing its claim to represent the interests of that whole sector.[18] Since the CV was clearly neither created nor abetted by the ruling German elites, it surely demonstrates how the extra-parliamentary system developed in the 1890s independently of any 'manipulation from above'.

A further feature of the 1890s was the strengthening of the politics of particular interests and the emergence of new political subcultures. Manfred Rauh, for example, has shown how the German states in the Bundesrat started in the 1890s vehemently to defend

[17] *Im Deutschen Reich*, vol. 2 (1896), 3, p. 170.
[18] For details see Borut, 'New spirit', chapter 6.

their particularistic interests. Then, as already noted, there was the emergence of a variety of new interest groups. Several historians associate this new 'particularism' not only with the emergence of mass politics but also with the disappearance of the all-powerful figure of Bismarck, a symbol of German unity and loyalty, from the political centre, and his replacement by the weak figure of Caprivi.[19]

One key feature of the new particularism was the development by several minorities of dense organisational networks, amounting in fact to specific subcultures which could take care of almost every need of their members from cradle to grave. Within the organisational network the minority members, rejected by the dominant culture, could find a spiritual home, social recognition and acceptance, which in turn bolstered their loyalty to the minority and its leading institutions. The most important minorities to develop such a network were the Socialists, the Catholics and Poles in the eastern provinces and in the Ruhr basin.[20] In the 1890s the Jews also started to develop an organisational network of their own, including associations devoted to the study of Jewish history and literature, Jewish student fraternities, a Jewish veterans' association (*Kriegerverein*) and more. This was, in part, an answer to their inferior social position, their inability to find acceptance in existing German organisations. But more importantly it manifested a new approach. At one time Jews had deliberately sought out the company of non-Jews in preference to ties with other Jews.[21] They now sought self-confirmation and a secure social position through association with fellow Jews.

---

[19] See Wehler, *Nationale Kampfverbaende*, p. 120, and see also Manfred Rauh, *Föderalismus und Parlamentarismus im Wilhelminischen Reich* (Düsseldorf 1973), pp. 121–129.

[20] I use the term 'subculture' as defined by Milton Gordon, *Assimilation in American life* (New York 1964), pp. 29–35 and 'The subsociety and the subculture', in David O. Arnold (ed.), *Subcultures* (Berkeley 1973, 3rd edn.), pp. 152f. This definition circumvents the objections raised by historians such as Richard Evans and Vernon Lidtke to using that term in the German context.

[21] This subject has hardly been touched by modern researchers, but see Shulamit Volkov, 'The dynamics of dissimilation: *Ostjuden* and German Jews', in Jehuda Reinharz and Walter Schatzberg (eds.), *The Jewish response to German culture* (Hannover, N.J., London 1985), pp. 195–211. The Jewish German newspapers obviously avoided discussing that social trend, but it is reported, as a novelty, by correspondents of Hebrew Jewish papers in Eastern Europe, who were not worried about German public opinion's reaction to their reports. See, for example, *Hatsfirah* (Warsaw) vol. 19 (1892), 110, 30 May, p. 451; vol. 21 (1894), 43, 4 March, p. 173.

Again, a close examination of the operational methods employed by the biggest group of organisations, those devoted to Jewish history and literature, reveals a striking similarity to the operational methods employed by organisations of the larger minorities: wide mobilisation efforts aimed at all sectors of society, including the lower strata and the formerly neglected groups of youth and women; the use of public mass media and mass agitation techniques for the enlistment effort as well as for reports of organisational activities; and – in the actual activity – efforts to find areas of common ground which would enable members with differing opinions to work together within one framework.

It is clear, then, that a new, far more assertive public style of Jewish politics was emerging in the 1890s. As might be expected, the beginnings of the new Jewish politics encountered considerable resistance from the established Jewish leadership, particularly within the big communities and first and foremost in Berlin. Indeed, efforts to bring about such changes in the early 1880s had failed because of the established leadership's opposition.[22] By the early 1890s, however, that resistance could no longer prevent the success of the new Jewish activists. The founders of organisations such as the CV or the societies for the study of Jewish history and literature, which formed their own national association in 1893, received wide public support, and succeeded in establishing their associations as the largest national Jewish organisations. By 1895 it was the Berlin community leadership (whose stand was undermined by strong opposition within the community itself) that backed down and expressed its support for the new organisations. German Jews had now found a new leadership, committed to a new style of politics.

III

Who were the men behind this dramatic change in Jewish politics? In my research, I have collected personal information on three groups who pioneered the new political style. Those groups are:
A Individual Jews that tried to counter anti-semitic propaganda, using mass propaganda techniques, between 1890 and 1895. In

[22] For an example see Schorsch, *Jewish reactions*, pp. 59–65; Ragins, *Jewish responses*, pp. 33–35; and for more details in Borut, 'New spirit', chapter 2.

all this group may have amounted to some 93 Jews, spread all over the Reich, except for Bavaria.[23]

B Executive members of the CV up to 1895. This group comprised 26 people (27 with the organisation's secretary), all but one from Berlin.

C Leaders of the associations for the study of Jewish history and literature. Within this group we can distinguish two subgroups: (1) executive members of the twenty-five local associations that were established up to 1895, in all some 167 people, from all over the Reich; (2) executive members of the national association: 11 people (12 with the secretary) also spread throughout the Reich.

For subgroup C1 information was available only about the professional composition of its membership. More extensive information was collected on the thirteen executive members of the Berlin association, which was the dominant association in Germany and the major force behind the expansion of the movement and the founding of the national association. This group will be designated subgroup C3.

Information on the members of these groups was not easy to come by, as most of them were not famous public figures, and were not mentioned in the standard biographical directories. Nevertheless, their occupations, often mentioned in the various reports concerning their activity, were easier to identify and near complete data are available on that subject. More extensive personal information was discovered about forty-two members of group A, twelve members of group B, seven members of subgroup C2 and five members of subgroup C3.

On the basis of these data, the Jewish activists from these various categories turn out to have a number of common characteristics. In the first place, they were predominantly employed in intellectual and especially academic professions. A second shared characteristic was a birthplace different from their place of residence at the time of their activism. In fact, most were born in the eastern provinces of Germany, and a significant number were born east of the German Reich. Finally, they were all still of a relatively young age at the time in which they were engaged in Jewish politics.

How did this profile compare with that of the traditional Jewish

---

[23] For information on this group see Jacob Borut, 'The rise of Jewish defence agitation in Germany, 1890–1895', *Leo Baeck Institute Year Book*, vol. 36 (1991), pp. 59–96.

leadership? For the purposes of this study, data were collected about executive members of the two biggest Jewish communities, Berlin and Frankfurt, as well as members of the Berlin community's *Repräsentantenversammlung* up to 1893 (the last year in which those leadership organs unanimously took the older approach to community issues). The data show that intellectuals and the academically educated were heavily over-represented in the Berlin community leadership organs, by about three times their weight in the total Jewish population in Germany. Although this concentration is not as heavy as among the activists, it still greatly reduces the significance of that factor. The results concerning birthplace were less conclusive: Frankfurt community leaders were mainly natives of their town, Berlin community leaders were divided between natives and immigrants from the eastern provinces, while the information found about a few members of the Berlin *Repräsentantenversammlung* indicates that this body was heavily composed of immigrants from the east.

This leaves age as the most significant distinguishing characteristic of the new activists. And the findings here are very clear: of the forty-two activists in group A about whom we have information, eleven were born after 1861, another eight between 1851 and 1860, and another eleven between 1841 and 1850. Thus 71.4 per cent of these activists were born after 1841. Of the twelve activists we have information about in group B, seven were born after 1850 and two more between 1841 and 1850, for a total of nine (75 per cent) born after 1841. In subgroup C2 three members were born after 1850, in fact after 1855, and three more (i.e. six out of seven) after 1840, and in fact after 1845. In subgroup C3 all five members about whom we have information were born after 1840, and three of them were born after 1855. In comparison, for the Berlin and Frankfurt community leadership organs we have information about nineteen members, all of whom were born before 1850, all but three before 1841. Indeed, the large majority – fourteen out of nineteen (73.7 per cent) – were born before 1830.

Those figures suggest clearly that generation, in the sense of age cohort,[24] was the single most important distinguishing characteristic

---

[24] On that term see I. Rossow, 'What is cohort and why?', *Human Development*, vol. 21 (1978), pp. 65–75. There has been some opposition by sociologists to the use of the term 'generation' to designate age cohort. See, for example, David Kertzer, 'Generation as a socio-

of the activists forming the new Jewish politics.[25] The dates also provide us with a clear demarcation line: the generations born in the late 1840s and 1850s led the way for change. The established leadership, opposing change, was composed of members of the generations born in the 1820s and even earlier.

As far as generational consciousness is concerned, we have to distinguish between activists in Berlin and those in the provinces. In the provinces, the activists encountered little opposition, and in many cases were supported in their efforts by local community leaders and local Jewish elites. In fact, many an activist belonged to those elites. In Berlin, on the other hand, the community leadership and many members of the local elites opposed, openly or behind the scenes, the efforts of the new activists. This was especially evident in individual efforts to combat anti-semitic agitation. It was in Berlin that several activists displayed a clear generational consciousness, claiming that it was up to the new generation to correct the mistakes made by their elders, who had failed to defend their needs against their enemies. 'Unfortunately so many Jews, in particular the older ones, take little heed of even their most vital interest', bemoaned the founders of a small organisation aimed at fighting anti-semitism through public rallies.[26]

There is ample evidence that the different kinds of approach adopted by the two leadership generations reflect divergent collective mentalities.[27] We believe those mentalities were heavily influenced by the respective generations' formative experiences, gained during their members' youth and early political and professional careers.[28] Those born in the 1820s grew up and entered

---

logical problem', *Annual Review of Sociology*, vol. 9 (1983), pp. 125–149. Among historians and most sociologists, however, this use is widespread, and we shall follow it.

[25] Jehuda Reinharz had already asserted the importance of the generational factor within the German Zionist movement. See *Fatherland*, pp. 144–146, and his articles 'Three generations of German Zionism', *The Jerusalem Quarterly*, vol. 9 (1978), pp. 95–110; 'Ideology and structure in German Zionism 1882–1933', *Jewish Social Studies*, vol. 62 (1980), 2, pp. 119–146. We have not dealt with the Zionists since they were a very marginal group at the time.

[26] Quoted in the *Berliner Volkszeitung*, vol. 40 (1892), 6, 8 January, 3rd page. For other expressions see Ludwig Jacobowski, *Offene Antwort eines Juden an Herrn Ahlwardt's. Der Eid eines Juden* (Berlin 1891), pp. 29, 31; Heinrich Meyer-Cohn, 'Vor 25 Jahre - eine Erwiderung', *Allgemeine Zeitung des Judentums*, vol. 58 (1894), 29, 20 April, pp. 338–340.

[27] On the importance of applying that term to generational research see Anthony Esler, '"The truest community": social generations as collective mentalities', *Journal of Political and Military Sociology*, vol. 12 (1984), pp. 99–112.

[28] See Marvin Rintala, 'Generations in politics', in David Sills (ed.), *International encyclopedia of the social sciences*, vol. VI (New York 1968), pp. 92–96; Marvin Rintala, *The constitution of*

politics during the times of the hard struggle for Jewish emancipation, a struggle that had its ups (the *Vormärz* era, the 1848 revolution) and downs (the reaction after 1849). The struggle was based
upon the support of the Liberal movement, without which it had no
chance of success. The Liberals clearly expressed their disapproval
of any Jewish separatism, and Liberal spokesmen openly expressed
the view that emancipation should lead to the disappearance of the
Jews as a separate group within German society. As well as having
to contend with such views from the Liberal movement, the Jewish
community of the pre-emancipation period also confronted political
authorities who were both powerful and authoritarian. And it was
an authoritarian government, led by Bismarck, that finally granted
the Jews their desired emancipation.

Emancipation was seen by German Jews, after the long fight for
it, as a most formidable achievement. It was not their achievement –
it was granted from above, and the effort to bring it had succeeded
only through the help of their Liberal friends, and only when those
concurred, and were not in a state of confrontation, with the
government. The lesson learned was that one should wait patiently,
not fight the all-powerful authorities, and justice would win in the
end.

The formative political experiences of the generations born in the
late 1840s and 1850s, however, were quite different. Emancipation
had been granted whilst they were still in their young adulthood,
or even in late adolescence. Emancipation was not, for them, a
climax, a reward for hard efforts, but more like an interim or even a
starting-point for building on. Any infringement on their deserved
rights was therefore hard to accept. Moreover, their formative
political experiences were not associated with a powerful government, but rather with a government that failed to assert its
supremacy over opposition groups: the Catholics in the *Kulturkampf*
and the Socialists. They also observed that in the debate over
protective tariffs massive interest-group pressure induced the
government to change its course sharply. The lesson learned was
that government could be challenged and that minorities could hold

silence: essays on generational themes (Westport, Conn. 1979). See also Richard and Margaret
Braungart, 'Political generations', *Research in Political Sociology*, vol. 4 (1989), pp. 281–319.
For some useful criticism of a tendency to limit the effects of formative experience to one
particular age group see Walter Friedrich, 'Bemerkungen zum Generationskonzept',
Deutsche Zeitschrift für Philosophie, vol. 38 (1990), 1, pp. 46–47.

their own even against the government. This, one might add, was an experience they shared with non-Jewish members of the same generational cohort, a fact which goes some way to explaining Germany's new political style in the 1890s.[29]

Of course, it might be argued that this socialisation model is in fact unnecessary. In times of change it is often the younger element who, being less settled and well established, react more flexibly to the new situation. But in the present case the huge majority of the relevant Jewish activists were settled and professionally and socially well established. The formative experience model is thus more convincing in explaining why it was members of this generation who were quick to grasp the political changes occurring in Germany in the 1890s and who responded to the contemporary wave of anti-semitism with a new style of politics for the defence of Jewish minority interests. Large segments of Jewish society, including parts of the provincial community leadership and elites, accepted and supported their initiatives, being aware of the changes that were taking place in the politics of the day, and acknowledging the usefulness of exploiting those changes for Jewish benefit.

The established big community leadership, on the other hand, which for many years ran Jewish politics according to the characteristics we described earlier, found it hard to accept a political style that was in complete contrast to their own formative experiences and belief-system. In former times, their opposition would have sufficed to block attempts for change. That by the 1890s some new, non-established young leaders could challenge the Jewish *Honoratioren* and succeed in spite of their antagonism, was itself one clear indication of the changes that had taken place in the intervening period.

IV

It seems probable that the generational factor was important not just in the Jewish sphere but in the emergence of the wider political style of 1890s Germany. A new generation came into politics, whose adolescence and young adulthood occurred at a time when the government did not seem as mighty as before, and when the old established agrarian elite had become economically weak, and when

---

[29] See, for example, Eley, *Reshaping the German right*, pp. 184–185.

its politics were clearly particularistic, aimed at its own economic benefit and not for the general welfare. Influenced by such formative experiences as the unsuccessful *Kulturkampf* and anti-Socialist campaigns and the governmental change of course in 1878 and by particularistic experiences gained from within their own milieu, political activists of the younger generation were ready to fight publicly for their own interests and take on the government if necessary. With the first successes the changes gained momentum, as members of the different groups and sectors came in growing numbers to recognise the new possibilities for interest group politics. Thus German politics were reshaped and the old *Honoratiorenpolitik* was replaced by a different style of open, noisy, particularistic politics. The suggestion here, then, is that what occurred within German Jewry was a particular case of a general phenomenon, indicating that Jewry should be analysed in a manner which accords with what its members wanted to be: not as a separate, distinct group, but as an organic part of German society.

CHAPTER 6

The 'front generation' and the politics of Weimar Germany

Richard Bessel

> Until 1930 we all failed to appreciate fully the First World
> War's political legacy: the decimation of the younger gener-
> ation in the war. The volunteers of 1914, who had wanted an
> ethical revival of the nations, lay for the most part under cold
> earth all over Europe. They could not be replaced. The loss of
> young men was so enormous that within twelve years the
> post-war generation formed the majority of Germany's male
> voters.[1]

Thus Heinrich Brüning looked back, in his memoirs, at the impact
of the front generation on the politics of the Weimar Republic.
Brüning was deeply influenced by his experiences in uniform during
the First World War, in particular by his membership in an elite
machine-gun unit and by the scenes he had witnessed as the war
came to an end. Indeed, this provided the starting-point for his
memoirs, which open with comments about his position *vis-à-vis* 'my
generation'. While Brüning reflected the widely held conviction that
the men who had fought in the war formed a special generation, his
understanding of their role in public life was in some respects
remarkably perceptive. True, he reproduced the contemporary
rhetoric about the 'volunteers of 1914' who 'lay for the most part
under cold earth all over Europe and could not be replaced'; yet he
displayed an appreciation that it was not the generation 'decimated
in the First World War' but the post-war generation which proved
most difficult for Weimar democracy to accommodate. In this way
Brüning's observations, written down half a century after the
Armistice of November 1918, neatly frame a discussion of the front
generation and the politics of Weimar Germany.

Generations are essentially imaginary concepts. They are per-

---

[1] Heinrich Brüning, *Memoiren 1918–1934* (Stuttgart 1970), p. 40.

ceptions of what individuals have in common; they are shared
public declarations of identity – of ways in which people identify
and represent themselves in the public sphere. A sense of generational identity (like a perception of class identity) can nevertheless
be a powerful political force. The 'front generation' – the self-
conscious public representation of those who experienced the First
World War – provides perhaps the clearest example we have of the
power of generational identity in politics. Certainly, there are few
instances where the idea of shared generational experience has
intruded more stridently into the political arena.[2]

                                    I

Although the war itself provided the experiences around which the
idea of the front generation coalesced, Germans born between
roughly 1880 and 1900 had a number of things in common in
addition to having been put into uniform during the Great War.
The front generation was the last cohort to have been socialised
during the empire rather than the war or the Weimar Republic. Its
childhood was characterised by relative stability and prosperity, its
adult life by upheaval, by war, revolution, political instability,
inflation. It was a generation a large proportion of whom did not
survive their 20s, and many of whom died violent, unnatural deaths.
It was a generation a large proportion of whom never had the
opportunity to form normal adult relationships and families – and in
this sense the women born between 1880 and 1900 formed part of it
no less than did the men. It was a generation which observed the
technology of mass production in the first decades of mature industrial society and subsequently observed the technology of mass
destruction in the first industrial war.

    The combination of socialisation in a relatively stable political
and economic environment and adulthood in an environment characterised by upheaval and instability led to what may be posited as a
key element of this generation's mentality: the longing for a stability
and comradeship which many believed had existed in the recent
past and which contrasted so sharply with the crisis-ridden present

---

[2] It is noteworthy that this period saw a general burgeoning of interest in generational
theories of cultural change. For a concise overview, see Herbert F. Ziegler, *Nazi Germany's
new aristocracy: the SS leadership, 1925–1939*, (Princeton 1989), pp. 67–70 and see Elizabeth
Harvey's essay in this volume.

of Weimar Germany. The formulations of men such as Edgar Jung –
that the war generation had discovered heroism and had become
not just a distinct generation but in fact new men[3] – highlight only a
part of the problem which the front generation posed for the
Weimar Republic. It was not simply the rhetoric about the community created in the trenches that made the image of the front
generation so potent, but also the attractions of a mythical past for
the last generation to be socialised during the empire and the first to
be thrown into the maelstrom of the wars and economic upheavals of
the twentieth century.

Of course, the idea of the front generation and the generation of
1914, about which so much has been written, was to a considerable
extent a literary invention – a product of the shock felt by middle-
class prophets of cultural renewal as they were plunged into industrial warfare side by side with the common people in the trenches.[4]
It was perhaps as much an expression of middle- and upper-class
intellectuals' embarrassed discovery of the poorer strata as of the
creation of 'a new man' in the classless community of the trenches,[5]
and a product of 1900 as much as of 1914 – of the challenge of
modernity which took shape around the turn of the century as much
as it was of the war itself.[6] Certainly the literary output of men who
regarded themselves as changed irrevocably by the war and set
apart from the rest of humanity by what they had experienced in the
trenches (both the horror of industrial warfare and the camaraderie
of a 'front community'), has done much to establish the concept of
the front generation in the popular and historical imagination. As
Robert Wohl has noted, when we imagine the army of returning
veterans during the 1920s as a generation of men crippled what we
are actually seeing is the representation of this group by Remarque
and Hemingway.[7] However, the front generation was more than its
representation in the literary output of a Walter Flex, Fritz von

---

[3] Edgar Jung, 'Die Tragik der Kriegsgeneration', *Süddeutsche Monatshefte*, vol. 26 (1930);
Edgar Jung, *Die Herrschaft der Minderwertigen* (Berlin 1927). See the discussion of this in
Ziegler, *Nazi Germany's new aristocracy*, p. 67; Walter Struve, *Elites against democracy: leadership
ideals in bourgeois political thought in Germany, 1890–1933* (Princeton 1973), pp. 317–351.
[4] See Robert Wohl's comments on Walter Flex, *The generation of 1914* (London 1980), p. 49.
[5] See Ernst H. Posse, *Die politischen Kampfbünde Deutschlands* (Berlin 1931), pp. 24–25.
[6] Two stimulating texts on this last theme are Modris Eksteins, *Rites of spring: the Great War and
the birth of the modern age* (New York 1989); and August Nitschke, Gerhard A. Ritter, Detlev
J. K. Peukert and Rüdiger vom Bruch (eds.), *Jahrhundertwende. Der Aufbruch in die Moderne
1880–1930* (2 vols, Reinbek 1990).
[7] Wohl, *The generation of 1914*, p. 223.

Unruh or Erich Maria Remarque; it also was a product of the often ambiguous experiences of millions of people who lived through the war.

Who, then, constituted the front generation? The answer which first comes to mind is the men who experienced combat during the First World War. But this apparently simple definition raises problems. For one thing, it excludes the majority of Germans – women – who were born during the period roughly between 1880 and 1900 and who lived through and were affected deeply by the First World War. For another, it raises the question of what is meant by the experience of combat during the First World War. What sort of experience was necessary for membership in the front generation: a few weeks or months in the trenches in northern France? Military service in occupied Poland or on the Eastern Front? A 'red badge of courage'? What, actually, is sufficient to link a generation together, both in the perceptions of those who count themselves among its members and as a concept accepted among the public at large?

According to statistics assembled in the *Sanitätsbericht* of the German army in the First World War, 13,123,011 men served in the army between August 1914 and July 1918.[8] This comprised 19.7 per cent of the population of the German empire in 1914. Of course, not all these men were in uniform at any one moment. On average during the four years of war somewhat less than half were in the army at any given time; of these, about two-thirds were in the *Feldheer* and about one-third were in the *Besatzungsheer*. The number of men in the army reached its peak in 1917, and fell off fairly rapidly after the March offensives of 1918.[9] Turnover was enormous, and it appears that only a small minority of the men in the army spent four uninterrupted years in the trenches. Death, injury, illness, capture and call back to work in Germany removed huge numbers of men from the ranks. Roughly two million German soldiers were killed: according to the *Zentralnachweiseamt für Kriegsverluste und Kriegergräber*, at the end of 1933 the number of confirmed war dead stood at 1,900,876 men from the army, 34,836 from the navy and another 1,185 who had died in Germany's former colonies;

---

[8] Reichswehrministerium, *Sanitätsbericht über das deutsche Heer (Deutsches Feld- und Besatzungsheer) im Weltkriege, 1914–1918*. Vol. III: *Die Krankenbewegung bei dem Deutschen Feld- und Besatzungsheer* (Berlin 1934), pp. 12, 31.

[9] See the month-by-month figures in Reichswehrministerium, *Sanitätsbericht*, vol. III, p. 8. For further discussion, see Richard Bessel, *Germany after the First World War* (Oxford 1993), pp. 5–14.

in addition, there were an estimated 100,000 men listed as missing in action whose fate remained unknown and were presumed dead. Furthermore, altogether 4,814,557 German soldiers were reported as having been wounded during the war, and there were 14,673,940 registered cases of illness among servicemen.[10] Most of the ill and wounded returned to the ranks; of those who were wounded, about three-quarters recovered and were reclassified as fit for active duty.[11] Over and above this, as many as 800,000 German soldiers were taken prisoner during the war, most of whom returned home between the autumn of 1919 and the summer of 1920.[12]

The experiences of warfare which these men had were diverse and often divisive. Military service during the early months of the war, when the German armies were plunging through Belgium and into northern France, was quite different from life in the trenches; the stationary warfare in Flanders was quite different from the fighting along the vast Eastern Front. The nature of trench warfare – and the majority of Germany's troops were stationed along the trench-carved Western Front – gave rise to divisions between the men up at the front and those behind the lines, out of the reach of enemy artillery. While there certainly did develop a sense of a 'front community' which linked men who shared a common experience in the trenches, there also arose deep animosities behind the lines, where military drill and the preferential treatment of officers pro-voked great resentment and friction between officers and men.[13]

Furthermore, it would be mistaken to believe that during the First World War the German army was a world unto itself, cut off from the home front. Most soldiers did not pass the war years continually in battle, at or near the front. Many spent long periods recovering

[10] Reichswehrministerium, *Sanitätsbericht*, vol. III, pp. 12, 31.
[11] *Ibid.*, p. 62. Robert Whalen, using the figures from the *Sanitätsbericht*, states incorrectly that of the wounded *who recovered* 74.7 per cent returned to active duty. See Robert Weldon Whalen, *Bitter wounds: German victims of the Great War, 1914–1939* (Ithaca, London 1984), p. 40. In fact the 74.7 per cent refers to the proportion of the *total* wounded (of whom more than one million died of their wounds) who subsequently were reclassified as fit for duty or who remained in the army. Only 344,576 (7.6 per cent) of the total who survived their wounds were reclassified as unfit for service.
[12] Eight hundred thousand was the figure given in German government discussions of the prisoners of war during 1919. See, for example, Hagen Schulze (ed.), *Akten der Reichskanzlei. Weimarer Republik. Das Kabinett Scheidemann. 13. Februar bis 20. Juni 1919* (Boppard am Rhein 1971), p. 25.
[13] See Wilhelm Deist, 'Der militärische Zusammenbruch des Kaiserreichs. Zur Realität der "Dolchstoßlegende"', in Ursula Büttner (ed.), *Das Unrechtsregime. Vol. I: Ideologie Herr-schaftssystem Wirkung in Europa* (Hamburg 1986), pp. 107–108.

from wounds or illness in military hospitals or in medical institutions or convalescent homes in Germany; many were moved from front to front as the course of the war altered – and this often meant travel through the Reich; many were called back to Germany during the second half of the war to provide badly needed labour in war industries; many were able to enjoy periodic leave in Germany; many were drafted and sent to the front only during the later stages of the war;[14] many were called to the colours, released, then called up again; and throughout the conflict there was constant rotation to relieve units in the front line. There was no typical experience of the First World War, no uniform experience of the front generation. The war meant many different things to the many men who fought it. The idea of a single front experience was a mythical creation of the post-war world. It represented an attempt to cover over divisions rather than to assert real unity of experience and perspective. As George Mosse has written in a revealing recent study, 'The reality of the war experience came to be transformed into what one might call the Myth of the War Experience, which looked back upon the war as a meaningful and even sacred event ... The Myth of the War experience was designed to mask war and legitimize the war experience; it was meant to displace the reality of war.'[15]

Nevertheless, the vast majority of German males born between 1880 and 1900 had *some* experience of the First World War in uniform. The roughly 13.2 million men mobilised at some stage during the war comprised about 85 per cent of the 15.6 million males in the German empire then eligible for military service.[16] Men in these birth cohorts who saw no military service – due to physical disabilities or to employment in key sectors of the war economy – were the exception. The soldiers came from all walks of life, although it would appear, from evidence of the origins of those killed, that men from rural areas were more likely to become soldiers than were industrial workers (who more often were held back to

[14] See Bessel, *Germany after the First World War*, p. 7.
[15] George L. Mosse, *Fallen soldiers: reshaping the memory of the world wars* (New York, Oxford 1990), p. 7.
[16] Whalen, *Bitter wounds*, p. 39. See also Rudolf Meerwarth, 'Die Entwicklung der Bevölkerung in Deutschland während der Kriegs- und Nachkriegszeit', in Rudolf Meerwarth, Adolf Günther and Waldemar Zimmermann, *Die Einwirkungen des Krieges auf die Bevölkerungsbewegung, Einkommen und Lebenshaltung in Deutschland* (Stuttgart 1932), pp. 57–64.

work in war industries).[17] The majority were single[18] – which means
that for the majority of members of the front generation marriage
and establishing a family came *after* their war experience. That is to
say, the attempt to settle into stable social and economic relationships occurred after the stable environment in which they had
grown up had been blown apart, first by war and then by revolution
and economic upheaval. For the front generation, the search for
stability occurred during a period of terrible instability.

II

Yet though the challenge of adjustment and reintegration was no
doubt considerable, the gap between military and civilian life
during and after the First World War was by no means so hard and
fast as has often been assumed. The conventional assumption has
been that the German soldiers who fought in the First World War
were men who 'had found an emotional home in soldierly comradeship' and who therefore, 'disillusioned', 'returned home in 1918
and 1919 and could not adjust to daily life'.[19] That no doubt was
true of some, but it was hardly true of all or even most of the millions
of German soldiers who returned home in 1918 and 1919. The vast
majority were able to put their war experiences behind them, find
employment, reintegrate into or establish their families, and 'adjust
to daily life'.[20] Even a crude comparison between the total number
of Germans who served in the armed forces during the First World
War and the (at most) 400,000 men (not all of whom had been in the
wartime army) who joined the *Freikorps* suggests that far more
veterans managed subsequently to lead unremarkable humdrum
lives than sought refuge in a life of violence in paramilitary uniform
as a result of an inability to adjust to civil society.

[17] See Statistisches Reichsamt, *Statistik des Deutschen Reichs*, vol. 276, p. xlix; Meerwarth, 'Die Entwicklung der Bevölkerung', pp. 69–70.
[18] Of the German soldiers killed during the Great War, 68.75 per cent were single. See Bessel, *Germany after the First World War*, p. 10.
[19] Jürgen Reulecke, '*Männerbund* versus the family: middle-class youth movements and the family in Germany in the period of the First World War', in Richard Wall and Jay Winter (eds.), *The upheaval of war: family, work and welfare in Europe, 1914–1918* (Cambridge 1988), p. 444.
[20] See Richard Bessel, 'Unemployment and demobilisation in Germany after the First World War', in Richard J. Evans and Dick Geary (eds.), *The German unemployed: experiences and consequences of mass unemployment from the Weimar Republic to the Third Reich* (London 1987), pp. 23–43. Generally, see Bessel, *Germany after the First World War*.

Yet they did vote. The men who experienced at least some part of the First World War in German uniform and survived to return to the Reich, formed a significant proportion of the electorate of Weimar Germany. Altogether, roughly 11 million German soldiers survived the war and returned to Germany. Even in 1932, after approximately 650,000 of the men in Germany born between 1880 and 1900 had died since 1919, the surviving members of what might narrowly be termed the front generation still numbered nearly 10.5 million men; they comprised more than one-quarter of the German electorate during the 1920s and, given the generally lower participation of women in elections, an even higher proportion of those who actually voted.[21] What is more, veterans of the First World War came to comprise the backbone of many party organisations in Weimar Germany – most famously of the Nationalsozialistische Deutsche Arbeiterpartei (NSDAP), but of the other political parties as well. It hardly could have been otherwise: in 1930 the men born between 1880 and 1900 were aged between 30 and 50, i.e. they were of an age when people normally establish themselves in their communities. They quite naturally assumed positions of importance in local organisations, or attempted to wrest control from their elders – from the generation of those who already had been adults during the empire and many of whom were approaching retirement from public life by 1930. Thus what may have been an inevitable generational conflict in the political arena was conducted by a group which also saw itself as the front generation.

But what difference did this really make? Can the political radicalism or the political divisions of the Weimar Republic be explained by reference to the front generation? Did the fact that so many of Weimar Germany's men experienced the First World War measurably affect the ways in which they acted in the political sphere? There is little evidence to suggest that it did. The main cleavages which characterised the German electorate were religious, occupational and geographical (i.e. town and country), and all the political parties attempted, in their own ways, to court the front generation and all heaped praise on the 'heroes' of the trenches. Indeed, since the veterans of the First World War comprised so large a section of the electorate in Weimar Germany it would have been highly unlikely for them to have been found largely in one political

---

[21] See Bessel, *Germany after the First World War*, pp. 270–271.

camp and not in another. However, one cleavage that the front generation obviously did parallel was that between men and women. The front generation may have been too large to parallel any particular political preference, but it was one way of describing the majority of middle-aged men in Weimar Germany.

Yet in many regards women also were members of the war generation. They had experienced wartime hardships on the home front in their millions. Their family lives had been disrupted profoundly as husbands, sons and fathers were called to the colours. Many women lost their own homes once husbands were called up and they were compelled to give up flats of their own and move in with parents or in-laws. More than half a million German women were widowed by the war.[22] For many women, in particular those who, as a result of the war, became dependent upon the German welfare system during the crisis-ridden years of the Weimar Republic, the scars left behind by the war remained for decades; as Karin Hausen has reminded us, the most vulnerable of the women who suffered as a consequence of the war, German war widows, especially those with children, 'paid the costs of World War I in installments of their daily lives'.[23] Women had borne the brunt of the catastrophic food shortages which plagued Germany during the war (while the men in the armed forces continued to be fed reasonably well); they had had to negotiate the thriving, and often painfully unfair, wartime black market; they had faced the double burden of having to run their households and care for their families while working long hours – in an often undernourished condition – to bring in necessary income in the absence of male breadwinners. They had worked in munitions industries in their hundreds of thousands, to be turfed out as soon as the war was over and the soldiers returned.[24]

---

22 Whalen, *Bitter wounds*, p. 95. Other estimates put the number of war widows in Weimar Germany at roughly 600,000. See Karin Hausen, 'The German nation's obligation to the heroes' widows of World War I', in Margaret Randolph Higonnet, Jane Jenson, Sonya Michel and Margaret Collins Weitz (eds.), *Behind the lines: gender and the two world wars* (New Haven, London 1987), p. 128.

23 Hausen, 'The German nation's obligation', p. 126. The longer-term negative consequences for women's living standards of having lost their husbands during the war can be seen in the study by Karl Nau of war victims in Darmstadt in 1930: Karl Nau, *Die wirtschaftliche und soziale Lage von Kriegshinterbliebenen. Eine Studie auf Grund von Erhebungen über die Auswirkungen der Versorgung von Kriegshinterbliebenen in Darmstadt* (Leipzig 1930). For details of the incomes of war widows in Darmstadt in 1930, see pp. 28–30.

24 The best discussions of German working women during the war are to be found in the work of Ute Daniel, especially her *Arbeiterfrauen in der Kriegsgesellschaft. Beruf, Familie und Politik im Ersten Weltkrieg* (Göttingen 1989). See also Ute Daniel, 'Fiktionen, Friktionen und Fakten.

Although the war profoundly affected the German women who lived through it, in the public imagination they were not included in the front generation. During the Weimar years Germany's women were confronted by an image of the front generation which explicitly excluded them and their experiences. As such, the potency of the front generation in the public language of politics in Weimar Germany – and particularly during the final years of the Republic – was another, powerful assertion that politics and the public sphere generally was a male realm.[25] To assert that politics should be an expression of the front generation was in effect to assert that women had little or no role in public political life. It is certainly of more than passing interest that the political party which ultimately exploited the myth of the front generation most successfully and whose leader was constantly presented (and presented himself) as a front soldier – that is, the Nazi party – was also most militantly anti-feminist.

III

The most visible intrusion of the front generation into German politics after 1918 was the activities of those officers who found a home in paramilitary and right-wing groups after the war. Much has been written of the men who returned to a defeated Germany 'deeply marked by their war experiences and hostile toward the civilian population, by whom they felt betrayed and abandoned', men who returned 'confused, embittered, angry, hungry, and with no hope of pursuing military careers because of the limitations placed on the German army by the Treaty of Versailles' and who 'soon found opportunities to use the destructive skills they had learned at the front'.[26] Their contribution to Weimar politics was significant. These were the men who led the *Freikorps* groups which campaigned against left-wing activists and Polish insurgents in the years after the First World War and occupied leading positions in the numerous military-style organisations (the *Kampfbünde*) which proliferated in Weimar Germany,[27] and many subsequently held

Frauenarbeit im Ersten Weltkrieg', in Gunther Mai (ed.), *Arbeiterschaft in Deutschland 1914–1918* (Düsseldorf 1985), pp. 277–323; Ute Daniel, 'Women's work in industry and family: Germany, 1914–18', in Wall and Winter, *The Upheaval of War*, pp. 267–296.
[25] On these themes, see especially Klaus Theweleit, *Männerphantasien* (2 vols, Frankfurt 1977).
[26] Wohl, *The generation of 1914*, p. 54.
[27] See James M. Diehl, *Paramilitary politics in Weimar Germany* (Bloomington, London 1977).

leading positions in the Nazi party. Furthermore, the self-conscious expression of front generation politics during the 1920s was not limited to the militarist antics of the fringe racialist right. Groups which could be regarded as mainstream (although also clearly on the right of the political spectrum) also saw themselves as representatives of the front generation. The most obvious example is the *Stahlhelm* (whose full title was *Stahlhelm*, League of Front Soldiers), whose members identified themselves as 'front soldiers' throughout the Weimar period and whose self-proclaimed purpose was to promote politicians 'who will depend on us front soldiers for support'.[28]

Yet as already indicated, many former front soldiers, who continued to identify themselves as such, were loath to subscribe to right-wing, militaristic politics. Many brought back from the trenches a profound rejection of the horrors of war. In fact, the largest organisation of veterans of the First World War as *veterans* was not a right-wing paramilitary formation, but an organisation which was largely social democratic: the Reich Association of War Disabled, War Veterans and War Dependants (*Reichsbund der Kriegsbeschädigten, Kriegsteilnehmer und Kriegshinterbliebenen*), which grew to a peak of 830,000 dues-paying members in 1922.[29]

No less than the right-wing formations so keen to glorify military traditions and to cultivate a particular vision of soldiers' experience in the First World War, the war's victims formed a major – both audible and visible – element of the front generation. Throughout the Weimar period the war victims vigorously and vociferously attempted to defend their interests. They constituted a substantial segment of the German population during the interwar years, and their collective voice was difficult to ignore. It has been estimated, for example, that roughly 2.7 million German soldiers returned from the First World War with some form of permanent disability. The financial obligations created for the German state by the war were enormous.[30] In 1926, for example, war-related pensions were being paid to 792,143 disabled veterans, 361,024 widows, 849,087 fatherless children and 62,070 children with no living parent.[31] The

---

[28] This is a comment by Franz Seldte, the leader of the *Stahlhelm*, given in his official biography (Wilhelm Kleinau, *Franz Seldte. Ein Lebensbericht* (Berlin 1933), p. 49), quoted in Robert G. L. Waite, *Vanguard of Nazism: the Free Corps movement in postwar Germany 1918–1923* (New York 1969), p. 267. On the *Stahlhelm* generally, see Volker R. Berghahn, *Der Stahlhelm. Bund der Frontsoldaten* (Düsseldorf 1966).

[29] Whalen, *Bitter wounds*, p. 150. [30] *Ibid.*, p. 95. [31] *Ibid.*, pp. 156–157.

scale of the human problems left behind by the war overwhelmed the state welfare services; the resulting pensions system, as Robert Whalen has described so colourfully, remained 'a maze of red tape' during the Weimar period, creating enormous difficulties for over-worked bureaucrats and enormous anger among the war victims whose cases sometimes took years to resolve.[32] Organisations of war victims claimed that their members were being short-changed; government officials claimed that pensions budgets had to be pruned. Consequently the idea of a front generation took shape in part through conflict with agencies of the Weimar state, as war victims sought to defend their interests as *war victims* in noisy public campaigns. Although it may not have reflected accurately the ambiguous realities of war experience, employing the concept of the front generation offered an auspicious context in which to present demands in the public arena. Who, after all, could denigrate the contribution of the front generation?

The conflicts inherent in the welfare programmes for war victims were exacerbated once the German economy went into a tailspin during the early 1930s. Spending on pensions was cut and payments were no longer calculated from the date of the application but rather from the date when the application was approved, which in effect made the victim pay for bureaucratic delays.[33] War victims responded with howls of protest, as hundreds of thousands demon-strated against the cuts. The problem was illustrated clearly by a letter from a disabled war veteran sent to the Prussian welfare minister in October 1931. After borrowing phrases word-for-word from a recent resolution of the Social Democratic Reich Association of War Disabled, War Veterans and War Dependants, he threat-ened to turn to the Nazi deputies Wilhelm Kube and Joseph Goebbels to raise the matter in the Reichstag.[34] The front gener-ation was making its presence felt in the political arena with a vengeance.

---

[32] *Ibid.*, pp. 155–165. [33] *Ibid.*, pp. 168–170.

[34] Archiwum Panstwowe we Szczecinie (APS), Oberpräsidium von Pommern, no. 3938: Bitte des Kriegsbeschädigten Walter Kosinsky um Zahnersatz und Nachzahlung von Militär-gebührnissen (Request from disabled war veteran Walter Kosinsky re replacement of teeth and back payment of allowances for military service) to the Preußischer Minister für Volkswohlfahrt, Stettin, 18 October 1931; *ibid.*: The Landeswohlfahrtsamt to the Ober-präsident, 11 January 1932. The text of the resolution of the *Reichsbund* from a protest demonstration in Stettin on 26 April 1931 may be found in APS, Oberpräsidium von Pommern, no. 3938: Reichsbund der Kriegsbeschädigten, Kriegsteilnehmer und Kriegshinterbliebenen, Gau Pommern, to the Oberpräsident, Stettin, 27 April 1931.

The idea of a front generation provided a public identity and platform from which war victims could pursue their interests. It was given shape by demands for 'justice' and reference to the promises made so liberally that the soldiers of the First World War could be confident of receiving the 'thanks of the Fatherland'. To be a member of the front generation was to be someone to whom German society owed a debt of honour. Yet it is difficult to imagine any payment which would have been regarded as satisfactory.[35] The debt of honour never could be adequately repaid, and consequently the front generation formed a public identity which ultimately was not terribly supportive of Weimar democracy.

Damaging as the political mobilisation of war victims was for the Weimar Republic, the idea of the front generation ultimately may have had an even greater impact upon the sorry politics of Weimar Germany through those too young to have fought in the war. Probing the contribution of this group is difficult and necessarily speculative, but it is worth considering the possible consequences of a widespread sense of guilt at not having shared the horrors of the trenches in a country where, increasingly, the exploits of the front generation were praised as the model of selfless heroism. There are signs which suggest that the myth of the front generation was potent less in mobilising those who actually experienced life in the trenches than in inspiring the post-war generation which had not seen combat in the First World War. One such piece of evidence is that efforts to recruit for *Freikorps* units and local citizens' militias (*Einwohnerwehren*) sometimes met with greater success among school-leavers, among whom the image of the heroic soldier held greater allure than it did among soldiers who had returned so recently from the senseless slaughter of the trenches.[36]

Another sign of the attraction of the idea of the front generation for those too young to be counted as its members was the mass following of the Nazi movement itself. Particularly among its activist

---

[35] For an extremely suggestive discussion of war victims' welfare in comparative perspective in Britain, France and Germany, see Michael Geyer, 'Ein Vorbote des Wohlfahrtsstaates. Die Kriegsopferversorgung in Frankreich, Deutschland und Großbritannien nach dem Ersten Weltkrieg', *GG*, vol. 9 (1983), 3, pp. 230–277, esp. pp. 250–258.

[36] Geheimes Staatsarchiv preußischer Kulturbesitz Berlin-Dahlem, Rep. 12/11a/2, ff. 189–90: The Magistrat to the Oberpräsident in Königsberg, Tilsit, 11 March 1919; Brandenburgisches Landeshauptarchiv Potsdam, Rep. 3B Reg. Frankfurt/Oder I Pol, no. 457, ff. 36–38: The Landrat to the Regierungspräsident in Frankfurt/Oder, Reppen, 11 April 1919; Waite, *Vanguard of Nazism*, pp. 42–44; Hagen Schulze, *Freikorps und Republik 1918–1920* (Boppard am Rhein 1969), p. 51.

core – in the SA, where military values and the so-called spirit of 1914 found particular expression – the vast majority of Hitler's supporters were of the post-war generation.[37] The young men who flocked to the Nazi formations in the early 1930s had been children at the time of the war. For them the war often had brought upheaval and insecurity, but they had not experienced the horrors of combat at first hand. Their experience of war was more likely to have come from films, cheap children's novels, and playing soldier with their school comrades. For members of this generation, war was youthful fantasy, not the dreadful reality of the trenches. Their idea of war could match more closely the images conjured up by the idea of the front generation than did the experiences of the men who actually had fought a war.

Similar conclusions are suggested by evidence in the *Deutschland-Berichte* (Germany Reports) of the exiled German Social Democrats after Hitler had come to power. When the German government reintroduced conscription in March 1935, different sectors of the population responded in quite differing ways. Whilst some observers noted 'ardent approval' among the older generation, especially since thereby 'the youth finally will learn discipline and order again', others registered misgivings. This was the case 'especially among older people', who feared a new war and were far from keen to see a new militarisation of life.[38] And from Saxony one informant wrote:[39]

The former participants in the War whom we could ask about their opinion on the introduction of general conscription gave expression in a very veiled manner that they were not keen to relive the years 1914–1918. War invalids and war widows spoke to the effect that better the Reich government should first meet its previous commitments and recompense all the victims of that last war before it creates new victims once again and spends money for armaments.

According to an informant from southern Bavaria, on the other hand, 'the young people appear to be very pleased that they are able to join up'.[40] The people most keen 'to relive the years 1914–1918' were those who had not been compelled to endure them the first

---

[37] See Richard Bessel, *Political violence and the rise of Nazism: the storm troopers in Eastern Germany 1925–1934* (New Haven, London 1984), pp. 33–45; Peter Longerich, *Die Braunen Bataillone. Geschichte der SA* (Munich 1989), pp. 89–91.
[38] *Deutschland-Berichte der Sozialdemokratischen Partei Deutschland* (Sopade) 1934–1940, Zweiter Jahrgang 1935 (Frankfurt 1980), pp. 276–282.
[39] *Ibid.*, p. 412.   [40] *Ibid.*, pp. 276–282.

time round. It was among this generation, that the idea of the front generation could remain unambiguously positive and war could be made to appear attractive. For the front soldiers of the First World War, the experience of combat – if they cared to remember it accurately – had been too complex and contradictory to confirm the idea of an heroic front generation. Yet for them as well heroic myth held its attractions, and it proved profoundly damaging for the Weimar Republic. Instead of discussing honestly the nature of the war and their participation in it, Germans retreated into talk about a mythical heroic 'front spirit'. The striking contrast between public descriptions of the front generation and the far less edifying facts of its actual conduct are extremely revealing; at issue was not what actually happened (for example, the breakdown of discipline and mass desertions which accompanied the end of the war), but what people were able to admit publicly (perhaps even to themselves) had happened.[41] The idea of the front generation thus was less a way to interpret the actual experience of the First World War than a means by which to retreat from the unpleasant realities of the war and the post-war period, and that is what made it politically so corrosive.

IV

The illusions which comprised so much of the public language of politics in Weimar Germany were dangerous not least because they helped fix the agenda in such a way as to favour some political currents and to disadvantage others. Not only did they help set an agenda which served the right; they also encouraged irresponsibility. In order to function, a democratic political system needs a certain degree of consensus recognising the limits within which policy decisions have to be made. As long as the truth about the 1914–1918 conflict, its causes and consequences, remained excluded from mainstream public discussion, it was both possible to accept and, indeed, to glorify war and impossible to face fully the harsh economic and political realities which confronted the Weimar Republic. The prominence given to the front generation in public discussions in interwar Germany both manifested and facilitated the flight from political responsibility. Responsible politics remained a

---

[41] For further development of arguments along these lines, see Richard Bessel, 'The Great War in German memory: the soldiers of the First World War, demobilization, and Weimar political culture', *German History*, vol. 6 (1988), 1, pp. 20–34.

hostage to myths about the First World War throughout the
tortured life of the Weimar Republic, and democracy eventually
paid the price.[42]

The idea of the front generation was not simply a vision of a new
egalitarian community which allegedly had been forged in the
trenches in northern France. It also was a myth which placed a
heavy burden on the first German democracy and attracted most
powerfully those who had escaped the horrors of the First World
War but who prepared the way for the Second.

---

[42] On the ramifications of the myth of Germany's innocence with regard to the First World
War see Wolfram Wette, 'Ideologien, Propaganda und Innenpolitik als Voraussetzungen
der Kriegspolitik des Dritten Reiches', in Wilhelm Deist (ed.), *Ursachen und Voraussetzungen
der deutschen Kriegspolitik* (vol. 1 of Militärgeschichtliches Forschungsamt (ed.), *Das Deutsche
Reich und der Zweite Weltkrieg)*(Stuttgart, 1979), pp. 25–173; Ulrich Heinemann, *Die
verdrängte Niederlage. Politische Öffentlichkeit und Kriegsschuldfrage in der Weimarer Republik*
(Göttingen 1983). More generally, see Richard Bessel, 'Why did the Weimar Republic
collapse?', in Ian Kershaw (ed.), *Weimar: why did German democracy fail?* (London 1990), esp.
pp. 123–128.

CHAPTER 7

The New Woman and generational conflict: perceptions of young women's sexual mores in the Weimar Republic

Cornelie Usborne

For contemporaries, the emergence of the New Woman was one of the most striking and challenging features of Weimar society. Contemporary discussion was set alight by the provocative behaviour and dress of a new generation of young women who seemed determined to break with established norms. For some observers, the New Woman's defining characteristic was the abandonment of motherhood. Many conservatives argued that because of the New Woman's fecklessness and irresponsibility the family was in crisis, moral depravity on the increase and society suffering from the effects of husbands and wives both going out to work. Others were conscious rather of a new female style. For them the quintessential New Woman was a pleasure-seeking glamour girl, dressed in short skirt or even in trousers, hair worn bobbed in a *Bubikopf*, wearing make up and smoking cigarettes.

Historians have been divided on how to treat the phenomenon.[1] For a while, there was a tendency to argue that there never really had been a New Woman. The conservatives' dismay was seen as exaggerated propaganda, stoking up public fears in order to defend reactionary viewpoints. Similarly, the image of the glamour girl was dismissed as media hype. Fashion changes there may have been, but they applied only to a small section of the urban population and certainly had little to do with a wider emancipation or change of values. Finally, it was argued, the suggestion that there was a new emancipated generation of young women ignored the persistent high levels of gender inequality; old assumptions and gender roles remained predominant. More recently, however, historians of

---

[1] E.g. Detlev Peukert, *Jugend zwischen Krieg und Krise. Lebenswelten von Arbeiterjungen in der Weimarer Republik* (Cologne 1987), pp. 95ff; Ute Frevert, *Women in German History* (Oxford 1989).

Weimar have acknowledged the very real changes to women's social position.[2] There has been a greater willingness to respect the contemporary view that many young women did indeed pioneer a new life-style and question traditional gender roles, thereby creating tensions between men and women, old and young.[3]

In line with this latter approach, the present essay argues that a new female generation, with profoundly different values and behaviour, *did* emerge after the First World War. At the same time, however, the contemporary images of the New Woman were not just mirrors on reality. The very fact that, as already intimated, those images were often contradictory shows how far reactions were coloured by the anxieties, beliefs and political agendas of the observers. The political right and left reacted differently from one another, as did older and younger people. Male commentators and female commentators often produced different arguments and pronouncements frequently contained a strong element of class bias.

In fact, as the present essay will show, the notion of the New Woman was able to excite such contemporary attention precisely because it triggered anxieties that went to the very heart of the social and political state of the nation. For the political left, and the sex and social reformers often allied to the left, the phenomenon of the New Woman was a mixture of promise and disappointment. On the one hand, it represented their considerable achievements in the fight for social and gender equality; on the other, it was a potential threat to social harmony and to the health of the next generation. For conservatives the New Woman was an almost wholly negative symbol, which illustrated the collapse of the patriarchal system and traditional sexual mores. It was widely felt that female emancipation, coupled with the impact of war and revolution, had weakened the moral fabric of the population, encouraging the spread of prostitution, venereal diseases, illegitimacy and abortion.[4] For all contemporaries, whether conservatives or reformers, the emergence of a younger generation of women demanding unprecedented civil and sexual rights aroused irrational, often unacknowledged fears of

[2] Cornelie Usborne, *The politics of the body in Weimar Germany: women's reproductive rights and duties* (London 1992), pp. 85, 95.

[3] E.g. Atina Grossmann, *Women, family and the rationalization of sexuality: German sex reform 1925–1935* (forthcoming) and '*Girlkultur* or thoroughly rationalized female: a New Woman in Weimar Germany?', in Judith Friedlander, Blanche Wiesen Cook, Alice Kessler-Harris and Carroll Smith-Rosenberg (eds.), *Women in culture and politics* (Bloomington 1986), pp. 62–80.

[4] See Usborne, *Politics of the body*, pp. 31ff, 82ff.

cultural anarchy and reflected the drama of a society undergoing the trials of modernity.

This essay, then, is about how the image of a generation – the New Woman – was constructed. It focuses particularly on the issue of sexual behaviour, because it was young women's sexual mores that were most likely to generate fears and controversy and it was in the area of sexual behaviour that differences and tensions between the generations were at their clearest. Thus the essay will examine first the way in which the New Woman was defined or perceived by sex reformers, by popular culture and avant-garde art and by the women's movement. It will then assess how far these definitions and perceptions corresponded to the reality of young women's lives in Weimar. Were older observers simply deluded or exaggerating, or had they indeed witnessed profound changes in female sexual mores? In answering this question, the essay deploys not only demographic and socio-economic data but also the testimony of young women themselves. Indeed, it will be argued here that historians should take young women's discourse more seriously, not just as a looking glass on social change, but also as a force which contributed to contemporaries' changing perceptions of female aspirations and behaviour.

I

A central role in our story is played by Germany's vociferous sex reform movement. The movement emerged prior to the First World War but became a popular force only in the Weimar Republic, and it played a key role in shaping public perceptions of the New Woman. Sexologists like Magnus Hirschfeld, who founded the World League of Sexual Reform (WLSR), were joined by left-leaning sociologists like Rudolf Goldscheid, who pleaded for 'sexual and reproductive rights as the highest achievement of political and economic human rights'.[5] The cause of sexual reform enjoyed support also from left-wing politicians such as the Communist Emil Höllein, from doctors interested in social medicine as was Max Hodann, and from feminists like Helene Stöcker, who founded the radical League for the Protection of Motherhood (*Bund für Mutter-*

---

[5] Rudolf Goldscheid, 'Zur Geschichte der Sexualmoral', *Die Neue Generation (NG)* (1931), 10–11, p. 180.

schutz, BfM).[6] While male sex reformers were concerned with a new sexual code in general, Stöcker and other members of the *Bund* addressed women's sexuality in particular. They campaigned for a New Morality, a celebration of erotic love and of all motherhood, whether this was sanctioned by marriage or not. According to Stöcker, a New Morality would replace the existing double standard in sexual mores and the repressive teaching of the church. It would also stimulate feminism since it was founded on women's sexual equality and reproductive self-determination.[7]

Public awareness of the BfM's campaign for women's 'sexual freedom' was considerably increased when other organisations like the WLSR began to lend it support. Left-wing sex reformers writing in the journal *Die Weltbühne* took up the BfM's campaign for easier divorce for women locked in loveless marriages but also advocated more controversial ideas such as free access to birth control, free love and temporary sexual unions in order to help the young discard outmoded ideals of chastity, monogamy and maternity. These reformers espoused liberated sex for women as part of a cultural revolution, transforming all society. As one contributor put it, 'we could become a new human race: mothers who want to be mothers ... fathers who respect their wife's longing for a child and children who are wanted and loved. A culture of love.'[8] Feminist sex reformers never tired of stressing that sexual fulfilment was women's 'greatest and most important source of vitality and joy'. Suggestions ranged from sex education in all elementary schools to 'schools of love' to teach men how 'to awaken women's sensuality' in such a way that 'it could reach maturity'.[9] Sexologists, the majority of whom were men, agreed with both principle and strategy. And to lend respectability to such schemes they carried out 'scientific' research and published impressive graphs to teach men the skills of timed mutual orgasm ostensibly to increase understanding between husband and wife.[10]

[6] Richard J. Evans, *The feminist movement in Germany 1894–1933* (London, Beverley Hills 1976), pp. 133ff.
[7] Helene Stöcker, 'Zur Reform der sexuellen Ethik', *NG* (1930), 3/4, p. 70 (originally published in 1905); Christl Wickert, Brigitte Hamburger and Marie Wienau, 'Helene Stöcker and the Bund für Mutterschutz', *Women's Studies International Forum*, vol. 5 (1982), 6, p. 611.
[8] Cited in Willem Melching, '"A New Morality": left-wing intellectuals on sexuality in Weimar Germany', *Journal of Contemporary History*, vol. 25 (1990), p. 80.
[9] Margarete Weinberg, 'Zur Problematik der Ehe', *NG* (1930), 5/6, pp. 183–187.
[10] E.g. J. R. Spinner, 'Die Bedeutung des Lustkurven für das Eheglück', *Liebe und Ehe*, vol. 1 (1929), July, pp. 53–58; *Die Liebes-Lehre. Eine Liebesschule für Eheleute* (Berlin 1929); cf. Atina

[handwritten margin note: Sexual reform supported by SPD, reforms, left-wing]

It would be wrong to suggest that the theme of the New Woman's sexual emancipation was restricted to the esoteric circle of sex reformers. Left-wing women's journals, such as the Communist party (KPD) organ *Weg der Frau* took up the clarion call for sexual enlightenment.[11] The Social Democrat (SPD) journal *Die Gleichheit* also supported sex reform, especially such schemes as 'companionate marriages'.[12] Some prominent Socialist women leaders called forcefully and publicly for sexual freedom for women. In a Reichstag speech in 1928, which was all the more daring for being given by an unmarried woman, Toni Pfülf defended every woman's right to be sexually active. She went on to argue that erotic fulfilment was women's 'natural destiny' and that exerting this right would help to destroy 'bourgeois hypocrisy and selfishness' and ensure the birth of a 'new sexual morality'.[13] Feminists in the SPD and KPD spearheaded the parliamentary campaign for legal equality of unmarried mothers and their children and for better access to birth control, including abortion, which they regarded as a precondition for sexual emancipation. They also strove to reform the civil code to ensure legal equality for women in divorce and marriage.

This latter was also a central concern for bourgeois feminists in the Federation of German Women's Associations (BDF). But they too did not shrink from the issue of looser morals among young women. They were quite ready to accept that extra-marital relationships need not necessarily be a sign of moral depravity. Marianne Weber, widow of Max Weber, was chair of the BDF from 1919 to 1923 and the BDF's self-appointed spokesperson on sexuality. She admitted that women could achieve 'sensual happiness' and 'the experience of transcendence mediated by love' in free unions.[14] This was a remarkable concession from somebody as devoutly religious as Marianne Weber and shows how seriously women activists engaged with the changed attitudes they perceived all around them.

Grossmann, 'The New Woman and the rationalization of sexuality in Weimar Germany', in Ann Snitow, Christine Stansell and Sharon Thompson (eds.), *Desire: the politics of sexuality* (London 1984), pp. 190–211.

[11] E.g. *Weg der Frau*, October 1931, p. 28, 'Gesundheit und Hygiene. Unbefriedigtsein und Geschlechtskälte'.

[12] E.g. Dr Emily Stricker, 'Die zukünftigen Mütter', *Die Gleichheit* (1919), 13, p. 33; Henriette Fürth, 'Die Bekämpfung der Geschlechtskrankheiten', *Die Gleichheit* (1920), 13/14.

[13] *Augsburger Postzeitung*, 19 April 1922; *Die Genossin*, vol. 6 (1929), 1, p. 21.

[14] Marianne Weber, 'Die Formkräfte des Geschlechtslebens', in *Frauenfragen und Frauengedanken. Gesammelte Aufsätze* (Tübingen 1919), pp. 205ff.

II

While debates by sex reformers and bourgeois feminists reached an
audience made up of the educated middle classes, the theme of the
New Woman and a new sexual code was also taken up by the mass
media of film, illustrated magazines and romances and thus
involved a very much wider audience, many of whom belonged to
the lower social strata. The icon of the New Woman in popular
culture was the new breed of female white-collar workers who more
than any other profession during the 1920s inspired visions of
sexually and economically liberated young women. The new office
and retail jobs, a consequence of the rapid rationalisation in industry, were in the public limelight because they constituted the fastest
growing sector of female employment and also because they attracted predominantly very young and single women who were encouraged to use their sex appeal for promotion. The young woman typist
was a frequent subject for popular novels.[15] Like the sales girl, the
heroine of numerous entertainment films,[16] she was commonly
portrayed as the chic young lady effortlessly combining daytime job
with evening amusement in the dance bar or cinema. She seemed to
embody the enlightened attitude towards women of the new
republic.

While the mass media were content to show this new career
woman in the guise of glamour girl, much of *Neue Sachlichkeit* art,
avant-garde films and fashion journals, catering for the middle
classes, offered a more contradictory message about the New
Woman: they showed her as an active participant in modern life,
with strongly masculine qualities, coolly confident about her erotic
power but also with feminine frailty, often in the passive role of
victim of society. Since many of the best known paintings of women
in the *Neue Sachlichkeit* style were by male artists, the paintings'
blurring of conventional gender demarcations hints not just at
women's changing sexuality but also at a crisis of identity on the

[15] Rudolf Braune, *Das Mädchen an der Orga Privat* (Berlin 1930); Christa Anita Brück,
   Schicksale hinter Schreibmaschinen (Berlin 1930). See also Renny Harrigan, 'Die Sexualität der
   Frau in der deutschen Unterhaltungsliteratur 1918–1933', *GG*, vol. 7 (1981) 3/4, pp.
   412–437; Heide Soltau, 'Moderne Heldinnen. Frauenlektüre als Spiegel weiblichen Seins',
   in K. von Soden and M. Schmidt (eds.), *Neue Frauen. Die Zwanziger Jahre* (Berlin 1988), pp.
   20–24.
[16] E.g. Irmgard Keun, *Gilgi – eine von uns* (Berlin 1931); *Das Fräulein von Kasse 12* (1927); *Die
   Privatsekretärin* (1931).

part of German men.[17] This would explain why some male artists introduced a note of misogyny, especially when depicting women who flaunted their sexuality.

Otto Dix is a good example. His *Portrait of the Dancer Anita Berber* (1925) shows Berber in the contradictory role of sexual predator and prey. It also reveals Dix's own uncertainty about female sexuality. Dix had been fascinated by Berber's lascivious body, her erotic movements and her indulgence in prostitution and bisexuality and this comes across well in the picture. Yet Berber appears not only as sexual adventuress but also as victim (of drug abuse). There is a hint of *Schadenfreude* at the dancer's physical decay, conveyed in the careful rendering of the ravages of opium and cocaine addiction from which Berber was to die only four years later at the age of 30.[18]

Female androgyny was a frequent theme in Weimar avant-garde art, mirroring this sense of insecurity about sexual roles of men and women. Dix's *Portrait of the Journalist Sylvia von Harden* (1926), for example, evokes confusing emotions by contrasting the mannish qualities of the sitter (her short hair, the masculine face and hand, the severe pattern of her dress) with the clear sexual signals she emits as a woman through her pose, sitting alone at a table as if inviting male company, her short hem line and silk stockings and above all the redness of her dress and the wallpaper, a colour traditionally associated with eroticism. The new medium of film, too, provided a perfect space for exploring definitions of female and male sexuality. Film historians have pointed out that avant-garde directors invited the spectator to 'relax rigid demarcations of gender identification and sexual orientation'.[19] As Thomas Elsaesser put it, Pabst's *Pandora's Box* (1928), for example, shows how 'male obsessions – repressed homosexuality, sado-masochism, an urge to possess, capture, limit and fix – confront feminine androgyny and feminine identity'.[20] Blurred sexual identities often add to a sense of suspense or even fear in the audience. For example, the heroine of Murnau's

---

[17] Cf. John Fout, 'Sexual politics in Wilhelmine Germany: the male gender crisis, moral purity, and homophobia', *JSH*, vol. 2 (1992), 3, pp. 388–421.

[18] Cf. Karl Toepfer, 'Nudity and modernity in German dance, 1910–30', *JSH*, vol. 3 (1992) 1, pp. 58–108, 96ff.

[19] Janet Bergstrom, 'Sexuality at a loss: the films of F. W. Murnau', *Poetics Today*, vol. 6 (1985), 1–2, pp. 185–203, quoted in Patrice Petro, *Joyless streets: women and melodramatic representation in Weimar Germany* (Princeton 1989), p. 157.

[20] Thomas Elsaesser, 'Lulu and the meter man: Louise Brooks, Pabst and *Pandora's Box*', *Screen*, vol. 24 (1983), 4–5, pp. 4–36.

Nosferatu (1919), Nina, shares with the vampire the mystical and sexual powers usually associated with male sexual drives and thereby embraces both roles of victim and perpetrator and, more worryingly, of feminine and masculine behaviour.[21]

Androgyny also featured frequently in illustrated journals. In 1926, for example, the fashion journal, *Die Dame*, in a display with the caption 'New evening wear for women', showed a boyish androgynous woman wearing a dinner jacket (with a short skirt) with her hands firmly in her pockets next to an androgynous young man in the same suit (but with trousers) and the same pose. Contemporaries, including many women, frequently interpreted this fashion as the expression of a cultural crisis.[22] The image of the masculinised New Woman was thus not just a male-generated fantasy and was much discussed among women themselves. Many women journalists opposed it. A *Berliner Illustrirte Zeitung* editorial from 1925 bore the title 'Now that's enough! Against the masculinisation of woman' and denounced the fashion of the 'page-boy cut' for 'denying the voluptuousness of the female body' and being 'morally embarrassing for male feelings'.[23] Analysing this outburst, Patrice Petro, the film historian, concludes that 'the tone of moral outrage suggests that something more than women's fashion was at stake in the dispute over the New Woman'. What was especially disturbing, she suggests convincingly, was the trend in which 'women seemed to renounce femininity and regress to an adolescent sexuality – and thus to deviate from the path of "normal" female sexual development'.[24]

III

Another forum of public discourse in which responses to, perceptions of and prescriptions for the New Woman were debated and defined was the women's movement. It was an indication of the importance contemporaries attached to questions of female sexual-

---

[21] Petro, *Joyless streets*, p. 157. See also Ludmilla Jordanova, *Sexual visions: images of gender in science and medicine between the eighteenth and twentieth centuries* (New York, London 1989), pp. 111ff.

[22] Anita, 'Die Vermännlichung der Frau', *Berliner Illustrirte Zeitung (BIZ)*, vol. 35 (1 August 1924), pp. 997–998, quoted in Petro, *Joyless streets*, p. 114.

[23] 'Nun aber Genug! Gegen die Vermännlichung der Frau', *BIZ*, vol. 15 (29 March 1925), p. 389, quoted in Petro, *Joyless streets*, p. 105.

[24] *Ibid.*

ity that even the powerful denominational women's movement felt obliged to confront the issue of, as it saw it, declining sexual standards and the various attempts by social reformers, sexologists and feminists to define new patterns of sexual behaviour.[25] Hedwig Dransfeld, leader of the League of German Catholic Women, urged women to work towards a moral revival which would 'guard the female body against exploitation as a sexual lure'.[26] To counter the various campaigns for free love and 'companionate marriage' Catholic women leaders pleaded for the upholding of absolute standards of female sexuality. Helene Weber, mother of the sociologist Max and a prominent member of Dransfeld's organisation, understood her era as a spiritual turning point in these questions which necessitated a 'passionate struggle for the victory of the spirit' and 'for religious forces'.[27] Protestant women fought a similar campaign. Margarete von Tiling, leader of the German Evangelical Women's Federation, wished to uphold clear differences between female and male sexual propriety. She rejected the idea that 'women have the same erotic needs as men' and even more the current theory that women needed sex because 'the sexual act *per se* ... signifies the unfolding of womanhood'.[28]

Although, as we have seen, many bourgeois and Socialist women leaders had acknowledged and seemed even to have applauded new life-styles among Weimar's young women, there was, nevertheless, much concern that these would be detrimental to women's interests and undermine the institution of the family. Criticism was usually guarded and phrased in conciliatory language, but older women activists in the middle-class women's movement nevertheless distanced themselves from the libertarianism of their younger sisters. Marianne Weber and her predecessor in the BDF's chair, Gertrud Bäumer, did accept, in principle, that pre-marital sex could enrich women's lives but feared that it rendered women more vulnerable by reducing them 'to objects of a stronger and more brutal sex

---

[25] On history and membership see Usborne, *Politics of the body*, pp. 72ff. Cf. Doris Kaufmann, *Katholisches Milieu in Münster 1928–1933* (Düsseldorf 1984) and *Frauen zwischen Aufbruch und Reaktion. Protestantische Frauenbewegung in der 1. Hälfte des 20. Jahrhunderts* (Munich 1988).

[26] Usborne, *Politics of the body*, p. 83.

[27] Helene Weber, 'Moderne Zeitfragen, I. Die Frage der Jugend', *Die Christliche Frau*, vol. 26 (1928), 6, pp. 105–108.

[28] Margarete von Tiling, 'Das Verhältnis der Geschlechter in der Mädchenerziehung', *Monatsblatt der Vereinigung Evangelischer Frauenverbände Deutschlands*, vol. 10 (1931), 10, pp. 151–153.

drive'. So they rejected the claims for female erotic freedom on a par with men and defended the notion of an inborn polarity of female and male nature. Unlike women, Weber asserted, men were ruled by their sex drives but the erotic experience meant less to them than to women. Just 'as man rules the material sphere, woman has been placed by nature on a higher plateau' and should not bridge this gap 'by descending to the man's level ... but should try instead to raise him up to her level through the pure, strong power of her love'.[29] Similar concern about young women's sexual mores were voiced also by Social Democrats[30] – despite their reputation as free thinkers and critics of the bourgeois family – and, perhaps even more surprisingly, by older radical feminists like Helene Stöcker.[31]

Stöcker's reaction is especially significant since in her youth she and other contemporary women sex reformers had themselves been regarded as New Women. The New Woman had indeed been a potent symbol of *fin de siècle* Europe[32] and in Germany gained notoriety with the *BfM* in Berlin and the Munich group of free lovers around Franziska von Reventlow and the von Richthofen sisters.[33] But when Stöcker and others in the *Bund* defended 'free love' they thought of a monogamous and long-term relationship not sanctioned by the church or the state but justified by their own rigorous system of ethics in human relationships. By contrast the younger generation of women seemed to indulge in promiscuity for hedonistic reasons and in order to avoid responsibility. Stöcker and others had fought for a new sexual equality not for selfish reasons but as an act of rebellion against outmoded bourgeois respectability. They had wanted to enhance human relationships, prevent human misery and improve the quality of offspring. Young women of the

[29] Marianne Weber, *Ethik*, vol. 5 (1928), pp. 72–81 and *Die Frau*, vol. 34 (1926/27), p. 466.
[30] See Usborne, *Politics of the body*, pp. 76ff; cf. Detlev J. Peukert, 'Der Schund- und Schmutz-kampf als "Sozialpolitik der Seele"', in Hermann Haarmann, Walter Huder and Klaus Siebenhaar (eds.), '*Das war ein Vorspiel nur ...* ', *Bücherverbrennung Deutschland 1933* (Berlin 1983), pp. 51–64.
[31] See Amy Hackett, 'Helene Stöcker: left-wing intellectual and sex reformer', in Renate Bridenthal, Atina Grossmann and Marion A. Kaplan (eds.), *When biology became destiny* (New York 1984), pp. 109–130.
[32] Cf. Elaine Showalter, *Sexual anarchy, gender and culture at the fin de siècle* (London 1982); Lucy Bland, 'The married woman, the "New Woman" and the feminist: sexual politics of the 1890s', in Jane Rendall (ed.), *Equal or different: women's politics 1800–1914* (Oxford 1987), pp. 141–164.
[33] Cf. Martin Green, *The von Richthofen sisters: the triumphant and the tragic mode of love* (New York 1974).

Weimar Republic displayed no signs of such zeal but seemed to be guided by fashion, mass media and consumerism.

But there were also other important differences between the older women's rights activists and young women of the Republic. To start with, the older generation of emancipated women were few in number, university educated, upper middle class and espoused radical ideas in support of women's rights and a better society. But the New Women of the 1920s were numerous, often lower middle class and not particularly interested in politics or ideology.

Older feminists had often been criticised for their failure to marry and have children just as the New Woman of the 1920s was accused of neglecting her 'prime' social duty of motherhood. But the reasons for staying single and/or childless for the two age groups were often different. The older generation had frequently sacrificed marriage and motherhood for the cause of feminism, whereas the younger generation appeared to spurn matrimony for reasons of self-interest and personal pleasure. For them remaining single no longer necessarily meant celibacy and marriage no longer presupposed childbirth.

Finally, the older campaigners, brought up as they were in the authoritarian climate of Wilhelmine Germany, had had to fight hard to advance women's rights, whereas the majority of young women lived in a republic which had brought with it a climate of change and openness, had granted women many new privileges and promised more. This often engendered complacency instead of commitment. As a result, there was much incomprehension among the older stalwarts of the women's movement and social reformers about young women's apparent apathy. New sexual mores were the easiest targets for criticism because they were the most obvious indicators of change. Thus older women were often united by their criticism of young women's sexual behaviour even though they were otherwise in different camps: Socialist feminists, middle-class women's rights activists, sex reformers and leaders of the religious women's movement.

Distrust between the generations was, it seems, mutual. Many young women of the 1920s spurned feminist campaigns and ideas as outmoded. They showed little respect for older members of the women's movement who appeared to them as old-fashioned spinsters pursuing legal and political reforms of little relevance to their own lives. The campaigns of neither Socialist nor bourgeois feminists

Mistrust between generations

to reform the law on prostitution or to extend maternity protection, which had important implications for women, could capture the imagination of the mass of the younger generation. Thus even those political parties most committed to women's emancipation and the BDF encountered apathy and found it increasingly difficult to attract young female members, a fact regularly bemoaned at party conferences and annual general meetings.[34]

The journals of the women's movement commented explicitly on the conflict between the generations from at least 1921 onwards and it also surfaced at many conferences during the 1920s.[35] In the journal of the BDF, *Die Frau*, which dedicated many articles to this theme, there was a consensus that young women of the 1920s simply availed themselves of their new-found rights without paying due respect to their elders who had achieved these through hard-won battles. Young women's lack of gratitude and commitment to organisations of any kind was criticised and attributed to their 'indifference, their egotistical preference for shallow pleasures, the quest for instant gratification'.[36] Women students, the supposed vanguard of feminists, came under particular attack for taking their privilege for granted. They were accused of laziness and gross indifference towards university education which had been, for the older generation of pioneering women students, an 'incredible life-enriching experience'.[37] Most older women activists agreed that female students' free and easy sex life and their tendency to use the university simply as a convenient place to meet men (as suggested by a number of social surveys) was deplorable. To Germany's first generation of women academics this seemed to have turned their own arduous campaigns of 'opening doors' into a charade.[38]

The question of young women's sexual frivolity was indeed one to fuel the generation debate not just among the organised feminists but also amongst women journalists and writers. In 1928, Vicky

[34] Irene Stoehr, 'Neue Frau und alte Bewegung? Zum Generationenkonflikt in der Frauen-bewegung der Weimarer Republik', in Jutta Dalhoff, Uschi Frey and Ingrid Schöll (eds.), *Frauenmacht in der Geschichte* (Düsseldorf 1986), pp. 390–402.

[35] See Stoehr, 'Neue Frau und alte Bewegung?', pp. 390–402.

[36] Paula Elkisch, 'Pädagogische Gedanken zum Geschlechterproblem', *Die Frau*, vol. 35 (1927/28), pp. 23–28; Annemarie Doherr, 'Zum Generationenproblem in der Frauen-bewegung', *Die Frau*, vol. 38 (1930/31), pp. 532–538.

[37] E.g. H. Thoeniessen, 'Die studierende Frau und das Geschlechterproblem', *Die Frau*, vol. 35 (1927/28); Maria Schlüter-Hermkes, 'Von der wissenschaftlichen Frauenarbeit', *Die Christliche Frau*, vol. 27 (1929), p. 110.

[38] Paula Elkisch, 'Pädagogische Gedanken zum Gechlechterproblem'.

Baum, for example, published a best-selling novel about the erotic dilemmas encountered by a science student, *Stud.chem Helene Willfüer*. One year earlier she had written a light-hearted article chiding the younger generation of women for being 'superficial', 'materialistic', depressingly factual about sexual relations and having 'love affairs ... at the drop of a hat'.[39]

There was much consternation within the women's movement that pre-marital sex was apparently widely practised not only by women students but by an ever younger age group of female adolescents of the educated classes. Teachers deplored the high level of sexual activity amongst female 'Lyceum students'. They were aware that many 'young women no longer recognise the just demand of sexual purity' because they claimed 'the same right as young men of their class have long possessed'. Naturally, young men encouraged this, it was claimed, because they obviously preferred 'healthy, educated girls to infected whores'.[40] Pedagogues were frequently driven to use highly melodramatic language. One high-school teacher described as commonplace the sight of young girls who had obviously overindulged in sexual activity: 'under-age girls, their faces marked by dissipation and by the lowest form of passion' offered a glimpse into 'an abyss' of immorality which filled conscientious teachers with 'wild fear'.[41]

Other women commentators expressed themselves more moderately but confirmed a dramatic change in sexual attitudes because 'even the educated young women of today have begun to imitate the pre-marital life ... of the men of their circles'.[42] The growing stress on rationality, so it was claimed, promoted an 'increasing gap between emotions and sexual drives'. The notion of a 'natural sex drive' was no longer thought to be the preserve of men nor was motherhood thought to be reserved for married women.[43]

[39] Vicki Baum, 'O, diese Eltern! Die Kluft zwischen den Generationen', *BIZ* 28 August 1927, pp. 1389–1390.
[40] Clara Thorbecke, 'Die sozialen Bedingtheiten der Pubertätsentwicklung bei der weiblichen proletarischen Großstadtjugend', *ZfW*, vol. 16 (1929/30), p. 26; E. Fuchs, 'Moderne Jugendprobleme', *Monatsblatt der Evangelischen Frauenverbände Deutschlands*, vol. 8 (1929), 7, pp. 128, 129, 133.
[41] Fuchs, 'Moderne Jugendprobleme', pp. 128–129.
[42] Dr Elisabeth Schmitt, article in *Die Frau*, June 1928, quoted in H. Weber, 'Moderne Zeitfragen', p. 163.
[43] Charlotte Buchow-Homeyer in her book about temporary marriages published in Berlin in 1928, quoted in Helene Weber, 'Moderne Zeitfragen, II', *Die Christliche Frau*, vol. 26 (1928), p. 162.

IV

Older women activists may have been worried by the sexual
behaviour of middle-class young women, but it was when they
turned their attention to the sexual mores of young working-class
women that they were truly appalled by what they discovered. A
new spate of research into the life-style of female workers revealed
behaviour unacceptable by bourgeois standards. Hildegard Jüngst's
1929 study of female adolescents employed in a chocolate factory is a
good example of the new trend to investigate not only working
conditions but also intimate behaviour of women working in industry.[44] The author found that factory work with its 'spirit of deperso-
nalisation and technological-rational utilitarianism' had disturbing
consequences: the only release for the young female workers was to
indulge in and even celebrate an 'unrestrained sexual drive'. Jüngst
declared herself deeply shocked by the 'shameless' way they com-
peted with one another to score the highest marks for a week-end's
erotic adventures and the openness with which they applauded
promiscuity and ridiculed fidelity. The author blamed the monoto-
nous working conditions and the deprivation and misery of home life
but she also deplored the influence of cinema and pulp literature for
instilling 'the poison of sexual provocation' in young people.[45] A
year later, the social anthropologist, Maria Kahle, known for her
work on German folk culture in former German territories in
Eastern Europe and German colonies, studied the life and attitudes
of young female workers in a biscuit factory in Westphalia with
similar results.[46] The author felt it wise to avoid open criticism of
these young women workers 'since they had never learnt about real
values in life' but her implied disapproval is all the clearer.[47]

A 1929 study of proletarian girls aged between 14 and 16, carried
out by a Berlin social worker, Clara Thorbecke,[48] bravely rejected
the conventional view of the proletarian milieu as 'unhealthy' and
'undesirable', believing instead that it merely reflected a necessary

[44] Hildegard Jüngst, *Die jugendliche Fabrikarbeiterin. Ein Beitrag zur Industriepädagogik* (Pader-
     born 1929).
[45] *Ibid.*, pp. 110, 90.
[46] Maria Kahle, *Akkordarbeiterin. Aus meinem Tagebuch* (Gladbach-Rheydt 1930).
[47] *Ibid.*, pp. 26, 29.
[48] Thorbecke, 'Die sozialen Bedingtheiten', pp. 22–32. Cf. Clara Thorbecke, 'Über den
     Sittlichkeitsbegriff in der sozialen Unterschicht', *Die Frau*, 1923, pp. 137–143; and Clara
     Thorbecke, *Reifungsprobleme der proletarischen weiblichen Großstadtjugend* (Berlin 1928).

adaptation to cramped housing and working conditions where physical intimacy was frequently witnessed and condoned. The author found to her surprise that young working girls were even prepared to tolerate flirtation or seduction by the boss, seeing such behaviour 'as just reward for good work'. Nevertheless Thorbecke was very concerned at the prevalence of early sex amongst her objects of study and believed all future erotic relationships would end up being 'shallow and merely sexual' and preclude the possibility of real love.[49]

Lisbeth Franzens-Hellersberg's study of the work and life-style of young proletarian women, *Die Jugendliche Arbeiterin*, published in 1932,[50] also devoted much attention to sexual habits. But in stark contrast to most other middle-class commentators, who expressed horror at the estimate of 'experienced teachers and social workers' that 90 per cent of all proletarian girls between 14 and 18 had had sexual relationships, the author was not shocked by what she saw. She concluded instead that 'it would seem that the primitive qualities of vitality are the only real signs of personal creativity in women workers'. The 'awareness of being young' was, she found, the most important weapon against the vicissitudes of working-class life and the consciousness of youth was, she claimed, invariably translated into 'erotic exploits'. Erotic adventures added glamour and crucial compensation for all the other shortcomings of life: they acted as status symbols among peers at work and gave the young working-class woman strength to endure humdrum and conflict at home.[51]

But Franzens-Hellersberg was also conscious of the negative effects of relying mainly on sex: in her view it rendered the young woman apathetic to the outside world and to her own fate. With erotic adventure as her main pastime she felt no need for close friendships with other young females, for political activity or for work in women's organisations and effectively denied herself any possibility of social commitment.[52]

v

These surveys seemed to confirm that a New Woman had emerged in the Weimar Republic and that a dramatic shift in attitudes had

[49] Thorbecke, 'Die sozialen Bedingtheiten', pp. 25–27.
[50] Lisbeth Franzens-Hellersberg, *Die jugendliche Arbeiterin. Ihre Arbeitsweise und Lebensform* (Tübingen 1932).
[51] *Ibid.*, pp. 9, 4, 8, 64.   [52] *Ibid.*, pp. 87–8, 72.

taken place. Traditional norms of sexual mores and propriety had apparently been discarded in favour of pleasure-seeking and promiscuity. Yet there is another way of reading the evidence. In the first place, it is not really certain that the girls' behaviour was so terribly new. According to Heidi Rosenbaum, pre-marital relationships had always been acceptable in proletarian circles as long as the intent of a future marriage was made clear. The practice harked back to rural customs when economic circumstances delayed marriage and steady relationships were thought to offer safe outlets for sexuality and to guarantee children.[53]

What was new, in fact, was not working-class behaviour but the fact that bourgeois women were for the first time carrying out research on the life-styles of working-class women. For one thing, the importance accorded in the Weimar Republic to social policy had stimulated new attempts to address the problems of juvenile delinquency and public health. In addition, Weimar saw a large-scale influx of qualified women into the social administration. These new female professionals played a key role in rethinking social policy, shifting the focus of investigation towards women's problems. Whereas male workers tended to be studied solely in their working environment, female labourers were now also investigated at home, during their leisure time and in their most intimate relationships and furthermore were judged according to moral-ethical norms.[54]

This is why the surveys of female factory work of the 1920s and early 1930s are such a rich source of information on attitudes to sexual mores. Yet the surveys' perception that proletarian adolescents represented a new generation of emancipated women, whose views and sexual behaviour were free from traditional constraints, was wrong in assuming not only that there had been a change in behaviour but also that this change was the consequence of a widening sphere for women. Even Lisbeth Franzens-Hellersberg, one of the most sympathetic observers of working-class women's behaviour, partly fell into this trap. It is true that as a (professional middle-class) member of the Social Democrats she tried quite successfully to avoid judging what she saw according to

53 Heidi Rosenbaum, *Formen der Familie* (Frankfurt 1982), p. 426.
54 Karin Jurzyk and Carmen Tatschmurat, 'Frauen forschen – Frauenforschung? Untersuchungen über Frauenindustriearbeit in den 20er Jahren', in Dalhoff et al., *Frauenmacht in der Geschichte*, pp. 238–253, 239.

'ethical-bourgeois value systems' and to remain open minded.[55] Indeed, she asserted that sexual activity, indulged in with conviction, was not necessarily corrupting and often a valuable aid against delinquency and prostitution. Yet when she depicted young proletarian women as apathetic and unpolitical she ignored their very limited opportunities to be active. Working-class girls had little occasion to take part in organisations or, for that matter, in having a 'good time'. As many as 90 per cent of them lived at home where they were expected to help in the kitchen, with mending and sewing and with child care. These duties were expected over and above the time spent in paid employment. If allowances are made for time spent travelling to and from work and in breaks and clearing up this amounted, on average, to no less than eleven hours.[56] Most young proletarian women led a life of hard work and drudgery that belied the notion of pleasure-seeking New Women.

Indeed, the notion of the sexually liberated good-time girl did not fit even the socio-economic group usually portrayed in the media as the very embodiment of the New Women, young female white-collar workers. In films and popular fiction, typists and shop-assistants were young and glamorous. But contemporary photographs of typist pools and department stores suggest that this was a myth. In reality, women employed in this newest sector of the labour market were neither symbols of female emancipation nor did they challenge accepted codes of moral propriety or gender stereotypes. As Ute Frevert has shown, white-collar work did little to raise women's work from low status and low pay. The enthusiasm for entertainment and provocative dress displayed by some employees was often no more than an attempt to compensate for dull and badly paid jobs. Just like young factory workers, white-collar workers were too poor to move away from home where parental control and domestic duties continued. Ironically, the modern notion of organised labour also reinforced the ideology of domesticity in that the majority of these employees regarded their job not as a career

---

55 Franzens-Hellersberg, *Die jugendliche Arbeiterin*, pp. 9, 4, 8.
56 Dr Hedwig von Schott, 'Die Arbeits- und Lebensverhältnisse der erwerbstätigen Jugend', *Christliche Frau*, vol. 27 (September 1929), pp. 268–280; compared to their brothers girls were clearly disadvantaged as far as distribution of housework, own rooms and own beds were concerned; time spent at work ranged from the fashion industry with 10 hours, 25 minutes to domestic service with 12 hours, 35 minutes.

but as a mere interlude until marriage, their 'proper' destiny in life.[57]

VI

So what was real about the New Woman, and what was it that had given rise to so much concern and discussion among the older generation?

Concern about young women's role in society has to be understood first within the context of demographic changes, changes so startling to contemporaries that their fears of 'sexual anarchy' and the disintegration of the family are hardly surprising. The German birth rate was declining at a faster rate than in any other Western country and by 1933 it had become the lowest in Europe.[58] This long-term change was reinforced by the impact of the First World War and the revolution: a huge deficit in the birth rate and a new tendency among young people to marry but not have children. Many Germans began to talk of 'racial suicide' and complain that women were refusing to perform their 'biological duty'. It is wrong to dismiss this simply as hysteria. At that time it was customary to regard the decline in German fertility as a reflection of national defeat and a hopeless future rather than understand it, as we do now with the benefit of hindsight, as part of a deeper process of social change which affected all industrialised countries.

Other statistics also helped fuel anxiety about the future of the family: there was a discernible rise in the post-war divorce and illegitimacy rate[59] which compared very unfavourably with other countries, notably England and Wales. There was also a low marriage rate amongst young women. It is true, marriage had not gone out of fashion in the new republic where a higher proportion of the adult population were married than ever before. But in the 20–25

---

[57] Ute Frevert, 'Vom Klavier zur Schreibmaschine. Weiblicher Arbeitsmarkt und Rollen-zuweisungen am Beispiel der weiblichen Angestellten in der Weimarer Republik', in A. Kuhn and G. Schneider (eds.), *Frauen in der Geschichte* (Düsseldorf 1979), pp. 82–112.

[58] Reinhard Spree, 'Der Geburtenrückgang in Deutschland vor 1939', *Demographische Informationen*, 1984, p. 62.

[59] In 1921 the divorce rate was 33 per 10,000 marriages compared to England's 6.8 (F. Burgdörfer, 'Statistik der Ehe', in M. Marcuse, *Die Ehe* (Berlin 1927), p. 82). For the reaction to this, see Usborne, *Politics of the body*, pp. 91ff. The illegitimacy rate in 1920–26 was 12.2 per cent compared with 8.7 per cent in 1906–10; see Peter Marschalck, *Bevölkerungsgeschichte Deutschlands im 19. und 20. Jahrhundert* (Frankfurt 1984).

age group a third fewer women were married than before the war.[60] This was a direct effect of the war. So many young men had died on the battlefield that there were now over two million 'surplus' women, most of marriageable age. Unable to find a husband, these women were viewed by contemporaries as a social problem. For one thing, they were unable to help regenerate the population. But they were also seen as posing a double threat: at work they were seen as competing with male breadwinners for jobs; after hours they were suspected of luring other women's' husbands into infidelity.

In addition, women's new-found rights in the Republic contributed to fears that male and female roles were being blurred and undermined and that the social and moral order was in danger. Since winning the active and passive vote in December 1918 and subsequently gaining access to all professions women seemed to be conquering a public sphere which had previously been regarded as an all-male domain.

Historians have, of course, questioned the extent of women's emancipation in the Weimar Republic and it is true that important constitutional promises of sexual equality were never fully realised.[61] But women's formal rights had dramatically improved since 1914 and were in advance of most other European countries. Most importantly, contemporaries had registered these changes and, depending on age group, gender and political outlook, were either inspired or unnerved by them. After all, German women members in the Reichstag and state diets were in absolute and proportional terms the most numerous in the world, and the increasing number of women in higher education and the professions was also impressive by international standards.[62]

Furthermore, women's participation in the economy seemed to challenge gender roles and undermine the institution of the family. Although there were few quantitative changes in women's employment during the 1920s there were significant structural changes. Many more women were working in traditionally male industrial

---

[60] Annemarie Niemeyer, 'Zur Struktur der Familie. Statistische Materialien', *Forschungen der Deutschen Akademie für soziale and pädagogische Frauenarbeit* (Berlin 1931), pp. 23–24.

[61] Cf. Helen Boak, 'Women in Weimar Germany: the "Frauenfrage" and the female vote', in R. Bessel and E. J. Feuchtwanger (eds.), *Social and political development in Weimar Germany* (London 1981), pp. 155–173; Renate Bridenthal and Claudia Koonz, 'Beyond *Kinder, Küche, Kirche*: Weimar women in politics and work', in Bridenthal, *Biology*, pp. 33–65.

[62] Maria Schlüter-Hermkes, 'Von der wissenschaftlichen Frauenarbeit', *Die Christliche Frau*, vol. 27 (April 1929) p. 115.

occupations, a fact which made them at once more visible and a greater challenge to accepted sexual roles.[63] Social hygienists were particularly alarmed about what they regarded as the detrimental effects of industrial labour on young women's reproductive health. But the domestic work which they recommended as the ideal occupation for women[64] had become increasingly unpopular on account of its low pay, low status and minimal protective legislation.

Apart from the declining birth rate, there was another aspect of demographic change that needs to be taken into account. The high birth rate of the pre-1914 period meant that in the post-war years there were in absolute and proportional terms more young people than ever before. This made them highly visible, be it in the labour and housing markets or in the criminal statistics.[65] This was especially true of young females. Between 1910 and 1925, the number of female adolescents aged 14 to 18 increased by 12.8 per cent, while the number of women aged 18 to 21 grew by 19.6 per cent.[66] It was precisely this age group, between school and marriage, whose sexuality seemed such a dangerous commodity to the older generation. Young women had also become more visible in the labour market. Between 1907 and 1925 the number of economically active young women between 14 and 25 had increased by 1,023,156 from 3,679,304 to 4,702,460, with the largest increase in the age group 20–25. In proportion to the population as a whole this constituted only a marginal increase (from 66 per cent to 68 per cent), but contemporaries were worried that over a million more economically active young women would have a disastrous effect on unemployment, the birth rate and family formation.[67] Finally, the exposure of young women's behaviour to public scrutiny was not unconnected to the fact that these demographic changes were an urban rather than a rural phenomenon and that the number of young women was outstripping that of young men in German

[63] According to the first post-war census of 1925 the number of women working in industry was nearly 3 million, a 50 per cent increase since the last census of 1907 (Olga Essig, 'Die Frau in der Industrie', *Quellenhefte zum Frauenleben in der Geschichte*, vol. 18 (1933), pp. 93–94).
[64] E.g. Max Hirsch, 'Die Gefahren der Frauenerwerbsarbeit für Schwangerschaft, Geburt, Wochenbett und Kinderaufzucht', *Archiv für Frauenkunde und Eugenik*, vol. 9 (1925), 4, pp. 318–348.
[65] Cf. Peukert, *Jugend zwischen Krieg und Krise*; E. Harvey, *Youth and the welfare state in Weimar Germany* (Oxford 1994).
[66] Schott, 'Die Arbeits- und Lebensverhältnisse', p. 269.
[67] Statistics computed from table of economic activity per age group in *Wirtschaft und Statistik* (Berlin 1929), p. 121; Peukert, *Jugend zwischen Krieg und Krise*, pp. 40–43.

cities.[68] Consequently, most enquiries into the life-style of female adolescents focused on Germany's large towns, especially the capital, despite evidence that the level of pre-marital conceptions and illegitimacy in rural communities continued to be very high.[69] These demographic developments help explain contemporaries' concern with young peoples' behaviour, and may at times have led observers wrongly to conclude that major changes of attitude had taken place. And yet there is plenty of evidence that a radical shift of behaviour *had* taken place and that a clear generation gap did exist in attitudes towards sexuality. This change was probably less marked amongst working-class women, who had traditionally adopted a freer approach to female sexuality than their middle-class counterparts. It was the latter who now demanded for themselves the same right of sexual experience traditionally granted to young men. For example, a well-known Berlin woman doctor reported that among her private patients there were many '16-year-old girls of good families who have regular intercourse. To find this among 17- or 18-year-old girls I find no longer surprising.'[70] And in 1932 a survey of 360 physicians on this subject carried out by Max Horkheimer and Erich Fromm of the Frankfurt Institute for Sociology found a consensus view that women of all classes tended towards sexual libertarianism.[71] Other studies asserted also that young men had accepted this; when girls from respectable families had abandoned the pretence of celibate lives before marriage this had 'not lessened their chances of future husbands'.[72] Wilhelm Reich, the psychoanalyst who had moved to Berlin in 1930, confirmed this finding in his study on sexual morality.[73]

VII

Finally, the testimony of young women themselves confirms the reality of the New Woman. There is, of course, considerably less

[68] Peukert, *Jugend zwischen Krieg und Krise*, p. 39.

[69] See Dr. med Erich Meyer, 'Beiträge zum Sexualleben der Landjugend', *ZfW*, vol. 16 (1929/30), pp. 106–111.

[70] Dr. med Hermine Heusler-Edenhuizen, 'Die sexuelle Not unserer Jugend', *Die Frau*, vol. 35 (June 1928), 9, pp. 605–609.

[71] Erich Fromm, Max Horkheimer, H. Mayer and H. Marcuse, *Studien über Autorität und Familie* (Paris 1936), pp. 272–291.

[72] Alice Rühle-Gerstel, *Die Frau und der Kapitalismus. Eine psychologische Bilanz* (Leipzig 1932), p. 199.

[73] Wilhelm Reich, 'Das Fiasko der Sexualmoral', reprinted in Reich, *Die sexuelle Revolution* (Frankfurt 1971).

sourcematerialfortheviewsofyoungwomenthemselvesthanforthoseof
their observers and critics; what there is needs careful interpretation. Adolescents' statements usually appeared in response to an
enquiry defined and worded by social investigators and it is likely
that this influenced their answers. Günter Krolzig's survey of more
than 2,000 mostly proletarian young people (1,700 males and 400
females), which investigated their attitudes to family life, is a case in
point.[74] Despite strenuous efforts to avoid it, there is considerable
evidence in the survey of gender bias. For example, boys generally
stressed the importance of sex education and freedom given at home
but none of the girls is quoted as having mentioned either issue. It
seems probable that girls were not uninterested in these issues but
were not encouraged to address them or their answers were simply
not printed. There is no information on the process of selection and
editing.[75]

But what Krolzig's survey does teach us is that this group of
youngsters believed there to be a large generation gap. The authority of the parents, particularly of the father, had waned and such
authority as the parents did exercise was resented. Female apprentices who reported tension at home blamed it mainly on 'unfair'
parental control of their free time. They also rebelled against stereo-
typed gender roles which prescribed that daughters but not sons
should help with housework. Other boys and girls expressed their
objection to parental control by spending their free time away from
their family and with their peers, especially with those of the other
sex. Indeed, most youngsters of 16 or over admitted to a steady boy
or girl friend and such friendships seem to have offered an excuse to
avoid family rituals. As one young female worker put it: 'I've got a
boy friend for Saturday and Sunday because I don't enjoy it among
the old fogies.'[76] If parents objected, girls would meet their boy
friends clandestinely.[77] But many expressed their anger at 'over-
strict' rules. Friendship with boys was a useful instrument in the
battle between the generations. But girls also thought of it as an
educational, even commercial asset. A 16-year-old hairdressing
apprentice declared, for example: 'I don't meet my boy friend very
often. I am not allowed to go out with him every Sunday. My
mother is suspicious and thinks something might happen. But she is

[74] Günter Krolzig, *Der Jugendliche in der Großstadtfamilie auf Grund von Niederschriften Berliner Berufsschüler* (Berlin 1930).
[75] *Ibid.*, pp. 7–9, 127.   [76] *Ibid.*, pp. 44, 76, 83–84, 142, 146.   [77] *Ibid.*, pp. 145–146.

wrong. I do not go out with bad intentions, but I can only learn from somebody who is intellectually superior.' The financial advantage of a boy friend was sometimes stressed quite unashamedly. A young factory worker of only 14 declared confidently: 'I don't need any money, because my boy friend keeps me. At Whitsuntide I'll give up work because I play tennis during the summer', and there were other examples of girls regarding boy friends in as unemotional a way as a stockbroker thinks of a commodity to be acquired and disposed of at will.[78]

The same kind of *Sachlichkeit*, Weimar's famous New Sobriety, pervaded the 1931 novel, *Gilgi, One of Us*, the first book by a young writer, Irmgard Keun. Her publishers hailed this as 'the most revealing self-portrait of the younger generation' and it became an instant best-seller. The dust jacket and publicity material displays a photograph of the author looking every inch the New Woman of Weimar Germany: in her early 20s, pretty, with short hair and self-confident.[79] Her novel's heroine, Gilgi, was a model of the New Woman, too: a self-assured and attractive typist, a modern woman working in a modern industry, the fashion industry (in her case underwear). The story obviously struck a chord with other young women who considered Gilgi *one of them*, as the title suggests. So successful was this novel that it was not only serialised in *Vorwärts*, the party sheet of the SPD, but it was also made into a film.[80] The novel's popularity undoubtedly stemmed from the author's shrewd combination of *Neue Sachlichkeit* sentiments and romance, which appealed to the educated middle as well as lower middle classes. Gilgi combined modern and traditional values: she is presented as the cool, ambitious career girl but also 'the little woman', all soft and weak once her 'dream' man arrives on the scene. Like most female white-collar workers in real life Gilgi is prepared to sacrifice career and financial independence for romantic love. But just when she seems to relinquish all control over her own life (when she becomes pregnant) she regains it. The advent of motherhood ironically stiffens her feminist resolve: she rejects an abortion, leaves her lover and courageously rebuilds her life as a single mother. The story cleverly introduces some of the key issues of Weimar feminism:

[78] *Ibid.*, p. 146.
[79] Irmgard Keun, *Gilgi – eine von uns* (Berlin 1931), jacket and flap copy.
[80] Ingeborg Franke, '*Gilgi*, Film, Roman und Wirklichkeit', *Der Weg der Frau*, February 1932, pp. 4–8.

women's economic and reproductive rights, free love and unmarried motherhood. The author also highlights traditional feminine qualities such as the heroine's motherliness (in putting her future child above all else) and a tendency towards sentimentality and unreality for which it was attacked by the Communist monthly *Weg der Frau*. This accused the author of whitewashing the degrading nature of female white-collar work and the life of most young employees during the Depression.[81]

Lack of realism in Gilgi's circumstances notwithstanding, her mode of representation nevertheless runs counter to the popular fiction for girls in Weimar Germany in which, as Elizabeth Harvey puts it, 'authority and convention' usually triumph.[82] Gilgi personifies many of those 'masculine' or androgynous features of New Woman which caused the older generation such anxiety. At only 20 Gilgi seems to have lost all innocence and idealism; she has a boyish appearance with 'slender legs, childish-slender hips'. Her life-style reveals the manly virtue of sober rationality. She is in 'full control of her little life', keeping a careful check on her health, looks and career. Her morning routine is as precise as clockwork. She rises every day at half past seven without fail to do her exercises by an open window. The rhythm is reminiscent of parade ground drill: 'Forward bends, up and down; the fingertips touch the floor, the knees are straight. That is the form. Up – down, up – down'.[83] Gilgi is also in control of her sexuality: when her boss shows his infatuation with her Gilgi coolly arranges for a girl friend to divert his amorous attention, acting in the calculating manner usually adopted by men engaged in commercial sex. Like so many men Gilgi embraces extra-marital relations: she carries on her affair quite openly and thinks of the resulting pregnancy as impractical but not immoral. 'You see', she explains to a young male friend trying to help, 'I don't really care. I am really terribly immoral, Pit. I simply lack one of the senses – where others have morality I have an empty hole. I simply do not understand why an illegitimate child should be immoral.' When she travels to Berlin to face confinement, unemployment, homelessness and loneliness her self-assessment again evokes ideals of

[81] *Ibid.*, pp. 4–8.
[82] Elizabeth Harvey, 'Private fantasy and public intervention: girls' reading in Weimar Germany', in Jennifer Birkett and Elizabeth Harvey (eds.), *Determined women: studies in the construction of the female subject, 1900–1990* (London 1991), pp. 38–67, here p. 47.
[83] Keun, *Gilgi*, blurb, pp. 7–8.

masculinity: 'I am really competent. And I have a very strong will
... I am very strong and healthy and have a thousand chances to
remain so.'[84]

One publication which confirmed for both contemporaries and
historians the impression that young working women had few illusions about the domestic bliss of marriage and motherhood was a
1930 survey organised by the German Union of Women Textile
Workers.[85] One hundred and fifty women textile workers described
the double, sometimes triple burden of waged and domestic labour
and child care which dominated their working day and their
weekends (*Mein Arbeitstag, mein Wochenende*). As Atina Grossmann
has pointed out, the study shows clearly that modern young women
saw home not as 'a haven in a heartless world' but an extension of
the market place: they adopted the language and attitude of time-
motion techniques which ruled their industrial work in order to
describe their household chores.[86] It must indeed have dismayed
population planners of both left and right to find that marriage was
never described as woman's true destiny nor motherhood as her
fulfilment. Single women rarely expressed a longing for matrimony
and married women thought of children not as a blessing but as a
burden. How could they be induced to heal the wounds of a society
suffering from the crisis of modernisation and the worst depression in
living memory?

VIII

The New Woman, emancipated and sexually permissive, became a
potent symbol of the rapid social and ideological changes which took
place in Germany after the First World War. On the one hand the
image was a myth carefully constructed by the mass media, fashion
industry, conservatives and young women themselves, but on the
other hand the material position and attitudes of young women had
undergone such a fundamental transformation as to make it a
reality: they had new political and social rights; they had made
inroads into 'male' jobs and dominated new white-collar work; they
believed in controlling their fertility and small families and had

---

[84] *Ibid.*, p. 236.
[85] Deutscher Textilarbeiterverband (ed.), *Mein Arbeitstag, mein Wochenende. 150 Berichte von Textilarbeiterinnen* (Berlin 1930).
[86] Grossmann, *Girlkultur*, pp. 69ff.

easier access to birth control; they were the subject of public discussion and of the media. Of all her attributes it was the New Woman's sexuality that assumed most importance and became the focal point of debate and the main target of social policy. This was partly because of fears over a declining birth rate and the health of the nation. It was also because sexual behaviour was seen as a barometer measuring the degree to which young women were rethinking the scope of their freedom and power and their role in family and society.

Although older contemporaries reacted to New Woman in many different and contradictory ways, it is clear that these differences were small compared with the real and perceived gap between them and the younger women who belonged to the New Woman generation. Conservatives, Liberals, Socialists and even sex reformers largely agreed that female sexuality should be regulated and harnessed to the institutions of marriage and the family, even if they disagreed sharply about the methods to be employed. The consensus even bridged the gender barrier. Older feminists did, of course, celebrate women's new rights and their freedom to separate sex from procreation but they shared with men the fear that young women were abusing this freedom for shallow pleasure and to the detriment of national regeneration. The real divide in opinion was thus between older and younger people. As such, the debate about female sexual morality revealed a conflict between the generations which remained unresolved until it was suppressed by the authoritarian rule of the Third Reich.

This emphasis on generational conflict should not blind us to the very real class divisions that remained. On the whole, the New Woman was a middle- or lower-middle-class phenomenon. Proletarian women had not undergone the same social transformation in relation to employment patterns, fashion and life-style. The various surveys on young working women's sexual habits should be read not as evidence of a lowering of proletarian standards of morality but rather of a new middle-class awareness of proletarian behaviour. On the other hand, the emergence of middle-class New Woman had in fact produced something of a convergence of behaviour among young women. The lives of young women from all classes were characterised by elements guaranteed to instill fear in the older generation, above all pre-marital sex, promiscuity (with its attendant dangers of VD and abortion), late marriages, the small family and part-time motherhood because of employment outside the home.

Finally, what is clear is that the fears aroused by the emergence of New Women were not just exaggeration or delusion but testified to the way in which young women were openly rebelling against the inherited moral code and their prescribed gender role. Whether working or middle class, they resisted the blandishments of popu- lation planners, sexual reformers and feminists. They rejected the paradigm of femininity associated with fecundity, motherliness and sexual innocence just as they rejected the ideal of feminist solidarity concentrating instead on personal pleasure and self-interest. They were indeed a challenge, as Grossmann puts it, both 'to the "old" proletarian mother of a large family and to the "old" single commit- ted women's rights activist'.[87] Thus they emerged as positive agents rather than passive victims, helping to shape a new social order.

[87] *Ibid.*, p. 67.

CHAPTER 8

Generations of German historians: patronage, censorship and the containment of generation conflict, 1918–1945

Peter Lambert

Recent commentators on the development of German historiography in the period between the Lamprecht controversy of the 1890s and the Fischer controversy of the 1960s and 1970s are generally agreed that German historicism showed striking resilience. The boundaries of the historicist orthodoxy had been set through a compromise between the exponents of the Prussian school of the 1850s to 1870s (notably Dahlmann, Sybel and Treitschke) and the neo-Rankeans whose intellectual agenda took shape as the contours of the Bismarckian empire were stabilised in the 1870s and 1880s. Where the former, as propagators of a quasi-revolutionary mobilisation, had emphasised the dynamic of the nation, the latter stressed the role of the state as a guarantor of stability – so long, that is, as it was based on the nation. The actions of 'great men' in the furtherance of (German) nation statehood, and the power-political 'epochs' and 'missions' of the nation state, continued to provide the central agenda for German historical writing during both the Weimar Republic and the Third Reich.[1] Historians whose own careers spanned empire, republic and Third Reich included Richard Fester (1860–1945), Friedrich Meinecke (1862–1954) and Johannes Haller (1865–1947).[2]

Intellectual challenges to the dominant understanding of history

---

[1] George G. Iggers, *Deutsche Geschichtswissenschaft. Eine Kritik der traditionellen Geschichtsauffassung von Herder bis zur Gegenwart* (Munich 1971); Hans Schleier, *Die bürgerliche deutsche Geschichtsschreibung der Weimarer Republik* (Cologne 1975); Bernd Faulenbach, *Die ideologie des deutschen Weges. Die deutsche Geschichte in der Historiographie zwischen Kaiserreich und Nationalsozialismus* (Munich 1980).

[2] Fester was an early modernist, Ordinarius at Erlangen (from 1899), Kiel (1907) and finally Halle (1908–1926); Meinecke was an Ordinarius successively at Strasburg (from 1901), at Freiburg (from 1906) and at Berlin (1914–28) and president of the Historische Reichskommission from 1928 until his forced retirement by the Nazis in 1935; Haller was Ordinarius in medieval history at Gießen (1904–06) and Tübingen (1906–1932).

were not entirely lacking in the years after the First World War.
They came respectively from a handful of Left Liberals and from the
overlapping schools of *Volkshistoriker* and *Ostforscher* whose political
sympathies were with *völkisch* currents. In the conflicts between
historicist orthodoxy and these heresies, generational combined with
political and methodological sources of antagonism. Left Liberals
like G.W.F. Hallgarten (born 1901) and Eckart Kehr (born 1902)
waged unequal struggles with their supervisors and examiners.[3]
Volkshistoriker like Hermann Aubin (born 1885) and Kleo Pleyer
(born 1898) perceived themselves as posing a generational challenge
to the staid statism of their elders.[4] From the late 1920s to the
mid-1930s, the Nazi student movement seemed likely to give an
added spur to a racist interpretation of history. Yet scholarly orthodoxy was maintained by historians like Fritz Hartung (born 1883),
Otto Becker (born 1885) and Heinrich Dannenbauer (born 1897),
who were prepared to continue to uphold the values represented by
their teachers.[5]

Some of the principal sources of a general methodological stag-
nation and of a high degree of conformity and continuity may, I
suggest, be sought in the bureaucratic and institutional context
within which academic history was produced. Alternative
approaches to the discipline failed to take root in the universities not
because of inherent scholarly weaknesses, but because they were
suppressed. Containment of conflict – ideological and generational –
was achieved by a judicious admixture of patronage and censorship.
Parameters of academic and political permissibility were set with

[3] See below pp. 174–176.
[4] Willi Oberkrome, 'Reformansätze in der deutschen Geschichtswissenschaft der Zwischenkriegszeit', in Michael Prinz and Rainer Zitelmann (eds.), *Nationalsozialismus und Modernisierung* (Darmstadt 1991), pp. 216–238 argues that the *Volkshistoriker* mounted a coherent
and interdisciplinary intellectual challenge to the dominance of statist historiography and
that their work provides moments of continuity with the new German social history of the
1960s. This thesis should be treated with some caution; see: Michael Burleigh, *Germany turns
eastward: a study of Ostforschung in the Third Reich* (Cambridge 1988), which argues forcefully
that however progressive they may have been in narrowly methodological terms, it is the
susceptibility of the *Ostforscher* to racism and Nazism that should be seen as their chief
characteristic; Winfried Schulze, *Deutsche Geschichtswissenschaft nach 1945*, *HZ*, Beiheft 10
(Munich 1989), p. 306, reminds us that only a comprehensive 'denazification of the concept
of the *Volk*' could permit 'a new approach to social history' after the war. Thus, the real
impact of the *Volkshistoriker* may have been further to delegitimise social history in the
decade and a half immediately following the end of the Second World War.
[5] Hartung was Ordinarius in modern history at Kiel (1921–23) and Berlin (1923–47), Becker
at Halle (from 1927) and then Kiel (from 1931). On Dannenbauer's academic career see
below, pp. 178, 181.

reference to the notion that professional historians had a corporate identity and collective responsibilities to the nation.

So what historians meant when they described themselves as belonging to a guild, and what ramifications this sense of corporate identity had will be my point of departure. A review of the politics of faculty appointments introduces another, institutional, moment. The routine of internal university power games provides a key to understanding why, by 1933, the composition of the professoriate had changed so little since the Kaiserreich's demise. The Nazi seizure of power adversely affected very few historians and the guild achieved a further lease of life until 1945. The general relationship of the guild to Nazism was marked by a 'structural resistance' similar to that shown by a variety of other sections of society.

I

No appointment to a full chair of history was conceivable in Germany after 1914 without due reference to qualities quite separate from anything that might be deemed specifically pertinent for an academic, since the task of the Ordinarius was commonly agreed to reach beyond the confines of academia. In recommending one colleague for advancement in spite of a modest record of publication, Fritz Hartung emphasised that 'quite simply, the main thing about a professor is that he should be a good chap (*ein Kerl*); the books come only in second place'. He was still more insistent that political judgement must be exercised in respect of an applicant and of the requirements of a particular faculty. This he held to be the logical consequence 'of the historico-political task of the historical professorship'.[6] Thus criteria for appointment to an Ordinariat were varied: academic achievement was only one among a number of considerations, and not necessarily the most significant so long as a nebulous standard of *Wissenschaftlichkeit* was discernible in the appointee.

Within the Wilhelmine and Weimar university systems, the relationship between the academic teacher and the student was marked by the overwhelming authority of the former. At the level of the Habilitation, it resembled a patron–client relationship: the

---

[6] Universitätsbibliotek Göttingen, Meyer papers no. 175. Hartung to Meyer, 25 September 1923.

metaphor favoured by the Ordinarien themselves in describing it was, tellingly, derived from nature. Hartung complained of Erich Marcks's academic offspring that 'strength of character has surely never been the characteristic of Marcks's students ... And the apples haven't fallen far from the tree at that.'[7] When Walter Frank attacked his former teacher, Oncken, in a now notorious polemic, Haller accused Frank of behaving in a manner that bordered on patricide.[8]

An equally distinctive mark of the guild's functioning was the pervasive influence of an interlocking series of patronage networks. While historians acknowledged a collective intellectual debt to Ranke and to Treitschke,[9] a number of lesser 'schools' built up around contemporary luminaries. Friedrich Meinecke was prodigious in the production of successors in the practice of history, who tended either – like Otto Becker – to follow his political line, or – like Hajo Holborn, Wilhelm Mommsen and others – to stand somewhat to his left. Otto Hintze and Hans Delbrück both ran salons during the Weimar years, attracting colleagues and political allies. On the right of the guild, no individual could boast a circle of students as wide and as able as Meinecke's, nor a salon as popular as Hintze's. Here, strength had perhaps less need of concentration. However, obligation and patronage defined, for instance, a loose grouping including Dietrich Schäfer, Richard Fester, Hartung, Georg von Below, A.O. Meyer and Adolf Hasenclever.[10] Even a self-professed 'outsider' (*sic*) of the guild like Haller, a Baltic German who ascribed his relative isolation to long periods spent abroad, could lay claim to an influential and politically surprisingly diverse group of successful *Doktoranden* and *Habilitanden* who included the Nazis Kleo Pleyer and Heinrich Dannenbauer, the conservative Fritz Ernst and the democratically orientated Ulrich Noack.[11]

[7] Bundesarchiv Koblenz (BAK), Fester papers no. 246. Hartung to Fester, 3 November 1922.
[8] BAK, Haller papers no. 29. Haller to Dannenbauer, 13 January 1935.
[9] This was even true of those on the left of the guild. Cf. Walter Götz, 'Heinrich von Treitschke zu seinem hundertsten Geburtstag' (1934), in his *Historiker in meiner Zeit. Gesammelte Aufsätze* (Cologne 1957).
[10] Fester was pivotal to this circle, having supported von Below and particularly Schäfer in the ultra-annexationist propaganda campaigns of the First World War and having taught, and aided the careers of, Hartung and Hasenclever.
[11] Fritz Ernst, *Johannes Haller – Gedenkrede* (Tübingen 1947) p. 11; Fester papers no. 190. Haller to Fester, 6 October 1920. Certainly, Haller's influence extended well beyond the small group named here and continues even into contemporary Germany. Cf. Heribert Müller, 'Der bewunderte Erbfeind. Johannes Haller, Frankreich und das französische Mittelalter', *HZ*, vol. 252 (1991), 2, pp. 265–317.

From less exalted students professors expected and often received striking marks of deference. Fester's position, in the eyes of one group of his students, was that of a *Führer* – in politics as much as in academic direction.[12] Inevitably, in reaction to this highly authoritarian and hierarchical system (in which the university was little less than an *Obrigkeitsstaat* in miniature) student tradition had developed classic inversion rites. The departure of an Ordinarius from his university was marked by something akin to an All Fools' Festival, invariably involving a clown – the *Kasperle* – and obliging the professor, as the celebrated victim of the event, to see himself caricatured by a student – 'an educative critique', as Hartung wryly observed on being subjected to the performance.[13] In this way, harmless channels were provided for any pent-up student hostilities.

From the collapse of the monarchies in November 1918 onward, historians perceived their academic community as being permanently under threat. A thorough-going democratisation of university life was widely expected of the new, democratic authorities in the first flush of their victory. And even with the benefit of hindsight, Haller looked back on the reformist aspirations of 1918–19 as on a rebirth of barbarism.[14] Even Friedrich Meinecke rushed to defend the bastions of 'our spiritual aristocracy'. Meinecke was adamant in insisting on the exemption of higher education from what he otherwise accepted as normative standards of academic accountability, on the need to 'separate politics from scholarship', and abjured any desire 'for one moment to do the unspeakable and create democratic scholarship'.[15]

Within this 'aristocratic' community, the discipline of history was held in markedly high esteem. While historians could not prevent the advent of sociology as a potential rival, their faculties suffered no resultant weakening, either in terms of their perceived competence to project the political will of the universities, or in simple numerical terms. On the contrary, as Bernd Faulenbach has pointed out, the external impression is of a flourishing discipline, represented by increasing numbers of practitioners through the Weimar years. By

---

[12] Fester papers no. 28. Hermann Lohmeyer to Fester, 20 September 1923.
[13] Meyer papers no. 175. Hartung to Meyer, 15 August 1923.
[14] Haller papers. 'Auf dem Katheder', unpublished autobiographical typescript, p. 244.
[15] Friedrich Meinecke, 'Die deutschen Universitäten und der heutige Staat', in his *Werke*, vol. II (Darmstadt 1957), p. 412.

1931, no fewer than 238 historians were active in German universities, compared with only 185 in 1910. However, the intellectual horizons of the guild had, by the birth of the Weimar Republic, narrowed considerably; the pre-war beginnings of academic diversification had effectively been brushed aside by the perceived primacy of power politics within historical discourse.[16]

The dominant notion of academic freedom was unrelated to any pluralist, tolerant conceptions; rather, it was an essentially medievally defined ideal of *Libertas*. What was at issue was the privileged position of the guild: its right to pursue a general intellectual direction of its own corporate choosing, its right to select its own membership and run its own affairs free from the interference of political authorities.

II

Rancorous, politically inspired disputes racked the guild throughout the duration of the Weimar Republic, dividing it into 'moderate' and 'extreme' nationalist camps and carrying over the arguments that had arisen in respect of war aims into the claustrophobic atmosphere of the committee room and the lecture theatre.[17] Old friendships collapsed and professional etiquette was dispensed with, as professors opened their quarrels to a wider audience. Georg von Below was unsparing in his onslaught on Meinecke, his protegé before 1914;[18] Johannes Haller and Walter Götz hurled abuse at each other in full view of a Tübingen student audience.[19] In 1926, Meinecke finally felt obliged publicly to admit that these hostilities inescapably affected all the 'territory of academic life' and accused 'our reactionary colleagues' of an unconscious political prejudice in their appointments.[20] He grossly understated his case.

In February 1919, Schäfer favoured Richard Fester with lengthy, unsolicited advice respecting the vacant Ordinariat in English at Halle, warning him of the candidacy of a pacifist, a brother of Walter Schücking. Such a move, Schäfer explained, would, 'in the

---

[16] Iggers, *Deutsche Geschichtswissenschaft*, pp. 305–308.
[17] On academics' controversies over war aims in the First World War see Klaus Schwabe, *Wissenschaft und Kriegsmoral. Die deutschen Hochschullehrer und die politischen Grundfragen des ersten Weltkrieges* (Göttingen 1969).
[18] Fester papers no. 190. Haller to Fester, 21 May 1920.
[19] Haller, as note 11, pp. 152–153.
[20] Meinecke, 'Die deutschen Universitäten', pp. 408–409.

patriotic interest, be painfully lamentable'. Schäfer's step was unprecedented, and undertaken with all the appearance of hesitancy and uncertainty as to its outcome. He carefully denied harbouring the least desire to get entangled with the affairs of another university:[21]

As far as I can recollect, I have never yet written a letter of similar content . . . You must forgive my writing such a letter: but what does one not learn to do for the fatherland! The Chair of English at Halle is an important political position.

Far from protesting against Schäfer's self-confessed infringement of the autonomy of a university with which he had no formal connection whatever, Fester undertook the organisation of a campaign to keep Schücking out. He thus violated a further custom, intervening in the business of another department and, in doing so, directly opposing the preference of the retiring Ordinarius, all on the grounds that 'all those who have not yet learned to crawl must hold together more than ever'.[22] From Schücking's former teacher Morsbach (Jena), he obtained the desired ideological ammunition: 'Schücking is a political fantasiser like his well-known brother and all the more dangerous since he can speak and write well . . . He is . . . an enemy of Prussia and of Bismarck.'[23] Fester then collected signatures for a petition to the Prussian minister of education, which denied that Schücking had 'a scientific character of inner firmness and free of fantasy'.[24] Thus, Fester turned a criticism made by Morsbach of Schücking *qua* politician into an onslaught on his academic reputation. The actual, exclusively political, motive was concealed from the minister.

It was not an isolated case: even so generally respected an historian as Gerhard Ritter could fall foul of similarly conceived machinations (Hartung saw to his exclusion, on solely political grounds, from the appointment list for the chair at Kiel).[25] Racial prejudice, too, was given free rein: Fester likened the appointment of a Jew at a Protestant German university to letting loose a pike in a goldfish pond.[26]

---

[21] Fester papers no. 255. Schäfer to Fester, 28 February 1919.
[22] *Ibid.* Fester to Schäfer, 27 June 1919.
[23] *Ibid.* Morsbach to Fester, 23 April 1919.   [24] *Ibid.* Fester to Becker, 2 June 1919.
[25] *Ibid.* no. 246. Hartung to Fester, 22 August 1923.
[26] *Ibid.* no. 255. Fester to Schäfer, 20 November 1919. The pseudo-medieval metaphor is characteristic of Fester's prose, but his anti-semitism was altogether modern.

III

Yet governmental preference ensured that 'Republicans of Reason' were able to exert an influence quite out of proportion to their numbers. In government-sponsored research projects and institutions they were propelled into positions which gave them unique access to, and often control over, vital records pertaining to the development of the Reich's politics from Germany's unification onwards. The publication of the documents of the Foreign Office was entrusted entirely to moderate interpreters of power politics. In the parliamentary commission of inquiry into the war guilt question and within the Historische Reichskommission, the weight of Delbrück, Meinecke and their friends was incomparably greater than in the guild at large. Ultra-nationalists and anti-democrats were reduced to a rearguard campaign of sniping criticism and obstruction – albeit one which was often conducted to remarkable effect.[27]

In the universities, the pattern of domination and control was very different. Fears that the guild would be flooded with an influx of democratic appointees, and that the Weimar authorities would turf incumbent Ordinarien out of their seats, proved very largely unfounded. Limited opportunities to rid universities of the most intransigent elderly adherents of the old regime were offered in 1920 by the introduction of a process whereby the emeritation of academics between the ages of 65 and 68 could be forced on them and the faculties. Yet ministers availed themselves only very rarely of even these limited powers. Schäfer and von Below both fell foul of this process (in 1921 and 1924 respectively), but when Fester became a victim of it in 1927, he was only the third noteworthy historian to have suffered so ignominious a retirement.[28]

In fact, Fester's compulsory emeritation and the manner of its accomplishment illustrates the failure of democratic political moments to secure inroads into academe, rather than its success. The Philosophical Faculty at Halle reacted with a storm of protest and the Deutschnationale Volkspartei (DNVP), through the inter-

---

27 Cf. Helmut Heiber, *Walter Frank und sein Geschichtsinstitut für das Neue Deutschland* (Stuttgart 1966), pp. 141ff. and the excellent discussion in Schleier, *Geschichtsschreibung*, pp. 141ff. and 143ff.
28 Schleier, *Geschichtsschreibung*, p. 162.

vention of Fester's Greifswald colleague Siegfried August Kähler, raised the issue on the floor of the Prussian *Landtag*. He perceived not only a gratuitous insult to the individual concerned but a threat to the independent development of the universities and, indeed, to the 'cleanliness of public life'.[29] Fester persuaded the faculty to draw up a shortlist for his successor headed by von Müller and including Fester's close friend Adolf Hasenclever. The ministry rightly interpreted the suggestions placed before it as a challenge to its intentions and rejected the list – at the cost of having to humble itself most conspicuously by asking Fester to undertake the cover for his own vacancy until a successor could be found. Meanwhile, the ministry put an alternative list of candidates to the faculty: Fester was entrusted with the formulation of the faculty's response. Inevitably, it was overwhelmingly negative. Nevertheless, where the ministry was steadfast in its commitment, faculty resistance must ultimately prove unavailing. Without in the least taking him to heart, Fester and his colleagues acceded to the appointment of Otto Becker as being the least of the evils they had been obliged to consider.[30]

In the saga of the Fester case, a still more overtly anti-republican challenge was orchestrated by the racialist students in Halle's Hochschulring deutscher Art. On 17 May 1927, up to a thousand of them joined a torchlit procession through Halle to accord their departing professor a final academic honour. A local student leader delivered a peroration ending with a ringing call to resistance: 'We students will not bow down! All out, lads! . . . For academic liberty, for the nationalist-racialist ideal, today and for ever: all out, lads!' The students demonstrated behind massed bands of the *Stahlhelm* which played military marches; in the working-class quarters of the town they were met by counter-demonstrators of the Reichsbanner organisation chanting *Freiheit*! Fester himself, standing amidst serried ranks of his colleagues, addressed his supporters from a balcony. He brought a brief and rather coded speech to a climax with three vivats in a scene depicted with relish by the conservative *Hallesche Zeitung* the following day:[31]

---

[29] Kähler in the *Hallesche Zeitung*, 24 March 1927. Cf. also his articles in e.g. the *Münchener Neueste Nachrichten*, 20 February 1927 and the *München-Augsburger Abendzeitung*, 2 March 1927.
[30] Fester papers nos. 9 and 10, *passim*.   [31] *Hallesche Zeitung*, 18 May 1927.

Vivat alma mater Fridericiana! Vivat Borussia Fridericiana! Vivat Germania Bismarckiana! Joyfully, like a vow, the 'Vivat' reverberates up to *Geheimrat* Fester from 800 students as a sign that he had been understood, and the song of the God who had caused iron to grow is sung.

The newspapers which had sprung to Fester's defence channelled their abiding sense of outrage at his departure into indignant attacks on the politics and professional qualities of his successor. Becker's inaugural lecture was held up to public ridicule as an absurdly narrow effort, unworthy of an Ordinarius.[32] His faculty found itself unable to evade the duty of replying, but its statement rejecting these attacks was so brief and so lame as rather to add credence to the insults.[33]

The effects of the occasional enforcement of early retirement – the sole means the authorities chose to employ in pursuit of the diminution of 'reactionary' influences on university life – thus gave precious little encouragement to democratic historians. The confrontation in Halle had advanced a single and at best ambiguous friend of the Republic. This had been achieved at the cost first of making the ministry appear ridiculous, and second of the propulsion of Becker into an embattled political position. Immeasurably worse was the resentment the affair had stirred up among students and, above all, among a majority of guild historians. Max Lenz's appraisal of the Fester case was characteristic: 'do it to the others: after all, some time the cup will overflow'.[34] As a result of his treatment, Fester became something of a *cause célèbre* on the right.[35]

Inadequate and inconsistent, the interference of republican authorities in academe was, without effecting anything approaching a transformation of the guild, a cause of much ill will. Those scholars who were dismissed scarcely suffered a commensurate loss of influence within their profession; even where their successors were of a different hue, they were never men of the left.

IV

Even the politically 'moderate' members of the guild – recent and half-hearted converts to republicanism all – frequently took an

---

32 Cf. *Hamburger Nachrichten*, 6 May 1927; *Deutsche Zeitung*, 18 May 1927.
33 'Die Philosophische Fakultät der Universität Halle-Wittenberg', declaration in *Hallesche Zeitung*, Beilage, 21 May 1927.
34 Fester papers no. 10. Lenz to Fester, 25 October 1926.
35 *Ibid.* no. 35. Meyer to Fester, 20 March 1930.

active part in a vendetta conducted by the profession against perceived leftist interlopers. The guild united to repudiate the historical
vision and obstruct the research and career prospects of the small
group of Left Liberal historians.[36] Common intellectual hallmarks of
the latter – they had no organisational identity – were a rejection,
whether explicit or implicit, of the tenets of the primacy of foreign
policy and a wide-ranging critique not only of particular politicians
and political currents of imperial Germany, but of the Wilhelmine
system as such. Unlike their historicist colleagues, the exponents of
Left Liberalism did not regard themselves as automatic opponents of
pacifism, internationalism or social democracy. The eclecticism of
George W. F. Hallgarten and of Eckart Kehr, for instance, encapsulated a willingness to explore and employ Marxist tools of analysis.[37]
Left Liberalism offered a piecemeal but none the less substantial and
intellectually effective challenge to the rigid orthodoxy of German
historicism. Yet the practical effects of this challenge on the writing
and teaching of history within the guild remained negligble. For it
was met not by the opening of a debate but by more or less
systematic political manoeuvring, by suppression and by outright
censorship. The guild closed ranks, meeting ideas with organisational repression.

There was an increasing propensity to refuse Left Liberals access
to the guild's leading journals. For decades on end, the *Historische
Zeitung*, for instance, failed even to review the cultural 'universal
history' of Kurt Breysig:[38] a wall of silence could prove a powerful
weapon. Indeed, the dead hand of the guild's active interventions
could bury work entirely. Hermann Kantorowicz's important work
on the war guilt question, ready for publication in 1929, was
effectively suppressed and did not appear in print until it was
rescued from Kantorowicz's papers by Immanuel Geiß in the mid-
1960s.[39] There is every reason to suspect that, without the interference of senior colleagues set on blighting their academic career

[36] Schleier, *Geschichtsschreibung*, Part 2: 'Die linksliberalen Historiker in der Weimarer
Republik', *passim*.
[37] *Ibid.*, pp. 468, 488.
[38] Bernhard vom Brocke, *Kurt Breysig, Geschichtswissenschaft zwischen Historismus und Soziologie*
(Lübeck 1971), pp. 123–124.
[39] Hermann Kantorowitz, *Gutachten zur Kriegsschuldfrage 1914*, edited with an introduction by
Immanuel Geiß (Stuttgart 1968). For a discussion of its censorship, see Geiß, 'Die
manipulierte Kriegsschuldfrage', *Militärgeschichtliche Mitteilungen*, vol. 2 (1983). Cf. also
Ulrich Heinemann, *Die verdrängte Niederlage. Politische Öffentlichkeit und Kriegsschuldfrage in
der Weimarer Republik* (Göttingen 1983).

prospects, the Left Liberal historians would have found a substantial reading public. Their political kindred spirits working in the genre of historical bellelettrism – Herbert Eulenberg, Werner Hegemann, Paul Wiegler and, most notably of all, the iconoclastic Bismarck-biographer Emil Ludwig – obtained a popular following.

The politically articulated case against Left Liberals fell broadly into three areas of controversy. First, they were condemned for espousing 'unpatriotic' opinions, which were held to have no place in German scholarship. Second, they were severely berated for any significant signs of class content in their historical analyses. Third, they were abused for any hint in their writing of sympathy with Jacobinical, pacifist or labour movement causes.

When Eckart Kehr applied to write a Habilitation at Königsberg under Hans Rothfels's supervision the outcome was both significant and characteristic. Rothfels cold-shouldered Kehr, his distaste for the latter's critical reinterpretation of totems of nationalist historiography quite overcoming any sympathy he might have harboured for his former student. Hermann Oncken was initially inclined to be amused by what he perceived as over-reaction on Rothfels's part. Querying his motives in dismissing Kehr, he wondered whether this was not an instance of a 'born Jew feeling moved to act as guardian of the conservative East Prussian nobility'. Ritter, however, determinedly defended Rothfels from Oncken's rebuke, replying to Oncken on 24 September 1931, immediately after having read Kehr's work:[40]

I would also have rejected Kehr ... It seems to me that this gentleman had better take his Habilitation in Russia rather than Königsberg. Because that, of course, is where he belongs: one of those 'noble Bolsheviks' who are really dangerous to our historical work.

Oncken did then go over to the growing lobby of academics concerned to try to scotch Kehr's career. He was to join Fritz Hartung in an unsuccessful bid to dissuade the Rockefeller Foundation from granting Kehr a scholarship to conduct research in the USA.[41] Unable to find funding or a publisher for his work in Germany, Kehr was, in effect, forced into emigration by the machi-

---

[40] Niedersächsisches Staatsarchiv, Oldenburg, Oncken papers no. 462. Ritter to Oncken, 24 September 1931.
[41] Iggers, *Deutsche Geschichtswissenschaft*, p. 309.

nations of his colleagues, among them leading lights of the Weimar circle and self-professed republicans.

The problems Left Liberals confronted in all their dealings with the exclusivist and intellectually ossified guild appear in stark contrast to relations between the professors and the several adherents of the myriad *völkisch* political groups and parties among their students. At Tübingen, at Halle (first under the auspices of Fester, then of Hans Herzfeld) and in Munich in particular, Nazis and other racialist circles flourished. In the latter case, Karl Alexander von Müller was able to gather an impressive array of Nazis around his evening classes on the causes and course of the First World War and on the German resistance to Napoleon. Goering, Hess and Baldur von Schirach were among Müller's admirers there, and Ernst Hanfstaengl (Hitler's first convert among the Munich upper classes and his foreign press agent after 1933) and Walter Frank were both supervised by him for their doctorates.[42] At Halle, Otto Strasser's *Doktorvater* was Richard Fester, whose students' letters in general testify to his careful nurturing of a sizeable group of ultra-racialist students.[43] Typical of these was Studienrat Werdemann's expression of pride in the overt anti-semitism with which he had chosen to conclude his doctoral thesis on Caprivi. He doubted:[44]

whether what I say at the end about 'parliamentarism', and how I say it (poison for the peoples, a tool of the mainly Jewish Big Capital in order to master them) is advisable, because one does not like to touch on this fact.

Whatever he feared might be the reaction of his examiners, he could comfortably afford to be candid with Fester at least.

There are many other instances of very warm relations between avowed Nazis or racist thinkers and members of the guild. In September 1944, just after joining the SS, Dr Fritz Wendt wrote to Richard Fester to acknowledge the latter's role in his personal development.[45] Ten years earlier, the racist activist, politician and collaborator with Walter Frank, Kleo Pleyer, had written in similar vein to acknowledge the magnitude of his indebtedness, academic and political in equal part, to Johannes Haller.[46] Yet Pleyer also alluded to differences in approach that existed between him and his

[42] Ernst Hanfstaengl, *Hitler: the missing years* (London 1957), p. 71.
[43] Fester papers no. 228. Otto Strasser to Fester, 4 November 1924.
[44] *Ibid.* no. 37. Werdemann to Fester, 23 October 1957.
[45] *Ibid.* Wendt to Fester, 17 September 1944.
[46] Haller papers no. 23. Pleyer to Haller, 13 May 1934.

erstwhile mentor. By 1936 the discordant note had come to pre-dominate. Haller refused to supply a reference supporting Pleyer's application for a chair at Berlin and accused him of dishonesty.[47] The scholarly dissonances were products equally of Pleyer's inter-disciplinary approach and of his racism. For Pleyer's advocacy of a 'new total science' first involved an intermeshing of history, soci-ology and ethnography, and second was predicated on the view that the *Volk* was the 'original life force' and pre-dated the state. Both ingredients of this witches' brew were in equal measure anathema to Haller and also to the Berlin faculty, which rejected Pleyer's candi-dacy.[48]

The cordiality which prevailed in relations between established academics and younger *völkisch* aspirants could thus not disguise an increasing ideological gap between them. For the guild, racialism was permissible as a colouring of or an adjunct to historicism – never as a substitute, as the sole or prime approach to historical under-standing. Before March 1933, the *völkisch* students had made few inroads into the guild; thereafter, as will be argued below, they were perceived as a distinct menace. The goodwill long accorded them must have been widely regretted. Nevertheless, the professors' mis-fortune was largely of their own making. Racialist historians would, after 1933, scarcely have been placed even to challenge the guild had they not been afforded research and limited career opportuni-ties by it in the past.

V

Prior to the Nazi seizure of power, not a single Ordinarius professor of History had joined the National Socialist party. Though many historians were willing to cooperate with the Nazis, and sympa-thised with several of their aims, they did not see in Hitler the sole or the necessary saviour of Germany – at least until after he had established his regime in power. Their brand of political conserva-tism ensured a continued general allegiance to the 'old order'. From the late 1920s on there emerged a generation of students which had not been formed by the experience of imperial Germany. Here, in

---

[47] *Ibid.* Haller to von Müller. Undated draft in reply to a letter of 9 December 1936.
[48] Cf. Heiber, *Walter Frank und sein Geschichtsinstitut*, pp. 242, 393ff. It should be emphasised that Pleyer's interpretation of history did not go unchallenged even among Frank's closest young collaborators. *Ibid.*, p. 501.

the perception of many university teachers, lay the root cause of the friction between themselves and a majority of their students, which marred their enjoyment of academic life during the first half of the following decade.

In the mid-1920s there were few signs of an impending crisis for the study of history. Student numbers were rising and the temperament and serious academic inclination of the rising generation seemed to bode well. In 1926 Haller could report with satisfaction of a substantial student following in Tübingen with 170 attending his lecture series on medieval Europe and 243 listening to shorter and more general lectures on state and church before the Counter-Reformation.[49] In relation to many of these students, Haller felt that generational discrepancies might be to their advantage rather than to his own. Those who – like Heinrich Dannenbauer – had participated in the war were the objects of his esteem, even of jealousy. Thus, he explained to Dannenbauer that while they had many experiences in common, 'you have one great advantage over my generation: the experience of the war in your youth, when it can form and further the individual. The war only afforded us old ones blows which could no longer harden, but destroy quite a lot.'[50] Shared experience of pre-republican Germany was thus a bond between teacher and student, whilst the nature of the differences of experience was certainly no bar to the development of cordial relations.

By 1929, however, academic standards were felt to be in decline and a new gulf opened with the arrival of students who did not in any way relate to the imperial past. Fritz Hartung complained that, even among his better students ('who are of course not entirely lacking') he was obliged to recognise 'how little now connects them with the old Germany'.[51] Dannenbauer – who, like Hartung, had fought in the war – noted of this younger generation that 'They have no idea of war and would be very ready to take it lightly, with patriotic dash and a horrifying underestimation of the opponent. Even among the wiser heads, the systematic change becomes distubingly noticeable in big words and arrogance.'[52] Their appointed

---

[49] Haller papers no. 29. Haller to Dannenbauer, 6 May 1926. It may be some measure of student commitment that individual sessions of the medieval Europe series lasted up to four hours!

[50] *Ibid.* 13 April 1926.   [51] Fester papers no. 246. Hartung to Fester, 15 March 1929.

[52] Haller papers no. 29. Dannenbauer to Haller, 10 May 1936.

positions as custodians and mediators of the past notwithstanding, established historians seemed at a loss to know how to address the problem.

As *völkisch* radicalism in general, and Nazism in particular, swept through student bodies, the self-confidence and turbulence of student organisations amounted to a direct challenge to professorial authority. An older generation had demonstrated student solidarity with the political stand of a Richard Fester: their teachers, and not they themselves, had provided the occasions and chosen the ground for political activity. The students of the early 1930s, by contrast, took political initiatives which they expected or demanded that exalted professors follow.[53] Clearly, many students were no longer even interested in what they had to say, and took it upon themselves to pester their teachers for syllabus changes. In response to pressure for innovation, Karl Brandi endeavoured to whip up some enthusiasm for social and economic history. 'The result: complete failure. This term, I am lecturing on the great turning points in German history, that is to say, I am telling a story. And I've got somewhere with that.'[54] Schwertfeger, to whose despairing 'heaved sigh' Brandi's note had been a reaction, fared still worse. Perhaps, he mused, he was being subjected to a boycott as a punishment for having supported Hindenburg for the presidency.[55] The irony of his situation struck him repeatedly: while his lecture series 'The history of war and the nature of defence' was attended by audiences of only ten students, hundreds participated in weapon-sports workshops.[56]

Haller found increasingly good reason to blame the disruption of university life directly on the interference of the Nazi party. Initially, he endeavoured to smooth things over by amicable discussion, believing a settlement to be potentially advantageous to both sides. Distressed at a prospect of a souring of relations between his colleagues and himself on the one hand, and the National Socialists (NSDAP) on the other, merely because of the policies on higher education formulated by the latter, Haller appears to have sought contact with Rosenberg in August 1932. His concern was that Nazi proposals for reform of the universities risked, 'irreparable alien-

---

[53] See Michael Stephen Steinberg, *Sabers and brown shirts: the German students' path to National Socialism 1918–1935* (Chicago 1977).

[54] BAK Schwertfeger papers no. 406. Brandi to Schwertfeger, 24 November 1932.

[55] *Ibid.* no. 530. Schwertfeger to Oberstleutnant August Frühling, 13 August 1931; 11 August 1934.

[56] *Ibid.* no. 406. Schwertfeger to the Rektor of Göttingen University, 18 November 1932.

ation between the NSDAP and the youth, especially the academic youth, belonging to it on the one side and the circles of the teachers and professors on the other side.'[57] Subsequent developments served only to increase Haller's misgivings. For himself, the parting of the ways came just two months later. In response to the receipt of a petition from Nazi students, Haller was moved to put the upstarts firmly in their place. First and foremost he informed them 'that, to put it bluntly, I find it unsuitable for students to present their teachers with a public declaration, in a finalised form of words, for their signatures'.[58] The request itself, then, was perceived by Haller as an affront to his professional dignity.

In some respects, academia did not recover from the upsurge of student discontent until after the demise of the Third Reich. Thus, in 1939, Fritz Hartung still found a great deal of which to complain:[59]

It no longer gives me any great pleasure to work with students. The over-estimation of physical activity takes effect ever more clearly in a retrogression not only of knowledge ... but also above all of spiritual training. Books are as good as not read any more, for a start because the student of today does not know how he should learn. The dogmatic attitude of our time, which smells the spirit of evil in criticism, also makes its presence strongly felt; one reads only one book about a subject and believes that without qualification. Even Macaulay was held up before me recently in a *Staatsexamen* as an authority on English history. That he had a particular political approach, and moreover one that is not accepted today, did not even enter the candidate's consciousness.

Nevertheless, Hartung's list of criticisms is arguably as significant for what it does not as for what it does bewail: if the students' mood was one of bellicosity, it was, by the later 1930s, no longer one of belligerence toward academic authority.

In the last years of Weimar, as we have seen, the professors had faced considerable pressures from Nazi students (though they had shown few signs of giving way to student demands). To a certain extent the situation worsened after March 1933, since the weight of ministerial interference was now added to that of the Nazi student organisations. But in fact the advent of the Third Reich seems to

57 Haller papers no. 9. Haller to Rosenberg, 18 August 1932.
58 *Ibid.* Haller to the Bundesleitung of the Nationalsozialistischer deutscher Studentenbund, 27 October 1932. Brandi and Schwertfeger reacted in similar vein to the initiatives of the NS Dozentenbund, cf. Schwertfeger papers no. 407. Brandi to Schwertfeger, 15 May 1933.
59 Fester papers no. 246. Hartung to Fester, 26 May 1939.

have coincided with abatement in the truculence of the Nazis' student supporters. The extension of the *Führerprinzip* to the universities was not the calamity that many academic traditionalists had feared it might be. Even in the potentially vulnerable role of Dean in a period of political turbulence, Hartung could afford to observe the antics of student politicians with detatchment and even wry amusement.[60] In just a year since the formalisation of the position of *Studentenführer*, Berlin had seen off no fewer than five occupants of the post, not one of whom had served his full term of office. A student leadership in hopeless internal turmoil was scarcely likely to mount an effective challenge to experienced administrators and academics versed in the manoeuvrings of university politics.

Encouraged by the odium of scandal surrounding the *Studentenführer* in Berlin, Hartung began, in August 1933, to discern an impending parting of ways between the mass of ordinary students and their official organisations; he grew quietly confident 'that the natural relationship between lecturer and student will soon be restored'.[61] By April 1934 he had seen ample confirmation of his view that the greater part of the student body was very willing to revert to academic pursuits. 'Those students who want to learn something are gradually offering resistance to the coercion and the regimentation.'[62] Over the next three years Hartung's optimism was borne out. Falling numbers and a student backlash against their radical leaders made it possible for him complacently to remark that 'working with the students and influencing them has become easier again'.[63]

Still active and combative in his retirement, Haller felt that by early 1934 the situation was ripe for a counter-offensive against the Nazi student leadership. With evident relish, he encouraged Heinrich Dannenbauer to publish a lecture stating their mutually held traditionalist intellectual convictions: this would present a challenge not only to prominent Nazi ideologues, 'but almost more to Schirach and co., for whom it is the youth that's at issue'.[64] Dannenbauer shared Haller's cautious confidence in the serious inclinations of academic youth. 'At bottom', he was persuaded, 'the people are good chaps and would like to work decently and

---

[60] *Ibid.* 23 August 1933. [61] *Ibid.* 28 August 1933.
[62] *Ibid.* 14 April 1933. [63]*Ibid.* 29 March 1937.
[64] Haller papers no. 29. Haller to Dannenbauer, 25 February 1935.

thoroughly & are sick to the back teeth of the official stuff and nonsense.'[65]

If the generation of students who were attending universities in the mid-1930s had burned up their radical energies, the professors remained anxious lest a new intake should prove less amenable to intellectual influence. The fear was that new students would prove hopelessly ignorant, and irretrievably indoctrinated by the regime. Haller, for example, was obliged to state an implicit preference for the schooling provided under Weimar and feared that, in 1934, he was dealing with the final generation of a youthful German intelligentsia. 'Whether the most recent generation, without having learned anything proper at school, and after being put through the mill of Hitler Youth and SA, will remain similarly sensible, I dare not say.'[66] It was a trepidation which Dannenbauer came to share, as he remarked in May 1936: 'what sort of people the future [one word] generation are will have to remain to be seen. From the circle of the older ones I hear unfavourable opinions; they are said to lack spirit, to be dull and – uncomradely!'[67]

Whatever the shortcomings of students whose historical consciousness and general education had in part been moulded after 1933 in Nazi schools, they were not the material of which a resurgence of anti-academic rebels was made. The wave of discontent of the early 1930s had been effectively withstood: no student challenge comparable in its comprehensiveness was mounted to trouble the still waters of German academia until the unrest (as strikingly familiar in form as it was dissimilar in content) of the 1960s. 'During cleaning-up work at the University of Heidelberg as a student in 1944', remembered Karl Ferdinand Werner, 'I found a stack of propaganda writings from the years 1933 and 1934. They were, as I read them, curios from the past, of a radicality which had later become unthinkable in the academic domain.'[68] This was telling testimony to the durability of professional authority and to the correspondingly short life-span of student aggression toward it.

---

[65] *Ibid.* no. 19. Dannenbauer to Haller, 10 May 1936.
[66] *Ibid.* no. 29. Haller to Dannenbauer, 11 November 1934.
[67] *Ibid.* no. 19. Dannenbauer to Haller, 10 May 1936.
[68] Karl Ferdinand Werner, *Das NS-Geschichtsbild und die deutsche Geschichtswissenschaft* (Stuttgart 1967), p. 46; Uwe Dietrich Adam, *Die Universität Tübingen im Dritten Reich* (Tübingen 1977), p. 204.

VI

Where the Weimar Republic had failed to democratise the guild, the Nazis failed to secure its ideological coordination. The respect of the guild and not the support of the party remained the goal of the vast majority of historians, whose general support for the *Volksgemeinschaft* stopped at the unversity gates. Thus, Heinrich Dannenbauer, the first Nazi appointee to an Ordinariat and one foisted on to an unwelcoming faculty by dint of party pressure, 'went native' after his appointment. Prior to Hitler's advent to power, Dannenbauer had been one of a small group of relatively young Nazi party members on the academic staff at Tübingen. As such, he fancied himself the target of an anti-Nazi conspiracy orchestrated by senior colleagues. In the summer semester of 1932, he had appeared to throw down the gauntlet to his elders when he had adopted a broadly *völkisch* tone in delivering a series of lectures on 'German consciousness in medieval history'. But, encouraged by Haller, he chose the occasion of his inaugural lecture as Ordinarius to spearhead the guild's refutation of racist interpretations of history, pronouncing attempts at explaining history 'on a racial basis' to represent 'the height of confusion' — and so helped not only to arouse the discomforting curiosity of the SS in 1935 but to secure for himself a reputation for integrity that endured into the Federal Republic.[69]

The composition of the guild, its political contours and intellectual horizons at the end of the Weimar interlude had been determined not only by the conceptual inertia of those of its members who had retained their chairs since 1918, but also by their collective ability to ensure continuity in the representation of their craft.

---

[69] Haller papers no. 29. Haller to Dannenbauer, 14 July 1934. On Dannebauer's subsequent defence of the guild's historicist positions, see Werner, *NS-Geschichtsbild*, pp. 48ff; Peter Lambert, 'The politics of German historians 1914–1945' (doctoral thesis, University of Sussex 1986), pp. 70–79.

CHAPTER 9

Gender, generation and politics: young Protestant women in the final years of the Weimar Republic

Elizabeth Harvey

Generational identity and generational conflict were concepts which exerted a powerful fascination in Weimar Germany. The sharp historical discontinuities since 1914 – the watershed of the Great War, followed by the revolutionary upheavals of the post-war period and later by the Depression – accentuated the contrasts between the formative experiences of one age cohort and those of its immediate predecessor.[1] A leader of young Protestant women observed in 1930 that 'in all the past centuries there has probably never been a time in which the image of youth has changed so rapidly and with such dramatic contrasts'.[2] By 1932, a contemporary commentator declared that the current generation of adolescents was unable to comprehend the outlook of their immediate elders, let alone understand the world in which their parents and grandparents had grown up.[3]

The sense of belonging to a generation marked by some key experience in adolescence like the outbreak of war, or the 'hunger winter' of 1916–17, or the inflation did not inevitably lead to a particular political outlook. But there were ideologues with backgrounds in the youth movement and links to the late Weimar *bündische Jugend*[4] who were convinced not only that generational divides were crucial in shaping Weimar society, but moreover that a

The research for this article was carried out with the financial support of Liverpool University's Research Development Fund and the German Academic Exchange Service.

[1] Hans Mommsen, 'Generationskonflikt und Jugendrevolte in der Weimarer Republik', in Thomas Koebner, Rolf-Peter Janz and Frank Trommler (eds.), *'Mit uns zieht die neue Zeit'. Der Mythos Jugend* (Frankfurt 1985), p. 32; Irmtraud Götz von Olenhusen, *Jugendreich, Gottesreich, Deutsches Reich. Junge Generation, Religion und Politik 1928–1933* (Cologne 1987), pp. 25–26.
[2] Adelheid Crome, 'Zur Geschichte des Jugendwerkes', *Jugendweg*, vol. 11 (1930), 1, p. 9.
[3] Dr Visser t'Hooft, 'Die Jugend 1927 und 1932', *Weibliche Jugend*, vol. 41 (1932), 11, p. 283.
[4] On the pre-war youth movement and the Weimar *bündische Jugend*, see Walter Z. Laqueur, *Young Germany: a history of the German youth movement* (New Brunswick 1984, 2nd edn.).

young generation, steeled by its hardships since 1914 and united behind suitable leaders, was destined to play a key role in politics. The 'generation of the disinherited' would become the 'generation of the chosen'.[5] In the final years of the Republic, as has been well documented by research, a rhetoric of generational politics flourished as the collapse of the institutions of Weimar democracy left a growing political vacuum.[6] Little came of initiatives by activists from the *bündische Jugend* to translate the 'will of the young generation' into a remoulding of the party political spectrum.[7] However, undeterred by their failure to unify the ranks even of organised youth, let alone mobilise mass support for a transformation of party politics, the self-styled representatives of a young political generation continued to cultivate a myth of youth as the force which would redeem the nation from its current state of weakness and discord.[8]

The *bündisch* cult of youth and youthful vigour, its scorn for Weimar politics and its ideas of a new *Reich* and an organic *Volksgemeinschaft* bore striking affinities with elements of the National Socialist message. These affinities have raised questions for research on the relationship between the 'generational politics' of the late Weimar Republic and the triumph of National Socialism, and it has been found that ideological affinities did indeed tempt many *bündisch* activists into sympathy with the new regime in 1933, even if the elitism of the *Bünde* sat uncomfortably with Nazi methods of mass mobilisation.[9] Enthusiasm for National Socialist ideas was also widespread in other bourgeois youth organisations: recent work on confessional youth organisations has stressed the ideological 'fit' between the world of organised Protestant youth and that of National Socialism, and the extent to which members of Protestant youth organisations welcomed the Nazi takeover.[10]

---

[5] E. Günther Gründel, *Die Sendung der jungen Generation* (Munich 1932), p. 441.

[6] Frank Trommler, 'Mission ohne Ziel. Über den Kult der Jugend im modernen Deutschland', in Koebner *et al.*, *Der Mythos Jugend*, p. 26; Larry Eugene Jones, 'German Liberalism and the alienation of the younger generation in the Weimar Republic', in Konrad J. Jarausch and Larry Eugene Jones (eds.), *In search of a Liberal Germany: studies in the history of German Liberalism from 1789 to the present* (Oxford 1989), pp. 287–321. See also Richard Bessel's essay in this volume.

[7] Larry E. Jones, *German Liberalism and the dissolution of the Weimar party system 1918–1933* (Chapel Hill, London 1988), pp. 326–337, 369–373, 380–383, 387–391.

[8] Trommler, 'Mission ohne Ziel', pp. 20–23, 40–44.

[9] Matthias von Hellfeld, *Bündische Jugend und Hitlerjugend. Zur Geschichte von Anpassung und Widerstand 1930–1939* (Cologne 1987), pp. 33–98.

[10] Von Olenhusen, *Jugendreich, Gottesreich, Deutsches Reich*, pp. 207–220.

Most writing on generational conflict in Weimar Germany has neglected questions of gender. In much of the literature of the time and in subsequent writing on the subject, the constructs 'youth front' and 'young generation' are simply assumed to be male.[11] However, some commentators of the period did take account of female experience. The youth psychologist Eduard Spranger, introducing an essay collection published in 1932 entitled *Female youth in our time*, declared that 'we have all experienced the profound change in the psychological constitution of the young woman of 1930 compared with that of the young woman of 1920'.[12] Adelheid Crome, a leader of young Protestant women, believed that the three decades since the turn of the century had seen the decline of the 'young lady', protected from the outside world and dependent on her family until marriage, and the rise of the modern educated young woman, endowed with political rights, earning her own living and taking a growing degree of independence for granted.[13] Helene Raff, writing in the *Süddeutsche Monatshefte* in January 1932, painted a similar picture of rapid social transformation reflected in a succession of female generations. She, however, stressed the negative as well as the positive aspects of emancipation: the economic difficulties faced by young women coming on to the job market in the Depression and the challenges they faced in building a new social identity for themselves.[14]

In the late Weimar years, it was quite plausible to conceive of young women in their late teens and 20s as constituting a 'young female generation', sharing crucial experiences of new rights and freedoms but also of political turbulence and economic hardship. Whether there was any prospect of young women uniting or becoming active in the public sphere on the basis of a shared generational identity was another matter. It was true that large numbers of girls and young women belonged to youth organisations ranging from groups of the *bündische Jugend* to party youth groups, confessional and sports organisations.[15] In 1928 1.4 million of the 4.3 million

---

[11] Gründel, *Sendung der jungen Generation*, pp. 22–63.

[12] Eduard Spranger, 'Einleitung', in Hertha Siemering and Eduard Spranger (eds.), *Weibliche Jugend in unserer Zeit* (Leipzig 1932), p. 2.

[13] Adelheid Crome, 'Zur Geschichte des Jugendwerkes', *Jugendweg*, vol. 11 (1930), 1, p. 9.

[14] Helene Raff, 'Das junge Mädchen von einst und heute', *Süddeutsche Monatshefte*, vol. 29 (1931–2), 4 (special issue: *Die jungen Mädchen von heute*), pp. 268–269.

[15] On women in the *bündische Jugend*, see Marion E. P. de Ras, *Körper, Eros und weibliche Kultur. Mädchen im Wandervogel und in der bündischen Jugend 1900–1933* (Pfaffenweiler 1988); Irmgard

members of youth organisations were female; in 1933 an estimated 42 per cent of female 14–25-year-olds were in some way 'organised'.[16] But while membership of such organisations could well expose young women to messages stressing collective youthful will and strength, and bring them into a milieu which promoted initiatives for and by youth, it did not necessarily provide any basis for political unity or mobilisation across ideological and class divides.

One commentator who considered the question of young women's response to the generational politics of the late Weimar years was Josepha Fischer, a leading expert on 'organised youth'. Writing in 1932, she took the view that any notion of forging a broad spectrum of an age cohort into a 'political generation', a task facing massive obstacles even if only young men were involved, was a lost cause where young women were concerned. Analysing trends among 'organised' female youth, Fischer underlined the factors which tended to counteract any sense of generational unity and unified political will among young women. In the case of boys and young men, she argued, the *bündische Jugend* had at least succeeded in promoting among a wide cross-section of organised male youth a common and widely accessible currency of activities and style. By the late Weimar period, Catholic, Socialist and *völkisch* boys alike were, for all their ideological differences, appearing in disciplined, uniformed formations emphasising their militancy and masculinity. No such unifying influences emanating from the youth movement, in Fischer's view, had shaped the life-style and outlook of 'organised' young women: there was no common culture springing from a shared sense of 'modern young womanhood' on which to base a female generational politics.[17]

Gertrud Bäumer, a leading bourgeois feminist, provided a rather different assessment in her article in the *Süddeutsche Monatshefte* in

Klönne, *Ich spring in diesem Ringe. Mädchen und Frauen in der deutschen Jugendbewegung* (Pfaffenweiler 1990). On women in Catholic and Protestant youth organisations, see von Olenhusen, *Jugendreich*, pp. 75–77, 97–99, 211–215; on women in the Socialist youth movement, see Martina Naujoks, *Mädchen in der Arbeiterjugendbewegung in der Weimarer Republik* (Hamburg 1984).

16 For 1928 figures, see 'Die Mädchen in den Jugendverbänden', in Emmy Wolf (ed.), *11. Jahrbuch des Bundes Deutscher Frauenvereine (1927–8)* (Mannheim 1928), p. 81. For 1933 figures, see Josepha Fischer, *Die Mädchen in den deutschen Jugendverbänden: Stand, Ziele, Aufgaben* (Leipzig 1933), p. 4.

17 Josepha Fischer, 'Probleme der heutigen weiblichen Jugendführung', *Das junge Deutschland*, vol. 26 (1932), 12, pp. 403–411.

January 1932 on 'Political and religious commitment among female youth'.[18] Bäumer, who kept a close watch on developments in the youth movement and among youth generally, had been a sponsor of one of the political experiments designed to give expression to the political will of the 'younger generation'.[19] Like Fischer, she emphasised the multitude of factors which divided and fragmented the young female generation.[20] Nevertheless, she found some unifying tendencies: 'over the last year, young people generally, including the girls, have become more determinedly political'.[21] The intensity of this politicisation varied greatly, as did the forms in which it expressed itself. However, Bäumer diagnosed as a general trend among female youth a growing concern with the fate of Germany and its people, and a belief that as young women they had a particular part to play in bringing about national recovery: they felt called upon, as young people did generally, to serve the nation at a time of emergency. Beyond the factors of class, educational background, confession and ideology which divided young women, Bäumer detected signs of a common response among young women to the political crisis which was influenced, among other things, by *bündisch* ideas.[22]

The tension between images of generational unity and those of intra-generational fragmentation in relation to young women during the Depression years provides a starting-point for the present essay. As a study of middle-class girls and young women in three Protestant organisations, it focuses on one part of the spectrum of 'organised' female youth in Weimar Germany. The members of the Protestant groups examined here were defined not only by their generation and gender, but also by their confession, class background and education. The extent to which these factors marked them off from the rest of their peer group may shed light on the intra-generational diversity upon which contemporaries commented. At the same time, investigating these groups provides a way of assessing the degree to which a broader sense of generational unity, with consequences for young women's actions in the public sphere, actually was forged by the twin crises of the Depression and the

[18] Gertrud Bäumer, 'Politische und religiöse Bindungen der weiblichen Jugend', *Süddeutsche Monatshefte*, vol. 29 (1931/2), 4, pp. 280–282.
[19] See Jones, *German Liberalism*, pp. 380–383.
[20] Bäumer, 'Politische und religiöse Bindungen der weiblichen Jugend', p. 280.
[21] *Ibid.*, p. 282.   [22] *Ibid.*, pp. 281–282.

disintegration of the Weimar Republic. The essay therefore looks at young Protestant women's responses to economic and political crisis, and raises the question of how far these responses might have been shared by a broader section of their peer group.

Two aspects of that reaction in particular are highlighted. First, the essay looks at the extent of the reception among young Protestant women of the 'generational politics' emerging in the late Weimar years. In order to explore the issues raised by Bäumer and Fischer, the essay asks how far the members of the Protestant young women's organisations examined here took up the ideas of a 'youth front' or 'youth mission' emanating from the ranks of the *bündische Jugend*, and explores Bäumer's notion of a growing commitment among young women to serving the nation in what appeared to be its hour of need. The second major focus is on the girls' response to National Socialism. It discusses the impact of Nazism on Protestant young women's organisations and their members both before and after January 1933, asks how far their response corresponded to the pattern of ambivalence and confusion seen elsewhere among middle-class youth organisations, and looks at the reasons why young Protestant women might have embraced or rejected National Socialist ideas.

I

This essay focuses on young women in three Protestant youth organisations: the *Weggenossenkreise*, the *Mädchenbibelkreise* and the *Christdeutscher Bund*. All three organisations recruited from the small minority of girls and young women who were educated beyond the standard of the elementary school (*Volksschule*) which the mass of children attended until the school-leaving age of 14.[23] Typical recruits ranged from schoolgirls in the upper forms of *Lyzeen* and *Gymnasien*, to university students, trainee social workers and probationary teachers in their 20s, drawn from the Protestant middle classes. The leaders and spokeswomen of the organisations, and the editors of the newsletters and journals, tended to be older: often they were teachers, theologians or the wives of pastors.

The *Weggenossenkreise* were a self-styled elite section of the massive

---

[23] In 1931, 13 per cent of girls aged 14–16 and 2 per cent of girls aged 16–19 were in full-time schooling. See Peter Lundgreen, *Sozialgeschichte der deutschen Schule im Überblick*. Vol. II: *1918–1980* (Göttingen 1981), pp. 118–119.

Evangelischer Reichsverband weiblicher Jugend (known until 1929 as the
Evangelischer Verband für die weibliche Jugend Deutschlands). Founded in
1893, the *Reichsverband* encompassed a vast network of groups with a
total of over 200,000 members in the late Weimar period.[24] The
Weggenossenkreise traced their origins to the study groups set up
within the *Reichsverband* by Guida Diehl before the First World War
for 'educated female youth'.[25] When Guida Diehl parted company
from the *Reichsverband* towards the end of the First World War,
taking her followers and her journal, the *Neulandblatt*, with her, a
gap was left which was filled in 1920 by the founding of a new
journal *Jugendweg*, and by the formation, under the leadership of
Adelheid Crome, of a new organisation for educated young women
within the *Reichsverband*.[26] By 1929 there were 299 groups of *Weggenossen*; its membership ranged from older schoolgirls to young
women in their 20s training for professional work, with students at
social work training schools forming a major contingent.[27]

The programme of the *Weggenossen* stressed 'living Christianity',
discipline, loyalty and a 'way of life befitting a genuine German girl'
(*echte deutsche Mädchenart*).[28] In line with the designated role of the
Weggenossen as the intellectual spearhead of the *Reichsverband* ('the
educated must lead the way!')[29] discussions of social, religious and
political problems were central to the life of local groups. The rest of
the programme included activities inspired by the youth movement
– hikes, folk singing and dancing – together with *Freizeiten* (holiday
courses and camps), and trips to the mass rallies of the *Reichsverband*.
The *Deutscher Bund der Mädchenbibelkreise*, founded in 1919,

---

[24] On the *Reichsverband* in the Weimar period generally, see Centralausschuß für die innere
Mission (ed.), *Handbuch der inneren Mission*, vol. I (Berlin 1929), pp. 166–173; Grete
Schemann, 'Evangelischer Reichsverband weiblicher Jugend', in H. Siemering (ed.), *Die
deutschen Jugendverbände. Ihre Ziele, ihre Organisation sowie ihre neuere Entwicklung und Tätigkeit*,
vol. III (Berlin 1931), pp. 133–141; Barbara Thiele, *Jugendarbeit als Spiegel des Zeitgeschehens
dargestellt am Beispiel der Arbeit des Burckhardthauses 1893–1965* (Gelnhausen, Berlin 1968),
pp. 43–80; Fischer, *Mädchen in den deutschen Jugendverbänden*, p. 5; Von Olenhusen, *Jugendreich*, pp. 211–215.

[25] On Guida Diehl's activities in the Weimar period, see Claudia Koonz, *Mothers in the
Fatherland: women, the family and Nazi politics* (London 1987), pp. 80–84.

[26] Leopold Cordier, *Evangelische Jugendkunde*. Vol. II: *Die evangelische Jugend und ihre Bünde*
(Schwerin 1926), pp. 405–407, 671–675; Adelheid Crome, 'Weggenossen im Verband',
Jugendweg, vol. I (1920), 20, pp. 153–156.

[27] *Handbuch der Inneren Mission*, vol. I, p. 167; Adelheid Crome, 'Weggenossen', in Ev.
Reichsverband weiblicher Jugend (ed.), *Unser Jugendwerk* (Berlin 1929), p. 20.

[28] Adelheid Crome, 'Die Weggenossenarbeit', *Weibliche Jugend*, vol. 38 (1929), 10, p. 262.

[29] Crome, 'Weggenossen im Verband', p. 154.

brought together in one organisation the bible study groups for 'educated girls' dating from before the First World War.[30] The movement initially retained links with the *Evangelischer Reichsverband*, but severed them in 1923. By 1929, the movement comprised 743 groups with a total of 14,000 members; by 1933, its membership was 15,000.[31] Like the *Weggenossenkreise*, the membership of the *Mädchenbibelkreise* (or MBK for short) spanned an age range which included teenagers and women in their 20s. The organisation's monthly journals, *Unser Blatt* for members over 18 and *Der helle Schein* for the 14–17-year-olds, had in 1929 circulations of 6,400 and 3,100 respectively.[32] These periodicals, to a much greater degree than the journals of the *Weggenossenkreise*, were concerned with bible interpretation and religious issues, but they also carried contributions on political and social questions and problems confronting the young Christian woman in her daily life.

The activities and literature of the *Mädchenbibelkreise* were unequivocally centred on the Gospel and its proclamation. The movement was 'neo-pietist', stressing the crucial experience of conversion and 'awakening', the importance of mission work and the role of the laity.[33] Members were to bear witness to its message in their daily lives, and selected recruits were trained for mission work: the movement took special pride in its two missionaries to China.[34] Adherents valued the clear focus of the movement, but critics found its approach to religious matters dogmatic and the scope of its activities narrow.[35] Nevertheless, the *Mädchenbibelkreise* movement offered its members more than just bible study: like the *Weggenossenkreise*, it included folk dancing, hiking and sports in its meetings, *Freizeiten* and rallies.

The *Christdeutscher Bund* differed from the organisations described above in two ways. First, it was a mixed organisation, within which

[30] On the *Mädchenbibelkreise*, see Cordier, *Evangelische Jugend*, pp. 417–421, 662–665; *Handbuch der Inneren Mission*, vol. I, pp. 177–179.
[31] *Handbuch der Inneren Mission*, vol. I, 177; Fischer, *Mädchen in den deutschen Jugendverbänden*, p. 6. The equivalent organization for boys, the *Bund deutscher Bibelkreise*, had a membership in the late Weimar years of around 20,000.
[32] *Handbuch der Inneren Mission*, vol. I, p. 178.
[33] On neo-pietism and its influence on Protestant youth organisations in the early twentieth century, see von Olenhusen, *Jugendreich*, pp. 198–199.
[34] M. Weller, 'Unsere Bundestagung', *Unser Blatt*, vol. 26 (1933), 7/8, p. 117.
[35] Cordier, *Evangelische Jugend*, pp. 664–665.

girls and boys under 18 formed separate groups.[36] Secondly, it identified itself as *bündische Jugend*, and accordingly adhered to the principle of the autonomy of youth ('youth is led by youth'). The *Christdeutsche Jugend* was founded by Leopold Cordier and other young Protestant pastors and theologians in autumn 1921 as a breakaway group from Guida Diehl's *Neulandbund*, an originally all-women group, which had in turn, as we have seen, broken away from the *Evangelischer Reichsverband* in 1917–18. The reason for the break with the *Neulandbund* was Guida Diehl's leadership, which was perceived as authoritarian and out of tune with the principles of the youth movement, while leading the *Bund* too far in a nationalist direction at the expense of its Christian dimension.[37] In 1927 the organisation renamed itself *Christdeutscher Bund*; it remained small and had by 1933 a total of 1,500 members (including male and female members).[38]

The aim of the *Bund* was to link the Lutheran essence of Reformation theology to the ethos of the youth movement. It sought to connect the idea of the responsibility of the individual believer before God with the youth movement principle of self-reliance and 'authenticity'.[39] A major focus of its activities was community education to promote a Christian way of life and youth movement values among young people outside the *Bund*, and to this end it ran courses and camps for young people at its residential centre in the *Jugendburg* Hohensolms, founded in 1924.[40]

Women over 18 did not form a separate section within the *Christdeutscher Bund*, but – under a predominantly male leadership – took part in its general activities and meetings. The 14–18-year-old members, both girls and boys, were organised as distinct sections, initially calling themselves *Jungstreiter* (young warriors or fighters). The debates over this name give some indication of the identity of the *Jungstreiter* girls. 'Whether the girl struggles inwardly and quietly, and the boy on the whole struggles outwardly, that still means they're both young fighters.'[41] 'We girls *particularly* must

[36] On the *Christdeutscher Bund* generally, see Cordier, *Evangelische Jugend*, pp. 580–589; Werner Kindt (ed.), *Dokumentation der Jugendbewegung*. Vol. III: *Die deutsche Jugendbewegung 1920 bis 1933: die bündische Zeit* (Düsseldorf 1974), pp. 574–577.
[37] Cordier, *Evangelische Jugend*, pp. 581–582.
[38] Kindt, *Die deutsche Jugendbewegung 1920 bis 1933*, p. 574.
[39] Cordier, *Evangelische Jugend*, pp. 533–537.   [40] *Ibid.*, p. 589.
[41] Else Ludwig, 'Zum Namen Jungstreiter', *Der Jungstreiter*, vol. 4 (1927), 10 (Ernting 1927), p. 80.

struggle and fight for our girlhood [*um unser Mädchentum*], for the sanctity of German women's honour ... Young fighters in the struggle for German womanhood!'[42] The *Junggstreiter* had a small membership and the largest and most active local girls' groups were in southern Germany.[43]

Despite the differences between the three groupings examined here, their leaders transmitted a number of basically similar messages to the membership through meetings, rallies, journals and newsletters. The connection between Christianity and patriotism was taken as read, the nation being portrayed as a God-given entity. The obligations of a German and a Christian, it was argued, were first and foremost to one's German brothers and sisters, and took precedence over duties towards mankind as a whole. Leaders and activists purveyed a version of recent German history as a catastrophe for Christian values and for the nation. A participant at a seminar organised in May 1919 by Adelheid Crome (founder of the *Weggenossen*) was told that 'you German girls must now above all love your Fatherland like a child loves its sick mother'.[44] A decade later, those readers of *Jugendweg* who had been too young to experience the revolutionary aftermath of the war were reminded of that era: 'Fatherland, freedom, government, law became concepts which could be interpreted one way one day and another the next ... the great mass of people threw themselves into dancing and a dizzying round of licentious pleasures. It was as if the gates of hell had opened. Where, now, was God?'[45]

Responding to the national crisis was, in the view of Protestant girls' leaders, a task for women as well as men. The granting of legal equality to women underlined their new responsibilities. A former leader of the *Mädchenbibelkreise* recalled the changes accompanying the founding of the Republic: 'With the new era came issues which directly affected the nation as a whole and the individual, and affected men and women equally: the technological age, Americanisation, Bolshevism, nationalism, marriage reform, the economic question. And in all of this the Christian, and the Christian woman

[42] Friedel Schneider, in 'Zur Aussprache', *Jungstreiter-Rundbrief der Mädels* (*JRM*) (1930), 5 (im Gilbhard 1930), 4.
[43] Lotte Brüggemann, 'Liebe Elisabeth Schmidt ... ', *JRM* (1931)1 (im Hartung 1931), p. 12.
[44] Grete Schemann, *Vierzig Jahre evangelische Jugendarbeit: Ein Weg zur deutschen Gegenwart* (Berlin 1933), p. 12.
[45] Erna Schatter, 'Aus der Zeit der Not', *Jugendweg*, vol. 11 (1930), 1, pp. 5–6.

too, found themselves more or less having to tread new ground [*Neuland*].'[46] Protestant women leaders had not wanted the vote and had not campaigned for it, but now that it was there Protestant organisations urged young women to use it along with their new legal equality to make their contribution to the defense of Christian values and the idea of the nation.[47] The supreme task and duty of women had always been to serve others, above all within the family. Now, it was argued, in these disorderly, bewildering and degenerate times, young Christian women would also have to serve through the wider sphere of political and public life.[48]

From readers' letters and reports in the journals and newsletters, it is clear that at least part of the attraction of being a *Weggenosse*, or a *Jungstreiter*, or a member of a bible study circle, was its programme of 'constructive leisure' which had little to do with political and moral duties. Belonging to such a group meant getting away from the family and being with one's peers. 'The family is where nothing happens – that's what a lot of members think about the family', observed a contributor to a journal of the *Mädchenbibelkreise*.[49] The organisations also offered opportunities for sports, skiing trips, hiking, and longer excursions to new places, often linked to travelling to national rallies. The chairwoman of the *Mädchenbibelkreise* made a special point in her portrait of the organisation for the youth organisations' journal *Das junge Deutschland* of mentioning that the national meetings for schoolgirls were held in attractive and historic cities such as Danzig and Dresden; Protestant girls proved enthusiastic tourists.[50]

At the same time, there are signs that ordinary members did concern themselves with the political and moral goals identified by the leaders of their organisations, albeit to varying degrees. In the case of the schoolgirls in the *Jungstreiter* and the *Mädchenbibelkreise*, there is, admittedly, little evidence of members in the 1920s directly

[46] Magdalena Muntschick, 'Zeitschrift und Bewegung', *Unser Blatt* (1932), 1, p. 9.
[47] On Protestant women's responses to the introduction of women's suffrage, see Doris Kaufmann, *Frauen zwischen Aufbruch und Reaktion. Protestantische Frauenbewegung in der ersten Hälfte des 20. Jahrhunderts* (Munich, Zürich 1988), p. 66; Jochen-Christoph Kaiser, *Frauen in der Kirche* (Düsseldorf 1985), pp. 106–109.
[48] Anna Mayer, 'Eine unserer Aufgaben in der Politik', *Jugendweg*, vol. 1 (1920), 5, p. 37; A. Mayer, 'Der Wirklichkeitssinn bei der Wahl', *Jugendweg*, vol. 1 (1920), 11, pp. 84–85; Julius Richter, 'Rüste zu schwerer Arbeit', *Jugendweg*, vol. 11 (1930), 16, pp. 121–122.
[49] Hilde Freytag, 'Abend in der Familie', *Der helle Schein*, vol. 8 (1932), 9, p. 125.
[50] Magdalene Fritzsche, 'Deutscher Bund der Mädchen-Bibel-Kreise', *Das junge Deutschland*, vol. 24 (1930), 9 (special issue, *Mädchenerziehung in den Jugendverbänden*), p. 431.

engaging with questions of politics and public life, but they seem to
have taken their moral mission to the *Volk* seriously enough. In the
case of the *Jungstreiter*, their 'struggling and fighting' in the 1920s
took place above all on the cultural battlefield. This meant standing
up for German culture against 'degenerate Western civilisation',
embodied in the taste of their classmates for bobbed hair, alcohol,
popular hit songs and American dances.[51] 'It revolts me', complained a *Jungstreiter* faced with the prospect of how her classmates
were planning to amuse themselves on a Rhine steamer excursion.[52]
Readers debated whether or not she should go or stay at home and
spare herself the experience.[53]

By contrast, a more direct interest in political questions was
evident among *Weggenossen* members, whose exchange of views took
place in contributions and queries to the journal *Jugendweg* in the
course of the 1920s. The questions they raised were wide ranging.
Should a woman today, having gained full political rights, force
herself to read the newspaper and overcome her antipathy to party
politics? Was it possible to distinguish between concern with the fate
of the Fatherland and an interest in party political debate?[54] What
did it mean to be a German nationalist: did it mean supporting the
German National People's Party? (Or hanging patriotic pictures on
the wall?)[55] Did women have a special mission in politics? What did
the legacy of the feminist movement mean for today's generation of
young women, which 'through the hard-fought achievement of
equal rights has been given an awesome and unprecedented share of
responsibility for the destiny of our people'?[56] It was the final
Weimar years from 1930 onwards, however, which were to push
political issues further up the agenda for the rank and file both of the
Weggenossenkreise and of the other groups.

[51] Anna Steinheil, 'Eine Anfrage an uns alle', *Der Jungstreiter*, vol. 4 (1927), 4 (Lenzing 1927),
  p. 31.
[52] A. Heider, *JRM* (1929), 1 (im Heuert 1929), p. 10.
[53] Responses in *JRM* (1929), 2 (Gilbhard 1929), pp. 11–12, and 3 (Christmond 1929), pp.
  3–7.
[54] 'Steine auf dem Wege' ('Ist es Pflicht, daß wir uns mit Politik beschäftigen?'), *Jugendweg*,
  vol. 4 (1923), 1, p. 8; responses, *Jugendweg*, vol. 4 (1923), 3, p. 24; more responses,
  Jugendweg, vol. 4 (1923), 5, p. 40.
[55] Irmgard Sabardy, 'Nationale Jugendbewegung', *Jugendweg*, vol. 3 (1922), 12, p. 96; Lina
  Jacobi, 'Nationale Jugendbewegung', *Jugendweg*, vol. 3 (1922), 19, p. 153; 'Von Weggenossen' (Henny Werneke's letter), *Jugendweg*, vol. 4 (1923), 7, p. 51.
[56] Elisabeth Neuloh, *Jugendweg*, vol. 4 (1923), 3, p. 24; Lotte Pudor, *Jugendweg*, vol. 4 (1923),
  9, p. 67; quotation from Asta von Fournier, response to Esther von Kirchbach, *Jugendweg*,
  vol. 10 (1929), 10, p. 160.

II

In the final years of the Republic, Protestant youth leaders noticed important changes coming over the rank and file of their organisations. Anna Paulsen, a leading figure in the *Weggenossen* and a teacher at the bible study seminar of the *Evangelischer Reichsverband*, observed in December 1930 that the *Weggenossen* were taking a growing interest in political affairs and social problems.[57] And Adelheid Crome, writing in autumn 1932, noted that discussions at *Weggenossen* meetings were increasingly concerned with women's role in relation to political and national life. 'The girls are gripped by these questions, we see that at the rallies and summer camps.'[58]

Anna Paulsen saw these changes as conditioned partly by young women's daily confrontation with the effects of the Depression. 'A powerful factor in this process is their personal experience of mass poverty and economic crisis, which raises the question of how things could be changed.'[59] As members of the bourgeoisie, they were conscious too of their own precarious economic position. A contributor to one of the MBK journals in late 1932 observed that the 'protective walls around our bourgeois existence are being shaken by the economic crisis, the distinctions of class and education are being levelled'.[60] The crumbling of protective walls or fortifications was an image echoed in a 1932 report by a working group set up by the *Weggenossen* on the theme of 'Serving the *Volk*': 'We have been wrenched out from all the security behind which we had dug ourselves in, from all the things meant to protect us against all the "chance events" of life. The things we used to rely on: ability, a career, good training, wealth, even if one still has them, are no guarantee of anything nowadays.'[61] Middle-class fears were fuelled by growing class conflict and the apparent strength of the organised left. In a 1931 article entitled 'The others', a member of the *Mädchenbibelkreise* reported back on her experience of a Socialist

[57] Anna Paulsen, contribution to survey on politicisation of youth organisations, *Der Zwiespruch*, vol. 12 (1930), p. 3; See also Barbara Thiele, 'Vaterländische Aufgaben der evangelischen Frau innerhalb der Mädchenvereinsarbeit', in Dora Hasselblatt (ed.), *Wir Frauen und die nationale Bewegung* (Hamburg 1933), pp. 51–52.
[58] Adelheid Crome, 'Jugendweg und Kreisarbeit', *Weibliche Jugend*, vol. 41 (1932), 10, p. 246.
[59] Anna Paulsen, contribution to survey on politicisation of youth organisations, in *Der Zwiespruch*, vol. 12 (1930), p. 3.
[60] G. Eisel, 'Unsozial?', *Unser Blatt*, vol. 25 (1932), 5, back cover.
[61] 'Bericht des Arbeitskreises "Dienst am Volk": Verantwortung und Dienst der evangelischen Frau', *Jugendweg*, vol. 13 (1932), 6, p. 94.

youth rally. Its demonstration of unity and strength appeared to her as a massive battle cry against the bourgeoisie, sustained, as she now realised for the first time, by 'a whole ideology and a whole culture'. The bourgeoisie, she concluded rather helplessly, had better start doing something about the conditions of the poor and the unemployed before it was too late.[62] Educated young Protestant women felt new sorts of insecurity not only as members of the bourgeoisie, but also as women. The career opportunities which had begun to open up were closing off again.[63] The anti-feminist backlash of the Depression years was taking its toll: sexist complaints that qualified professional women would take away men's jobs added to the pressures on women students.[64] A teacher in her early 30s described in *Jugendweg* the plight of her *Abitur* class, faced with the message from careers advisers: 'all professions overcrowded' and she contrasted their gloomy situation with the opportunities that had been open to her own generation of women.[65]

If personal insecurity was one factor leading young Protestant women to concern themselves more than hitherto with political and social problems, they were also responding as members of youth organisations to the sense of momentum created by 'youth initiatives' of various sorts. These initiatives ranged from practical projects identified with the young generation to the ideological offensive centred on notions of a 'youth front' transforming politics. The idea of youth's mission was picked up in different ways by young Protestant women and their leaders. In the case of the *Weggenossen* leadership, it meant promoting in the pages of *Jugendweg* new political groupings such as the *Christlich-Sozialer Volksdienst*, with its pledge to break the mould of Weimar party politics and to articulate the 'will of the young generation'.[66] In the case of the *Mädchenbibel-*

---

[62] Agnes Strauß, 'Die andern', *Der helle Schein*, vol. 7 (1931), 3, pp. 56–57. According to the report, the rally was organised by the *Sozialistische Arbeiterjugend* (youth organization of the German Social Democratic Party).

[63] Jill Stephenson, *Women in Nazi society* (London 1975), pp. 148–151.

[64] Marieluise Schlüter, 'Die Studentin im neuen Staat', *Jugendweg*, vol. 14 (1933), 7, pp. 103–104. On the campaign against women's education and employment rights in the Depression, see Stephenson, *Women in Nazi society*, pp. 130, 152–154. On the position of women students in the Depression, see Michael Kater, 'Krisis des Frauenstudiums in der Weimarer Republik', *VfSW*, vol. 59 (1972), pp. 207–255.

[65] Helene Rogge, 'Alles überfüllt', *Jugendweg*, vol. 12 (1931), 1, pp. 4–5.

[66] Heinz-Dietrich Wendland, 'Um Staat, Politik und christliche Partei', *Jugendweg*, vol. 11 (1931), 7, pp. 99–102; Adelheid Crome and Anna Paulsen, editorial comment, *Jugendweg*, vol. 13 (1932), 2, pp. 29–30. On the Christlich-Sozialer Volksdienst, see Klaus Scholder, *The Churches and the Third Reich*. Vol. 1: *1918–34* (London 1987), pp. 139–140.

kreise, members were encouraged to seek out their contemporaries on the other side of the ideological and class divide.[67] MBK members undertook fact-finding missions into the alien territory of left-wing youth organisations. However, building bridges and constructing a 'youth front' in the climate of 1932 was easier said than done. One MBK member, having taken part in a Communist study group in 1932, came back alarmed and discouraged by the intellectual rigour, energy and commitment of the young Communists she had encountered. They could argue much better than *Bibelkreis* members, and their experience was much wider: 'What do we really know', she lamented, 'about the brutal misery of a working-class woman's life!' No wonder, she observed, that they were recruiting young people so rapidly: they offered a strong, lively community, a combative style, and an inspiring idea.[68]

An apparently more promising initiative to unite youth of different classes in a miniature *Volksgemeinschaft*, and one which fired the enthusiasm of a great range of youth organisations in the final eighteen months of the Weimar Republic, was the voluntary labour service.[69]

As originally envisaged by groups in the youth movement such as the *Deutsche Freischar*, work camps, set up in an environment removed from the conflicts and corruption of the city, would unite youth of all classes in useful manual labour and inspire a reshaping of society and the state.[70] The Brüning and Papen governments borrowed the rhetoric of the work camp movement to clothe the publicly subsidised voluntary labour service, and the bandwagon of the voluntary labour service gathered momentum throughout 1932.[71]

Though the official programme remained for some time overwhelmingly oriented towards young men, by late 1932 a movement was emerging to develop labour service opportunities for women.[72]

[67] Wally Schreiber, 'Selbstzweck', *Unser Blatt*, vol. 25 (1932), 5, back cover.
[68] 'J.', 'Mitläufer oder Mitkämpfer', *Der helle Schein*, vol. 8 (1932), 4, p. 55.
[69] On the voluntary labour service, see Henning Köhler, *Arbeitsdienst in Deutschland. Pläne und Verwirklichungsformen bis zur Einführung der Arbeitsdienstpflicht 1935* (Berlin 1967); Peter Dudek, *Erziehung durch Arbeit: Arbeitslagerbewegung und Freiwilliger Arbeitsdienst 1920–35* (Opladen 1988); on the female labour service before and after 1933, see Dagmar Morgan, *Weiblicher Arbeitsdienst in Deutschland* (Mainz 1978).
[70] Dudek, *Erziehung durch Arbeit*, pp. 133–168.   [71] *Ibid.*, pp. 178–190.
[72] Morgan, *Weiblicher Arbeitsdienst*, pp. 26–52; Stephenson, *Women in Nazi society*, pp. 84, 103.

Young women from the *bündische Jugend* participated in work camps, organised schemes themselves, and exhorted others to support the movement.[73] Women school-teachers, social administrators and teachers of social work were particularly active in promoting the labour service to their colleagues and juniors through the columns of the professional teaching and social work journals.[74] These enthusiasts presented participation in a labour service scheme, and especially employment as a camp leader, as a way of harnessing the otherwise wasted talents and energy of unemployed newly qualified teachers and social workers.[75] The 'service' aspect of labour service harmonised smoothly with the established and traditional ethos of the 'feminine' caring and educational professions. At the same time, the labour service also promised to break new ground for young women, offering an escape into a new social and physical environment, within which women would have to carve out new roles for themselves and make their mark on the new forms of community life.[76] A member of the committee on labour service set up by the union of women teachers (*Allgemeiner Deutscher Lehrerinnen-Verein*) stressed that the women's labour service involved 'a healthy social adventurism' and required 'pioneers for various sorts of new territory'.[77]

Protestant young women's organisations were quick to promote

[73] On the role of *bündisch* women in organising and promoting work camp initiatives, see Lore Lommel, 'Arbeitslager Pilchowitz', and Magdalene Keil, 'Mädchenarbeitslager Loos', in *Der Boberhauskreis. Rundbrief Nr. 15* (December 1972), pp. 7–10.

[74] 'Aufruf! Auf zum Dienst!', *ADLV-Zeitung*, vol. 49 (1932), 31 (FAD-Sondernummer), p. 359; 'Freiwilliger Arbeitsdienst für Mädchen', *ADLV-Zeitung*, vol. 49 (1932), 31, pp. 360–361. On the feminists' contribution to the debate on women's labour service in the final Weimar years, see Susanne Dammer, *Mütterlichkeit und Frauendienstpflicht. Versuche der Vergesellschaftung 'weiblicher Fähigkeiten' durch eine Dienstverpflichtung (Deutschland 1890–1918)* (Weinheim 1988), pp. 267–268.

[75] Käte Darmer, 'Junglehrer(innen) und FAD. Bericht über das erste Schulungslager für Junglehrer, 5.-27. Juni', in Hohndorf bei Löwenberg (Schlesien), *ADLV-Zeitung*, vol. 49 (1932), 25, pp. 293–294; Lina Wolff, 'Freiwilliger Arbeitsdienst für sozialpädagogische Berufsarbeiterinnen', *Vereins-Zeitung des Pestalozzi-Fröbel-Hauses*, vol. 44 (1932), 179, pp. 20–21.

[76] For a similar argument formulated in relation to women in the *bündische Jugend*, see E. Harvey, 'Serving the *Volk*, saving the nation: women in the youth movement and the public sphere in Weimar Germany', in Larry Eugene Jones and James Retallack (eds.), *Elections, mass politics and social change in modern Germany* (Washington, DC, Cambridge 1992), pp. 214–219.

[77] Hilde Lion, 'Die Zusammenarbeit der Lehrerin und der Fürsorgerin', *Soziale Berufsarbeit*, vol. 12 (1932), 10, p. 119; Hilde Lion, 'Erwerbslos, aber nicht arbeitslos', *ADLV-Zeitung*, vol. 49 (1932), 1, p. 9.

the voluntary labour service programme.[78] In doing so they echoed arguments used elsewhere, but they added their own religious dimension. Labour service would be service not only to the Fatherland, but also to God, and it would bring opportunities for mission work. It was members of the *Mädchenbibelkreise* who made this argument most forcefully. One member, reporting in *Unser Blatt* on her experiences cooking on a men's scheme in Kiel, declared that working together with the unemployed of all classes and backgrounds had overcome ideological division and created the chance to raise religious questions.[79] This view was repeated by another contributor in November 1932, who argued that practical help to the unemployed would pave the way for getting across to them the message that real help could only come from God; perhaps, she speculated, one could persuade them that in God's kingdom nobody need be 'unemployed' at all.[80]

Some youth organisations looked beyond the voluntary labour service to create kinds of community enterprise that would serve the welfare of the nation on a more permanent basis. An idea to which they continually returned was that of agricultural settlement in Germany's underdeveloped rural east. This idea was also taken up by women.[81] Settlement was the topic of the moment for women's organisations of all kinds, declared a woman government official from Stettin in August 1932, who had been instrumental in getting women appointed in the Köslin district of Pomerania as 'settlement assistants'.[82] She and others promoted the idea of agricultural settlement to young women teachers and social workers as a chance to employ, in a new and challenging environment, their special womanly capacity to serve and care for others. Women coming from outside with pedagogical talents could infuse fresh energy into village life organising kindergartens, girls' groups and mothers' circles.[83]

[78] See Anon., *JRM* (1931), 1 (Hartung 1931), pp. 18–19; Lotte Petersen, '"Ostsiedlung" und FAD', *Christdeutsche Stimmen*, vol. 13 (1933), 1/2, p. 29; Anneliese Arndt, 'FAD für Mädchen in Hohensolms', *Christdeutsche Stimmen*, vol. 13 (1933), 3, pp. 52–54.
[79] Agnes Strauß, 'Dienst am Arbeitslosen', *Unser Blatt*, vol. 25 (1932), 9, inside back cover.
[80] Lilly Schütz, 'Freiwilliger Arbeitsdienst und Gemeinde', *Unser Blatt*, vol. 25 (1932), 11, p. 162.
[81] Dammer, *Mütterlichkeit und Frauendienstpflicht*, pp. 269–272.
[82] Änne Sprengel, 'Ländliche Siedlungspflege in Pommern', *Soziale Berufsarbeit*, vol. 12 (1932), 8, pp. 89–92.
[83] 'Tagung über "die volkserzieherische Aufgabe der Frau auf dem Lande und in den Siedlungen"', *ADLV-Zeitung*, vol. 49 (1932), 29, p. 341; Hilde Grünbaum-Sachs, 'Lehrer-

Protestant young women's organisations, too, took up the idea of agricultural settlement.[84] As in the case of the voluntary labour service, the Protestant journals portrayed the task of agricultural settlement with a particular religious slant. Marie-Elisabeth Arlt painted for *Jugendweg* readers a lyrical vision of rural settlement life and domestic piety: 'A modest house ... simply and practically furnished, German craftsmanship ... the young housewife with the delicate features and the work-worn hands a picture of health and of pleasure in her work. The eyes of the children raised expectantly to their father. And the tall man, his face tanned by sun and wind, about to open the holy bible.'[85]

Part of the fascination of the rural settlement issue for youth organisations was its link with the economic and ethnic struggle of Germany's eastern regions. As such, it became an obvious focus for the nationalism and concern with border issues which characterised a wide spectrum of bourgeois youth organisations from the relatively 'liberal' *Deutsche Freischar* to the extreme right. Apart from fuelling the rural settlement movement, a nationally inspired awareness of the 'crisis of the German east' also fed into other 'borderland' youth activities, which snowballed in the final years of the Republic and led to tens of thousands of young people travelling to eastern border areas to see these regions and their problems for themselves.[86]

Young Protestant women became caught up in this movement. An increasingly demonstrative nationalism, typically expressed as outrage at the Versailles settlement, pervaded Protestant girls' organisations after 1930. Writing in the winter of 1932–33, Barbara Thiele noted that the *Evangelischer Reichsverband* had over the past year no longer had to make efforts to inculcate patriotic values into its young women members. On the contrary, the problem now was

innen für Siedlerberatung', *ADLV-Zeitung*, vol. 49 (1932), 18, p. 209; 'Studienfahrt in das Siedlungsdorf Treskow', *Vereins-Zeitung des Pestalozzi-Fröbel-Hauses*, vol. 44 (1932), 182, pp. 17–25; Nohl, 'Die pädagogische Osthilfe', *Die Erziehung*, vol. 7 (1931/2), 8, pp. 456–461.

84 Lotte Petersen, 'Ostsiedlung und Freiwilliger Arbeitsdienst', *Christdeutsche Stimmen*, vol. 13 (1933), 1/2, pp. 28–29; Marie-Elisabeth Arlt, 'Die Scholle: Ein Wort zur Berufsfrage', *Jugendweg*, vol. 13 (1932), 1, p. 13; T. Iffland, 'Siedlungsarbeit im Jahre 1932', *Jugendweg*, vol. 13 (1932), 9, pp. 138–141.

85 Arlt, 'Die Scholle', p. 13.

86 Ernst Bargel, 'Grenz- und auslandsdeutsche Arbeit der jungen Generation', in Will Vesper (ed.), *Deutsche Jugend: Dreißig Jahre einer Bewegung* (Berlin 1934), pp. 237–252; 'Grenzland-fahrten und Auslandsbeziehungen der bündischen Jugend', in Kindt, *Die deutsche Jugend-bewegung 1920 bis 1933*, pp. 1529–1546.

how to cope with the force of the 'national movement' sweeping
through its ranks. 'There is a healthy revulsion against the oppression of our people under foreign rule, a conviction: this cannot go
on, and a will to help build something new.'[87] Items evoking the
'mutilated' Fatherland with its 'bleeding borders' (blutende Grenzen)
and discussing the fate of the German-speaking minorities in
Poland, Denmark and the South Tyrol, the plight of the Saarland
and the problems of East Prussia became increasingly prominent in
Protestant girls' journals and featured in the programmes of semin-
ars and rallies.[88] These concerns could also shape the everyday
rituals of group life. A Jungstreiter newsletter carried a report on one
group's mountain hike in the summer of 1930 in the Bavarian forests
near the Czech border. The girls gathered at the summit for a short
patriotic ceremony: 'after a three-fold "Heil!" to our German compatriots in Bohemia and singing the German national anthem we
began the descent'.[89]

The MBK promoted the cause of 'Germandom under threat' with
particular vigour. Its journals carried reports from members living
in the 'lost lands' of the Memel area and north Schleswig, and a
piece by a Baltic German.[90] In the summer of 1932, the regional
leader of the East Prussian MBK invited members from the rest of
Germany to take part in a fact-finding visit to East Prussia which
would mix patriotic tourism with an adventurous political mission.[91] The focus shifted to the problems of Silesia in October 1932,
when the national conference of schoolgirl members of the MBK was
held in Breslau: the notice advertising the conference urged
members to 'come to us in the hard-pressed East. Give us strength in
the struggle for our Germandom!'[92]

Apart from symbolic demonstrations of solidarity, there were also

[87] Barbara Thiele, 'Vaterländische Aufgaben der evangelischen Frau innerhalb der
    Mädchenvereinsarbeit', in Hasselblatt, Wir Frauen und die nationale Bewegung, pp. 51–52.
[88] Martin Donath, 'Volk ohne Raum', Jugendweg, vol. 12 (1931), 3, pp. 40–43; Martin
    Donath, 'Grenzland und Kreuz', Jugendweg, vol. 14 (1933), 6, pp. 86–88; Rudolf Homann,
    'Eine Reise in den deutschen Osten', Christdeutsche Stimmen, vol. 12 (1932), 4/6, pp. 62–66;
    Pfarrer Eichstädt, 'Reisebrief aus Wolhynien', Der helle Schein, vol. 7 (1931), 9, pp.
    131–135; Anna Lawton, 'Quer durch Deutschland', Unser Blatt, vol. 25 (1932), 1, pp. 5–8.
[89] 'Unsere Ferienfahrt 1930', JRM, 1930, 6 (Neblung 1930), p. 13.
[90] Waltraut Nadolny, 'Umkämpftes Deutschtum', Unser Blatt, vol. 25 (1932), 5, pp. 79–80;
    J. Lorentzen, 'Nordschleswig', Unser Blatt, vol. 25 (1932), 6, pp. 90–92; M. Urban, 'Die
    baltische Lage und ihre Predigt', Unser Blatt, vol. 25 (1932), 5, pp. 77–79.
[91] Gertrud Sagadlo, 'Ostland – Ostfahrt', Unser Blatt, vol. 25 (1932), 4, p. 64.
[92] Der helle Schein, vol. 8 (1932), 6, back cover.

opportunities for more tangible service to the borderlands and struggle for the national cause. From 1929 onwards, a few young women from the MBK took temporary teaching jobs in an adult education college in the *Grenzmark* region near the Polish border, a 'spiritual power station' (*Kraftwerk für Menschenherzen*) supplying 'energy' to Germans living near to the Polish corridor. The women taught courses on German history and politics, promoted German culture and 'gave young Germans the inner strength for their struggle' against Poland and Catholicism.[93]

In the final years of the Republic, young Protestant women were making a twofold discovery of the *Volk*: on the one hand, the discovery of the common German people, their social inferiors, plunged into social misery, and on the other hand the discovery of the downtrodden German people, their compatriots, a nation enslaved by hostile foreign powers. Seeking to locate themselves as young people and as women in relation to the *Volk*, to the movement for new forms of community life and to the national struggle in the east, their organisations became more explicitly political than before. These changes may have made young Protestant women's groups seem to an increasingly politicised younger generation of women more in tune with the times. However, 'politicisation' also exposed the organisations to a new danger, since it opened them up to direct competition with unambiguously political youth groups, above all with those of the National Socialists. Those members of Protestant youth organisations who were most receptive to the 'social' and 'national' message were likely to conclude that it was being proclaimed and practised more radically and effectively elsewhere.

III

After 1930, young women members of Protestant organisations who had been converted to National Socialism began to stir up political debate at group meetings and rallies. By the summer of 1932, according to an organiser from the *Evangelischer Reichsverband*, 'there was no group in which the national question did not bring upheaval, no summer camp and no rally which did not discuss topics such as "Christians and National Socialism", "Our attitude to National

---

[93] Hilde Freytag, 'Eine Grenzland-Volkshochschule', *Der helle Schein*, vol. 7 (1931), 12, p. 192.

Socialism", "May we wear the swastika alongside the badge of our *Verband?*" and so on'.[94]

Nazi sympathisers indicated a range of motives for their conversion. For the anonymous contributor to a *Weggenossen* working party newsletter on 'Serving the people', it was the National Socialist promise to enhance the status of women in the home and to make it easier for women to marry and have children.[95] For Erna Schatter, a *Weggenosse* old enough to have experienced as a young woman Germany's defeat and the revolution, it was Nazism's onslaught on the alleged corruption and incompetence of the Republic's politics and on the decadence of Weimar culture, its passionate nationalism, and its unswerving pursuit of the 'politics of the impossible'. In her version of Nazism, its religious dimension was clear: 'where there is faith', she declared, 'all is possible'.[96] For the *Jungstreiter* Elisabeth Schmidt, a Bayreuth schoolgirl, Nazism's appeal lay in a variety of factors: its radical nationalism (her own nationalism had been fired by a holiday in France),[97] its social egalitarianism, which contrasted with the social exclusivity of the *Christdeutscher Bund*[98] and its sense of the mission of youth. 'We are the young generation on whom the legacy of the two million dead now rests', she told an audience of *Jungstreiter* girls at a rally in the summer of 1931.[99] What she had found in the Nazi movement was comradeship, hard work and asceticism, and she emphasised that the comradeship between the sexes among young party workers was entirely pure. Thoughts of the opposite sex, of marriage and family were banished for the duration of the struggle; only once the Third Reich had come about could such thoughts be permitted.[100]

Nazi enthusiasts encountered some criticism from their fellow members in Protestant groups. A student member of the *Christdeutscher Bund* reproached pro-Nazi *Jungstreiter* for neglecting the interests of other nations and damaging the cause of peace.[101] A debate with a Nazi speaker in June 1932 brought the condemnation by a group of women members of the *Christdeutscher Bund* of Nazi

[94] Thiele, 'Vaterländische Aufgaben der evangelischen Frau', p. 51.
[95] 'Aus dem Rundbrief. Arbeitskreis I', *Jugendweg*, vol. 13 (1932), 3, pp. 45–47.
[96] Erna Schatter, 'Zu: Volk ohne Raum', *Jugendweg*, vol. 12 (1931), 4, p. 56.
[97] Elisabeth Schmidt, 'Zur Aussprache', *JRM* (1930), 5 (Gilbhard 1930), p. 7.
[98] Elisabeth Schmidt, speech to Klausenmühle meeting, summer 1931, reproduced in *JRM* (1931), 5 (Christmond 1931), p. 17.
[99] *Ibid.*, p. 18.   [100] *Ibid.*
[101] Ria Jost to E. Schmidt, *JRM* (1930), 6 (Neblung 1930), pp. 9–12.

notions of 'racial fitness', and an affirmation of the right to life of the handicapped child.[102] For many *Weggenossen* as well as *Christdeutsche*, the fundamental issue appeared to be whether National Socialism put the *Volk* and the race above God; given the efforts of the Nazi movement in the final stage of its quest for governmental power to affirm its basic conformity with Christianity, this question caused much soul-searching.[103]

Meanwhile, as the debates continued, converts to Nazi ideas were deserting their Protestant groups. It is hard to tell how substantial this loss of members was, though it is clear that organisers and leaders were alarmed. A much-quoted estimate by Udo Smidt, leader of the male *Bibelkreise*, put support among male *Bibelkreis* members in 1931 for National Socialism at around 70 per cent.[104] Cordier, leader of the *Christdeutscher Bund*, cited this estimate and warned that 'the young people who counted' were turning their backs on Protestant organisations.[105] A member of the *Christdeutscher Bund*, writing a few days after the Nazi takeover in 1933, observed that 'our *Jungstreiter* group has dwindled rather in size, since a number of girls have left and have gone to political youth groups, BDM, etc.'.[106] In the summer of 1932, a leading *Weggenosse* remarked that 'the lively and able young pupils' from the academic secondary schools (*höhere Schulen*), 'are for the most part striving to join the *völkisch* movement and the political youth organisations'.[107]

A detailed account of how the young women's organisations examined here reacted to the Nazi takeover and to Nazi policy towards Protestant youth organisations during the first year of the regime would be beyond the scope of this essay. However, some trends can be outlined briefly. The period between January and December 1933 were months of uncertainty for Protestant youth

---

[102] Anneliese Arndt, 'Die Stellung der Frau in der Gemeinschaft. Bericht über die Hohnsolmser Arbeitstagung vom 4.-5. Juni 1932', *Christdeutsche Stimmen*, vol. 12 (1932), 10/11, p. 151.

[103] Gertrud Willms, '"Dienst am eigenen Volk" (Bericht. Arbeitskreis I)', *Jugendweg*, vol. 12 (1931), 4, p. 60; Anneliese Arndt, 'Die Stellung der Frau', *Christdeutsche Stimmen*, vol. 12 (1932), 10/11, p. 152.

[104] For Smidt's estimate, see Scholder, *Churches and the Third Reich*, vol. 1, p. 131.

[105] Leopold Cordier, 'Zur gegenwärtigen Lage der evangelischen Jugendarbeit', *Evangelische Jugendführung*, vol. 3 (1931), 3, pp. 68, 70. On Cordier's fears concerning the support for National Socialism among Protestant youth, see von Olenhusen, *Jugendreich*, pp. 175–176.

[106] T. Klein to Ella Nassauer, 3 February 1933. ADJB, Akte A2–124/6.

[107] Martha Voigt, 'Die Arbeit an der Jugend höherer Schulen', *Weibliche Jugend*, vol. 41 (1932), 7/8, p. 177.

organisations. Politically divided after their initial, predominantly positive reaction to the Nazi takeover, and confused by the speed of events, Protestant youth leaders struggled to find an appropriate response to a regime which at first led them to believe that Protestant youth organisations might retain their autonomy alongside the Hitler Youth.[108] Such hopes were dashed when, in December 1933, in line with an agreement signed against the protests of Protestant youth leaders between *Reichsbischof* Müller and Reich Youth Leader von Schirach, the Protestant youth organisations affiliated to the *Evangelisches Jugendwerk* were ordered to incorporate all their members under the age of 18 into the Hitler Youth.[109] The agreement destroyed the autonomy of Protestant youth organisations; thereafter, Protestant youth was allowed a separate identity only in the form of parish-based groups which were not to organise sports or other leisure activities.

During these months, the girls' organisations and their leaders seem to have veered between a sense of being on history's winning side, following the victory of radical nationalist politics and the apparent restoration of Protestant Christianity as a pillar of state power, and a sense of weakness and impending defeat confronted with the battalions of the Hitler Youth. Reports on the Whitsun 1933 rally of the *Mädchenbibelkreise* in Wernigerode portrayed a membership at one with the nation and united as never before. Members cheered the announcement of a uniform, introduced for the first time to underline the strengthening of the collective spirit; they *marched* (another innovation) up to the castle, and on the hilltop sang a psalm, cheered the Fatherland and the *Führer*, and finished with the national anthem 'with right arms and hearts uplifted'.[110] In contrast to this picture of confidence and enthusiasm, a few months later an ex-leader of the MBK was writing a long and tortured article for the membership which expressed doubts and fears about the role of Protestant girls and women in the new state. 'Do we really have a mission in the *Volk*?' she asked. 'We schoolgirls from *höhere Schulen*? At this moment in the history of our *Volk*?'[111] Similar questions were being asked in the course of the summer by the young

---

[108] Johannes Jürgensen, *Die bittere Lektion. Evangelische Jugend 1933* (Stuttgart 1984), pp. 28–36; Scholder, *Churches and the Third Reich*, vol. 1, pp. 573–574.
[109] Scholder, *Churches and the Third Reich*, vol. 1, pp. 574–578.
[110] M. Schetelig, 'Unsere Missionsbundestagung 1933', *Der helle Schein*, vol. 9 (1933), 6, pp. 116–119; M. Weller, 'Unsere Bundestagung', *Unser Blatt*, vol. 26 (1933), 7/8, p. 118.
[111] Magdalene Muntschick, 'Mädels im neuen Staat', *Der helle Schein*, vol. 9 (1933), 10, p. 148.

women in the *Christdeutscher Bund* and its *Jungstreiter* groups.[112] A discussion at the Wülzburg rally for *Jungstreiter* in August 1933 considered whether the *Jungstreiter* could still justify their existence as an organisation. One suggestion was to give up as a separate organisation and to join the BDM:'we can help the girls there to find the forms of group life they are seeking and we can influence them with the spirit of our group'.[113] Others disagreed and wanted to carry on as a separate organisation: younger members out of loyalty to the organisation, older members out of scepticism about their power to influence the BDM if they were to join it.[114] But in the end, once the fate of the organisation was sealed, the *Jungstreiter* leader Ella Nassauer still appealed to members to try and bring their message to the masses: 'there will always be some in the BDM whom you can interest in religious questions'.[115]

IV

The women in Protestant youth groups formed only a tiny segment of their age cohort; the organisations which have been examined here were small and socially exclusive; they were conscious of being set apart from the mass. In the final years of the Weimar Republic their membership was not expanding and the organisations appeared to be reacting to developments rather than shaping them. What significance, then, can these organisations and their membership have for a consideration of generational formation or generational identity among young women in Weimar Germany?

This essay has argued that, in the final years of the Weimar Republic, the members of Protestant young women's organisations became increasingly aware of the gulf separating them from the *Volk* and increasingly concerned to bridge it. The Depression, mass youth unemployment, escalating political conflict, and the mobilisation of young people by National Socialism became inescapable realities even for the most sheltered middle-class girl or young woman.

Generational ideology and youth-based initiatives provided one

---

[112] The *Christdeutscher Bund* decided at its Whitsun rally in 1933 on a merger with the *Bund Deutscher Jugendvereine* to form the *Bund Christdeutscher Jugend*. D. Toboll, 'Die Christdeutsche Jugend (Christdeutscher Bund)', in Kindt, *Die deutsche Jugendbewegung 1920 bis 1933*, pp. 574–575.

[113] 'Die Bayreuther', 'Freizeit der Jungstreiter auf der Wülzburg', *JRM* (1933), 4 (Scheiding 1933), p. 17.

[114] *Ibid.*   [115] Ella Nassauer, editorial, *JRM* (1934), 2 (Ostermond 1934), p. 12.

framework within which young Protestant women could express their new-found awareness of the *Volk* and their desire to reach out beyond the confines imposed by class and ideological barriers. Ideas propagated by spokesmen of the youth movement about a united front of youth to combat the crisis inspired young Protestant women to try and forge links to young people in different ideological camps. When young Protestant women took part in a Communist study group, or considered the merits of joining the BDM to take their message there, they were reaching out beyond the well-defined community of their own organisation to seek contact with others within their peer group. As they sought to develop programmes of political and social action, Protestant young women's organisations adopted initiatives launched by other youth groups which aimed to mobilise the energies of youth in the national cause. The ideas of labour service, of rural settlement and of the national struggle in the east were on the agenda across the spectrum of bourgeois youth organisations. Protestant young women's groups, like other youth organisations at the time, were thus responding to ideas which were 'in the air', which were transmitted from one group to another, and given a particular nuance by each group according to its ideological stance.

Ideologies of gender provided an additional framework within which young Protestant women expressed their desire to dedicate themselves to national goals. The young educated women who belonged to the Protestant organisations examined here sought opportunities in the final Weimar years to demonstrate a special female competence in the spheres of culture, welfare and pedagogy. This competence could serve to justify a role for women in the public as well as the private sphere, notwithstanding the attacks on women's rights by right-wing parties in the Depression. Here, too, the numerically insignificant Protestant young women's organisations appear to have been part of a wider trend among educated young middle-class women in the Depression years. In taking up concepts such as 'service' (*Dienst*), 'struggle' (*Kampf*) and the search for new 'space' or 'territory' (*Raum*), Protestant young women were taking up slogans which were becoming current among other women's groups in the *bündische Jugend* and among groups of young professional women such as teachers and social workers. These slogans, associated with projects such as social work in new rural settlements, or with pedagogical projects in Germany's eastern border lands, appeared to guarantee to qualified young women who faced reduced chances on the job market an adventurous and active role within new environments, alongside men but not competing with them, performing tasks consistent with safe and comfortable notions of femininity while breaking new ground in a literal and metaphorical sense.

In the final years of the Republic, young Protestant women in the organisations described here grasped at opportunities to merge with the trends of the moment, to join in the national 'mission of youth', and to find their place within the national community as young women. This urge to identify with broadly based generational initiatives, and beyond them with a restored and idealised *Volksgemeinschaft*, was shared by other groups of educated young women.

However, as far as young Protestant women were concerned, their urge to identify with the *Volk* coexisted in some tension with their desire to retain their autonomy as organisations with a religious basis and, setting themselves apart from the mass, to assert their distinct identity as Christians in a godless world. For a moment, in early 1933, it seemed that these contradictions were resolved: as young Protestant women, they were at last marching in step with the youthful masses both for Germany and for God. The causes and initiatives which as young women they had taken up in the final Weimar years were being supported by the new regime and expanded, promising new opportunities to harness young women's energies. The illusion of harmony, however, was soon shattered. The conflict between loyalty to Christian values and the pull of the national movement was ultimately resolved only by force from the new regime.

CHAPTER 10

The Hitler Youth generation and its role in the two post-war German states

Alexander von Plato

The term 'Hitler Youth' conjures up images of a paramilitary organisation turning boys into men – 'hard as Krupp steel and quick as lightning'. And the girls, so the cliché would have it, were educated to be good German mothers, happy within their domain of home and hearth, a domain subordinate to the larger world of men just as the League of German Girls (BDM) was a subdivision of the larger organisation of the Hitler Youth (HJ). That, at any rate, is the conventional picture. But such a crude caricature tells us little about the real experiences of the millions of boys and girls who were members of the HJ or about the significance of those experiences for shaping social behaviour and attitudes in the two post-war German states.

How, then, did the almost nine million boys and girls in the HJ and BDM[1] experience the Nazi youth organisations? Accounts of the period tend to dwell on 'camp fire romanticism', on the appeal of a 'youthful community', on sport and games, sometimes on paramilitary drill or political education. Only rarely do they tell us whether the HJ was accepted or rejected by its members. Until very recently, the historiography of the Third Reich neglected such central questions as what in retrospect was seen as positive or negative in the HJ. How did the HJ generation subsequently interpret and deal with the experiences of those years? How did those experiences shape their subsequent lives and, through them, the society in which they lived? In other words, what did it mean for the two post-war Germanies that an entire generation had gone through the experience of the *Jungvolk* (DJ – the 10–14-year-olds section of

Translated by Mark Roseman. For reasons of space, some longer interview extracts in the original German text have not been included in the translation.

[1] In 1939 8.7 million of the 8.87 million 10–18-year-olds were enrolled in HJ or BDM, used here as a generic term to include the *Jungmädel*.

the HJ), the HJ or the League of German girls, or had spent time in the Reich labour service or the girl's labour year? And not just *any* generation – it was this generation, after all, whose energy, zeal and loyalty was to be decisive in reconstructing East and West Germany after the war.

During the last ten years or so, the recognition that these questions were not being answered in the conventional literature stimulated a number of historians to turn to oral history, in particular to life-history interviews, in which Germans of the HJ generation were asked about their experiences in the Third Reich.[2] The present essay is an attempt to distil from this work, and in particular from the projects in which the author was personally involved,[3] a number of hypotheses with respect to the nature and impact of the HJ experience.

I

On the basis of these oral histories we can provisionally divide the HJ generation (the generation of Germans born between 1919 and 1931) into three broad groups: the large group of *Durchmogler*, i.e. the pragmatists and opportunists who went with the flow, sticking out neither one way nor the other; the small group of opponents who roundly rejected the HJ; and the medium-sized group of the

---

[2] Amongst many other bibliographies and surveys see Peter Alheit, Wolfram Fischer-Rosental and Erika M. Hoerning, *Biographieforschung. Ein zwischenbilanz in der Soziologie* (Bremen 1990); Karin Hartewig, 'Oral history in Germany', in *BIOS. Zeitschrift für Biographieforschung und Oral History* (special issue on the 7th International oral History Conference 1990); Bernd Parisius and Franz-Josef Brüggemeier, *Ergebnisse einer Erhebung über Bestände und laufende Projekte zur Oral History in der Bundesrepublik* (Hagen 1983); Gerhard Paul and Bernhard Schossig (eds.), *Die andere Geschichte. Geschichte von unten. Spurensicherung, ökologische Geschichte, Geschichtswerkstätten* (Cologne 1986); Alexander von Plato, 'Oral History als Erfahrungswissenschaft. Zum Stand der "mündlichen Geschichte" in Deutschland', *BIOS*, vol. 1 (1991).

[3] These comprised a number of surveys conducted from Essen and Hagen University. See Lutz Niethammer (ed.), *'Die Jahre weiß man nicht, wo man die heute hinsetzen soll.' Faschismuserfahrungen im Ruhrgebiet* (Berlin, Bonn 1983); Lutz Niethammer (ed.), *'Hinterher merkt man, daß es richtig war, daß es schiefgegangen ist'. Nachkriegserfahrungen im Ruhrgebiet* (Berlin, Bonn 1983); Lutz Niethammer and Alexander von Plato (eds.), *'Wir kriegen jetzt andere Zeiten.' Auf der Suche nach der Erfahrung des Volkes in nachfaschistischen Ländern* (Berlin, Bonn 1985); Nori Möding and Alexander von Plato, 'Siegernädeln. Jugendkarrieren in BDM und HJ', *Schock und Schöpfung* (1986); Nori Möding and Alexander von Plato, 'Nachkriegspublizisten. Ein Erfahrungsgeschichtliche Untersuchung', in Peter Alheit and Erika M. Hoerning (eds.), *Biographisches Wissen. Beiträge zu einer Theorie lebensgeschichtlicher Erfahrung* (Frankfurt, New York 1989), pp. 38–69; Lutz Niethammer, Alexander von Plato and Dorothee Wierling, *Volkseigene Erfahrung. Eine Archäologie des Lebens in der Industrieprovinz der DDR* (Berlin 1991); Alexander von Plato and Wolfgang Meinicke, *Alte Heimat - neue Zeit. Umgesiedelte, Vertriebene und Flüchtlinge in der SBZ und DDR* (Berlin 1991).

enthusiasts, who took the movement and its ideals whole-heartedly on board. However, as soon as one tries to allot particular individuals to one or other group, it becomes clear that these are at best ideal-typical categories. They cannot do justice to a reality that was far more confused and ambivalent. In most accounts positive and negative perceptions exist side by side; for example, individual positive memories may exist with a broader recognition of the horrific shadow side of National Socialist rule. And as the life that was being related changed course in this or that direction, our respondents often shifted their perception of the past. So what conclusions *can* we draw about the HJ experience?

It is worth noting at the outset that the interviews reveal very similar perceptions among respondents from both East and West Germany. In oral histories from both sides of the former border, positive experiences of the Nazi years coexisted with more negative memories and judgements. More than that, the myths and images which surfaced about the Third Reich – Hitler building the autobahns or putting an end to unemployment; the image of a happy, carefree youth and its ostensible ignorance, or at best half-knowledge about the concentration camps, and so on, were the same whether the respondent was from the FRG or the former GDR.

Among many positive features, interviewees mentioned that the HJ and BDM helped youngsters discover new regions and places. Camping trips, day hikes, sporting competitions in other regions, the special child evacuation programmes to 'bomb-free' areas during the war, and the various compulsory labour schemes, all increased the geographical mobility of German youth.

Perhaps the most important positive experience was the fact that socially, too, the HJ and other institutions helped youngsters discover new territory. Because the HJ aspired to bridge class barriers, many of its members were able to meet youngsters or adults from different backgrounds and thus break out of their own milieus. Ambitious HJ members could rise up through the ranks. Sometimes working-class children found themselves in authority over youngsters with a grammar-school background. Those who performed well in the HJ might well also find their social mobility enhanced outside the organisation. A good HJ record could open up opportunities for youngsters whose parents' social status would in the past have denied them much chance of advancement. For example, successful HJ members might be able to get into one of the National

Socialist political academies or into a better school; they might be able to obtain an apprenticeship in a sought after occupation or gain entry into a white-collar profession. For many youngsters, the old adage from the working-class milieu of the 1920s 'them up on top, us down below', no longer seemed to fit.

The HJ also encouraged youngsters to take on positions of leadership and responsibility. At some time or other almost all boys and girls took on some office or higher rank, be it in the DJ or the HJ. Those who joined the *Jungvolk* as 10-year-olds, for example, moved in only their second year into positions of seniority over the new entrants. Thus the old youth movement principle that 'youth should be led by youth' became a reality for many young people. Those promoted received new badges and insignia as marks of their authority. The chevrons and frogging were highly important for the self-esteem of those involved, And, again, outside the HJ, too, the uniform or the higher rank brought recognition. Many of our interview partners mentioned the fact that when you wore the uniform you 'were somebody' and could not just be dismissed as a child.

Many of the respondents – and not just the enthusiasts – dwelt on the fact that they had been involved in useful and socially meaningful activity. They helped on farms or in land reclamation or collected metal for recycling; they looked after elderly members of the community, collected for the Nazis' 'winter help scheme', knitted for the poor or sent parcels to soldiers at the front. Because of the blanket condemnation of the HJ in the post-war period, our interviewees were at pains to emphasise this positive useful side. Respondents of both sexes believed that their HJ activities had been a lot more worthwhile than the activities of modern youth who 'just hang around outside discos' and did nothing useful.

In this context the HJ generation also argued that there had been a stronger 'social side' to National Socialism than later generations and most outsiders have been willing to acknowledge. Such things as the training competitions, for example, the fact that there were no school fees for the poor, the introduction of coeducation, competitions for the most social factory or more generally working for 'the community' were cited as examples.

Sometimes what emerged as the positive features of the HJ were simple facts such as the opportunity for young adolescents to meet members of the opposite sex and to enjoy a certain amount of freedom from the prudish moral codes of the parental household. For many children from strictly religious households, an important part of their experience was the fact that the anti-clericalism of the National Socialist movement helped strengthen their own resistance to parental values. They looked favourably on the removal of the confessional schools and the introduction of coeducation, and found it easier to resist regular church-going. However, the accounts here are contradictory. Some criticised the 'fanatics' in the HJ who arranged meetings on Sundays deliberately so that the youngsters could not go to church; others, however, recalled a more cautious policy from HJ leaders who, after some initial radicalism, kept Sunday mornings free so that church-going was possible – something which the youngsters themselves were not always keen on. The different levels of personal religious conviction clearly helped to shape the different perceptions of the movement here.

Another important point which has now become well established in the historical literature is that despite the official National Socialist ideology on woman's role in society, girls and young women in the youth movement gained new experiences and responsibilities very much outside the domestic sphere. The experience of exercising authority within the organisation collided with the official image of women as mothers, tied to church, children and the chip-pan.

Politically the HJ enjoyed widespread support for its opposition to the Versailles Treaty and to the humiliation of Germany. The Nazis' arguments here were their biggest plus points, followed by their successful war against unemployment.

It is important to note that many of our respondents distanced themselves in their testimonies from these positive features, even if they generally had 'happy memories' of their own youth in the Third Reich. And most, including many who did not belong to the category of the HJ's opponents, also had more negative experiences and assessments to relate.

One common criticism was that the HJ's activities often encroached on time our respondents would rather have spent with their families. Many would have preferred to stay at home rather than go along to drill practice, were dragged off on hiking trips unwillingly or were homesick during their evacuation. This might at first sight seem a rather unpolitical criticism, but in fact it raises issues that lay at the heart of the regime's claims on the individual. What was involved, after all, was a conflict between family and state, between the private and public sphere. And there was also the issue of the alienation between parents and children. Parents were often very guarded about revealing their views to their children, for example on political matters; for their part, some youngsters were critical of the 'hypocrisy' of their parents, although in retrospect they were often more forgiving once they understood more about the real nature of the National Socialist system.

Another closely related criticism raised by many ex-HJ members – and again by no means purely those openly hostile towards HJ – was that the continual meetings and assignments intruded into other aspects of their private life, school work, for example, or studying for their apprenticeship. Others would rather have spent time with the new girl or boy friend than gone along to yet another HJ or BDM meeting, or would have preferred to go to church rather than to the sports tournament. Some resolved the conflict between different demands on their time by doing the bare minimum required, and abiding by the principles 'don't stick your neck out' and 'don't get noticed' – principles which were to prove useful later in military service and in the post-war period.

What was being criticised here was often not just the fact that external demands were being made on one's time, but also the actual values and activities to which one was being committed. Bookworms, other hopeless cases on the sports field and the physically handicapped all had to reckon with ridicule and abuse as weaklings. Their negative experience often led them, at least implicitly, to reject the image of manliness embodied by the HJ and with it the emphasis on the body and sporting achievement. The collective appeared as a frightening vehicle for the stronger to impose themselves on the weaker. In response the weaklings devised their own survival strategies – for example, showing achievement in other areas such as in music, or at school.

Children from Christian, pacifist or Socialist/Communist homes in particular rejected the HJ's military drill and training and its idealisation of soldiering, as indeed the cultivation of military traditions at school. They found it hard to endure such rituals as raising the flag, the morning assembly, greeting the teacher with a military report on the presence and absences of the class by the 'platoon commander' (class representative), and the singing of military songs. It was even harder when at home their parents criticised these militaristic rites, in which the children nevertheless had to take part.

Often they did not know what to think, or learned to lead a sort of double life, switching between the values of their parents and those of school and HJ. A few of the respondents experienced the humiliation of having to march behind the others without uniform because their parents had refused to buy or make the HJ outfit. More common were the cases where children begged their parents to provide a uniform for so long that the father or mother finally gave in – perhaps to avoid getting into danger themselves, or to protect their children from taunts that they were too poor even to afford a uniform.

A few had also learned 'something' about the persecution of the Jews, the imprisonment of Communist relatives, euthanasia or sterilisation of the sick – knowledge which led them to adopt a more critical attitude towards other aspects of National Socialism as well.

The experiences and judgements described here were bound to have considerable significance for the later lives of the HJ generation and thus also for the development of post-war German society. To take one obvious example, members of this generation found it very hard to square their experience of the Third Reich with the political reorientation being demanded of them by the Allies. They were particularly alienated by the notion of the collective guilt of all Germans because they felt that they themselves had been deceived by the Nazis and used as cannon fodder. Most had formed, as we have seen, their own complex picture of positive and negative experiences and were now outraged by the blank negative judgement being cast on the Third Reich. Even those who had never regarded themselves as Nazis found that it was no longer permissible to mention even the 'positive things' about the Third Reich without being treated as such. This taboo was even stronger in the East than in the West, although it was soon evident that, at least externally, the new regime organised youth in a similar way to the old one.

II

No matter how the ex-HJ members entered the post-war period – be it returning from the front, from evacuation or from the anti-aircraft battalions – they found the old values were no longer applicable or acceptable. For the *Flakhelfer* generation (the anti-aircraft auxiliaries who gave their name to the later generation of HJ members) the fact that they had been socialised in the HJ only relatively late on in the Third Reich, and had become disillusioned with the regime when still relatively young, meant that they found it comparatively easy to reorientate themselves.[4] For their somewhat older compatriots who had been at the front or had already begun or even completed an apprenticeship, things were more difficult. They felt themselves isolated, confronted by the occupying powers or by an older German establishment which had already held authority in the Weimar Republic. They saw the big and little lies with which the adults fudged their way through the denazification panels[5] and found that the old enemies on the left had suddenly become the new 'untarnished' political leaders – particularly in the East.

This led to different reactions. Some, probably the smaller group, looked for a new clear ideological framework and found it in the organisations and theories of the Socialist movement. Others though rejected all collective and state-sponsored youth organisations. Many resolved never again to join a political party (though this resolve was sometimes abandoned in later life). A common reaction was to reject all statements of high ideals or emotive rhetoric. Many found it hard to accept the new political leaders or indeed a great many features of the emerging post-war system. Interviewees often spoke of their whole world 'falling apart'. They felt that they had been misled and ill used by the Nazis. Particularly in the West (though recent events may have produced a similar reaction in the former GDR) the key lesson drawn by many members of the HJ generation was just how easily the individual can be manipulated.[6] Schelsky's 'sceptical generation' was thus probably more of a disappointed generation than a sceptical-critical one.[7]

In political terms the young men and women of the HJ generation were rather passive. They came to terms with the challenges of the post-war period less by seeking out a new *political* homeland or ideology than by individual and pragmatic responses pursued within the narrow sphere of their lives. This tendency was

[4] Heinz Bude, *Deutsche Karrieren. Lebenskonstruktionen sozialer Aufsteiger aus der Flakhelfer-Generationen* (Frankfurt 1987); Rolf Schörken, *Jugend 1945. Politisches Denken und Lebensgeschichte* (Opladen 1990).
[5] Alexander von Plato, 'Eine zweite "Entnazifizierung"', in Rainer Eckert, Alexander von Plato and Jörn Schütrumpf, *Wendezeiten - Zeitenwände. Zur 'Entnazifizierung' und 'Entstalinisierung'* (Hamburg 1991).
[6] Today, this feeling is very probably widely shared in the GDR as well.
[7] Helmut Schelsky, *Die skeptische Generation* (Düsseldorf 1963, special edition).

undoubtedly encouraged by the sheer difficulty of surviving in the immediate post-war period. When you were worrying about getting enough to eat it was hard to take the world of high politics very seriously. On the other hand it also clearly reflected the way in which this generation had experienced the Third Reich and the lessons it had drawn from that experience.

In fact, the legacy of the HJ experience was ambiguous. On the one hand, the HJ had encouraged many members and particularly those who had taken on significant responsibilities within the movement, to be very active. It had conveyed the powerful experience that for those willing to put in the effort to the collective, the reward could be considerable personal advancement. The dissolution of the HJ consequently left a vacuum in the post-war period that cried out to be filled with new activity.[8] On the other hand, however, the disillusionment with National Socialism led, as we have seen, to a widespread rejection of collective organisations. Certainly many were sceptical about committing themselves to a new political cause. The question, then, was how to apply the energies awakened by the HJ – how to achieve advancement and recognition in the uncertain new world of the post-war period.

The resulting ambivalent outlook was probably extremely significant in explaining the particular pattern of behaviour which emerged in both Germanies after the war. Both societies seem to have been characterised by a willingness to put in enormous effort in return for recognition and personal advancement. At the same time, the question what or who this effort was being expended *for* was of only secondary importance. The lesson the HJ generation drew from the past, then, was *Pflichtbewußtsein*, a willingness to do one's duty, or better *Leistungsbereitschaft*, a willingness to give it everything one had, largely irrespective of whatever state form or political system happened to be in operation at the time.

At the same time, the social side of past experience had not been forgotten. Because they were politically so disillusioned many members of the HJ generation chose to focus their energies on social

---

[8] Alexander von Plato, *'Der Verlierer geht nicht leer aus.' Betriebsräte geben zu Protokoll* (Berlin, Bonn 1984); Nori Möding, '"Ich muß immer engagiert sein – fragen Sie mich bloß nicht, warum." Überlegungen zu Sozialisationserfahrungen von Mädchen in NS-Organisationen', in Niethammer and Von Plato, *'Wir kriegen jetzt andere Zeiten'*, pp. 256–304.

and unpolitical organisations such as the church or the unions.[9] It was in this social sphere that they found or constructed a continuity which legitimated their past activities and established a link between past and present. Later, it is true, many of these activists were to find a new spiritual home in the SPD or CDU, but in the first instance it was the ostensibly unpolitical organisations – the churches, the unions, the Red Cross and so on – which absorbed their energies and established a bridge between the HJ and their later political activity. In working-class areas it was above all the trade union movement which performed this bridging function, allowing the HJ generation to be active but politically neutral. Party-political neutrality was, after all, one of the cornerstones of the post-war German union movement.

This combination of political abstinence with a sort of pre-political or unpolitical activism was characteristic of both West and East Germany. The phrase 'we always did our duty' was by no means restricted to respondents from West Germany. In the GDR, too, the new state was able to draw on the same enormous reserves of energy and commitment and that applied also to women, who were speedily drawn into the production process.

In working-class areas during the Nazi period, many members of the HJ generation saw their Socialist parents run into difficulties with the regime. Later, after 1945, they saw the Nazi notables themselves in similar circumstances, now pleading for the so-called Persil certificates which would give them a whitewash at the denazification tribunal. Thus the reluctance to engage in collective activity was reinforced by the lesson that it was dangerous to put your political beliefs on public view and far safer to adopt a cautious policy of wangling your way through without being noticed. Some may well have learned to use the party card for cold-blooded political and personal advantage – a pattern of behaviour that was far from being restricted to East Germany. But in the West, it does seem as if the majority response of the HJ generation to the challenges and imponderables of the post-war era was to seek out the unpolitical middle ground, rather than to try and extract personal capital by tactically brandishing a new party card.

---

[9] I can still remember my anger when in my interviews former HJ leaders claimed a direct continuity from their social work in the HJ to their activities in the union and the SPD. Today it seems to me that such apparently self-serving, defensive constructions form an

What both East and West Germans of this generation had learned was that hard work and following orders was the best protection against the dangers emanating from the political system. Those who performed conscientiously and well had proved to be the most secure from attacks by the Nazis, from call up to the front, from the various traps of the post-war period or the demands of Germany's rulers – no matter whether they smoked Machorka or Lucky Strike.

It is important to note that the relationship between post-war behaviour and perceptions of the Nazi era was double sided. On the one hand, as we have just seen, the Nazi experience had encouraged the HJ generation to adopt unpolitical individualistic strategies to deal with the post-war era. On the other hand, this approach to life in the post-war era in turn encouraged many Germans to look back on the Third Reich, and particularly its youth organisations, and regard it as a very unpolitical system. Not just former HJ functionaries, but also people whose role in the Third Reich had ranged from that of workers to industrial leaders, from doctors to officers, from members of the German Christian church to officials of the National Socialist welfare organisations all tended in the post-war era to emphasise the 'unpolitical' nature of their activity. This tendency to depoliticise the past acted as a bond of understanding[10] between individuals from very different social classes and backgrounds and with very different roles in the Third Reich.

These observations help to explain the 'community of silence' which emerged in East and West against the Allies and against the new domestic political elites. There was a feeling of having been unjustly deprived by the new elites of the 'good experiences' of the past. At the same time, there was a feeling that no one else had a right to judge the 'bad experiences', and certainly not the émigrés from Moscow and London who had returned to take up the political reins in the post-war era.

They also help us understand the double lives led by citizens of the Soviet Zone and GDR: the difference between public statements and private views had been learned already. Only the political packaging had changed. One of the big mistakes of the GDR leadership was to believe that the public declarations of loyalty manifested a genuine anti-fascist reorientation. In reality, the

essential backcloth to understanding post-war German society, and should not be simply dismissed.

[10] Möding and Von Plato, 'Siegernadeln'.

majority had gone along with the new movement out of fear, for other pragmatic considerations, or perhaps out of a sense of duty or an authoritarian obedience to the state. Right up to 1989, the GDR leadership was to misinterpret what was in reality the post-war equivalent of the Good Soldier Schweik trotting along to the new political tune as a genuine political embrace of their particular brand of anti-fascism.

In the FRG as in the GDR, the experiences, values and norms of the HJ generation collided with those of the new post-war political elites. The latter had for the most part quite different experiences and outlook. Most were stamped by anti-fascism, and many had been in exile, bringing with them a political awareness which dated back to Weimar. Yet they found they could use the values and behaviour of the younger generation they had left behind in Nazi Germany. In the interests of reconstruction, the diligence, energy and desire for personal advancement of the HJ generation, perhaps also their social commitment, and certainly their willingness to adapt and fit into the new social system, all proved invaluable.[11]

III

In the West, the youth amnesty and the possibilities for rapid personal advancement meant that the younger generation's initial insecurity and uncertainty in the post-war period was soon dispensed with in the new certainties of the cold war era. In many respects, the task of confronting the Third Reich was left to a future generation – which then in the 1960s attacked the older generation for its role in the Nazi era.[12]

But what about the Soviet Zone and GDR? Beyond the common characteristics already identified, to what extent did the HJ generation show specific, distinctive patterns of reacting to the past and dealing with the reality of the post-war period?

Let us take the example of Frau T, born in 1923 in a city in Thüringen. We interviewed her when the former GDR was still in existence. Frau T in many ways exemplifies the pattern of 'blind activism' which we have already observed. By the end of the war she was already disenchanted with National Socialism. She found

---

[11] See also Michael Buddrus's essay in this volume.
[12] See Heinz Bude's essay in this volume.

herself alone, many of her friends having been killed or disappeared, and like many women of her generation never married. As a single woman without children it was easy for her to be called in to every kind of activity where help was needed. Recruited into the textile industry in 1947, pressure was applied on her to join the trade union and here she found a ready field of activity to which, as she emphasised, there was a strong cultural and social dimension. Outside the union, too, Frau T worked hard, training to receive the qualification of *Industriekaufmann*. She became the right-hand man of the boss and a member of the plant union leadership. But, like others of her generation, her entry into politics was delayed – she joined the Socialist Unity party (SED) only in 1961 and did not leave the church until 1963, after the death of her parents.

The tendency to be active without being closely involved in the goals or philosophy of the organisations for whom the activity was being carried out, is particularly apparent in the case of the German–Soviet Friendship Society, an organisation which Frau T joined despite having had very negative experiences of Soviet troops during the period of the invasion. But joining the Society was the 'done thing'. In fact, Frau T had difficulty explaining to the interviewer exactly why she had become a member – and this is true also for her attempt to convey why she entered the SED in 1961. What emerges is a pattern of pragmatic adaptation to the path of least resistance, coupled with a desire to be active and a simultaneous habit of subordination to the wishes of the 'leadership' – in this case the firm's management and the party leadership. And, at the end, 'war dann alles in Ordnung'.

A striking example of the fluidity and flexibility of her ideological commitment came when Frau T explained at one stage that she had become a Socialist because of her contact with the proletariat. In the same breath, however, she made clear that the actual manual workers in the factory had been fairly hostile to the ideas of the party and that it was the white-collar workers who had convinced her. When, in the interview, Frau T was alerted to the contradiction she qualified her argument, asserting that perhaps half the workers had been convinced Socialists. And yet, in the same breath, she returned once more to the original theme.

Like many of her contemporaries Frau T praised the social policy of the GDR and criticised the FRG for its lack of compassion, although at the same time complaining about the lack of consumer goods in the East. She also praised aspects of the GDR which in the West were among those most strongly criticised – the sense of order, and the fact that there were so many fewer demonstrations than in the FRG. The relative lack of freedom in the GDR seemed barely an issue for her.

Frau T is by no means an exception. Her attitudes to the party, the relationship between East and West, to the authoritarian regime in the GDR, to the more pronounced role of women or the church correspond to those of many of our respondents. Of course, emphases vary. Some identify more strongly with the HJ, others with the Free German Youth. Some were more traumatised by the defeat and its aftermath than others. Some were taken up more readily by the new state. Whereas in Frau T's account of the negative side of the Third Reich, she had tended to emphasise the racial persecution of the Jews, many other GDR respondents dwelled more on political oppression. GDR respondents were more conscious than Western counterparts of the deaths of millions of Soviet prisoners of war in German hands and of the political persecution of the Communists. The differing patterns of memory here clearly reflected the influence of the occupying powers and political leaderships in the two countries.

Like many, many other interviewees, Frau T emphasised how hard she had worked to help reconstruct the country after the war. Even more than the FRG, the GDR had been dependent on the commitment and effort of its citizens to get the economy going again. Yet at the same time, it was in the Soviet Zone and the GDR that the political reorientation demanded of the Germans was at its crassest. Activity and energy were in demand, but also political subordination and adaptation. Thus it is in the GDR that we find at its best defined the characteristic mixture of political passivity and pragmatism, on the one hand, and a great willingness to make sacrifices and expend enormous effort in the interest of reconstruction, on the other. The problem, of course, was that although the members of this generation were very cautious and reserved in their approach to politics, the new system demanded of them strong formal commitments to its ideals. Again and again in the interviews one heard fine sounding statements of principle which it was clear had little real meaning for the respondents. On the other hand, when they came to talk about their own pragmatic behaviour they sounded thoroughly credible. This contradiction between covert values and actual behaviour must have been a source of real strain not just to the society of the GDR but also to the individuals themselves.

The SED leadership seems to have recognised early on that in order to reconstruct East Germany successfully, it was going to have to take every qualified person without worrying too much about their former commitment to National Socialism. Conversely, the HJ generation had to learn to accept the defining conditions of post-war society – Soviet dominance, division of Germany, SED rule.

This is the key to what I would call a 'covert conservative alliance' between the new leadership, which wanted to rebuild the country after the ravages of war, and anyone who was willing to get stuck in and wanted to improve their personal circumstances. The leadership offered upward mobility to new positions of authority and prestige and demanded in return acceptance of the post-war conditions. Those who responded to this invitation offered in return an energetic commitment to the project of reconstruction and quiet support for the regime, seasoned with not a little pragmatism. The alliance was covert in the sense that the ideological differences between political leadership and its mobile, pragmatic following were never openly stated. Instead, an illusion of unity was demonstrated through anti-fascist and Socialist rituals. It was conservative in that what it emphasised was economic performance and effort, upward mobility, adaptation and obedience – values which amounted to anything but the 'new Socialist individual' who figured so prominently and so misleadingly in the GDR's reconstruction literature. Nevertheless, there *was* scope for many of the social aims which the HJ generation felt they had brought with them from their Nazi days to be revived. And indeed, there is little doubt that the experiences in the HJ played a considerable role in helping to create the social climate of the GDR.

Particularly after the migration of millions of qualified workers and bourgeois elites to West Germany, the GDR became a society of upward mobility and retraining on a massive scale. There was virtually no one among our interviewees who had not at some point after gaining their initial professional qualification gone back to do further training and gain a further qualification or even gone back into higher education.

The, perhaps more familiar, story of the FRG offers many parallels.

In the West just as in the East we find the dominance of the individual perspective – with an emphasis on personal advancement, a willingness to work hard and a strong awareness in the post-war era of the need to rebuild the country's economy. And, again as in the East, this economic drive was tempered with a strong social ideology which added social welfare elements to the principles of the capitalist market economy. The National Socialist era was increasingly shrouded in silence, as the cold war, with its battle against left-wing totalitarianism, allowed past involvement in right-wing totalitarianism to be forgotten. The 1960s then saw bitter challenges to this conservative side of the reconstruction process.

IV

In the Federal Republic economic success was a key precondition for the acceptance of the new state. In the GDR, by contrast, economic success was always precarious. At the beginning of the 1970s, Honecker pushed for greater economic success and a greatly expanded welfare state. Honecker's strategy collapsed in the 1980s as the SED state lumbered into bankruptcy. What this meant was that it was increasingly difficult to extend the covert alliance to the next generation. As the benefits of the SED's policies came to seem more fragile and endangered, as the possibilities for upward mobility became more limited, as the economic situation became more catastrophic, the younger generation turned against the system which their parents had helped to construct. Even before the construction of the Berlin wall this was evident in the huge numbers of qualified youngsters who fled to the West.

In retrospect, the short phase of growth after the construction of the Berlin wall in 1961 and Honecker's social policy of the 1970s had given the regime a temporary lease of life. Possibly the regime had enjoyed a certain boost because of the worldwide growth in support for Socialist ideas at the time of the Vietnam war, and because of the emergence of a more pronounced anti-fascist climate in West Germany. Soon, however, the social policy could no longer be financed. There was a lack of technical innovation and East German industry fell hopelessly behind the Western standard. And when Gorbachev and the Soviet Union dropped the GDR it was above all the GDR's discontented youth who went furthest in their rejection of the state.

For GDR citizens of all generations the fall of the Berlin wall brought a new regime and a new political reorientation process. For the HJ generation this was the third time that they had been expected to adjust to a new political framework. How they adjusted to *this* challenge would be a new chapter in Germany's post-war history.

CHAPTER 11

The BDM generation: a female generation in transition from dictatorship to democracy

Dagmar Reese

When I think of my early childhood and how, well, how lower middle class and how narrow it was, I'd have to say – it was the war that made the difference! No, it was actually even before the war . . . That seven years age difference between me and my sister – we often talk about it – my sister doesn't swim, my sister doesn't do exercises – although some people around then *did* do that sort of thing – I mean, it's partly simply the way she is – but it's also the whole attitude and how things were then. She grew up, you know, with hair in a bun and pointed shoes and high heels and all that . . . even now, if she's going on about something, I say, well, you're a lady and I'm not. And, you know, that *is* somehow the difference between us. They were all like that, not just her . . . that's what it was all about, that's how it still was, you know, sort of having a rod up your back and everything tightly strapped in. And then when I was older everything was a bit freer and, you know, I'd almost be tempted to say that perhaps the political change [i.e. the Nazi seizure of power – translator] had something to do with it . . . because it was like that then, everything was more sporty, you wore flat heels and, yes, you went swimming. For my sister that would have been impossible, pretty well. She did then begin swimming, true, but going to swim with a mixed youth group and stuff like that – well she didn't do that. But that's how it was with me.[1]

Of all the different generations of German women born since the turn of the century, it is the BDM generation – the cohort born

Translated by Mark Roseman. The author would like to thank the Förderprogramm Frauenforschung of the Berlin Senate which gave financial support to the research on which this piece is based.

[1] The quotation is taken from one of a series of interviews which I conducted as part of my PhD with women living in Minden/Westphalia and in the Berlin suburb of Wedding. The woman in this interview was born in Minden in 1920.

between the end of the First World War and the beginning of the 1930s, socialised in the Third Reich and organised in the Nazi League of German Girls (BDM) – which most closely corresponds to Karl Mannheim's stringent theoretical definition of generations.[2] Never before or since has an entire cohort of young women been socialised under such similar conditions. As the Nazi dictatorship extended its control over the public sphere and progressively over the private sphere, girls and young women from different social and regional backgrounds were increasingly united by the powerful common experiences of their generation.

The BDM, which was the female subsidiary of the National Socialist Hitler Youth (HJ), was a crucial agent in this process. From 1936 onwards, membership of the BDM became compulsory for girls.[3] But it was not only the BDM itself which helped create the BDM generation. Other important socialising instances were the Reich Labour Service, the War Auxiliary service, the Land Year and the various other agricultural and labour service schemes. And there was also the war itself. This was, after all, the generation of women which found itself more actively involved in the war effort than perhaps any other group of women before it. Overall, the wealth of shared experience and the common destiny of this cohort of women created a uniform identity and justify the notion of *the* BDM generation.

The following essay attempts to sketch in the experiences and identity of this generation. But in doing so, it aims to ask some more far-reaching questions about recent German history, and particularly the history of German women. One of the issues that will be explored here is how the National Socialist approach to young women should be placed in relation to the longer-term modernisation of women's role in society. In pursuit of this question, the essay begins by describing new gender paradigms which evolved at the turn of the century and which were to have a powerful influence on National Socialist policy. It then goes on to reaffirm recent research that, contrary to popular opinion, National Socialism did

---

[2] Karl Mannheim, 'Das Problem der Generationen', *KVfZ*, vol. 7 (1928), pp. 157–80, 309–50.
[3] The Hitler Youth Law of 1 December 1936 (RGBl. I 1936) declared the Hitler Youth to be the state youth organisation and jointly responsible with parents and schools for the upbringing of German children. In this essay the term 'BDM' is used to describe both Nazi girls' organisations, i.e. the *Jungmädel* and the BDM proper. See also p. 238.

not represent a return to outdated gender roles.[4] On the contrary, the aim of the National Socialist state was to mobilise young women and exploit to the full their productive and reproductive capacities. This in turn required the removal of the patriarchal, regional, religious and social restrictions which had traditionally confined the female role.

And yet the BDM generation was 'modern' only in a very limited sense, and here the essay moves on to look at the legacy of the Nazi experience for women in the post-war period. It will argue that because these young women's 'emancipation' became tainted by its association with National Socialism – or, put more broadly, because the 'secular' process of social modernisation and the specifically National Socialist impact had become intertwined – it was almost impossible after the war for the BDM generation to draw on its experience in a productive way.

A third theme of this essay is that the ambivalent legacy of the Nazi experience for women, while in some ways the result of factors specific to the Third Reich, also manifested a more general point that for women the promise held out by generationally based movements or programmes had always been highly problematic. The use of 'Generation' as slogan and battle cry in the hands of the German youth movement and others had come to imply that age was the decisive criterion in defining an individual's social identity, overriding, amongst other things, differences of gender. Young women were thus able, be redefining themselves as 'youth', to break though certain gender restrictions. But they did so only at the price of suppressing any awareness that this liberation was possible for them as *women*, rather than as 'youth'. For older women, indeed, the notion of generation had little to offer. Thus the problem of identity faced by the BDM generation after 1945 was caused not just by the fact that it was the Nazis which had engineered this transition. By choosing the life-style and values of youth, the young women of the 1930s had been able to attain greater equality with boys and to rebel against socially accepted definitions of what it was to be a woman. But this flight from their own gender identity into the freer category of generation could only ever be partially successful and, indeed, the price was that they undermined at least part of their claim to be treated as equal individuals.

---

[4] Ralf Dahrendorf was the first to recognise this; Ralf Dahrendorf, *Society and democracy in Germany* (London 1968). On the latest debates, see Michael Prinz and Rainer Zitelmann (ed.), *Nationalsozialismus und Modernisierung* (Darmstadt 1991).

I

When bourgeois society emerged, it did so – at least in Germany –
based on what was actually a relict of feudalism.[5] At the heart of
bourgeois society were ties of kinship: the bourgeois family structure
was elevated to a quasi-natural form of social organisation, in which
– as in a feudal organisation – the constituent parties, in this case the
sexes, adopted different roles, and these roles in turn provided the
basis for their mutual interdependence.[6] There was from the start,
therefore, a contradiction between the new principles of bourgeois
society and the 'feudal' family structure on which it was based. The
development of modern natural law, with its emphasis on the
freedom of the individual, stood in sharp contradiction to the
existence of such polar sexual roles, which restricted women to the
emerging private sphere. Just at a time when men were socially and
legally becoming self-determining subjects, with rights and freedoms
as individuals, women were paradoxically being consigned to a
prescribed, immanent role.[7] It was inevitable that as bourgeois
society developed further, these persistent feudal and corporative
elements in marriage and the family – as, indeed, in many other
areas of social life – would not remain unchallenged.[8]

The establishment of such polar gender roles was initially the
preserve of the new bourgeois elites. Those elites then spent much of
the nineteenth century propagating their bourgeois family ideal
among the lower classes.[9] However, just as the bourgeois model of
the family was attaining near universal acceptance, it was itself
being undermined from within. Once again, a new set of role models
was being developed by the elites of the time, and at the turn of the

---

[5] Max Horkheimer, 'Autorität und Familie in der Gegenwart', in Horkheimer, *Zur Kritik der
   instrumentellen Vernunft. Aus den Vorträgen und Aufzeichnungen seit Kriegsende*, edited by Alfred
   Schmidt (Frankfurt 1967), pp. 269–287.
[6] See Gisela Bock and Barbara Duden, 'Arbeit als Liebe – Liebe als Arbeit. Zur Entstehung
   der Hausarbeit im Kapitalismus', in *Frauen und Wissenschaft. Beiträge zur Berliner Sommer-
   universität für Frauen im Juli 1976* (Berlin 1977), pp. 11–199; Karin Hausen, 'Die Polarisier-
   ung der "Geschlechtscharaktere". Eine Dissoziation vom Erwerbs- und Familienleben', in
   Werner Conze (ed.), *Sozialgeschichte der Familie in der Neuzeit Europas. Neue Forschungen*
   (Stuttgart 1977), pp. 363–393; Claudia Honegger, *Die Ordnung der Geschlechter. Die Wissenschaften vom Menschen und das Weib* (Frankfurt, New York 1991).
[7] Anna Dorothea Brockmann, '"Gehört mein Bauch mir?" Die Herausforderung des Selbst-
   bestimmungsbegriffs durch die neuen Reproduktionstechnologien', *Beiträge zur feministischen
   Theorie und Praxis*, vol. 24 (1989), pp. 105–118.
[8] Ulrich Beck, *Die Risikogesellschaft. Auf dem Weg in eine andere Moderne* (Frankfurt 1986).
[9] Jacques Donzelot, *Die Ordnung der Familie* (Frankfurt 1979).

century the pace was set above all by intellectual elites within the reform movement and the women's, labour and youth movements. Within these groups we find the psychological foundations being laid for a transformation of modern society.

Of course, the transition from one prevailing notion of sexual roles to another is never clear cut or instantaneous. At any one time, several different 'images' or 'constructs' of gender will compete for predominance. In turn of the century Germany this was undoubtedly so, and yet it is equally clear that the model emanating from the youth movement enjoyed a decisive influence. Organised youth was by no means of one mind on issues of gender or sexuality; but what the various groupings had in common was the basic assumption that girls' primary attribute was that they were young rather than that they were female. For the girls themselves this created – admittedly only for a temporary phase of their lives – the freedom to break through existing gender barriers. They were given scope to extend, sometimes even to develop for the first time, their own individual personalities.[10]

Elisabeth Beck-Gernsheim has described the process by which women were gradually freed from the traditional limitations of the bourgeois modern as a transition from 'existing for others' to 'laying claim to a life of one's own'.[11] Like the emergence of the bourgeoisie from feudal ties, the modernisation of women's role took the form of a process of individualisation. To this modernisation process, the youth movement made a definite, though ambivalent contribution: above all, it operated with a notion of basic equality between the sexes – if only for a limited phase of their lives.

But in aligning themselves with the broader category of youth, young women sacrificed all claims to a specific identity as women. This was clearly evident in the ideal of the female comrade as formulated by Marianne Weber for the first women students, and Elisabeth Busse-Wilson for the young women of the youth movement.[12] Their ideal of female comradeship was strongly influenced

10 Dagmar Reese, 'Emanzipation oder Vergesellschaftung. Mädchen im "Bund Deutscher Mädel"', in Hans-Uwe Otto and Heinz Sünker (eds.), *Politische Formierung und soziale Erziehung im Nationalsozialismus* (Frankfurt 1991), pp. 203–225.
11 Elisabeth Beck-Gernsheim, 'Vom "Dasein für andere" zum Anspruch auf ein Stück "eigenes Leben". Individualisierungsprozesse im weiblichen Lebenszusammenhang', *Soziale Welt*, vol. 34 (1983), pp. 307–340.
12 Elisabeth Busse-Wilson, 'Liebe und Kameradschaft', in *Grundschriften der deutschen Jugendbewegung* (Cologne, Düsseldorf 1963), pp. 327–334.

by bourgeois conventions, not least in the renunciation of sexuality, and at the same time offered new bonds of solidarity which – and this is the decisive point – no longer ran along gender or class lines but along generational ones.

This ideal of comradeship between men and women, developed in the late nineteenth century in the context of the various reform movements, deserves a little closer attention.[13] It was an ideal of female equality, originally formulated for marital relationships or other partnerships between men and women. But the 'rational' model of equal partnership was incapable of dealing with the emotional unpredictability of love and sexuality. It is beyond the scope of this essay to expand on this, but the important point here is that out of the challenge to find an appropriate model for relations between the sexes three main positions emerged. First, there was the idea of trying to reconcile comradeship and sexuality. Many of those who advocated this were in fact trying to achieve a more 'rational' and controlled sexual life for men and women.[14] Secondly, there was a clear rejection of comradeship. This rejection was justified by arguments about the differentness of women and of their specific interests.[15] Finally, there was the youth movement's conception, which we have already encountered, namely of a non-sexual comradeship of limited duration, restricted to youth.

Of the three models, it was the latter which was to be the most influential, not least because it provided a number of advantages. In the first place, it responded to young women's individual ambitions without fundamentally challenging the whole structure of gender relations. Secondly, the limitation to the emancipation that was offered – that it applied only to youth – did not seem to be one imposed by politics or ideology but to be almost 'natural', determined by age. Finally, the potential threat of female emancipation was blunted also by the fact that the young women had to subordinate their interests to the common cause of the youth movement. The young female comrades, like their counterparts in the Socialist

---

[13] Dagmar Reese, 'Die Kameraden. Eine partnerschaftliche Konzeption der Geschlechterbeziehungen an der Wende vom 19. zum 20. Jahrhundert', in Dagmar Reese, Eve Rosenhaft, Carola Sachse and Tilla Siegel (eds.), *Rationale Beziehungen. Geschlechterverhältnisse im Rationalisierungsprozeß* (Frankfurt am Main 1993), pp. 58–74.

[14] This was the approach taken by Helene Stöcker, the *Bund für Mutterschutz*, the sexual reform movement of the 1920s and the political left. On all of this, see Cornelie Usborne's chapter in this volume.

[15] The position taken by Gertrud Bäumer and the moderate women's movement.

movement, often found themselves committed to goals and ideas which they had little hand in shaping.[16]

The female comrade's relationship to society was different from that of the traditional bourgeois woman. In the traditional female role, women were seen as being withdrawn from society. They were the embodiment of 'otherness', of the private sphere opposed to public society, sometimes even of a utopia. Now, however, women were conceived as being far more part of society, though only during their youth, i.e. in the period before marriage or at least before the first child.[17] This gave the young women a different frame of reference and set of values. The new girl of the youth movement exhibited quite different qualities from the bourgeois lady – she was physically active and interested in physical exercise; her approach to life was practical and rational. She could cope with new challenges and was agreeably unpretentious. In the eyes of men, the new youthful model was more predictable and easier to handle: no smelling salts or migraines any more. For their part, the young women enjoyed the limited freedom now open to them.

II

Before the First World War, the female youth movement remained restricted to the few thousand girls of the *Wandervogel*. But during the Weimar years, the ideas and style of this small avant-garde spread to a large number of different organisations, including denominational groups and the youth wing of the labour movement.[18] At the same time the older established women's associations complained about their failure to recruit younger members.[19] A change in orientation had clearly taken place among young women, even if on the whole restricted to the larger towns and the social elites, including the elites of the labour movement.

It was against this backdrop that the National Socialists made

[16] Michael Rohrwasser, *Saubere Mädel, starke Genossen* (Frankfurt 1975).
[17] The latter in the case of the companionate marriage. See Ben B. Lindsey and Wainright Evans, *Die Kameradschaftsehe* (Berlin, Leipzig 1928).
[18] Irmgard Klönne, *Ich spring in diesem Ringe. Mädchen und Frauen in der deutschen Jugendbewegung* (Pfaffenweiler 1990), p. 215. See also Marion E. P. de Ras, *Körper, Eros und weibliche Kultur. Mädchen im Wandervogel und in der bündischen Jugend 1900–1933* (Pfaffenweiler 1988).
[19] Irene Stoehr, 'Neue Frau und alte Bewegung. Zum Generationenkonflikt in der Frauenbewegung der Weimarer Republik', in Jutta Dahlhof, Uschi Frey and Ingrid Schöll (eds.), *Frauenmacht in der Geschichte. Beiträge des Historikerinnentreffens 1985 zur Frauengeschichtsforschung* (Düsseldorf 1986), pp. 390–400.

their first attempts at mobilising young women. As early as 1929, at a special Hitler Youth congress in Nuremberg, a motion was put forward calling for the so-called sister groups to be affiliated to the Hitler Youth. In justification, the proposers of the motion argued that other right-wing associations were now beginning to provide women with political training and 'to draw them into closer cooperation with the men'.[20] This proposal, though supported by the girls within the movement, was rejected by both the boys of the Hitler Youth and the women in the National Socialist women's organisation, the *Deutsche Frauenorden* (DFO). The Hitler Youth's attitude was similar to that of many other young men's organisations and reflected a general tendency towards separation of the sexes which had emerged in the *bündische* youth since the First World War. For their part, the women of the DFO were worried about losing potential new recruits to the girl's organisation and thus about losing influence within the movement. For the girls, however, membership of the Hitler Youth held two attractions: first, that they, like the boys, would be treated as part of youth, a 'German' youth, and would be given a real role in building up a new 'German' Reich. Secondly, the activities and outlook of the youth wing of the party were far more to their taste than the kind of work done by the DFO. For example, the DFO was prone, as in 1931, to call for youthful volunteers to 'do the washing for the SA'[21] or it offered first-aid courses and the like. In general, the DFO's leaders believed that their special contribution as women lay in placing the traditional female skills at the movement's disposal.[22] The BDM had a quite different tone, particularly once Trude Mohr, an experienced youth leader from the *bündische* youth and later national official in the BDM, had established a position within the movement. Under Mohr's influence, the BDM adopted much of the style of the Weimar youth movement: 'You heard it! Girls to the Hitler Youth! Forget the warnings of the stick-in-the-muds – come and join us! We must become one people!'[23] The BDM engaged in activities and pastimes very similar to those of the established youth movement: excursions, sport, evening meetings with crafts and singing and so on.

The decision to emulate the youth movement was not just of

[20] Bundesarchiv Koblenz (BAK), NS 26/352.   [21] *Angriff*, 2 April 1931.
[22] BAK, Sammlung Schuhmacher, G viii/ 251, p. 3, 2 December 1931.
[23] *Angriff*, 1 July 1931.

programmatic significance, but had important consequences for the balance of power within the Hitler movement as well. Trude Mohr headed the Gau Brandenburg and its relative success was manifest in a membership of 155 girls at the beginning of 1932, making it the second largest district in the Reich. In November 1932, the party accorded the BDM the status of sole Nazi organisation for girls. The BDM, with its strong youth movement character, had proved far more effective than the women's groups in attracting young support. The *Bund* appealed to the youngsters precisely because it did not embody the traditional 'feminine' values.

It was not just Mohr who benefited from the BDM's success, but also the National Socialists' overall youth leader, Baldur von Schirach. Schirach controlled the Hitler Youth to which the BDM was now affiliated. The clear losers in the power struggle were the older women in the National Socialist movement, those early 'rebels against emancipation', in Claudia Koonz's words, who were obsessed with their position and status within the party.[24] In the summer of 1931 the local women's groups, the women's working groups and the DFO had come together to form the National Socialist Women's Organisation (NSF), under the leadership of Elsbeth Zander. After the BDM had been declared the sole Nazi girls' organisation, the NSF moved in autumn 1932 to create *NS-Mädchenschaften* whose task it was to organise the 18–21-year-old girls. In a letter from 23 February 1932, Lydia Gottschewski, the BDM's national leader, made clear that the BDM regarded the rapid proliferation of these groups as a threat. In March 1933, the BDM therefore increased the upper age limit for members to 21 and the *NS-Mädchenschaften* were dissolved. At the same time, Lydia Gottschewski replaced Elsbeth Zander as NSF leader. Gottschewski's combination of the two positions might suggest that both organisations were now working hand in hand to mobilise young women, but what had happened, in fact, was that the BDM had succeeded in neutralising the older women's influence.

On the other hand, the BDM itself was not impervious to outside influence and it was forced to make concessions to the more traditional views of women's proper role. This was particularly true towards the end of the 1930s when the BDM had already started

---

[24] Claudia Koonz, 'Nazi women before 1933: rebels against emancipation', *Social Science Quarterly*, vol. 56 (1976), pp. 553–563. See also Claudia Koonz, *Mothers in the Fatherland: women, the family and Nazi politics* (London 1987), pp. 51–90.

losing some of its original appeal to German girls. A visible sign of the changes was that the brown skirt of the pre-1933 era, reminiscent of the SA uniform, was later replaced by a blue skirt and white shirt.[25] In later years the BDM was also banned from taking part in shooting practice. And yet in 1933 von Schirach had said on this question:[26]

Some people say that shooting courses, which the BDM has held from time to time, are unfeminine. I do not agree with that at all. I take the position that small-bore shooting is a sport like any other. I really cannot understand how there can still be people in Germany today who see something unfeminine in girls engaging in this sport. It trains them to have a steady hand and to appraise a situation coolly, it teaches them correct timing and how to control their nerves. We must not allow ourselves to be put off by old men or by old women who come running to us saying that young girls can only be educated by their mothers.

The BDM's programme thus contrasted markedly with that of the DFO. The latter continued to operate within the nineteenth-century conception of gender polarity, engaging in activities that conformed to the traditional range of female duties. The BDM, on the other hand, stood for the seemingly unpolitical goal of forming 'fresh and cheerful girls'.[27] It thus manifested and sustained the paradigm shift in gender roles which had begun at the turn of the century. By categorising girls as part of youth, and by legally enforcing this categorisation through to the remotest corners of the Reich,[28] the National Socialists accelerated the process of liberating young women from the traditional bonds of the family. They unleashed this change even in those areas where cultural, religious or political barriers had previously hindered it. For the great majority of women, the Nazis thus completed the individualisation process which for men had taken place at the time of the emergence of bourgeois society. But this was a highly ambivalent 'individualisation'. Just as the concept of the free and equal individual had originally meant nothing more than the ruthless and untrammelled

25 *Verordnungsblatt der Reichsjugendführung*, vol. 1 (1933), Folge 14.
26 BAK, NS 26/ 336, 25 November 1933, p. 6.
27 Jutta Rüdiger, former Reich official of the BDM in a letter to the author, 26 October 1982.
28 With the passing of the first and second executive decrees on the Hitler Youth Law on 25 March 1939 compulsory membership in the Hitler Youth was now binding. The decrees meant that the legal guardians of youngsters who opposed the law could now be punished either by fines or imprisonment. See Arno Klönne, *Jugend im Dritten Reich* (Cologne 1982), pp. 48f.

exploitation of human beings by other human beings, so now the formal equality between boys and girls within the category 'youth' meant only that the limited leeway for individuality, which had been a necessary byproduct of gender polarity, ceased to exist. The BDM might not train girls in femininity, motherhood, or the polar roles of the old gender model. Instead, it schooled them to be flexible and serviceable, a schooling that was based on the isolation of the individual and, for boys and girls alike, on physical training, discipline, rationality and efficiency.

III

The creation of a genuinely homogenous generation by the Nazis began with the dissolution of all other youth groups. On 5 April 1933, the Nazis took over the Reich Committee of German Youth Associations, the umbrella organisation of all youth organisations, in which between 5 and 6 million youngsters were organised. The first to be excluded from the organisation were the Socialist and Jewish groups. Soon the left-wing youth organisations were banned outright, followed by their right-wing counterparts – many of which opted for direct absorption into the Hitler Youth.[29] The 'coordination' of all youth work by the Nazis was accelerated by Hitler's appointment of Baldur von Schirach, hitherto Reich Youth Leader of the National Socialists (NSDAP), to youth leader of the German Reich on 17 June 1933. Henceforth, all youth policy measures came under Schirach's control. Schirach used his new power to dissolve the *bündische* organisations. At the end of 1933 an agreement was reached with the Protestant Reich Bishop Müller, which laid down that members of the Protestant youth association should also be members of the Hitler Youth. At the same time the Protestant groups restricted their activities to purely spiritual matters. The Catholic youth, the second most important denominational grouping, was initially protected from the depredations of the Hitler Youth by the Reich Concordat. However, an agreement between the Hitler Youth and the Reich Sport Leader meant that all sports were now tied to membership of the Hitler Youth. Similar pacts were sealed with the Reich Food Estate, the Working Group of National Socialist Women Students (ANSt), the National Socialist

[29] *Ibid.*, p. 20.

Welfare Organisation (NSV) and the German Labour Front (DAF). The net was being drawn ever tighter. In the 1933–34 period the Hitler Youth achieved an enormous increase in membership, from 15,000 to 1.5 million members. Girls made up initially only a small proportion but between 1933 and 1939 their share grew from a quarter to a half of all members. Even before 1936 the growth in girls' membership had outpaced that of the boys'.[30] With the passing of the 1936 Hitler Youth Law the Hitler Youth was now the state youth organisation. The annual enrolment of 10-year-olds became bureaucratic routine; only in the big cities and sometimes in rural districts was there any possibility of eluding the organisation.

For women born 1927 or later we can therefore presume BDM membership, so long, that is, as they were in a position to make a written declaration that they were of 'German extraction'. Every year, the local government registration offices drew up a list of 10-year-olds and summoned them to join the youth organisation. Enrolment involved acquiring a uniform – a further, symbolic step in the creation of a BDM generation. It was important that not all of the uniform could be bought. Neckerchief and woggle could be attained only by passing the *Jungmädelprobe*, the test taken by young girls six months after joining the BDM's junior division, the *Jungmädelbund*.

Not only was the external appearance of the BDM girls the same everywhere in the Reich, but the uniformity extended to the pattern of duties and activities in the youth organisation. The most important element was a weekly evening meeting – afternoons for the *Jungmädel* – the structure and content of which was defined centrally. From 1936 onwards BDM officials received printed guidance on the ground each meeting should cover. In addition, there were trips, sporting events, marches and, during the war, collections of all sorts. Of course, everyone's experience of the BDM was different, not least because of the idiosyncrasies of each local leader, but the common elements were far stronger than the differences. The BDM experience was particularly powerful for those girls who rose up the ranks within the movement. If we assume that by the end of 1935

[30] In 1935 the BDM membership grew by 20.7 per cent or 97,773, the HJ by contrast only by 5.5 per cent or 43,361. BAK, NS 26/358, Statistik der Jugend. See also Gabriele Kinz, *Der Bund Deutscher Mädel. Ein Beitrag zur außerschulischen Mädchenerziehung im Nationalsozialismus* (Frankfurt am Main, Bern, New York, Paris 1990), p. 25; Martin Klaus, *Mädchenerziehung zur Zeit der faschistischen Herrschaft in Deutschland*. Vol. II: *Der Bund Deutscher Mädel* (Frankfurt 1983), pp. 232–233.

some 4 million youngsters were organised in the Hitler Youth, then it is easy to see that with group sizes ranging between 15 and 20 youngsters some 323,000 young men and women were required as leaders. The BDM itself (i.e. excluding the *Jungmädel*) was, with 568,717 members, the smallest of the youth organisations, and yet in 1935 it alone had a need for around 33,000 leaders. After the passing of the Hitler Youth law in 1936 the rapid growth of membership, particularly in the *Jungmädel*, only increased the need for leaders.[31] Often the youth organisation turned to youngsters from local elites to fill the leadership positions – not least because only the pupils of grammar or equivalent schools had the free time to carry out the afternoon duties of *Jungmädel* group leaders. Amongst such middle- and upper-middle-class girls the BDM had perhaps its biggest impact. The young women developed their leadership qualities, learned how to assert themselves and get things done, and how to fit into hierarchically structured organisations. For many girls these were new and dramatic experiences.

The forging of a distinctive BDM generation was given significantly extra impetus both by the experience of war, and by the various forms of 'national service', in the RAD and War Auxiliary. In a number of important ways the BDM had prepared the ground for these various forms of service. The BDM's strong emphasis on sport, which according to Baldur von Schirach was supposed to account for two-thirds of its activities, made the girls physically resilient. The BDM experience also provided the girls with the qualities of responsibility, versatility and efficiency required to help keep civilian life going and maintain public order during wartime. Moreover, the massive use of girls in agricultural and factory work in the context of RAD and War Auxiliary Service would probably have been inconceivable without the BDM. The *Bund*'s frequent trips and camps away from home prepared a generation of girls for the separation from the family in places far removed from their home towns which wartime service often entailed. It gave them some preparation, too, for the sort of odyssey which Sybil Gräfin Schönfeldt has described when, as a 17-year-old she was forced to cross Germany alone, after her RAD camp was threatened by an imminent Russian advance. Many other young women were faced

---

[31] Dagmar Reese, *'Straff, aber nicht stramm -Herb, aber nicht derb.' Zur Vergesellschaftung der Mädchen im Bund Deutscher Mädel im sozialkulturellen Vergleich zweier Milieus* (Weinheim, Basel 1989), p. 73.

with similar tests.[32] Of course, the experience of war did vary for different girls, but hardly any were unaffected by it. Many rose to the challenge, extinguished incendiary bombs, tended to the wounded, 'organised' food and grew accustomed to death and destruction.

IV

The BDM, then, had produced – if we may crudely generalise for a moment – a generation of hard-working, resilient and unselfish 'pals', women early torn from their families, who had learned to assert themselves and who had put their backs to the wheel without demur. That is certainly how this generation was seen after 1945 and, indeed, how it saw itself. In distinct contrast to preceding generations of women, there was also a strong sense among the young women of the BDM generation of having been thrown back on their own resources. 'We stand alone' and 'we have to make our way alone', as one contemporary put it.[33] Yet after the war the odd fact is that this generation of young women remained strangely silent. A chorus of youthful voices could be heard through the pages of the numerous youth magazines sponsored by the occupying authorities. Almost none of them were female. Even contemporaries were struck by the silence. 'Why are young women silent?' was the headline above a major article in the youth magazine *Horizont*.[34] Even if few satisfactory answers were forthcoming at the time, the very fact of the question being asked indicates that contemporaries had expected something different. There was a widespread feeling that the absence of girls and young women from the public stage after 1945 somehow did not match with the new public presence they had attained during the Nazi period.

Why was it then that young women failed almost completely to build on the emancipatory processes unleashed by National Socialism and war?

A key reason was undoubtedly the fact that this 'emancipation' had been directed from above rather than struggled for below, a characteristic not only of the BDM but, in more muted form, more generally of the way in which the state had been responsible for the

---

[32] Sybil Gräfin Schönfeldt, *Sonderappell. 1945 - Ein Mädchen berichtet* (Munich 1984).
[33] *Horizont*, vol.1 (1945–46), 10, p. 14.
[34] *Horizont*, vol. 2 (1947), 10, pp. 8–9.

modernisation of women's position since the nineteenth century. German girls had not striven for the new opportunities open to them in the BDM; they were simply the passive recipients. They had had virtually no influence on the content of the groups' activities; the programme had been fixed from above. Even the composition of each group had been the result of an official bureaucratic procedure; they were not groups held together by friendship, by an idea or by a goal. Self-fulfilment was by and large possible only via upward mobility, i.e. through a career as youth leader.

A second and equally important factor was the way in which the question of guilt for National Socialist crimes became entangled with girls' experience in the Third Reich. At first sight, the lively discussion of the guilt issue in the authorised youth magazines in the occupation period would suggest that an active and productive altercation with the past was being pursued, at least amongst youngsters from the educated bourgeoisie. And there is no doubt that discussions of the guilt issue served to strengthen younger Germans' sense of generational identity. For, rather than, say, trying to attain a reconciliation with National Socialism's victims, the articles' chief theme was an ongoing dispute between 'German youth' and the parental generation. The young contributors were reacting angrily to the many paternalistic and pedagogic 'calls to youth'[35] addressed by older Germans to the supposedly 'mesmerised and ideologised' younger generation. One young man wrote of the parental generation:[36]

During its life-time, this generation has sworn three different oaths of loyalty and broken all three. It has unleashed, or at least not prevented, two wars. It has thus shown neither integrity nor intelligence and has no right to sit in judgement on the youth of this country, a youth whose only crime is perhaps that it ever listened to the crazy commands of the older generation.

But whilst it may have strengthened generational identity, this very attempt to turn the search for the guilty into a generational question served not only to exculpate the younger generation (and, indeed, to allow the *older* generation to bury its own past in an exaggerated 'concern' for the young) but also allowed the question

[35] Manfred H. Burschka, 'Re-Education und Jugendöffentlichkeit. Orientierung und Selbstverständnis deutscher Nachkriegsjugend in der Jugendpresse 1945–1948. Ein Beitrag zur politischen Kultur der Nachkriegszeit' (doctoral thesis, Göttingen 1987), p. 99.
[36] *Horizont*, vol. 1 (1945–46), 6, p. 10.

of personal responsibility to be avoided.[37] The real past, with all its complexity, disappeared behind the intergenerational acrimony. Moreover, for girls in particular, the confusion of the generational and the guilt questions, had further consequences. The BDM had been attractive for girls precisely because it treated them primarily as young people rather than women. For them, even more than for the boys, National Socialism was associated with the breaking down of traditional barriers. In the post-war era, they thus faced the problem that their personal emancipation was associated with a criminal regime, from implication in which, as a generation, they were trying to extricate themselves. The memory of their own new freedom become interwoven with the growing awareness of the catastrophe of genocide and national collapse. The result was, as Christa Wolf has written, a fragmented self: 'The past is not dead; it is not even past. We detach it from ourselves and pretend to be strangers.'[38]

Thirdly, precisely because their self-perception was so much more generational than gender based, the young women of the BDM generation failed to develop a response to the fact that their material situation and career prospects after the war were far poorer than those of their male contemporaries.[39] The enormous surplus of women over men meant that for many the traditional perspective of marriage and family was simply unavailable. Many realised, as Hilde Thurnwald noted in her study of Berlin families, that they

[37] The generation conflict on the guilt question lasted until round 1948. The disappearance of the debate thereafter was probably the result of a number of factors – the decline of the youth press, the general amnesty for youth, but above all the cold war, which offered new opportunites to suppress awareness of one's own guilt.
[38] Christa Wolf, *Kindheitsmuster* (Darmstadt, Neuwied 1977), p. 9.
[39] On the situation of women in the post-war period and on policy towards women, see Antje Dertinger, *Frauen der ersten Stunde. Aus den Gründerjahren der Bundesrepublik* (Bonn 1989); Annette Kuhn (ed.), *Frauen in der deutschen Nachkriegszeit* (2 vols, Düsseldorf 1985–86); Antje Dertinger (ed.), *Frauen in der Geschichte V*, (Düsseldorf 1984); Sibylle Meyer and Eva Schulze, '"Als wir wieder zusammen waren, ging der Krieg im Kleinen weiter." Frauen, Männer und Familien im Berlin der vierziger Jahre', in Lutz Niethammer and Alexander von Plato (eds.), *'Wir kriegen jetzt andere Zeiten.' Auf der Suche nach der Erfahrung des Volkes in nachfaschistischen Ländern* (Berlin, Bonn 1985), pp. 305–326; Sibylle Meyer and Eva Schulze, *'Von Liebe sprach damals keiner'. Familienalltag in der Nachkriegszeit* (Munich 1985); Sibylle Meyer and Eva Schulze, *'Wie wir das alles geschafft haben'. Alleinstehende Frauen berichten über ihr Leben nach 1945* (Munich 1988); Sibylle Meyer and Eva Schulze, *Auswirkungen des II. Weltkrieges auf Familien. Zum Wandel der Familie in Deutschland* (Soziologische Forschungen, H. 18), (Berlin 1989); Hans-Jörg Ruhl, *Frauen in der Nachkriegszeit 1945–1963* (Munich 1988); Renate Wiggershaus, *Geschichte der Frauen und der Frauenbewegung in der Bundesrepublik Deutschland und in der Deutschen Demokratischen Republik nach 1945* (Wuppertal 1979).

would have to seek fulfilment through their careers.[40] What was difficult for them was not the idea that they would have to work or shape their own lives independently, but that their career choices would not be complemented by a partner and children. Moreover, qualifying for a career was extremely difficult in the post-war era. In the first place, the food shortages, overcrowding and damage to housing stock made housework a very difficult and time-consuming business. In some areas, notably Berlin, these shortages continued into the 1950s.[41] Older girls, in particular, found an enormous burden being placed on their shoulders which left little time for studies or training. Secondly, there was a distinct shortage of suitable career opportunities. University places were often held back for returning soldiers. The range of occupations open to women continued to be very narrow. Helmut Schelsky noted in the 1950s that young women were confronted by a peculiar job and career situation' in which 'they were being forced to accept employment in old-fashioned production conditions which matched neither their aspirations nor their values'.[42] For women, then, the 1950s were characterised by a sharp discrepancy between ideology and social reality.[43]

Only in one area did girls break from solidarity with their male peers and act on their own initiative, namely in creating relationships with members of the occupying forces. Of course, the motives for such friendships were initially often those of narrow self-interest: above all the chance of obtaining scarce foodstuffs for themselves and their families, cigarettes and other luxury goods.[44] But it would be an over-simplification to see these material motives as the only reason for forming such relationships. Responding to complaints from German men that 'some of you do it for cigarettes, others do it for amusement while we stand around outside in our reconditioned uniforms', one young woman responded:[45]

[40] Hilde Thurnwald, *Gegenwartsprobleme Berliner Familien* (Berlin 1948), p. 120.
[41] See *ibid.* and also *Die Lebensverhältnisse in Deutschland 1947. Eine Studie des Hilfswerks der evangelischen Kirchen Deutschlands* (Stuttgart 1947); O. W. Haseloff, *Bericht über eine Repräsentativerhebung unter Berliner Jugendlichen im Alter von 10–21 Jahren* (Berlin 1953).
[42] Helmut Schelsky, *Die skeptische Generation* (Düsseldorf 1963, special edition), p. 267.
[43] See Angela Delille and Andrea Grohn, *Blick zurück ins Glück. Frauenleben und Frauenpolitik in den 50er Jahren* (Berlin 1985), p. 63.
[44] See the figure of Carla in Wolfgang Koeppen, *Tauben im Gras* (Frankfurt 1980) (first published in 1951).
[45] *Benjamin*, vol. 1 (1947), 5, p. 19.

Such criticism hits those of us hardest who least deserve it. Those who love the person Edward or John and not the Englishman Edward or John. Those for whom it is perhaps quite a problem that Edward is an Englishman. It's true, there's more to eat in England, housing conditions are better and clothes can be bought now and then. But in England there are also new relatives who may see it as a disgrace to have a German in the family. You have to struggle not only to speak English but also to think English ... But obviously you men can't imagine what it's like, otherwise you might feel something like respect. But even you must see that 'shaving off their hair' is no solution.

Friendships between young German women and men from the occupying troops or other foreigners were subject to massive moral condemnation. The fact that material motives always played some role made it easy to condemn them. But above all, the reaction was about the injury to the national honour, which really meant injury to male honour. Not a word was wasted on the injuries being perpetrated on female honour: in none of the youth magazines was there even one article on the numerous rapes[46] to which particularly this generation of women was liable.[47] In this moral climate, few women or girls were willing to defend themselves against the charge that as 'chocolate girls' they were undermining the 'national honour' and their own reputation, and certainly few did so with the vigour of this correspondent:[48]

Even if my opinion on the problem of the 'reputation of the decent girl' should unsettle narrow patriots, I hope that they will at least have the courage to examine it with rigorous honesty. Everything is open to more than one interpretation. I can remember some evenings during the war as a female auxiliary at staff headquarters. As we returned to our quarters, exhausted after a taxing day's work for the war effort, we would see German soldiers and officers strolling past, arm in arm with some elegant, well rested foreign dame. I have seen communications from the highest

[46] See Erika M. Hoerning, 'Frauen als Kriegsbeute. Der Zwei-Fronten Krieg. Beispiele aus Berlin', in Niethammer and von Plato, *'Wir kriegen jetzt andere Zeiten.'*, pp. 327–344; Annemarie Tröger, 'Between rape and prostitution: survival strategies and chances of emancipation for Berlin women after World War II', in Judith Friedlander (ed.), *Women in culture and politics: a century of change* (Bloomington 1986); Ingrid Schmidt-Harzbach, 'Eine Woche im April. Berlin 1945. Vergewaltigung als Massenschicksal', *Feministische Studien*, vol. 3 (1984), 2, pp. 51–65.
[47] According to Heimann many girls had experienced rape and suffered from sexual diseases. In Berlin/Neukölln 10 per cent of girls were affected. Siegfried Heimann, *Die Falken in Berlin. Erziehungsgemeinschaft oder Kampforganisation? Die Jahre 1945–1950* (Berlin 1990), p. 130.
[48] *Benjamin*, vol. 1 (1947).

ranks responding to the numerous applications for permission to marry a foreigner. The commanding officers were instructed to remind their officers and soldiers of the qualities of the German woman. In France, Russia and Italy I experienced the same thing again and again: foreign women were much more attractive than we were and all the German men were basically 'unhappily married' ... and now it really is a joke in bad taste when German men get worked up about the fact that German girls let themselves be spoiled by the Tommies. 1. The surplus of women means that not all girls can marry a German man. 2. It will do our men good for once to have to be gentle, tactful and chivalrous to gain our attentions. And you can't just stop trends, certainly not with insults. And cultured races can be found even outside Germany's borders.

But this was a rarity. A striking comment on the times was that in Berlin between 1945 and 1946 the number of women reported to the police on suspicion of prostitution rose by more than 500 per cent.[49] We can only speculate on what these figures really mean, but it seems plausible that as much as reflecting a genuine increase in prostitution, they also reflect a criminalisation of those aspects of female behaviour which drew forth envy and hostility.

V

Let us conclude, as we began, with the testimony of a young girl from the BDM generation. This is a girl who tried after the war without success to gain a place at university. The places were in short supply and were given by preference to former soldiers. Against the background of her own experience, she tried to find an answer to the question: 'why have young women remained silent?' 'I think', she wrote, 'we girls had higher hopes and have been more deeply disappointed. Be just and give us complete freedom! We will find courage and be silent no longer!'[50] Her answer encapsulates the dilemma facing an entire generation. This was a modern female generation, in Beck's terminology a modernised generation, i.e. it had been stripped of its feudal character and its identity was based on and part of an individualised society. And yet these women were not really free. Their emancipation from feudal restraint had been predicated on their submission to the demands of a criminal state. In retrospect, there was no pride or self-confidence to be won from this

---

[49] 2,661 reports in 1945, 17,732 in 1946. See *Berlin in Zahlen* (1950), p. 242.
[50] *Horizont*, vol. 2 (1947), 19, p. 12.

experience. And the post-war period offered no sphere of activity which might offer a new source of confidence and independence. On the other hand, the transformation of women's position which the Nazis had effected could not now be reversed. The BDM generation remained in a sort of limbo land, torn between conservative and modern conceptions of womanhood, alienated from its own experiences and desires, and silently adapting to the realities of post-war German society.

CHAPTER 12

A generation twice betrayed: youth policy in the transition from the Third Reich to the Soviet Zone of Occupation (1945–1946)

Michael Buddrus

For a regime wishing to impose its blueprint on society, winning over the support of youth, or at least neutralising youth's potential for opposition is crucial. Nowhere does this principle seem to have been taken to heart more than in Germany. From the Kaiserreich onwards, German elites devoted enormous energy to influencing the behaviour, life-style and attitudes of the young. Every administration and political party from the extreme left (Karl Liebknecht: 'He who has the young, has the army') to the extreme right (Joseph Goebbels: 'He who has the young has the future'), from party politicians to priests, and from senior civil servants to military figures tried to win young people over to their political goals. Perhaps the most distinctive feature of the German scene was the huge number of associations, leagues and clubs created by the adult world for young people. This development was triggered by the existence of the independent German youth movement, which from the Kaiserreich onwards prompted the established elites to found their own alternatives for young members. From these roots the attempt to shape youth through an organised youth movement broadened and intensified, reaching its highpoint in the Third Reich and the GDR.

Because of the energy and attention devoted to it, youth policy in Germany offers historians a fascinating arena in which to observe the relationship between regime and society. This is particularly so in the phases of breach and transition – in 1914, 1918–19, 1933, 1945

Translated by Mark Roseman. Lengthier extracts of many of the abridged quotations from GDR sources contained in this essay can be found in the author's 'Die doppelt betrogene Generation. Zu einigen Aspekten der Jugend und der Jugendpolitik in der SBZ/DDR 1945–1952' which appears in the 1993 issue of the *Jahrbuch für historische Bildungsforschung*.

or 1989–90. For one thing, those were the periods when successive regimes' efforts at mobilisation were especially concentrated and energetic. For another, the mixture of change and continuity that characterised the movement from one historical epoch to another can then be most clearly observed. The present piece analyses one of those transitional phases, namely, the period immediately after 1945, and looks at the way in which the new regime in East Germany tried to mobilise and integrate the Hitler Youth generation into post-war society.

I

What was the psychological state and social condition of German youth as the war came to an end? There is little doubt that the Nazis' comprehensive youth programme had left a deep impression. More than any previous regime, the Third Reich had created a unified youth, with mentality, attitudes and values that transcended differences of class and region. This was the result not just of the Hitler Youth and Nazi education policy; the war too had offered powerful, common experiences that further cemented the identity of this generation. Of course there remained important differences between young people, differences of family background, of gender, of regional identity and so on. But with the exception of the tiny minority in active opposition, of Jews and other persecuted groups, it seems justified to talk of *the* Hitler Youth generation.[1]

For most of this generation, the Nazis had undoubtedly engendered considerable identification with the regime, particularly with the figure of the *Führer*, an identification which lasted until the end of the war. There was no broad opposition movement and the fascist regime remained fully operational until early 1945. Indeed, even at the end some youngsters remained willing to sacrifice all for a last ditch defence of the regime. For others, though, the war gradually brought disillusionment. Many felt betrayed as they saw the chances for personal advancement and national glory crumbling with the deteriorating military position.

[1] See amongst many other studies Arno Klönne, *Jugend im Dritten Reich* (Cologne 1982); Michael Buddrus, 'Zur Geschichte der Hitlerjugend 1922–1939' (doctoral thesis, Rostock 1989); Arno Klönne, 'Deutsche Jugend im Zweiten Weltkrieg. Lebensbedingungen, Erfahrungen, Mentalitäten', in *Deutsche Jugend im Zweiten Weltkrieg* (Rostock 1991), pp. 25–32, here pp. 29ff; Rolf Schörken, *Jugend 1945. Politisches Denken und Lebensgeschichte* (Opladen 1990).

Most young people experienced 1945 not just as the collapse of National Socialism but also as the destruction of the German nation, an experience that produced a deep sense of shock, betrayal and uprooting. As Ernst Friedländer was one of the first to observe, the generation of 15–30-year-olds experienced 1945 as a much more fundamental break with the past than had their predecessors in 1918.[2] And yet, under the surface, many of the values and mentalities upon which the Nazis had based their ideology, and which in many cases pre-dated the Nazi period, persisted and were to have a profound influence on the post-war period.[3]

The end of the war saw the division of Germany into occupation zones, and as a result the experiences of different groups within the Hitler Youth generation became much more diverse. In the Western zones, this disorientated and disillusioned generation at least had the reassurance of seeing the old social system re-established relatively rapidly. Those in the Soviet Zone of Occupation and later the GDR had to contend with a far more radical transformation of social structures. Nationalisation, the introduction of the planned economy, and the sovietisation of culture, education and political system followed each other thick and fast, requiring from the younger generation a far more complex process of readjustment.

At the same time, the youth of the Soviet Zone of Occupation found themselves confronted with great social hardship. Disease was rife. Tuberculosis was a major killer, accounting for over one-third of deaths among young people. A survey of 4,700 unemployed youngsters in Saxony in May 1946 found that 4,218 were unfit for work, above all because of chronic malnutrition. Moreover, many youngsters lived in broken families. Twenty per cent had lost their fathers in the war. And the younger generation itself had been badly depleted by death, injury or internment with the result at the end of 1945 girls made up 75 per cent of the age group 18–25. Of those

[2] Ernst Friedländer, *Deutsche Jugend. Fünf Reden* (Hamburg 1947).
[3] See Arno Rose, *Werwolf 1944–1945* (Stuttgart 1980); Karl Heinz Jahnke and Michael Buddrus, *Deutsche Jugend 1933–1945. Eine Dokumentation* (Hamburg 1989); Matthias von Hellfeld and Arno Klönne, *Die betrogene Generation. Jugend in Deutschland unter dem Faschismus. Quellen und Dokumente* (Cologne 1985); *Jugend unterm Schicksal. Lebensberichte junger Deutscher 1946–1949*, selected and edited by Kurt Hass (Hamburg 1950); Winfried Maaß, *Die Fünfzigjährigen. Porträt einer verratenen Generation* (Hamburg 1980); Rolf Schörken, *Jugend 1945. Politisches Denken und Lebensgeschichte* (Opladen 1990) pp. 21, 137, 146.

young men who did return from the front, more than a third were injured.[4]

If that were not enough, a further source of hardship and disorientation lay in the very high mobility. By 1948 many hundreds of thousands of young people had entered the Soviet Zone, having fled or been expelled along with their families from Poland and Czechoslovakia. At the same time hundreds of thousands of children and youngsters fled sometimes with, sometimes without their families into the Western zones. The impact of all these losses and mobility on the population structure can be gleaned from the fact that in 1946 girls still accounted for 65 per cent of the 2,272,696 youngsters aged between 14 and 25. The Soviet Zone resembled a gigantic transit camp, whose catastrophic economic situation only added to the general difficulties.[5]

It was small wonder that the majority of young people appeared disorientated and apathetic. 'The basic mood of young people in the post-war era', writes Klaus Wasmund, '. . . can best be characterised as a general disorientation crisis, a crisis which manifested itself in a general distance to politics and indeed a political cynicism, and a cautious and reserved attitude towards the forces of democratic renewal.'[6] And yet in many East German towns and villages there was a minority of youngsters who were willing to be politically active. These youngsters often came from families with an anti-fascist background or had been members of the pre-Nazi youth movement and had now returned from prison, concentration camp or exile. They began to create youth organisations, often reviving the political or cultural goals of the Weimar youth movement. Alongside Communist youth associations and Young Socialist Workers' leagues, there were (though only briefly) occupational and

[4] See Vorstand des FDGB Groß-Berlin (ed.), *1. Geschäftsbericht des Freien Deutschen Gewerkschaftsbundes Groß-Berlin* (Berlin 1947), p. 48; Karl Heinz Jahnke, 'Zum Anteil der FDJ an der Gründung der Deutschen Demokratischen Republik', *Wissenschaftliche Zeitschrift der Universität Rostock, G-Reihe*, (1970), 6/7, p. 431; Zentralrat der FDJ (ed.), *Geschichte der Freien Deutschen Jugend* (Berlin 1983), p. 79.

[5] See Vorstand des FDGB (ed.), *Geschäftsbericht des Freien Deutschen Gewerkschaftsbundes 1946* (Berlin 1946), p. 208; Wolfgang Zank, *Wirtschaft und Arbeit in Ostdeutschland 1945–1949. Probleme des Wiederaufbaus in der Sowjetischen Besatzungszone Deutschlands* (Munich 1987), pp. 18 ff., 58 ff.

[6] Klaus Wasmund, 'Leitbilder und Aktionsformen Jugendlicher nach dem Zweiten Weltkrieg in Deutschland bis zu den 6oer Jahren', in Dieter Dowe (ed.), *Jugendprotest und Generationenkonflikte in Europa im 20. Jahrhundert Deutschland, England, Frankreich und Italien im Vergleich* (Bonn 1986), p. 217.

denominational groups, as well as unpolitical Esperanto, hiking and naturist groups. The question was, however, whether these first attempts to create a politically pluralistic youth movement would find the support of the Soviet occupying authorities and the Communist party.

II

The answer was not long in coming. Spontaneous local activities had no place in the planning of the Soviet occupying authorities and of the German Communist party (KPD) which the occupiers licensed and controlled. In July 1945 the head of the Soviet Military Administration (SMAD), Marshal Zhukov, banned these spontaneously formed youth groups and allowed the formation only of so-called anti-fascist youth committees. These committees were to be based in the town halls of the large and medium-sized towns and to be composed of the 'most active anti-fascist young men and women'. The SMAD's policy was designed as the first step towards the eventual formation of a single, Communist-dominated youth organisation.[7]

The following weeks and months saw the creation of many such committees in towns across the Soviet Zone. Initially, they, too, were characterised by considerable openness. Though headed by former members of the proletarian youth movement, particularly young Communists, or by youngsters who had been trained in Soviet POW camps or Antifa schools, the committees showed a willingness to leave matters of high politics to one side and concentrate on day to day issues most immediately affecting post-war youth. Many thus proved effective at mobilising the energies of their members and by the end of 1945 they had engaged some 10 per cent of East German youth.[8] However, this brief period of innocence soon came to an end. By the end of 1945, the many regional committees with their loose structure were brought together under five so-called anti-fascist state youth committees, whose representatives in turn made up the central anti-fascist youth committee in Berlin. The

---

[7] Institut für Geschichte der Arbeiterbewegung. Zentrales Parteiarchiv, Berlin (formerly SED-Archiv), (henceforth IfGA/ZPA), IV 2/16/6.

[8] See Michael Buddrus, 'Zur Einbeziehung ehemaliger HJ-Mitglieder in die Arbeit der Antifaschistischen Jugendausschüsse im Jahre 1945', *Beiträge zur Geschichte der FDJ* (1987), 9, pp. 55–61; Schörken, *Jugend 1945*, p. 142.

latter committee was to make up the core of the leadership of the Free German Youth movement (FDJ), created on 6 March 1946 and named after the groups set up during the 1930s by Communist exiles in Prague and Paris.

Like the Nazis in 1933, the politicians of the Communist and Social Democratic parties in 1945 invoked an ostensible (and largely fictitious) wish on the part of the younger generation for unity to justify their policy of creating a single, unified youth organisation open to all. Communists and Social Democrats argued that history had shown the division within the labour movement before 1933 to have been a fatal mistake. Thus there were now to be no separate Socialist or Communist youth organisations[9] (a decision which led to considerable protest on the part of both younger and sometimes also of older members of the two parties). Even when a unified party was formed in 1946 – the German Socialist Unity party (SED) – it still made great capital out of its unwillingness to create a separate party youth organisation. Social Democrat leaders in the Soviet Zone played along with this concept and were able to agree with the Communist representatives on goals, tasks and organisational structure of the future FDJ and that the two parties should be equally represented in the organisation's leadership.

The Christian Democratic and Liberal parties (CDU and LDPD) were forbidden to create their own youth organisations. To integrate youthful adherents of these parties and more generally young Christians of both denominations, it was agreed that four representatives of these groups should be allowed to join the FDJ leadership. In December 1945, Erich Honecker declared that 'Differences of belief and *Weltanschauung* should, in our view, not be a source of dissension. We believe in full tolerance in such matters.'[10] Yet, in reality, the SED's hold on the organisation grew. By January 1949 almost 20 per cent of the 460,000 FDJ members belonged to the SED, whilst as early as 1948 40 per cent of FDJ leaders held a party card. In April 1949 the CDU and LDPD representatives were ousted from the FDJ secretariat and the church liaison office was wound up. From then on until 1990 the FDJ's top leadership

<hr>

[9] Six days after the SPD's decision of 19 June 1945 not to create its own youth organisation, the Communists followed suit in the interests of a 'unified and free youth movement'; Walter Ulbricht, quoted in *Partei und Jugend. Dokumente marxistisch-leninistischer Jugendpolitik* (Berlin 1986), p. 230.

[10] Erich Honecker to the leaders of the youth committees, 3 December 1945, cited in *Partei und Jugend*, p. 241 ff.

consisted solely of SED members, a phenomenon that soon characterised the middle and lower levels of the organisation's functionaries as well. As a last step in the consolidation of power in the youth
movement, 1952 saw Christians subjected to massive repression
and driven out from the movement.[11]

The FDJ's evolution conformed closely to the policy worked out
by the exiled KPD at its so-called Brussels party conference of
summer 1935. Within the context of the hotly debated popular front
policy,[12] the KPD and the Communist International had laid down
that in a future Communist Germany the KPD should play the
dominant role in youth policy, but do so through the medium of a
unified anti-fascist and ostensibly democratic mass youth organisation which 'without reference to ideological, religious or other
differences should rally all non-reactionary, anti-fascist progressive
forces in the younger generation'. In reality the party continued
dogmatically to assert its right to control the youth organisation,
whilst outwardly maintaining the tactic of the popular front.[13]

One of the key dilemmas confronting leading Communists in
Germany 1945–46 was that in their view 'anti-fascist, progressive
forces of the young generation' were almost non-existent. Given that
most of the younger generation had been members of the Hitler
Youth, who was left to build the 'youth organisation of the new
type'? Up till 1945 the KPD proceeded from the strict assumption
that members of any sort of Nazi organisation, whether youth or
adult, were to be regarded as fascists and excluded from any form of
cooperation. This blanket condemnation was apparent in the KPD
Central Committee's (ZK) first proclamation of 11 June 1945:
'Hitler alone can not bear all the guilt for the crimes committed
against humanity. The ten million Germans who voted for Hitler in
free elections, despite the warnings that we Communists gave also
carry their share of guilt ... as do all those German men and women

[11] Jugendarchiv beim Institut für zeitgeschichtliche Jugendforschung, Berlin (formerly FDJ-Archiv), henceforth (JA) IZJ, A 424; Secret paper on the persecution of the *Junge Gemeinde*, 25 July 1952, in JA IZJ, A 2517; Manfred Klein, *Jugend zwischen den Diktaturen* (Mainz 1968); Heinz Lippmann, *Honecker. Portrait eines Nachfolgers* (Cologne 1971); Wolfgang Leonhard, *Die Revolution entläßt ihre Kinder* (Frankfurt 1955).
[12] Herbert Wehner, *Erinnerungen 1928–1942* (Berlin 1990).
[13] See, for example, the speech by Anton Ackermann, 'Der Kampf der Partei um die werktätige Jugend', in *Die Brüsseler Konferenz der KPD (3.-15. Oktober 1935)* (Berlin 1975), pp. 370f.

who passively stood by as Hitler seized power ... and all those who later followed him.'[14]

In the period immediately after the defeat of fascism there was a strong consensus between ordinary Communist party members and the leadership both on the question of who was guilty and on the policy of permanently excluding all National Socialists, particularly all adult Nazis, from cooperation. The *Tägliche Rundschau*, the organ of the SMAD and the KPD leadership, wrote in October 1945, that 'individuals who have been politically and morally infected by fascist ideology can in many cases never be won back, and certainly not in a matter of weeks or months'. Those who have been 'infected' by fascism will 'whether consciously or unconsciously, always have a destructive impact'.[15]

However, this consensus was soon to end. With their pragmatic sense of day to day realities and with an eye both to potential gains in the political sphere and to the country's manpower needs, the KPD leadership rapidly moved to a new position. In autumn 1945, the KPD, supported by the SMAD, though against the resistance of many ordinary Communists and Social Democrats, began to re-employ former nominal NSDAP (Nazi party) members, in particular highly skilled workers, scientists, engineers and administrators.[16] Soon the party leadership moved on from economic to political integration. It called for voting rights for ordinary NSDAP members and argued that 'former party members who are genuinely and sincerely willing to join in the rebuilding of Germany' should, after a successful probation period, be reintegrated into 'normal political life'.[17] As the 1946 autumn elections moved ever closer, the SED leadership intensified its efforts to win the support of former Nazi party members and put great pressure on the SED rank and file to adopt the new course.

Naturally enough, many SED members, particularly those who had remained in Germany during the Nazi period, protested against the new policy. The Association of Victims of the Nazi regime, for example, argued that they could not work alongside their former

---

[14] Quted in *Partei und Jugend*, pp. 223f.   [15] *Tägliche Rundschau*, 18 October 1945.
[16] See Frank Thomas Stößel, *Positionen und Strömungen in der KPD/SED 1945–1954* (Cologne 1985), pp. 107ff., 246ff.
[17] See the corresponding arguments from Walter Ulbricht and Wilhelm Pieck in *Tägliche Rundschau*, 6 March 1946, 6 June 1946, 12 June 1946 and 21 June 1946.

persecutors.[18] But the party leadership, returning from its Moscow exile, brushed the protests aside. Accusing the non-*émigrés* of lacking theoretical training and of possessing no knowledge of the 'further development of the scientific theory of Marxism-Leninism', Ulbricht imposed the Moscow line, suppressing the great variety of expectations and activities to be found within the rank and file.[19]

As far as youth was concerned, this shift in policy took place more rapidly and, thanks to the rather different tactics of the party, met with much less resistance. Recognising that the creation of a new 'unified anti-fascist-democratic mass youth organisation' under covert Communist leadership was impossible without the involvement of former HJ members, leading Communists and SMAD youth officers agreed in autumn 1945 that for pragmatic reasons German youth was to be given a general amnesty. The Hitler Youth generation, according to the new formula, had been misused by the Nazis. Walter Ulbricht, for example, pronounced to party functionaries as early as 24 June 1945 that 'German youth has been exposed to nothing but the evil influence of Nazi propaganda' and that he had 'faith that German youth, with the help of experienced anti-fascists [i.e. the Communists – M.B.], would contribute enthusiastically ... to the construction of a healthy social order'.[20] Erich Honecker, too, made similar noises. Only recently released from Nazi imprisonment, Honecker had been chosen to head Communist youth policy and had been rapidly schooled in Moscow's new line. 'German youth', Honecker declared, 'has been through the criminal school of Adolf Hitler' and has been 'misused for acts of shame'.[21] 'We extend the hand of cooperation to every ordinary member of the former Hitler Youth and League of German Girls and invite them to join in the task of reconstruction, because they, like our whole people, have been deceived and misled ... similarly we offer the hand of friend-

---

[18] See Stößel, *Positionen und Strömungen*, pp. 419f. In 1954 around 14 per cent of SED functionaries had been in the NSDAP or one of its affiliated organisations, though there were strong regional variations. See IfGA/ZPA, IV 2/5/25, IV 2/5/1371.

[19] See Stößel, *Positionen und Strömungen*, pp. 22f.

[20] Walter Ulbricht, 'Das Programm der antifaschistisch-demokratischen Ordnung', in Ulbricht, *Zur Geschichte der deutschen Arbeiterbewegung. Reden und Aufsätze*. Vol. II: *1933–1946* (Berlin 1963), pp. 441f.

[21] Erich Honecker, 'Neues Leben – Neue Jugend', in *Tägliche Rundschau*, 8 June 1945.

ship to all lesser HJ and BDM officials as long as they are honest and sincere in their commitment to Germany'.[22]

Yet though they might pragmatically advocate the rehabilitation of German youth, the KPD leadership continued to make very undifferentiated and crass assumptions about the guilt of all but active resistance fighters among the younger generation. Indeed, the Communists hoped that by extending an amnesty to the young, declaring faith in them and yet simultaneously reminding them of their guilt, they would induce young Germans to seek absolution by throwing themselves whole-heartedly behind the new order. In the words of Erich Honnecker, SMAD and KPD were, 'in a spirit of great generosity', giving a 'younger generation, which had never enjoyed the right to organise itself freely and democratically, the chance with the help of the Youth Committees to cleanse their lives of fascist influence and to join together in shaping the future'.[23] Former Hitler Youth members had 'no higher duty' than 'to be the generation which made good the evil which the Nazi leaders have wrought on our people'.[24]

The reintegration of the Hitler Youth generation was to be paralleled and facilitated by a huge programme of reeducation. In effect the Communists planned to engage in the same sort of indoctrination as the former Hitler Youth, though now in the opposite political direction. Erich Honecker's formula for dealing with the past was a mechanical brainwashing operation, to free 'the hearts and minds of our young people' from 'chauvinistic debris' and thus 'to wash clean the name of Germany'.[25] Elsewhere Honecker spoke of the need to 'reawaken in German youth that awareness of right and wrong, truth and lies, ethical behaviour and wrongdoing which the Nazis had destroyed, to remove Nazi ideology from their hearts' and to 'mould German youth into honest and decent human beings'.[26]

In April 1946 with an FDJ membership of just 175,000 members, the KPD (later SED) Youth Secretary, Paul Verner, tried to instil

[22] Erich Honecker, 'Die Jugend als aktiver Teilnehmer beim Aufbau einer antifaschistisch-demokratischen Ordnung' (December 1945), in Honecker, *Zur Jugendpolitik der SED. Reden und Aufsätze von 1945 bis zur Gegenwart* (Berlin 1985), pp. 22f.
[23] Statement of Erich Honecker on the proclamation by the SMAD on the creation of youth committees, 31 July 1945, cited in *Partei und Jugend*, pp. 232ff.
[24] Erich Honecker in July 1945, cited in *Partei und Jugend*, pp. 231ff.
[25] Erich Honecker, 'Neues Leben – Neue Jugend'.
[26] Erich Honecker cited in *Partei und Jugend*, pp. 232ff.

in leading party comrades a more differentiated picture of the Hitler Youth generation and to modify the party's approach. He warned against one-sided judgements and exaggerated expectations, arguing that the great majority of young people 'have been led to despair by the challenges which face them' and see 'no future for themselves'. If you want, he argued,

to paint a picture of young people's ideological position, then neither black or white will do. You need the whole spectrum. Between good and evil, positive and negative, there are many fine gradations. One part of our youth is firmly committed to building a new homeland but we also have great numbers of young people who stand back and remain apathetic. Finally, we have the great mass of young people who are simply driven by events. This should not surprise us. In the 12 years behind us Nazi ideas have been deeply implanted in the minds of our young people. We will have to dig deep and hard to eradicate fascist thinking.[27]

And Verner reiterated the invitation extended to former young National Socialists:

Many members of the Free German Youth were formerly in the Hitler Youth or the BDM. To all those HJ and BDM members, who are still not in the new movement, the FDJ extends the hand of friendship and calls on them to: march with us! Come into the Free German Youth, place your youthful energy in the service of progress, for our people and our country. Those, however, who belonged to the full-time leadership corps of the Nazi youth corrupters have no place in the organisation of the FDJ. They have no place in freedom – their rightful place is in prison.[28]

Other leading party functionaries too repeated and extended the offer made to the Hitler Youth generation. In June 1946, Honecker suddenly and emphatically declared that 'youth can not be equated with war crimes. Youth was misused . . . and misled'.[29] Otto Grotewohl went a step further and, partly in response to the West's approach to dealing with Germany's past, rejected the idea of 'holding youth responsible for things for which they can hold no responsibility. We reject any suggestion of holding youngsters responsible for thoughts and actions which they had no role in disseminating or initiating. And we reject also the high sounding

---

27 Paul Verner, 'Bericht über die Jugendarbeit der Partei', in *Bericht über die Verhandlungen des 15. Parteitages der Kommunistischen Partei Deutschlands, 19.-20. April 1946* (Berlin 1946), pp. 119ff.

28 *Ibid.*

29 Erich Honecker, 'Rede auf dem 1. Parlament der FDJ', 8 June 1946, cited in *Partei und Jugend*, pp. 273ff.

phrases, of which they're so fond in the west, to the effect that we need a political amnesty for youth. We don't need an amnesty for you, since we never for one moment condemned you, and we are not going to condemn you now.'[30]

Another – and somewhat more effective – result of the new commitment to win over young people were the 'four rights' proclaimed by the FDJ. At its first congress the FDJ, in consultation with the SED, announced 'in the name of the younger generation' that 'all democratic organs had the duty' to ensure youth 'political rights, the right to work and leisure, the right to education, and the right to happiness and enjoyment'.[31] These 'basic rights of the young generation' did indeed enjoy considerable resonance among young people and placed the bourgeois parties, with their more traditional approach to youth policy, under some pressure.

Yet overall the drive to recruit young Germans to the youth committees and, from March 1946, to the FDJ did not produce the hoped for results. And a similar poor response met attempts to persuade young people to join the Communist party, later the SED. In the immediate aftermath of the formation of the SED in April 1946 the share of party members under 21 was only 6 per cent. Even in the early 1950s almost 70 per cent of SED members were over 40, a fact which caused considerable consternation among the party leadership.[32]

III

It was apparent that the party was unable to communicate with much of the younger generation. The Communist leadership's mechanical and global condemnation of the past, the lack of real understanding for the experiences and situation of young Germans, influenced and vitiated their message.[33] For Honecker and the KPD leadership it was utterly inconceivable that young people might have had positive memories of the Third Reich. They were not prepared to confront the many youthful experiences and influences, by no means all of them of an inhumane character, which had

[30] Otto Grotewohl, 'Ruf an die Jugend', in Grotewohl, *Im Kampf um die eigene Deutsche Demokratische Republik. Reden und Aufsätze.* Vol. I: *1945–1949* (Berlin 1950), pp. 24ff.

[31] *Dokumente und Beschlüsse der FDJ*, vol. I (Berlin 1951), pp. 12f.

[32] IfGA/ZPA, NL 62/83.

[33] *Dokumente und Materialien zur Geschichte der deutschen Arbeiterbewegung*, Series III, vol. I, May 1945–April 1946 (Berlin 1959), pp. 37f.

helped form the young generation. Only for the period before 1933, when free and independent organisations existed in Germany, would the Communists accept that there had been 'great experiences' which 'many of us remember with pleasure'.[34] Many youngsters, who felt that during the Nazi years they had only done their duty, did not understand what it was they were supposed to have done wrong.

Paul Verner partly acknowledged this when he argued that the party was not even speaking the same language as those who had been socialised in the Third Reich. Terms with which the latter generation had grown up such as blood, race, state, courage, hardness, will, honour, loyalty, faith, but also fate, discipline, order, camaraderie, effort (*Leistung*), commitment and sacrifice were now all suspect. Words like people (*Volk*), Socialism, Fatherland or freedom had all gained a new meaning. Verner was very conscious that 'the great majority of the younger generation understand little of the language of today. Democracy, for example, is a slogan on which different people place very different interpretations.'[35] And just like the term 'democracy', which had been used pejoratively in the Third Reich to describe the 'Western plutocracies', so also the word 'Socialism' had undergone a change of meaning that was hard for young people to grasp. On the one hand the word was closely linked with their own past in National Socialism, and thus to be condemned; on the other hand they were being asked to subscribe to a new Socialism, this time ostensibly the true one. 'The young men and women who joined our party over the last year' argued Verner 'did not come as Socialists. Their concept of Socialism is very vague ... and clouded by the pseudo-Socialism of the Nazis.'[36] The only point of orientation that had retained some integrity, even though it had been misused, was that of Fatherland. Yet for the Hitler youth generation in the Soviet Zone, the Fatherland was defeated, divided and occupied by the Russians, the enemy of yesterday.[37]

---

[34] Erich Honecker, *Zur Jugendpolitk der SED*, p. 32.
[35] Verner, 'Bericht über die Jugendarbeit der Partei', p. 255.
[36] *Ibid.*, p. 257.
[37] See Hermann Weber, 'Zum Transformationsprozeß des Parteiensystems in der SBZ/DDR', in Weber (ed.), *Parteiensystem zwischen Demokratie und Volksdemokratie. Dokumente und Materialien zum Funktionswandel der Parteien und Massenorganisationen in der SBZ/DDR 1945–1990* (Cologne 1982), pp. 39f. On the language of post-war youth see, for example Urs Widmer, *1945 oder die 'Neue Sprache'. Studien zur Prosa der 'Jungen Generation'* (Düsseldorf 1966).

Partly in recognition of this communication gap, the SBZ's leaders tended, once the initial enthusiasm of victory had given way to more tactical considerations, to avoid the term 'Socialism'. It was reactivated only in 1952. Thus Honecker's manifesto 'Youth and Socialism' from March 1946[38] was quietly buried. Instead, the SED tried to present itself as the 'party of youth' in the hope of gradually winning over the Hitler Youth generation to authentic Socialism. The manifesto of the SPD-KPD congress of unity made the following appeal to young people: 'German youth is our hope. In your hands lies the future of our Fatherland. Our *Weltanschauung* must become the creed of the younger generation. In it you will find the highest ideals ... The Socialist Unity Party, this young party full of life and energy is thus your party, the party of German youth' and 'We address ourselves particularly to youth', so that 'it will recognise in our party its great guide and leader.'[39] But, the party was soon to learn that young Germans, having so recently followed one 'party of youth' and its great 'guide and leader', were not ready to attach themselves to a new one.

If failure to understand and respond to young Germans' real attitudes and needs was one reason for the SED's recruitment difficulties, another was that large sections of the party rank and file were hostile to the new 'youth cult'. The lowering from 18 to 16 of the minimum age for joining the party intensified many older members' fear that they would be pushed aside by new youthful cadres. Even comparatively senior party figures could be found expressing solidarity with the old comrades and deliberately denying younger recruits responsibility and access to decision making. Young people were often prevented from attending party training schools, and thus from attaining the prerequisite for further advancement. Many rank and file members refused to cooperate with the FDJ, arguing that many of its members had Nazi pasts and that the younger generation was not yet politically mature.[40]

Leaders from a series of local, town and factory party groups, and also many younger party members, demanded a separate SED youth organisation. They had perhaps failed to recognise that this was in fact what the SED was covertly trying to achieve with the FDJ. Some SED members rejected the broad church approach and

[38] See *Partei und Jugend*, pp. 251f.
[39] *Protokoll des Vereinigungsparteitages der SPD und der KPD* (Berlin 1946), pp. 170, 204.
[40] For more detail see Stößel, *Positionen und Strömungen*, pp. 187ff., 328ff., 521ff.

'ideological mish-mash' of the FDJ, arguing that Weimar had shown young people to be easy prey for an authoritarian leadership unless they enjoyed the 'firm theoretical foundations' and the 'political experience' which a Communist youth group could give them. But the SED leadership for its part rejected 'what is on the surface the attractive idea of creating a separate youth organisation, ideologically firmly linked to the party'. On the one hand, as we have seen, they hoped that the FDJ would act as a transmission belt, allowing them to influence a far larger section of the youthful population than just the few Communist sympathisers. 'We have a responsibility even for those youngsters who remain aloof from the party' and we 'cannot afford to isolate the most conscious and progressive young people in their own organisation, cut off from the rest of their generation'.[41] Thus young party members should make their influence felt within the FDJ. On the other hand, the young party and FDJ members were entrusted with an analogous task within the SED. 'Lacking political experience, more easy to influence and motivate, they had the task of bringing older members into line with the leadership's wishes', and particularly of ensuring that the leadership's production targets were met. 'They could do that better from within the main party organisation than from a separate body.'[42]

Records remain of a few of the meetings held between the central FDJ leadership in Berlin and the heads of the five state divisions. The minutes of those meetings testify eloquently to the problems facing the attempt to integrate young people into the movement. The regional leaderships found themselves caught between what were often unrealistic demands from on high and the real situation on the ground. Functionaries from Saxony, among other regions, complained in October 1946, for example, that a large number of local SED leaders had 'rejected' the FDJ as an 'unnecessary organisation'. In Thuringia by contrast the complaint was that the youngsters rejected the FDJ as the 'youth party of the SED'. In Brandenburg the party had not whole-heartedly recognised the FDJ and wanted to create 'its own Socialist youth organisation'. In Saxony-Anhalt, the 'young comrades ... are turned away by their elders'

---

[41] *Bericht des Parteivorstandes der SED an den 2. Parteitag* (Berlin 1947), pp. 113ff.
[42] Stößel, *Positionen und Strömungen*, pp. 329ff.

often with the argument that 'we were involved in politics long before you were even born'. In Mecklenburg a speaker had been applauded when he stated that 'the FDJ is the same rabble as the HJ'. In Rostock of the 800 SED members aged 16–25 not even 80 were in the FDJ. The state heads noted also that many of the FDJ officers were incapable of winning over youth. Successes among young workers – the group whose interests the FDJ saw itself mainly as representing – were limited ('only dances and alcohol drew them in'), whilst the student body was seen as 'a rallying point for everyone who is against SED and FDJ'.[43]

The state chiefs noted many reasons for the reluctance to join SED and FDJ. Though the church had not yet declared open opposition, it was already apparent that the 'representatives of the Catholic church reject the FDJ's aspiration for total mobilisation' and would cooperate with it only in some committee representing various separate youth movements. Many young people rejected not only the SED but any one-party system, with the argument that 'it would be a disaster for our people if one party should get an absolute majority'.[44] And there was also the deterrent effect of the actions of the occupying power, giving rise in many parts of Germany to difficulties in 'combating the anti-Soviet tendencies amongst our youth'. 'The Russians' were seen as making inordinate demands on young people which 'could not be reconciled with the FDJ's declared basic rights for youth'. For all states and provinces it was clear that 'Wherever the Russians are to be found relations are bad. Heavy work and long hours ... many arrests' and the general view that 'the SED is a servant of the Russians'.[45]

This was the difficult situation confronting leading FDJ functionaries. Often they lacked the ability, the time or the power to assert themselves. Small wonder that they moaned continually at the poor response to their (generally sincere and well meaning) efforts at winning over young people. At least up to the end of the 1940s, SED and FDJ leaders found themselves permanently running up against young people's 'tendency to be non-political', their 'count me out'

---

[43] 'Vertrauliche Auszüge aus den Besprechungen der FDJ-Führung 1946/47', in JA IZJ, A 3822.
[44] *Ibid.*   [45] *Ibid.*

attitude and their corresponding rejection of a state youth organisation.[46]

IV

Integrating young people in FDJ and KPD/SED was one main goal of the Communists. The other was to harness their energy in the interest of economic recovery. At a time of dire shortages, black marketeering, growing youth criminality and low labour morale, a more effective and energetic deployment of young labour seemed essential. In July 1945 Honecker argued that 'the creation of a serious, responsible attitude towards work on the part of the younger generation' is the 'prerequisite for the success of reconstruction'.[47] As in their approach to the membership of the SED, the party leadership wanted not only to ensure that young people put their full effort into industrial and agricultural production but also to use youthful energy to put pressure on the older generation.

In addition, the Communist party leadership wanted to use a mobile younger generation to achieve a more egalitarian society. Just as in the ethnic community of the Third Reich, youth was assigned the role of catalyst in achieving the 'unity of the people'.[48] Thus, just a couple of years after the end of the Nazi dictatorship, the SED party executive laid down that 'When we talk of the unity of the people, we must be clear in our minds that it is youth above all which can and must become the adhesive to bind our people together.' Youth must fulfil this potential 'in order to remove in the future all those barriers and prejudices which still divide the working people of this country today'.[49] Finally, the Communists also wanted to ensure that 'tens of thousands of really capable young men and women are found for the teacher training schools' in order to build a 'living bridge from school to the youth movement'.[50]

As we have seen, one of the Communists' strategies for encouraging young people to put their backs to the wheel was to cultivate a

---

[46] The level of organisation fluctuated sharply in the 1947–48 period, attaining 37 per cent in autumn 1949. It was only in the 1960s that it reached the 50 per cent level. In the 1970s the percentage of youngsters in the FDJ reached 70 per cent but by then FDJ membership was obligatory for almost any form of personal advancement.
[47] Cited in *Partei und Jugend*, pp. 230ff.
[48] See Buddrus, 'Geschichte der Hitlerjugend', pp. 78f.
[49] *Bericht des Parteivorstandes der SED an den 2. Parteitag* (Berlin 1947), p. 114.
[50] Erich Honecker, 2 December 1945, cited in *Partei und Jugend*, p. 245.

guilt complex (this despite the fact that youth was at the same time being told that it was victim of Nazi crimes). To be a builder, carpenter, joiner, roofer, farmer or to help with the harvest should be 'an honour' for former members of the HJ, argued Honecker. Through their 'work on the bomb sites, in the restored factories, on building sites, in apprentice workshops and in the harvest' they could demonstrate their desire to make a fresh start. Together, through work and through their activities in the FDJ they could 'prove that they have learned from the past'.[51]

But more tangible incentives were also on offer, most notably the FDJ's and SED's propagation of the slogan 'equal pay for equal work', given legal force by the SMAD in their Military Government Order 253. This had an electrifying effect on many youngsters, less on ideological grounds than because they saw in it the chance to improve their standard of living. The slogan 'equal pay for equal work' was instrumentalised by the 'Young activist movement'. SED and FDJ created numerous young brigades and set them the task of surpassing production norms by up to 300 per cent and thus forcing up the output of the older workers. The party leadership well knew where the 'weakest point in the solidarity of the workers' was to be found: it was the younger workers, used by the SED in 'rate-buster brigades' to trigger a generation conflict in the workplace. The party's overt justification for their policy was that 'the young will follow a big ideal with a passion' and 'are more easily won over to the new'. In effect, however, the SED was exploiting the fact that the young had been socialised in the Third Reich: here was a generation that had grown up when great ideals and enthusiasm had counted for a great deal, whilst the traditions and values of the German labour movement had counted for nothing.[52]

Thus Grotewohl announced that the new slogan was 'Make way for youth', and that it 'must be adopted by every progressive person ... in the economic, the social or the political sphere'.[53] Many factory managers, brigadists and master craftsmen, indeed many factory party leaderships and union leaders, actively or passively, resisted the young activist movement. They saw it as undermining workers' solidarity and putting too much pressure on older colleagues. They demoted younger workers, dissolved youth brigades,

[51] Erich Honecker, 'Neues Leben – Neue Jugend'; see also *Partei und Jugend*, pp. 230ff.
[52] See Stößel, *Positionen und Strömungen*, p. 371.
[53] Grotewohl, *Reden und Aufsätze*, p. 181.

hindered the introduction of new working methods and thus in part stymied the efforts of SED and FDJ and the genuine engagement of many youngsters.[54] Nevertheless, the SED's policy (later officially denied) of fomenting generational conflict brought both tangible economic results and facilitated the political and economic integration of post-war youth.

The success of the mobilisation campaign was, however, far more limited than the SED had hoped. As the state chiefs of the FDJ noted, most youngsters 'had great interest in learning a trade and becoming skilled workers', but they were not persuaded by the ideological dimensions of the SED's economic programme. Young people were of the opinion that 'they were working not for reconstruction or peace' but 'only for reparations'. What motivated them was the personal situation. When they were assured of a stable living standard they 'work gladly. Food and clothing are their priorities.'[55]

V

The SED was not entirely to blame for the failure to build a more genuine relationship with German youth. The difficult venture of making a fresh start was hindered from the start by a series of difficult challenges. Even with the best will in the world it was not possible to reconcile the expectations and hopes of the East German population with the interests of a Soviet Union that had been ravaged by the Nazi war machine. Moreover, for all the shortcomings of the SED's policies, and whatever the parallels between totalitarian policies of Nazis and Communists, there is little doubt that the socialisation of youth in post-war East Germany did not have the aggressive and inhumane character of that of the Third Reich.[56]

The fact remains, however, that SED and FDJ leaders conspicuously failed to communicate with the generation that had grown up during the Third Reich and the war. The leaders had spent the Nazi period in Soviet exile, in Nazi camps and prisons or in resistance to the Third Reich. Their socialisation, experience and outlook was

---

[54] On this point see Stößel, *Positionen und Strömungen*, pp. 371ff., 471ff.
[55] 'Vertrauliche Auszüge aus den Besprechungen der FDJ-Führung 1946/47', in JA IZJ, A 3822.
[56] See Michael Buddrus, 'Aspekte der Jugendpolitik', in Helga Gotschlich *et al.*, *Kinder und Jugendliche aus der DDR. Jugendhilfe in den neuen Bundesländern* (Berlin 1991) pp. 21–28.

poles apart from that of the Hitler Youth generation. Perhaps a genuine dialogue might have bridged the gap – but the Communist leaders did not seek it. Even when they were sincerely trying to communicate, they remained stuck in a language that took no account of the needs of youth or the realities of the younger generation's experience and situation. Instead, they invoked a pathos and idealism, trussed up in the inimitable vocabulary of Communist party rhetoric, which left the young listeners cold.

Moreover, the leadership knew and felt themselves to be on the side of the victors and treated the youngsters of the Hitler Youth generation undifferentiatedly as the losers. The Hitler Youth generation, true enough, was now generously given the chance to 'prove itself' in building a new Germany, but the price was that it had to bury its entire past, a past which in the eyes of the youth functionaries consisted solely of 'darkness and barbarism'. For many youngsters, this mechanical condemnation of their past constituted a theft of their own identity, and they reacted accordingly. The FDJ leadership was surprised and alarmed to discover, for example, that young people were increasingly 'opposed to the Nuremberg trials. They are not always in favour of war criminals being hanged' and they 'discuss with one another' 'whether a judgement was fair or not'.[57]

Young people's reaction here was not surprising. Their knowledge (like much of adult German society) of Nazi crimes was limited and they refused to accept what they heard, or their own share of responsibility. Moreover, for many youngsters, the contact to their former HJ leaders remained their only stable social ties and finally, of course, the men who now sat in the dock at Nuremberg had until very recently been the models whom they had looked up to.[58]

One of the key weaknesses of Communist policy was that it left no room for a genuine individual process of dealing with the past. The prisoner of war camps and Antifa schools, the youth committees and FDJ offered collective discussions rather than encouraging individuals to find their own way. The FDJ and SED leaders were, despite their protestations to the contrary, hostile to genuine individual attempts to deal with the past. Instead, the Communists

---

[57] JA IZJ, A 3822.
[58] See Buddrus, 'Zur Einbeziehung ehemaliger HJ-Mitglieder', p. 57.

wanted their organisations to be the new locus of group solidarity and belief. They wanted young people simply to substitute a new world view for the old Nazi one. They wanted, just as had the Nazis, to offer a system that would explain everything and would engender just as deep an identification with the new regime as with the old.[59] The new leaders could not or did not want to recognise that an entire generation had lost its political credulity.

Unwilling to allow genuine discussion about the past, and faced with a situation in which they did not even speak the same language as their youthful charges, the Communists introduced a sort of 'anti-fascism by decree'. Over night the younger generation were deemed to have become anti-fascists, indeed victims of National Socialism, an 'amnesty' gladly accepted by most of its beneficiaries. But this precluded a genuine catharsis. The great majority of youth – indeed of the population as a whole – who had followed Hitler right to the end might welcome the amnesty which the SED now offered, but their official relabelling as anti-fascists in a society relabelled as Socialist meant that the real, painful process of learning about and understanding one's own responsibility for the events of the past appeared unnecessary and indeed impossible. Over the following years, East Germany was swamped by a flood of more or less credible heroic biographies chronicling the epic struggles of fighters against National Socialism; the Nazi era came to seem like a period of permanent victory over fascism. Thus both population and leaders of East Germany took part in a form of communal self-deception.

What this indicates is that the Communists' relationship to German youth had two, rather contradictory, dimensions. On the one hand, as the leadership admitted with striking candour in 1953, the FDJ had 'not succeeded in persuading the great mass of young people to take an active part in the struggle to realise the aims of party and government' and had recently suffered a 'serious loss of influence among the younger generation'.[60] Since 1949 and particularly since 1952 tens of thousands of youngsters had joined the hundreds of thousands of their older compatriots fleeing the GDR in

59 See Everhard Holtmann, 'Die neuen Lassalleaner. SPD und HJ-Generation nach 1945', in Martin Broszat, Klaus-Dietmar Henke and Hans Wollner (eds.), *Von Stalingrad zur Währungsreform. Zur Sozialgeschichte des Umbruchs in Deutschland* (Munich 1988), p. 186; Schörken, *Jugend 1945*, pp. 109f.
60 JA IZJ, A 2498.

a bid to escape the intrusions of state and SED. It was against this background that the FDJ decided in 1953 on 'Measures of the organisation to hinder the flight of young people from the Republic'.[61] On the other hand, the Communists' self-deceiving 'anti-fascism by decree' actually facilitated the integration of youth, and indeed of the wider population. Through rapid identification with the anti-fascist 'victors of history', the population was spared the discomfort of genuinely recognising its role in the past. The suppression of uncomfortable memories, the one-sided blaming of Nazi crimes on monopoly capitalists and militarists, encouraged at least a partial identification with the new regime: the *Führer* is dead, long live the *Generalsekretär*! Alongside the survival of a traditional willingness to submit to authoritarian rule, this was a key reason for the fact that the imposition of the new dictatorship in East Germany was accepted with so little resistance.[62]

---

[61] JA IZJ, A 2525.
[62] On the survival of authoritarian values, see *Bericht des Parteivorstandes der SED an den 2. Parteitag* (Berlin 1947), pp. 99, 111; Schörken, *Jugend 1945*, p. 16.

CHAPTER 13

The generation conflict that never was: young labour in the Ruhr mining industry 1945–1957

Mark Roseman

As the war ended, surviving members of Germany's former trades union leaders set about re-establishing collective interest representation for the workers. Alongside uncertainties about future Allied policy or the employers' position, many unionists were worried about what the response of the Hitler Youth (HJ) generation would be. After all, no German aged 26 or less in 1945 could have had any experience of a trades union. Indeed, those born at the end of World War 1 and who thus entered the labour market during the slump, frequently went from unemployment to Reich Labour Service to military service to wartime call up without ever being part of a normal industrial workforce at all.[1] Youngsters that did manage to gain some industrial experience knew only the emasculated Councils of Trust and the German Labour Front. If they managed to assert their interests in the boom conditions of the late 1930s and early 1940s they did so only on an individual, not an organised collective basis. In addition, the young generation knew nothing of Weimar's subculture of workers' political and cultural organisations, banned since 1933. Terror had made it in many cases too dangerous for parents to communicate an anti-Nazi view to their children even in private.[2]

Particularly worrying for older labour leaders in 1945 were the many signs that the Nazis had been at least partially successful in

I am very grateful to Dick Bessel and Dick Geary for their comments on the manuscript. Footnotes have been kept to a minimum. For fuller references see my *Recasting the Ruhr 1945–1958: manpower, economic recovery and labour relations* (Oxford 1992).

[1] Detlev Peukert, 'Kolonie und Zeche. Arbeiterradikalismus, Widerständigkeit und Anpassung der Bergarbeiter zwischen Faschismus und Wirtschaftswunder', *Sozialwissenschaftliche Informationen für Unterricht und Studium*, vol. 8 (1980), pp. 24–30.

[2] An excellent overview is provided by Uli Herbert, 'Zur Entwicklung der Ruhrarbeiterschaft 1930 bis 1960 aus erfahrungsgeschichtlicher Perspektive', in Lutz Niethammer and Alexander von Plato (eds.), *'Wir kriegen jetzt andere Zeiten.' Auf der Suche nach der Erfahrung des Volkes in nachfaschistischen Ländern* (Berlin, Bonn 1985) pp. 19–52.

creating out of young Germans a generation of willing followers. In the HJ, in national service and in wartime military service the Nazis drilled youngsters from all social backgrounds to accept the discipline of hierarchical organisations. At the same time, the Nazis' propaganda and social policy enjoyed considerable resonance. Whilst many young Germans proved increasingly indifferent to the wave of propaganda continually emanating from the regime, there is ample evidence that many were at least partially impressed by notions of a national-racial community, overriding class divisions. The effectiveness and strength of a national movement set on national goals and not weakened by internal division, was widely appreciated as were the real and symbolic upwards social mobility offered by the HJ, by other party organisations and by military service during the war. In their attitudes, and in matters of personal style, too – clothing and leisure habits for example – young workers showed that they were breaking from their proletarian inheritance.[3]

What, then, was the impact of the HJ generation on workforce and labour relations in the post-war period? How did the older employers and union officials, most of them socialised in the quite different conditions of the Weimar republic, react to this younger generation? Was the position of the labour movement significantly weakened by the presence of a group of workers with no union traditions, socialised amidst the *Volksgemeinschaft* propaganda of the Nazi period? In fact, did the Nazis leave a sort of lasting gift to post-war German capitalism, undermining the class politics of Weimar and making it a more effective capitalist economy by deproletarianising the young workforce?

I

The mining industry offers a central, though not always typical, example with which to pursue these questions. For a start, what happened in mining mattered. Labour relations and strikes in mining had traditionally exerted an enormous influence throughout

[3] Günther Mai, '"Warum steht der deutsche Arbeiter zu Hitler". Zur Rolle der Deutschen Arbeitsfront im Herrschaftssystem des Dritten Reiches', *GG*, vol. 12 (1986), 2, pp. 212–234; for the Ruhr Michael Zimmermann, 'Ausbruchshoffnungen. Junge Bergleute in den dreißiger Jahren', in Lutz Niethammer (ed.), *'Die Jahre weiß man nicht, wo man die heute hinsetzen soll'. Faschismuserfahrungen im Ruhrgebiet* (Berlin, Bonn 1983) pp. 97–132. A lot of my thinking on the Nazi period draws on the oral history work carried out by Alexander von Plato and his colleagues. See the references in note 4 of von Plato's essay in this volume.

, other branches of industry. And whilst mining's overall economic significance was gradually waning in the long term, it enjoyed in the reconstruction period an importance second to none. Secondly, mining saw a particularly large influx of younger labour after the war, producing a very sharp age gap between the HJ generation and the older members of the workforce. Tensions and conflict might be expected to be as great here as in any other sector.

In 1945 the mining industry offered an extreme example of a more general problem: the depletion through call up and wartime losses of the younger and productive elements of the workforce. During the war, as German workers were called to the front, there was increasing resort to foreign conscript labour. By the beginning of 1945 foreigners amounted to some 40 per cent of the underground workforce. In 1945, liberation of these *Fremdarbeiter* and a general flight of German workers to the country meant that the underground workforce was almost 50 per cent under strength.[4] The depredations of war were all the more serious because even before the war had begun to make its demands recruitment problems in the interwar period had left the mining workforce increasingly over-aged.[5]

For our generational questions this had the important consequence that in 1945 only a tiny proportion of the workforce was young enough to have been socialised in the Third Reich. In 194 only 14 per cent was under 30![6] There was no large 'indigenous' generation, recruited as youngsters during the 1930s. The ' number of young men who came to the mines after 1945 di newcomers to the industry, coming sometimes with experie other areas of employment and very often after activ service. Thus the rift between those socialised in the ⌐ and those whose youth had occurred in Weimar or t¹ very largely overlapped with a division between es† and newcomers to the industry.

In the period up to 1957 the mines hired a h¹ When movement from pit to pit and rehiri⌐ employed in the mining industry have been ⌐ a million new recruits passed through the period. Much of the new intake did no⌐

[4] Deutsche Kohlenbergbauleitung (ed.), *Zahlen der* vol. 1, p. 20.
[5] Roseman, *Recasting*, pp. 24 and 162–166.
[6] Calculated from Oberbergamt Dortmund (⌐ table, 'Altersgliederung der Bergarbeiter ir

probably between 40 and 50 per cent of the underground workforce
was composed of individuals who had joined the industry since
1945.[7] The vast majority of these newcomers belonged to the HJ
generation. In 1946–47, the year of biggest intake, between 50 and
75 per cent of recruits were born between 1922 and 1930. At most a
quarter of those joining the industry were born before 1917–18. For
1948–50, between 80 and 90 per cent of recruits lay in the age
range 17–25, i.e. had been born between 1923 and 1933. It was
only in the course of the 1950s that this cohort in turn was sup-
plemented by the *Kriegskinder*, born too late to experience anything
of the Third Reich apart from its collapse. But even in 1957, getting
on for a third of the mines' intake had been born between 1920 and
1933.[8]

The generation gap between the newcomers and the established
workforce was accentuated by the fact that, because of the pre-war
recruitment problems already identified, there were relatively few
miners in the established workforce aged under 40. Those over 40
made up a huge 55 per cent of the underground workforce in 1946,
a figure still over 40 per cent in 1950 and only dropping rapidly
after 1951.[9] Whilst the younger age-range expanded rapidly due to
the influx of new blood, the middle years of 30–40, which might
have eased the differences between old and young, remained very
much under-represented.[10]

Equally important was the fact that the newcomers' social backgrounds often differed substantially from those of the established
workforce. In the period from late 1946 to 1950, mining was one of
the few reasonably well-paid employment opportunities around;
the result was that men flocked to the pits from all over Germany.
Between a quarter and a half of all recruits to the mines came from
outside the Ruhr and of the latter between a half and two-thirds
were expellees and refugees. Of these, a significant minority came
from non-working-class backgrounds. For example, one survey discovered that in the 1945–48 period some 15–20 per cent of expellees
taken on as miners had come from white-collar occupations or self-

[...]ng figures based on unpublished statistics from the Statistik der Kohlenwirtschaft e.V.,
[...]

[...]lated from the logbook of the mines' reception camp, Essen Heisingen, which is in the
[...]ion of the Gesamtverband des deutschen Steinkohlenbergbaues, Essen.
[...]ted from *ZdKW*, vol. 7, p. 38; vol. 16, p. 47; vol. 26, p. 47; vol. 39, p. 50.
[...]om table 'Altersgliederung der Bergarbeiter im Ruhrbergbau', in ObaD, *Jahres-
[...]8.*

employment.[11] Thus in mining (as indeed, to a lesser extent, in other occupations) generational differences overlapped with regional and social differences, a point to which we shall return.

II

To what extent did this army of new miners from the HJ generation weaken organised labour's position or blunt the militancy of labour politics? This is hard to answer for the very immediate post-war period since there were in a sense no organised labour relations. The mines were in Allied hands, and labour policy determined by the British military government. Both employers and German labour were in considerable disarray, the employers unnerved, the union-ists preoccupied with re-creating their organisation. It was not until 1946 that a functioning zonal trade union organisation was authorised by military government.

During this period, indeed until the late autumn of 1946, the British tried unsuccessfully to conscript labour into the Ruhr mines. Thousands of unwilling new recruits were dragged to the pits, equipped with threadbare work clothing and equipment and then set to work. Most slipped away within a few days of arrival. Only a tiny fraction of those conscripted stayed for any length of time and those that did stay refused to do much work. Small wonder, when in the chaotic economy of the post-war period, the reichsmarks in the miners' pay packets were increasingly valueless. In such a situation, the main efforts of employers and organised labour lay in trying to protect the interests of the established workforce against unruly and unhappy newcomers. At the face, pit deputies knew no other response to the conscripts than to adopt the sensitive human rela-tions techniques that had already been tried out on Soviet POWs. Needless to say, this hardly tempted young labour to stay.[12]

From the end of 1946, however, with both the Miners' Union (Industrieverband Bergbau, IVB – from 1949 IGB) and employers better organised, with new incentive schemes on offer which made mining work genuinely attractive, and with a rapidly expanding youthful element in the workforce, the situation stabilised. But though they might welcome the end to conscription, the unions saw much to worry them. The mines were taking on around 12,000 men

[11] For the statistics see Roseman, *Recasting*, pp. 257–258.   [12] *Ibid.*, pp. 23–58.

a month in 1947 and the IVB grew increasingly anxious about the young new miners' organisational and political reliability. In particular, those who came from outside the Ruhr and lived in the hostels, with few contacts amongst the other workers, appeared to the union to create potential divisions in the workforce which employers would be able to exploit. Trade union organisation was very low among such men, the IVB estimating it at around 50 per cent. From all over the Ruhr came union functionaries' complaints about the newcomers' ignorance of the purpose and value of trade unions.[13]

There were other worries, too. Several cases of miners found smoking underground graphically illustrated the way undisciplined, ill-informed young newcomers threatened the workforce's well-being. In some cases, too, young miners' absenteeism and under-production were affecting group earnings and thus the pay of their older established colleagues.[14] Yet so worried was the union about the emergence of a permanent split in the workforce that it refused to sanction punitive action against misbehaving young newcomers. For example, despite the extreme dangers associated with smoking underground, unions and works councillors were reluctant to endorse a hard line. It was not until the beginning of 1948 that the OBAD instituted body searches for smoking materials at the pit head, and even then the IVB and a number of works councils opposed them. Instead, the union emphasised education and persuasion as the way to change the young trainees' behaviour.[15]

In the course of 1948, and particularly after the June reform established a functioning currency, the pace of new recruitment slowed down and there were some indications that the intense coal scarcity of the immediate post-war years might soon be replaced by a glut. This led to fear of possible redundancies and increased anxiety about the potential impact on the workforce of newcomers with little trade union background. In June 1948, an American investigating team commented that it 'is reliably reported and quite

[13] IGB district reports for 1947 and 1948 from districts I, IV and V; Archive of the Industriegewerkschaft Bergbau und Energie, Bochum (IGBEA) BR4, H. Gutermuth, Works Council Division report for 1948, no date.
[14] German Mining Museum, Bochum (BBA) 32, 882, report on meeting of production committee deputy chairmen, 25 June 1947.
[15] Archive of the Landesoberbergamt Dortmund (ALD) 15200/3119/47, German Mines Supplies Organisation (GMSO) circular, 25 November 1947; 15200/355/48, Oberbergamt circular, 31 January 1948 and subsequent circulars.

apparent that considerable resentment is felt against the "outsiders" ... There is a very real fear of the possible future competition for jobs by those who can remember former periods of unemployment and low wages.'[16] Unionists feared that employers would exploit the situation to mount a general assault on the union and accused management of bringing in 'new comrades, not to increase the output, but as unschooled trade unionists to divide the workforce'.[17]

The IVB's concern was triggered not only by potential job losses but also by the youngsters' behaviour in the new conditions of the post-currency reform era. Apart from the fact that hostel inmates continued to be hard to organise, a frequent complaint about young miners was that they were trying to maximise their earnings irrespective of the cost to health or safety. Older men on contract wages faced an agonising choice between taxing their health by keeping up with the pace being set at the face or accepting loss of earnings for the sake of easier work. And there were safety costs, too. Union officials and works councils continually complained about infringements of safety regulations and about the 'rate-busters' (*Gedinge-Kaputtmacher*) from the mining hostels. In other pits, however, the youngsters were condemned for being *Drückeberger*, that is, for not working hard enough. The effect of both tendencies among young miners was often to undermine group solidarity and the group contract system.[18]

III

Though young newcomers undoubtedly generated many such headaches for labour representatives, a fundamental and rather unexpected feature of the post-war situation in the mining industry was that the IVB's position was relatively protected from such matters.

[16] Westfälisches Wirtschaftsarchiv, Dortmund (WWA) S22, BICO BISEC 11/104–1/39, Special Intelligence Report, 'Some German views of the political, economic and sociological aspects of Ruhr coal mining', 19 June 1948.
[17] Quotation from General Blumenthal Mine IGB branch chairman. papers in the collection of Michael Zimmermann, Alte Synagoge, Essen, File 'Betriebsratsprotokollen 1948–1951', Minutes of the workforce meeting of 18 July 1948.
[18] Archive of the German Trade Union Federation, Düsseldorf (DGBA) File 'IG Bergbau. Monatsberichte der IG Bergbau 1949', reports for April, May and June; Carl Jantke, *Bergmann und Zeche. Die sozialen Arbeitsverhältnisse einer Schachtanlage des nördlichen Ruhrgebiets in der Sicht der Bergleute* (Tübingen 1953), pp. 40, 45, 57; Helmut Hohmann, 'Lagerleben und Einzelgedinge', in IGBE Bezirk Ruhr-Nord, Recklinghausen (ed.), *Jahre die wir nicht vergessen 1945–1950. Recklinghäuser Bergbau-Gewerkschaftler erinnern sich* (Recklinghausen no date [1980]), pp. 169–170.

Initially, of course, it had little bargaining power over wage levels. They were set by the Allies in Berlin. But at the pit level, local unionists and works councillors enjoyed a great deal of influence. Managers, worried about being denounced to a denazification panel over their treatment of forced labour, and conscious that the British expropriation of the mines in 1945 might herald a period of public ownership in which the unions had a say, were willing to accord the workers' representatives considerable responsibility. At many pits, works councillors were able to insist on a *de facto* closed shop.[19]

In the course of 1947–48, it is true, many of these threats to the employers receded. Management regained confidence. The introduction of a hard currency enabled it to restore a more rigorous link between output and remuneration and to take a harder line in face wage negotiations. And yet at higher levels, it remained much more circumspect and conciliatory. For a start, the German body created by the Allies to run the coal mining industry, the Deutsche Kohlenbergbauleitung (DKBL), contained some union nominees. Far more important than their influence, however, was the fact that the employers were embroiled in discussions with the Allies about the future shape of the mining industry and, from 1950, about the Ruhr's place in a European Coal and Steel Community. Union support was vital if the German side were to present a united front in their discussions. Moreover, the industry was in a number of ways dependent on regional and federal state financial aid, and both regional and federal administrations, for their own reasons, were disinclined to alienate the IVB. The *Land* NRW, with its relatively left-wing CDU inclinations, found itself frequently in dispute with the DKBL, and sought union backing when it took these disputes to the bizonal, later federal administration or to the Allies. The federal government, too, was anxious not to antagonise the IGB – particularly during the period 1950–51, when Adenauer was involved in the delicate discussion over the Schuman plan. Finally, after 1951–52, the introduction of codetermination – itself again really a

<hr>

[19] Michael Zimmermann, *Schachtanlage und Zechenkolonie. Leben, Arbeit und Politik in einer Arbeitersiedlung 1880–1980* (Essen 1987), p. 213; Lutz Niethammer, 'Privat-Wirtschaft. Erinnerungsfragmente einer anderen Umerziehung', in Lutz Niethammer (ed.), *'Hinterher merkt man, daß es richtig war, daß es schiefgegangen ist'. Nachkriegserfahrungen im Ruhrgebiet* (Berlin, Bonn 1983) pp. 17–107, esp. pp. 69–73; IGBE Bezirk Ruhr-Nord (ed.), *Jahre die wir nicht vergessen* esp. p. 100; BBA 32, 740, minutes of directors' meeting, 8 August 1947; 32,882, memo 'Betrifft: Ernährungsverhältnisse', 23 May 1947.

product of the federal government's need to avoid a showdown with the unions at a time of delicate foreign negotiations – led, with time, to an extension of labour influence on management decisions within the plant.[20]

These factors very much limited the degree to which the employers could exploit the weakness or attitudes of inexperienced young labour. For example, in 1948 there were several indications that the industry would like to have carried out a rapid programme of redundancies of older labour both to cut costs but also to intimidate the workforce. There was plenty of precedence for such a policy from the interwar period. And yet, because of the constraints noted above and the influence of the state labour administration, the employers in fact adopted a very measured approach to redundancies. Union fears thus proved unnecessary.[21]

Perhaps the most interesting example of employers' attempts to influence young labour, and of the constraints that prevented their success, was the apprenticeship programme. The apprentices recruited after the war were, it is true, for the most part not strictly from the HJ generation but more properly belong to the generation of *Kriegskinder*, the generation whose first abiding impressions of wider society were under the conditions of total war and its immediate aftermath. Yet this generation, too, represented an opportunity for the employers to break the continuity of labour politics and shape a new workforce.

Influenced by the rationalisation movement that gripped German industry in the interwar period, the mining apprenticeship had been developed in the 1930s less for technical than for social and political reasons. The most important goal had been to give mining the status of a skilled profession and thus make it more attractive as a career. Moreover, the employers' hope was that together the new status conferred by the formal certification of skill and the close supervision and indoctrination which would accompany the train-

---

[20] Hauptstaatsarchiv Düsseldorf (HSTAD) NW53, 643, WAM to NRW Minister-Präsident, 14 July 1948; Minister-President to Bishop, NRW Regional Commissioner, 24 July 1948; Landrat Ernst to Arnold, 18 August 1948; NW73,47, WAM to IVB, 28 October 1948; NW 10,83, WAM IIIB 5 305, memo, 3 April 1951; Norbert Ranft, *Vom Objekt zum Subjekt. Montanmitbestimmung, Sozialklima und Strukturwandel im Bergbau seit 1945* (Cologne 1988), p. 43; G. Müller-List, 'Adenauer, Unternehmer und Gewerkschaften. Zur Einigung über die Montanmitbestimmung 1950/1', *Vierteljahreshefte für Zeitgeschichte*, vol. 35 (1985), 2, pp. 288–309.

[21] Roseman, *Recasting*, pp. 294–298.

ing would lead to the creation of a more 'responsible' workforce, as Rudolf Schwenger put it, code for one more docile and responsive to employers' wishes. In this the mines were part of a larger trend in the Third Reich to 'deproletarianise' through skilling.[22]

Though the apprenticeship was formally certificated in 1941, it was only in 1946–47 that the opportunity presented itself to recruit young apprentices on a large scale. Apart from attracting new labour, the mines saw in the apprenticeship a possible solution to three worrying problems. First, there was the very high degree of wastage in the immediate post-war period. A new status-conscious and self-confident young miner, it was hoped, would remain in the pits once training was complete and create a new stable and loyal workforce.[23] Secondly, there was a widespread feeling that the young, and particularly the war generation, were a politically and morally endangered generation. Often uprooted from their native homes, in many cases having lost fathers, with little memory of ordered conditions, it was felt that they had no sense of normal civilised life and values and would be liable also to political extremism. Senior employers repeatedly emphasised their belief that the apprenticeship, both by communicating a sense of worth and purpose, and because of the careful supervision and segregation from the rest of the workforce that it involved, could help shape the personality of the individual and inure him against the dangers of radicalism.[24] And this linked to the third aspiration of influencing the overall balance of power within the workforce and weakening 'radical' elements. A large new influx of youngsters from the provinces, untainted by connection with the Ruhr, might give the employers the chance to alter the nature of the Ruhr labour force.[25]

The employers expended considerable effort and ingenuity on

[22] *Ibid.*, pp. 168–169; Michael Zimmermann, 'Ausbruchshoffnungen. Junge Bergleute in den dreißiger Jahren', in Lutz Niethammer (ed.), *'Die Jahre weiß man nicht, wo man die heute hinsetzen soll'. Faschismuserfahrungen im Ruhrgebiet* (Berlin, Bonn 1983); Rudolf Schwenger, *Die betriebliche Sozialpolitik im Bergbau* (Munich, Leipzig 1932), here cited in ALD 16300, GMSO Circular no. 138, November 1945, annex 2; John Gillingham, 'The deproletarianisation of German society: vocational training in the Third Reich', *Journal of Social History*, vol. 19 (1986), pp. 423–432.

[23] HSTAD NW41, 761, Senft, Report on the conference of training directors at the DKV Haus, Essen, 15 January 1953.

[24] HSTAD NW41, 747, Sozialamt der evangelischen Kirche, 'Vorschläge zum Bau und zur Führung von Knappenheimen', 15 October 1951; NW41, 746, Dr Herwegen, 'Entwurf für die Tagesordnung einer Heimleiter-Tagung', no date [1948/9].

[25] See the complaint by a young IGB member, Roman Mrug, in DGBA, Protokoll-Sammlung, 'Protokoll des 1.Verbandsjugendtags der IGB', Bochum 1950.

trying to keep the apprentices, particularly those coming from outside the Ruhr, over whom *in loco parentis* the collieries had the most control, separate from the rest of the workforce and away from union influence.[26] New apprentice villages with in all over 5,000 places were set up well away from the existing towns. At the same time, to prevent labour representatives gaining access to the apprentices, the employers tried to get supervision of hostels into the hands of the church. 'I do not need to tell you', wrote the DKBL's Lorenz Höcker to the director of the miner Emscher-Lippe, 'that in our view the Christian spirit must shine out everywhere, but particularly in the homes. In the end it is the only force against the spirit (*Ungeist*) prevailing in the East – and not only in the East!'[27] A secret war developed, with employers and conservative allies within in the state social ministries trying to prevent workers' representatives from gaining access to the youngsters, while Social Democratic and Communist figures in the union movement did everything they could to prevent the church from obtaining control over the hostels.[28]

The employers, with the help of state officials, also provided a lot of political, moral and cultural education to the young hostel inmates. Apart from trying to instil pride and interest in mining, they wanted to convey the value of having roots in the locality and the notion that the secure personality had no need to change jobs. There was also more explicitly political education, in which above all a sense of authority and order was on the agenda. As Herwick, the director of apprenticeship education declared, 'We hope ... to form people who will later be too ashamed to say in the tram "Democratic freedom means everyone can do what they want".'[29]

And yet for all the efforts to shape a new kind of miner, the constraints inhibiting a really decisive thrust against the union movement were overwhelming. In the first place, the Works Council Law of 1946 gave local labour representatives a clearly defined role

---

[26] For the following see Mark Roseman, 'The organic society and the "Massenmenschen": integrating young labour in the Ruhr mines, 1945–1958', *German History*, vol. 8 (1990), 2, pp. 163–195; Roseman, *Recasting*, pp. 222–232.

[27] BBA 35, 267, Höcker to Premer, 3 June 1950.

[28] See IGBEA, File 'Jugend', August Enderle to August Schmidt, 12 May 1949 and subsequent correspondence and circulars.

[29] Archive of the Westfälische Berggewerkschaftskasse, photocopied extract from *Mitteilungen der WBK*, No. 3, 1950, Lecture from the Bezirksschuldirektor, Herwick, 'Unsere Bergberufschule als Erziehungsschule'. And see Roseman, *Recasting*, pp. 238ff.

in training and welfare matters.[30] Where the church gained control, it was true that labour for a while had problems of gaining access to hostels. But after the introduction of codetermination, with training matters passing into the hands of the union-approved labour director, such difficulties ceased. The labour directors were often keen to see the churches continue to run the hostels because it left them with more money for other aspects of the social budget, and the churches accepted agreements which gave unions plenty of access.[31] In fact organising the apprentices was never a great problem for the unions and by the end of the 1940s apprentice membership levels averaged between 80 and 90 per cent.[32]

Secondly, for reasons of cost, competence and keeping away the unions the employers had devolved the task of providing the young miners' political and moral education to a mixture of state officials and voluntary bodies. These officials, many of them drawn from adult education, were very concerned to maintain balance and what they saw as party political neutrality. There was certainly an emphasis on authority, on a return to 'Christian values' and a rather stiff moralising. There was also a rather ambivalent coexistence between the desire to recreate an organic society, in which everyone knew their place, and a commitment to democracy. But whilst there was criticism of 'radicalism' and 'totalitarianism', there was never any attempt to attack the labour movement as such. Indeed, state officials usually provided for at least some lectures from unionists. In short, the employers were simply not in a position to use apprentices as a vanguard against the union movement.[33]

IV

No doubt partly because of such restraints on employer's action, but also because the legacy of the Nazi era turns out to have been rather different from our initial assumptions, we find little evidence that young labour itself was particularly hostile to the union or any less

[30] Control Council Law no.22, Works Council Law, esp. Article v (f); see *Military Government Gazette for the British Zone*, vol. 9 (1946), pp. 197–199.
[31] IGB Bezirksleitung Essen (ed.), *Geschäftsbericht 1954/1955* (Essen [1956]), p. 117; IGB (ed.), *Jahrbuch 1956* (Bochum [1957]), p. 252.
[32] See district and central union annual reports in the library of the IGBEA and the DGBA Protokoll-Sammlung.
[33] On all this, see Roseman, 'The organic society'; and Roseman, *Recasting*, pp. 240ff.

interested in principle than older members in a strong organised representation for labour's interests.

The first and most obvious indicator is, of course, union membership. As we have seen, apprentice membership averaged between 80 and 90 per cent as early as the late 1940s. In some regions apprentice membership was nearer 100 per cent. The much lower figures among young adult miners were usually the result of the hostel inmates not thinking of any extended career in mining. When wastage reduced towards the end of the 1940s, union membership picked up and by 1951 the percentages in the hostels were in the 90s.[34] True, the union had problems again in the mid-1950s with wastage once more high and the employers refusing for a while to dock union dues at source. The IGB was forced to go out and confront its members with the monthly unpleasant duty of coughing up their contribution. As a result, membership fell, in some areas as low as 40 per cent in the hostels. But this was clearly primarily influenced by the short-term perspective of the young workers, rather than any underlying attitude to the union.[35]

On the question of what new young labour actually thought of the union, the evidence is, as Bernd Parisius has observed, somewhat contradictory.[36] Carl Jantke, in his 1950s participant observation study *Bergmann und Zeche* contrasted the older miners' close ties to the IGB with the younger recruits' more critical attitude.[37] Other studies and surveys, however, do not really corroborate his findings. The responses to a number of contemporary opinion surveys at mining hostels revealed a generally favourable attitude towards the union amongst the new miners. The IGB itself commissioned a survey of members' attitudes towards the end of the 1950s which identified the fact that virtually all the miners, even non-union members, believed the IGB was doing a valuable job.[38] On the few occasions that the union threatened strike action, it received widespread support throughout the industry. In the vote at the end of 1952 on potential industrial action over the introduction of the

---

[34] IGB Bezirk IV Bochum, *Jahresberichte* for the years 1949–51. See note 33.
[35] See annual reports for IGB Bezirk v 1954–55, p. 53 and vi for 1951–52, p. 31 and 1953, pp. 24–25.
[36] Bernd Parisius, 'Arbeiter zwischen Resignation und Integration. Auf den Spuren der Soziologie der 50er Jahre', in Niethammer, *'Hinterher merkt man'*, pp. 132–140.
[37] Jantke, *Bergmann und Zeche*, pp. 141ff.
[38] Unpublished EMNID survey conducted in April 1958 in the library of the IGBE, Bochum. See also Roseman, *Recasting*, pp. 306–309.

seven-and-a-half-hour day, the IGB achieved extremely high (over
90 per cent) votes in favour of strike action. In what was virtually
the only mining strike since the currency reform, the so-called
Reusch strike of 1955, the response was also very good. Even
substantial numbers of apprentices took part. In general, then, the
union does not seem to have faced any special problem in winning
the youngsters' allegiance.[39]

Within the collieries, it is true, there were many complaints that
workforce solidarity was being undermined by the youngsters'
behaviour. But these differences could rarely be attributed to the
result of a different socialisation. Often thinking of staying in mining
for a few years only, many young men wanted to earn as much as
they could in a short period, before turning to a more convivial
occupation. Other complaints, for example about those youngsters
who did not pull their weight, reflected the relative freedom of the
young worker from financial responsibilities and was a perennial
problem for labour. It was a life-phase, rather than a cohort difference, and had a long pedigree. The only special circumstance about
the post-war period was that with many of the youngsters away from
home in cheap subsidised hostel accommodation, they neither had
the financial nor moral pressure from parents to force them to keep
to the straight and narrow. Damaging though these intergenerational tensions may have been on the local level, they did not represent
any fundamental difference of outlook. It was a rejection of mining
as a career, rather than a different perspective on the rift between
capital and labour, which turns out most to have divided young
from old.

In fact, if there was a genuine difference in outlook, it was rather
in the other direction. The young miners were less willing to suffer
the sort of treatment and management behaviour which older
miners took for granted. We will return to this point later, but
certainly we can say at this point that they did not form a more
pliant generation.

It is hard to say with certainty what the political allegiance of the
new miners was. In the early post-war period, a large number of
groups looked with considerable unease at the young newcomers.
The employers thought they might prove a hotbed of political

---

[39] IGB, *Jahrbuch 1952* (Bochum [1953]), p. 208; archive of the Gesamtverband des deutschen
   Steinkohlenbergbaues, Essen (GDSTA), File 'Arbeitsausschuß 1948–1958', minutes of the
   Working Committee on Training Questions, 3 February 1955.

radicalism. The Social Democrats feared that they might be 'canon-fodder' for the Communists or might be seduced by neo-Nazi groups, and there were periodical scares about neo-Nazis in the mining hostels. But most of these fears proved unjustified. Behind the scenes of union party-political neutrality a bitter struggle to win the new miners' allegiance was fought out between KPD and SPD. The result was a clear victory for the Social Democrats, not least because of the influence of the refugees. By 1950, the KPD's influence was very much on the wane. In 1951, the KPD again made a concerted effort to win support from young miners, but by the end of 1952 its hopes had evaporated. Whether the youngsters were however tilting the balance, say, away from Christian representatives to SPD, or vice versa, is impossible to say. It is also hard to determine whether the Communists were being rejected for being too radical, or simply for being linked to the Soviet Union. What is clear is that the steady extension of Social Democratic representation in the works councils and union was certainly not hindered and was probably fostered by the young miners.[40]

v

We started out with a hypothesis that the Nazi-indoctrinated youngsters might have held back the union movement and weakened workforce solidarity. But the preceding information has painted a rather different picture. Could the union in fact have done *more* with young labour than it actually did? There is little doubt that the IVB, too, was, like the employers, subject to powerful institutional constraints impinging on its freedom of action. In the early years, the presence of military government made any strike a highly political matter – though this did not prevent miners from engaging in protest actions in 1946, 1947 and, under DGB auspices, in 1948. Later, the industrial relations legislation of the Federal Republic introduced a growing set of rules circumscribing the

[40] Archive of the SPD, Friedrich Ebert Stiftung, Bonn WW68, 'Protokoll der Ruhrbergbau-Konferenz am 31.8.1947 in Bochum', no date.; N25, vol. 1946–8, SPD Bezirk Westliches Westfalen, Report on the works council' elections in mining, Dortmund, 10 November 1947; N171, various KPD circulars from 1951–52; Michael Clarke, 'Die Gewerkschaftspolitik der KPD 1945–1951, dargestellt am Beispiel des IVB/IGB im Ruhrgebiet' (dissertation, Bochum University 1982), p. 56; also issues of the Communist journal *Unser Weg* for October 1951, March 1952 and May 1952, in possession of Ernst Schmidt, Alte Synagoge, Essen.

ability of unions to engage in conflict. And yet the overriding story of the IVB/IGB is not that it was prevented from mobilising the HJ generation – but that it did not want to do so.

Initially, Communist members, who were very strong at the local levels of the IVB, were keen to generate an activist, engaged, young cadre within the union. The increasingly dominant Social Democrat and Christian Democrat leaders by contrast expected a far more passive, disciplined role from union members.[41] Of course, the union continued to expend considerable energy on ensuring that as many new recruits as possible became union members. In keeping with its general style, however, the IGB leadership had no ambitions to mobilise the young miners for action or to develop out of the young single men an activist potential. The later IGB deputy Hans Alker, for example, was carpeted as youth secretary when he had the temerity to speak out against the *dirigiste* style of the union and the lack of democracy at union conferences. In addition, union leaders and even many works councillors were extremely willing to work cooperatively with the employers on even the most difficult of issues. Senior IGB figures waxed lyrical about the virtues of social partnership and in fact shared many of the employers' fundamental aims and views.[42] On key questions of public ownership of the mines, on codetermination and other matters, it is true, labour and employers held irreconcilable views, but that did not prevent the two sides from often making common front *vis-à-vis* the Allies in the negotiation over the reorganisation of the mining industry.

The evidence here, then, is that the absence of strikes and the emergent commitment to social partnership in the post-war period had little to do with the impact of the HJ generation. Where that generation might have weakened workforce solidarity, other factors served to limit the damage to the union or the degree to which employers could take advantage. In any case, as we have seen, there was little evidence that young labour could not be won for a forceful representation of miners' interests. Social partnership as it emerged in the post-war era was, in fact, a long cherished dream of the rather conservative miners' leaders. What had changed most since Weimar were probably the labour market and institutional pressures on the employers to cooperate with the union, coupled with, at least until

---

[41] Hans-Eckbert Treu, *Stabilität und Wandel in der organisatorischen Entwicklung der Industriegewerkschaft Bergbau und Energie* (Frankfurt 1979), pp. 69ff.

[42] See Roseman, *Recasting*, pp. 181ff, 300–302.

the late 1950s, a more favourable market for coal than had existed in the late 1920s. If the HJ generation had contributed actively to creating the new pattern at all, then only by helping to reduce Communist influence.

VI

Did the members of the HJ generation then have no impact on the mining workforce and on labour relations in the industry? Whilst overt generation conflict was limited to the sort of piecemeal tensions noted earlier, I believe that more quietly and over time the HJ generation did leave an enduring mark.

In the first place, there is some evidence that they challenged management behaviour which had long been characteristic of the mining industry. For, whilst in social policy matters a spirit of social partnership might prevail, within the mines themselves and particularly below ground, the pit militarism of an earlier era persisted. True, as Michael Zimmermann has argued, generational change can be observed on the management side as well. A new breed of manager which had entered the profession in the Third Reich was more conscious of the need for a different approach.[43] The DAF had had some influence here, with special training courses for pit deputies to override the old *Grubenmilitarismus*.[44] But the courses had enjoyed little support from senior management and change had not progressed very far by 1945.

Into this environment streamed hundreds of thousands of newcomers. Some simply buckled down and accepted the prevailing style and there were indeed occasionally complaints from established miners that the newcomers, particularly the expellees, were *too* compliant. But many other observers identified the contrary tendency among younger expellees and other young outsiders, namely, that they stood up to the deputies and management with a resolution and an effectiveness that had been lacking in the community.[45] An investigation of the face wage bargaining in the post-war period discovered that not infrequently it was the young newcomers

[43] Zimmermann, 'Ausbruchshoffnungen', pp. 113–115.
[44] Helmut Trischler, *Steiger im deutschen Bergbau. Zur Sozialgeschichte der technischen Angestellten 1815–1945* (Munich 1988), p. 335.
[45] See for example Walter Köpping, 'Als Betriebsobmann auf "Julia" 1947–1949', in Walter Köpping (ed.), *Lebensberichte deutscher Bergarbeiter* (Oberhausen 1984), pp. 404–405; Günther Eckerland, 'Lagersprecher', in *ibid.*, pp. 407–410.

who through their self-confidence and ability to put across their point of view became the spokesmen of the entire face.[46]

Where did that confidence come from? First, as we have seen, the upheavals at the end of the war had brought into the mines a significant leavening of men from other social backgrounds. Such men were used to quite different treatment to that handed out in the mines. Secondly, many had served in the military. There were many contemporaries' reports that 'we've had that sort of treatment in the barrack room and we're not standing for it again'. Quite a lot of the young men had exercised considerable authority in HJ and Wehrmacht and were not now going to be treated like the lowest private.[47]

With this experience behind them, the newcomers brought a new resolve into the workforce not to accept the rough and ready style of the deputies or allow themselves to be cheated in the piece-rate calculations. Many did not restrict their actions to answering back or complaining to the management, but steered their protest in the union.[48] As important as their willingness to stand up and fight, however, was their readiness to leave. This, of course, had much to do with the fact that they were young and single, and therefore less tied to the job. But it was also because, for the reasons just outlined, they were less willing to put up with rough treatment. Moreover, many had come to the Ruhr after the most incredible odysseys, first as retreating soldiers, then as discharged soldiers or ex-POWs trudging hundreds, sometimes thousands, of miles until they found their families, then further great treks with or without other family members in search of work. No doubt there were plenty who now hankered after stability, but they were, by and large, not frightened of moving.[49]

As the pits' labour losses steadily increased during the 1950s, a whole series of studies were commissioned to discover what was driving them away. The striking fact was that poor treatment by

---

[46] Hans Walter, 'Zehn Jahre Gedingeschlichtung im westdeutschen Steinkohlenbergbau', *Glückauf*, vol. 94 (1958), 43/4, pp. 1537–1546.

[47] Interiew with former unionist Walter Köpping, 16 August 1983; Jankte, *Bergmann und Zeche*.

[48] Interviews with Walter Köpping and Hans Alker. See also Federal Archive, Koblenz B102, 33091, Federal Economics Ministry Memo, Ref III A - 10934/56, annex 5: 'Alarm im Bergbau'.

[49] Lutz Niethammer, 'Heimat und Front', in Niethammer (ed.), '*Die Jahre weiß man nicht*', pp. 163–232.

lower management figured almost as frequently in explanations for quitting the industry as did the physical working conditions. All other complaints, even those about inadequate pay, were of subsidiary significance.[50] Though the industry found it very hard to change, there is little doubt that this steady drain of labour, and the well-attested reasons for the losses, did put a great deal of pressure to introduce a new management style. There is no room here to go into the sorts of changes that did begin to emerge, but it was surely a telling shift in managerial attitude that in 1955 the Ruhr employers decided in their recruitment material to substitute the polite form *Sie* for the informal *du* with which management had traditionally addressed the workers.[51]

Apart from their resourcefulness and expectations of better treatment, the other widely attested distinctive feature of the young miners from the HJ generation – and also of the younger *Kriegskinder* – was that they mistrusted any ideology, social flim-flam or political or religious rhetoric. This was another reason why the employers' attempts to create a stable workforce after the war met with such failure. The employers' attempts to impart a flavour of the mysticism and romance of working underground and to convey the Germanic virtue of *Heimatverbundenheit* or becoming rooted to community and soil were met with derision or indifference.[52] As the social workers in the hostels soon recognised, appeals to the 'German spirit' and lofty perorations on the 'Christian world view' served only to repel a sceptical younger generation.[53]

But the union, too, found the younger generation here disappointing and hard to place. The social scientist Theo Pirker, then a young activist in the union movement and himself a member of the HJ generation, noted very clearly this clash of outlook and ideologies. When older unionists talked of the harmonious ideal of social

[50] See Institut für Sozialforschung, 'Die subjektiven und objektiven Abkehrgründe bei sieben Zechen des westdeutschen Steinkohlenbergbaues in ihrer Auswirkung auf die Sicherung des Belegschaftsstandes unter Tage' (unpublished Ms Frankfurt 1955); Roseman, *Recasting*, pp. 253–263.

[51] Staatsarchiv Münster, File Arbeitsamt Dortmund 46, Außenstelle Bergbau circular no. 6/55 to labour exchanges, 26 October 1955; GDSTA File 'Arbeitsausschuß, 'Merkblatt für die Werbung von Neubergleuten', Hamborn, 20 December 1954.

[52] On all this, see Roseman, 'Organic Society'.

[53] See 'Der "Lager Mensch" – Symptom einer Entwicklung', in *Die Neue Zeitung*, 7 August 1951; GDSTA File 'Unternehmensverband 662–668', Ruhrarbeitsgemeinschaft für die kulturelle Bergmannsbetreuung paper, 'Bergarbeiterbetreuung', no date 1951]; Roseman, *Recasting*, pp. 249–250.

tnership, invoked the pathos of the labour movement or conjured
_ _ the image of the miner of bygone times, they could be as sure as
their bourgeois counterparts of losing their younger audience:[54]

I find it absurd that often I sit down at conferences or negotiations with
representatives of the older generation and discover that I am in fact the
realist although I, as the younger party, actually have more right to allow
myself some illusions.

And as the members of his generation moved up the union ladder,
the IGB became much more hard headed and pragmatic, not
necessarily more conflict oriented, but certainly more interest
driven, and no longer pursuing a global vision of harmony with the
employers. It was not least thanks to their influence that during the
1960s, the nature of the industry's social policy changed substantially, losing much of its patriarchal quality.[55]

VII

Ultimately, though, what did *not* happen was far more interesting
than what did. Despite the huge influx of youngsters from the HJ
generation neither the employers' nor the unions' fears were
realised. There was no bitter or radicalised younger generation, no
KPD or neo-Nazi stronghold in the hostels. There was no weakening
of the union movement – indeed, the IGB emerged far more solid
and better organised than had been the Communist, Catholic and
Social Democratic unions in Weimar put together. There was not
even any great conflict between the generations. Independent
surveys found no major difference between the generations in basic
attitudes towards the IGB.[56]

Why did the HJ generation fit in so quietly and so easily? In
retrospect, it is clear that disillusionment with the collapse of the
Third Reich, with the way Nazi leaders allowed the fatherland to go
to ruin, with the revelations that started emerging afterwards and
with the sudden volte face of the parent generation, left the younger
generation distrustful of any ideology.[57] They were not easy prey for
any radical party, and certainly not for the Communist party when

[54] Theo Pirker, 'Die Jugend in der Struktur unserer Gesellschaft', in DGB, Abteilung Jugend
(ed.), *Protokoll der Arbeitstagung der Gewerkschaftsjugend 25–30.11.1951* (Düsseldorf 1951),
p. 25.
[55] Ranft, *Vom Objekt zum Subjekt*, p. 218.
[56] Unpublished EMNID survey, Part 2, p. xxvii.
[57] See Dagmar Reese's essay in this volume.

many of them had experienced at first hand the Eastern Front, the Red Army and the expulsions.

Secondly, the presence of the Allies, and the parallelogram of forces between Allies, German state, labour movement and employers, created a situation in which the old Weimar labour movement elites were able to act with unusual freedom from the rank and file. Their power derived at least as much from the political and moral stature accorded them by the Allies, and the corresponding need for German employers to have the unions on their side in negotiations, as it did on their ability to get the workers out on the streets. The HJ generation witnessed a labour relations framework take shape around them without them having very much to do with it.

On the other hand, and this, too, facilitated the integration of the young workers, the trajectory taken by the labour movement leaders was in many ways quite attractive to the HJ generation. Shorn of some of the more flowery rhetoric of social partnership, a firm, well-organised representation of interests in a reasonably well-institutionalised framework, with conflict as a last resort, struck a chord with younger miners. This was, after all, a resourceful generation of youngsters, who, even if they had not grown up with unions, knew the power of big organisations.[58]

And finally there was the safety valve of mobility. For those who were willing to fit in, the mines themselves offered plenty of scope for advancement. Both the union and management hierarchies were desperately short of new blood. Talented youngsters found themselves being besieged with offers from one side to train as a functionary in the union schools and from the other to attend the Mining School and become a mining engineer. It was a mark of the new style of young worker that they were often tempted in both directions.[59] But if they did not like the conditions, they could always leave and find employment elsewhere. Unemployment in North Rhine Westphalia never went above 5 per cent,[60] and from an early stage in the post-war period it was clear that there would be ample opportunities to earn a living. And in the end, the biggest problem for the managers and unions posed by the HJ generation was not that they were radical or undermined the workforce, but that they would not stay.

[58] Pirker, 'Jugend in der Struktur', p. 25.
[59] As was Hans Alker, who in the end opted for the union and went on to become its deputy chairman. Interview with the author, May 1984.
[60] Calculated from *Statistisches Jahrbuch für die Bundesrepublik Deutschland* (1955), pp. 114–115.

CHAPTER 14

The German Kriegskinder: origins and impact of the generation of 1968

Heinz Bude

One of the paradoxes of the historical process is that there is no necessary connection between the motives for an action and its outcome. When a new social group or collective actor emerges on to the historical stage, for example, the motives that prompt it to act will rarely suffice to explain its historical impact. Hegel wrote of the 'transformation' (*Verkehrung*) of subjective intentions into objective meaning; sociologists speak of 'unintended consequences'. The basic principle of historical change is that the meaning of any historical action always extends beyond the purely subjective dimension of those involved.

The discrepancy between motive and outcome applies particularly to the great epoch-making social movements and the fate of the groups which unleashed them. Often the actors' motives derive from a historical situation which is then overturned by the processes they themselves have unleashed. A new order emerges, and those who had helped bring it about find their own actions and identity being seen in a new light and a new social context. The motives of the historical actors stem from one historical-social order; but the evaluation of its impact is carried out in another. This paradoxical relationship presents a particular challenge to the collective identity of the social groups involved. What from their point of view might appear as a failure, may in the context of the historical process they have generated be seen as a success, albeit one which has little to do with the original purpose of those involved. Alternatively, by focusing on the enduring impact of the social movement, its instigators may lose sight of what it was that originally galvanised them to form together and to act. What in reality at the time may well have been the rather parochial protest of a small group becomes in retrospect

Translated by Mark Roseman.

[handwritten margin note: the process cannot be shewed by the reality of the intention]

the heroic beginnings of fundamental social change. We should therefore not be surprised that those involved in such major social movements often end up deceiving themselves as to who they are and what they have done or that they lack a historical sense of their origins and their success.

This is exactly the problem now facing the members of the 1968 generation, i.e. those born between 1938 and 1948, who at the time of the 1968 revolts were aged between 20 and 30. They are now seen as the prime movers in a social movement which effected a fundamental revision of life-styles in Western societies. They are perceived to be the catalysts of a cultural transformation which produced new models of behaviour and decisively shaped our contemporary 'political culture',[1] our 'normal forms of behaviour' in everyday interactions,[2] and more generally the values governing our 'rational choice'.[3] This almost overwhelming success story weighs heavily on the 1968 generation's self-perception. A quarter of a century after 1968 the heroes of the revolts now stand as agents of a major evolutionary trend. But what was their real achievement and what were the formative influences that defined this generation?

[handwritten margin note: praised on cultural transformation but is that more of a by product than intended change]

Though all advanced nations acknowledge the importance of the cultural revolts of the 1960s, they differ markedly in the way in which those revolts have been absorbed and interpreted.[4] In the French republican tradition it was an obvious step to make a connection between 1789 and 1968.[5] In the motherland of eccen-

---

[1] This is the argument in Ronald Inglehart's celebrated enquiries into changing values; R. Inglehart, *The silent revolution; ibid., Kultureller Umbruch. Wertwandel in der westlichen Welt* (Frankfurt, New York 1989).

[2] In the tradition of Norbert Elias's civilisation theory, the literature talks of processes of informalisation, which are seen as being linked with the changes in the societal balance of power that were achieved by the 'middle-class radicalism' of the student movement. See Frank Parkin, *Middle class radicalism* (Manchester 1968); Hermann Korte, *Eine Gesellschaft im Aufbruch. Die Bundesrepublik Deutschland in den sechziger Jahren* (Frankfurt 1987).

[3] We could with Lionel Trilling argue that 'authenticity' has replaced 'sincerity' as the key objective of life investment, see Lionel Trilling, *Das Ende der Aufrichtigkeit* (Munich 1980).

[4] Unfortunately the internationally comparative study from Ronald Fraser *et al.* has little to say on this subject. Oral history here fails to master the voluminousness of the material. See Ronald Fraser (ed.), *1968: a student generation in revolt: an international oral history* (New York 1988).

[5] For example in the following quotation from Paul Veyne: 'May 68 will be the last revolution of the 19th century and the first "cool" revolt of the 21st century. The word "cool", incidentally, is used to mean everything and nothing – a sign of its importance, just as in

[handwritten note at bottom of page: across the world it had different national contexts]

tricity, by contrast, the student movement was just part of 'swinging London' and could be seen as an expression of untrammelled liberalism.[6] In Italy 'the movement' was perceived as the continuation of a populist tradition of wars of liberation against alien rulers – an interpretation that subsequently created a certain level of toleration for the terrorism of the Red Brigades.[7] And in Japan, where in the late 1960s there were wild outbursts of angry militancy, the student protests were evidently tolerated as the expression of a youthful elite which, once it had cooled down, was accepted in to leading positions in politics and economy.[8]

Only Germany has seen 1968 as a decisive caesura in its post-war development. This was recently confirmed by no lesser figure than the Federal President on the Day of German Unity. At the ceremony marking the official union of the two states, Weiszäcker had this to say about West German development since the war:[9]

> Over the years the people have developed an affinity for their polity, free from artificial feelings or nationalist pathos. Of course, in the 40 year history of the Federal Republic there have been some deep-seated conflicts between generations, social groups and political tendencies. Yet these conflicts, though fiercely pursued, have lacked the destructiveness which so burdened the Weimar Republic. Despite all the wounds they inflicted, the youth revolts at the end of the 1960s contributed to a deepening of the democratic engagement in our society.

Though the president referred to a history of social conflicts, he in fact named only one, the youth revolt at the end of the 1960s. This emphasis is indicative of the problem for the 1968 generation that we have already identified. Here we have the highest representative of the German people trying to explain to his compatriots why in the course of time they have developed an 'affinity' for their own country. And in this context the student movement is mentioned. The movement certainly 'inflicted wounds', concedes the former World War 2 soldier Richard von Weiszäcker, but led to a 'deepening' of the 'democratic engagement'. The 1968 generation thus seems finally to have found its place in the Federal Republic's family

1760 people spoke of the "sensitive soul"'; Paul Veyne, *Aus der Geschichte* (Berlin 1986), pp. 32f.

[6] See Karl Heinz Bohrer, *Ein bißchen Lust am Untergang. Englische Ansichten* (Munich, Vienna 1979).

[7] Guido Viale, *Die Träume liegen wieder auf der Straße* (Berlin 1979).

[8] Based above all on verbal reports by the sociologist Theo Pirker.

[9] Quoted from the Sonderdruck of the official Bulletin from 3 October 1990.

album. It is, so we learn, thanks to their protest that Germany became a political entity with which its citizens could identity 'free from artificial feelings and nationalist pathos'. We are forced to conclude that it was only in 1968 that the Federal Republic became a Western, liberal country.

In Germany, in other words, the 1968 generation is seen not just as a cultural avant-garde but as Germany's saviour from its National Socialist past. By participating unreservedly in the international movement of youth at the end of the 1960s, it brought to an end the fanaticism of the German soul. Germany since then is civilisation, society, voting rights and literature and no longer culture, soul, freedom, art.[10] But is this really so? Do those born between 1938 and 1948 really form the westernising cohort of the Federal Republic? Does this historical mission not demand too much of the 1968 generation?

II

The interpretation which I would like to advance in this essay is that in fact the Federal Republic's 1968 generation is much more German in its character than many of its members would like to admit. The generation which is seen, and indeed sees itself, as having unleashed the cultural westernisation of the Federal Republic is in its temperament and mentality in fact a generation of *Kriegskinder*, children of the war. It is here that the biographical roots of their identity must be sought. As evidence for my interpretation I would like to adduce a painting by the artist Georg Baselitz, which dates from 1962–63.[11] It is called 'Die große Nacht im Eimer', and is reckoned to be one of the artist's most important early works. The painting's significance derives in part from its role in the success of its creator. Together with Markus Lüpertz, Anselm Kiefer and Jörg Immendorff, Georg Baselitz belongs to a group of German painters who attained world fame in the 1980s as protagonists of a new German art. After the ironic affirmation of pop art, this new

[10] I.e. the inversion of that famous statement from the preface to Thomas Mann's *Betrachtungen eines Unpolitischen* (1918, reissued Frankfurt 1988), p. 23.
[11] This is not to argue that pictures want to 'say' something. If they did, then a written communication would suffice. Thus the struggle to interpret a picture must always recognise that between 'the figurative order of the picture and the discursive order of language there is always a free space which can never be filled'; Sarah Kofman, *Melancholie der Kunst* (Graz, Vienna 1986), p. 22.

style, with what was seen as a characteristically Germanic, tragic mood, was much sought after. After years in which Joseph Beuys had been the only well-known name, there was now the first time since the war German art of international renown.

The starting-point for my investigation is first that Baselitz, Lüpertz, Kiefer and Immendorff all belong to the 1968 generation, and secondly that these painters are now seen as expressing something important about the mood of Germany. What is it, then, that this generation has to say? And what does Georg Baselitz's 'Die große Nacht im Eimer' tell us about the life experiences of what became known as the 1968 generation? Of course, the interpretation of one painting can never suffice to explain the mood and experience of an entire cohort of the population. And yet I believe that, when interpreted alongside other types of social and psychological evidence from the post-war period, Baselitz's work offers important insights into the formative experiences and preoccupations of his contemporaries.

In 1963, the picture received its first public showing in the (West) Berlin gallery of Michael Werner and Benjamin Katz. The exhibition triggered a public scandal when, together with the painting 'Der nackte Mann' (The naked man) 'Die große Nacht im Eimer' was confiscated by the state prosecutor on charges of sexual immorality. The investigation and prosecution of the then 25-year-old painter Baselitz and the two 24-year-old gallery-owners kept the courts occupied until charges were dropped in spring 1965. But the storm in the media brought little return to the artist. True, there were many visitors, but they were interested in scandal not paintings. Over a two-year period Baselitz sold a single water colour and one small painting which went to an art dealer he had befriended.

The scandal was not just a moral but perhaps even more an artistic one. In the 1950s and early 1960s the art world in West Germany was dominated by abstract painting, informalism and tachism. After the enforced isolation of the National Socialist period, painters sought to re-establish ties with the international modern art movement and with the Ecole de Paris which at that time was seen to be its centre. Art should no longer try to reproduce the external world, according to the modernist doctrine, but should aim rather at evoking appearances or impressions. There was a general sense that to move from figurative to abstract painting was to step in the direction of progress and freedom. At the opening of the second 'documenta' at Kassel in 1959, those attending were reminded that in societies where men were not free, modern art was not allowed. Thus the system confrontation of the post-war era had found its aesthetic analogue: the West was committed to abstraction and freedom; the East to realism and repression.

In view of this commitment to the principle of abstract act, the representation of a recognisable figure and one, in addition, in an all too obvious physical state, was a provocation. In essence the judgement of the moralists and the art world was the same: 'Die große Nacht im Eimer' was the coarse and stupid outburst of a 'hooligan'.[12] A 'kick in the balls for the Germans' was what the Munich art dealer Franz Dahlem was later to call it.

Baselitz himself described the scandal retrospectively in these terms:[13]

The general view was, and this was the oh so wonderful thing about the 1950s and 1960s, that every one said – all doors are open. There is no problem. We are free. We live in a free society. You don't have to hold anything in. There are no taboos. And then this ridiculous picture.

III

Georg Baselitz, whose real name was Hans-Georg Kern, was born in 1938. Like his near contemporary Rudi Dutschke he hailed from eastern Germany, in this case from a village in Saxony with the name Deutsch-Baselitz, or Groß-Baselitz as it was known in the Nazi era. Three kilometres through the forest was the neighbouring village of Wendisch-Baselitz, inhabited by Catholic Sorbs. But the young Baselitz had little contact with the Sorb children, above all for reasons of religion. His background was, as one would expect of Germans from the east, out and out Protestant, with many pastors and teachers in the family. Baselitz remembers a childhood full of legends, of tales of the earth and what lay beneath. Everything sinister but also everything friendly came from the earth. Nothing from the heavens. That changed only towards the end of the war when the bombers arrived with their cargo.

[12] In the years 1956–58, West German public opinon was very much concerned with the so-called *Halbstarkenkrawallen* or hooligan riots. See Curt Bondy *et al.*, *Jugendliche stören die Ordnung. Bericht und Stellungnahme zu den Halbstarkenkrawallen* (Munich 1957).

[13] In Georg Baselitz, *Georg Baselitz im Gespräch mit Heinz Peter Schwerfel* (Cologne 1989), p. 50.

Baselitz's father is described by his son as a man of great shyness. He was a school-teacher and the family lived in the school house. The correct and respectable father had little understanding for the wildness or the rigorousness of his son. But evidently he was no tyrant, since the young Baselitz succeeded again and again in forcing him into having to defend his conventions. Of Baselitz's mother we learn nothing.

From 1956–57 Baselitz studied painting at the Hochschule für Bildende und Angewandte Kunst in East Berlin. After an argument with the professors over his predilection for Picasso, Baselitz was removed from the college. He was told to go and prove his worth as a worker. When he refused to do anything but paint pictures, his residence permit for Berlin and his ration card were taken away. So Baselitz crossed over what were then still open frontier points to West Berlin and entered the Hochschule für Bildende Kunst, where he studied from 1957 to 1964.

In no other West German town did the war's scars linger as long as in West Berlin, the town on the 'front line'. Markus Lüpertz (born 1941) artist and friend of Baselitz, described the Berlin of the early 1960s thus:[14]

In its early days, Berlin was a hole, culturally an absolute provincial small town. It was like a great empty sea bed slowly filling up from thousands of different directions and with thousands of different ideas. There was, of course, the great legacy from the 'twenties'. But the most important thing was that, slowly, a bubbling mass of young people began to form, people trying to find their way. The town itself gave nothing. It was pure legend, a museum, and not a museum of what you could see, just a museum of assertions.

These assertions were revived in those days by people who were sentimental enough to take the town for what it was. The assertions were, however, challenged by people like me, who came into this town as if was a desert, waiting to be populated.

This empty space, left behind by history, provided the social movements of the late 1960s with an arena in which to experiment. It was here that a unique mixture emerged, composed partly of debates and ideas revived from the 1920s, or 'those "twenties"', as Adorno called them,[15] and partly of new elements of pop culture – though the light-heartedness of pop culture usually had to take

[14] Markus Lüpertz, *Markus Lüpertz im Gespräch mit Heinz Peter Schwerfel* (Cologne 1989), p. 25.
[15] Thedor Adorno, 'Jene zwanziger Jahre', in Adorno, *Eingriffe* (Frankfurt 1963), pp. 59–68.

second place to political seriousness, as a glance at the persona of Rudi Dutschke reminds us. It is not surprising that once the anti-authoritarian phase of the student movement had run out of steam at the beginning of the 1970s, Berlin was the place where a whole system of putative party organisations emerged. The 'ruins of Berlin' provided a fitting backdrop to the ghostly conflicts between Maoist, revisionist, Trotskyite and 'spontaneous' cadres.

IV

This might all have remained an exotic bloom shut away in the glass case of Berlin had it not been for the fact that contemporary society chose to give the 'students' revolt' all its attention.[16] In the transition from the period of reconstruction and stabilisation after the Second World War to a new period of transformation and democratisation, social change was, you might say, simply waiting for a group to carry it out. As early as 1964 the normally conservative weekly paper, *Christ and Welt*, had carried the series 'The German education catastrophe'. This series of articles, written by the Heidelberg Professor for Religious Philosophy and former Heidegger pupil Georg Picht, caused an enormous stir in West German public opinion. Picht argued that a crisis in education must inevitably lead to a crisis in society:[17]

Our economic and social policy, our entire administration and our defence all rest on the foundations provided by the educational system. Since these foundations are beginning to collapse our entire state is like a giant standing on clay feet.

What Georg Picht called a 'giant on clay feet', Dahrendorf termed a 'rigidified hierarchical society', while the Mitscherlichs in their analysis of the German soul, *Die Unfähigkeit zu trauern* (The inability to mourn), complained that contemporary society was characterised by a 'psychological immobility in the face of burning societal problems'.[18] All these metaphors indicated a growing acceptance of the need for social mobilisation. All that was lacking

---

[16] Kai Hermann, *Die Revolte der Studenten* (Hamburg 1967). The series first appeared in *Die Zeit*. Many analysts have emphasised the media's decisive role in the emergence of the student movement. The classical essay in this area is Todd Gitlin, *The whole world is watching: mass media in the making and unmaking of the New Left* (Berkeley 1980).

[17] Georg Picht, *Die deutsche Bildungskatastrophe* (special issue of *Christ und Welt* 1965), pp. 56f.

[18] Alexander und Margarete Mitscherlich, *Die Unfähigkeit zu trauern* (Munich 1967), p. 38.

was the group to be in the vanguard. When the nation then set itself the task of carrying out a major educational reform, and thus gave education priority over other aspects of societal reform, the role of avant-garde in social modernisation was effectively handed over to youth.[19]

Another essential part of the background to the growth and impact of the student movement was the practical and direct pressure exerted by the very large numbers of youngsters coming up through the system.[20] The sudden growth of the student population forced a rapid expansion of the universities. The potential mismatch between the new supply of graduates and the employment opportunities available was resolved not least by a concurrent expansion in the welfare state. Between 1965 and 1975 the number employed in public administration rose by more than a third and many of the new jobs were in the higher levels of the administration. Indeed, in this ten-year period the number of higher civil servants actually doubled. Thus a whole generation of university graduates was able without any great struggle to obtain leading teaching, planning and administration positions in the welfare state and to apply their new ideas there. The fact that immediately after this generation employment opportunities were in effect doubly hit, first because the expansion of jobs came to a rapid end, and secondly because so many of the men in senior positions were relatively young, explains why the members of the 1968 generation are not particularly well loved by the generation that followed them.

The circumstances surrounding the 1968 generation's rise to prominence confirm one of the arguments made by theorists of social movements, namely that social movements emerge when a favour-

---

[19] On the reform see Ludwig von Friedeburg, *Bildungsreform in Deutschland. Geschichte und gesellschaftlicher Widerspruch* (Frankfurt 1989). This new role accorded to youth was parallelled by a striking change of orientation in studies in the sociology of youth. Whereas in Schelsky's 'sceptical generation', youth was seen as a force for social stabilisation, a decade later Leopold Rosenmayr was writing about 'Youth as a factor for social change'. See Helmut Schelsky, *Die skeptische Generation* (Düsseldorf 1963, special edition) and Leopold Rosenmayr, 'Jugend als Faktor sozialen Wandels. (Versuch einer theoretischen Exploration der Jugendrevolten)', in Friedhelm Neidhardt *et al.* (eds), *Jugend im Spektrum der Wissenschaften* (Munich 1970), pp. 203–228.

[20] In an insightful analysis of the links between population and social development 1945–78, Rainer Mackensen noted that 'in no other phase did young people have such an impact on the world of work as in the early 1970s'; Rainer Mackensen, 'Bevölkerung und Gesellschaft in Deutschland. Die Entwicklung 1945–1978', in Joachim Matthes (ed.), *Sozialer Wandel in Westeuropa. Verhandlungen des 19. Deutschen Soziologentags Berlin 1979* (Frankfurt, New York 1979), p. 458.

able political situation allows a minority suddenly to adopt the role of spokesman for society as a whole.[21] What made the situation so favourable in 1968 was above all the fact that in the early 1960s there had been a political block on any sort of reform. This had created such impatience that there was now a widespread readiness for change. No one, wrote the liberal sceptic Ralf Dahrendorf in his broadside against the Adenauer state, would wish on Germany the sort of constitutional political instability that had characterised the last years of Weimar. On the other hand, there were equal dangers in an over-rigid society. No political change was possible if political and electoral decisions were made out of blind loyalty by men and women hide-bound to tradition; and change was and had to be a permanent guest in all human society. If it were artificially held back, then not only would the gates of progress close, but the energies of change would build up until they burst forth in uncontrolled and explosive forms. In the 1960s, then, people were waiting for the 'breach'[22] in the dam and looking around to see who would blow the first hole.

V

When Georg Baselitz painted 'Die große Nacht im Eimer' he did so under the influence of authors such as Baudelaire, Lautréamont, Beckett and, above all Antonin Artaud. Baselitz turned to these works in a hunger for pictures which the artistic universe of abstract art could not satisfy. These authors created a literature which tried to represent the intrusion into language of the non- or pre-linguistic.[23] Words are continually disrupted and interrupted by other forms of articulation, providing us with signs of energetic bodily interventions and withdrawals. This literature demonstrates how, to use the language of Freud, a 'primary process' continually obtrudes into the 'secondary process' of language. Against the symbolic

---

[21] See Sidney Tarrow, 'Kollektives Handeln und politische Gelegenheitsstruktur in Mobilisierungswellen. Theoretische Perspektiven', *Kölner Zeitschrift für Soziologie und Sozialpsychologie*, Vol. 43 (1991), pp. 647–670.

[22] A term later used to describe the events of 1968 in Edgar Morin, Claude Lefort and Cornelius Castoriadis, *La Breche. Premières réflexions sur les évènements* (Paris 1968).

[23] Julia Kristeva writes in this context of a 'revolution of poetic language' in which two systems of giving meaning collide with each other: the 'symbolic' system of the well-formed character and the 'semiotic' of bodily marks. Julia Kristeva, *Die Revolution der poetischen Sprache* (Frankfurt 1978).

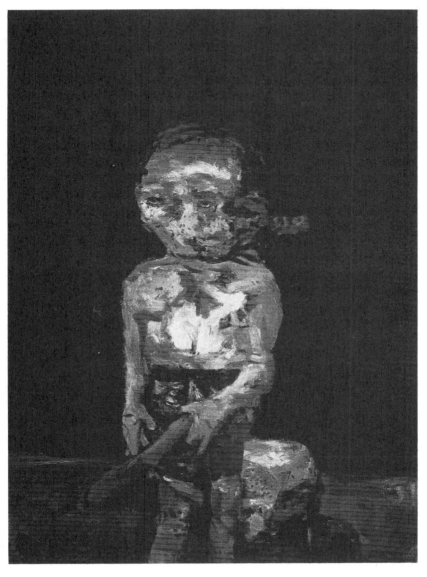

Georg Baselitz, 'Die große Nacht im Eimer'. Reproduced by permission of the artist

prohibition by the father, which is the starting-point for all language, an earlier and different experience continually asserts itself, whose theatre is the 'struggle' between the body of the child and the body of the mother. It is, then, a literature about the origins of the first gestures which create a relationship to the world.

In the first phase after crossing to West Berlin and his new teacher Hann Trier, Baselitz found it an enormous liberation to be able to paint relatively abstract pictures which had no connection to anything other than themselves. These meant for him the final break with representational art in the sense of Socialist Realism. But soon paintings began to appear with some curious feature – a nose perhaps, an over-sized foot, a small bag or a tear. And these unsettling partial objects gave rise to paintings which caught something, a mood or a feeling, which destroyed the heroism of abstract art. Baselitz had discovered a new aesthetic which enabled him to pose certain questions about the position of the artist in West German society. Above all, was the sublime indifference of abstract really the artist's only possible answer to fascism and war?

As Michael Baxandall has remarked, to describe a painting is to reproduce not the picture itself but one's own thoughts about it.[24] Accordingly, the thoughts reproduced here have been organised around three aspects of the picture: its title, the nature of the figure depicted, and the use of colour.[25]

In the picture's title, 'Die große Nacht im Eimer', 'große Nacht' or 'big night' could mean several different things. It might mean the big night – the night of a great occasion or celebration, a night of dance and drinking and intoxication. It could imply a night of love in which the lovers give themselves over to lust. But the German 'große Nacht' also leaves open the possibility of a more negative connotation, a long terrible night full of nightmares, in which the boundaries between dream and reality have become blurred. Whatever the case, something big has happened that still leaves an impression. But the big night is 'im Eimer', a phrase which literally means 'in the bucket', but figuratively 'up the spout'. The morning after, the 'big night' has somehow turned out to be an illusion, and there is a painful sense of loss. In 'Eimer' there are even overtones of 'Nachteimer' or chamber-pot. In any case, everything is up the

---

[24] Michael Baxandall, *Ursachen der Bilder. Über das historische Erklären von Kunst* (Berlin 1990).

[25] The following interpretation first appeared in Heinz Bude, 'Das Bild eines Kriegskinds', *Merkur*, vol. 45 (1991), 9/10, pp. 959–964.

spout. The big night has ended in a big awakening. In the light of day everything looks different. What will happen now?

The figure stands like a statue, divorced from contact with any immediate surroundings. Like a statue, it stands out against the background, confronting the observer with an unsuggestive absoluteness. It is not clear what lies behind the figure. Perhaps a chair or a drum or a chamber-pot.

The ambiguity on this latter point points to the larger, troubling question of whether we are looking here at an adult or a child. The upper half of face and head is clearly that of an adult. But below the level of the eyes the face is unformed. The mouth is completely absent. The figure cannot speak, and can express itself only through its physical posture.

The giant head rests on a slim torso. The gawky stiffness of the legs remind us once again of a child. The figure is not without strength, but the stance is not quite firm. From the overall physique, we might guess it to be a boy of about six years of age. The short trousers certainly suggest this, though they are strangely tight.

This scene is certainly not one of curious or lusty masturbation. The massive penis protrudes from a narrow fly. The boy is not masturbating but holds the erect penis in his hand. It looks to be so heavy that the boy might almost fall over. But he retains his balance.

The organ is both burden and weapon. What can the boy do with this enormous organ? At the most he could use it as a club and angrily hit out with it. There is no trace of narcissistic pride in this beautiful big penis which could drive any rival to flight. It appears more like an alien and removable attachment to the child's body. That's not mine, the boy appears to be saying, it belongs to someone else.

After the 'big night' has gone 'up the spout', the child shows its enormous organ, alien and dangerous in its erect state. The question is who is the audience for this scene? Is there someone there who could tell the boy what is happening to him? The picture allows no doubts. The boy's gaze is uninvolved and focuses on nothing.

The colour is applied without skill or care. The mouth has simply been smeared on. The colours of the ground graduate from light green to dark green leading to a dark and damp area, where moss and fungus grow. The colour is not firm or aggressive, rather soft and yielding. It expresses no strategy or clear message but vague feelings and hidden moods.

VI

In 1987 the French analyst Haydée Faimberg published an essay
which stands out from the general run of psychoanalytical writing.[26]
In it, she describes a particular form of identification which she calls
the 'telescoping' of generations. In her case study, she asks her
patient where his mind wanders to when he loses concentration. His
lack of involvement in everyday life reveals itself to be the counter-
part of an intensive inner involvement. She discovers the personal
history of someone else, which has somehow become the patient's
own history. As one would expect from a psychoanalyst's pen, it
emerges that it is the history of the patients' parents. The son is
caught up in an identificatory trap and the parents' history has
become transposed as his own. In reversal of the normal laws of
socialisation, the child begins from early in its life to take on the task
of interpreting and solving its parents' problems. Issues which for
reasons of shame, despair or guilt the parents find insupportable are
devolved on to the child. This is something different from the
well-known phenomenon of the parents' 'delegating' feelings that
are too strong for them or projecting wishes on to the child which
they can not fulfil for themselves. What is being delegated in this
case is the task of interpretation. Even when still an infant, the child
is called upon to show sympathy and understanding for the predicament of their parents and to give reassurance. The child
becomes the guarantor for a secret world of the parent. In the end,
the child protects the parents' real history by making that history its
own, albeit in a concealed fashion. The identification between the
parents and children is complete and there is no room to acknowledge the real discontinuities in generational experience.

   This account can serve as a description of the story of the
Kriegskinder born around 1940. During the bombing raids, even
small children aged 2–3-years-old had to reassure their mothers with
the beating of their hearts. They had to smile to show that everything was all right. The children offered their resonant space to save
the mothers from their secret fears and their weariness at the
struggles of everyday life.

   After the war things became even more confused. When the father

---

[26] Haydée Faimberg, 'Die Ineinanderrückung (Telescoping) der Generationen. Zur Genea-
logie gewisser Identifizierungen', *Jahrbuch für Psychoanalyse*, vol. 20 (1987), pp. 114–142.

returned home, the mother let the child understand that she had lost the man she had once loved and married. The man who had returned was not the same as before the war. In the child's eyes the father had thus lost his position in the family: he might shout and rage all he could, but all he did was to add new proof to the secret judgement of the mother. On the other hand, the children understood their father. They sensed his need and had an inkling of what he had been through. When he returned from the war, standing on the threshold waiting to be let in, they saw this grey man with curiosity and sympathy. This poor and needy man, whom the mother pursued with rage bred of disappointment, what did he want? Sometimes the children and their father ended up more like brothers and sisters, sealing a bond of mutual assistance against the 'big mother' figure. Now not just the mother's survival but survival of the whole family was in the children's hands. They had a double task, of confirming each parent's own experiences against the judgement of the other, and yet of bridging those differences and holding the family together. For the *Kriegskinder*, then, the history of their parents was a burden which threatened to squash their own history. They acted as containers for expectations – not their own but the expectations of their parents.

This predicament – the combination of a psychological emptiness on the one hand, and a psychological overburdening through overemphasising with the parents, on the other – is the subject of 'Die große Nacht im Eimer'. It expresses a traumatic stimulus. The boy can hardly bear the sign of his own manhood. In despair he tries to defend his own psychological space against the invasiveness of his parents. At the same time there is a desire to lash out wildly, to strike out with this huge penis.

In his classical essay on the question of generations, Karl Mannheim writes about the 'sedimentation' of experience.[27] For Mannheim, generational identity arises from contemporaries' common early experiences. In his view, the decisive binding experiences occur during adolescence. But this is almost certainly to put them far too late in life. The origins of the 'self-system'[28] date back to a much earlier stage of personal development. Glen H. Elder and his col-

---

[27] Mannheim, 'Das Problem der Generationen'.
[28] See Harry Stack Sullivan, *The interpersonal theory of psychiatry* (New York 1953).

leagues showed how, for a given cohort, social change produces specific, common patterns of experience even, and indeed particularly, in early childhood.[29] Elder's research on the vulnerable child can easily be combined with Mannheim's theories on the sedimentation of experience. The important point is Mannheim's insight that each phase of experience in one's later life is structured and interpreted according to a key set of early experiences. In other words, the experiences which are collected in the course of one's life are not simply added together but are continually being reorganised and restructured in relation to some deeply anchored biographical starting-point. Individuals or groups may find themselves growing up into a new historical epoch, but they will continue to evaluate the occurrences and phenomena they encounter in the light of earlier experiences, which stem from a quite different epoch. This explains how it is that the bonding and identity of particular cohorts persists across the passage of time and social change.

The history of the cohort that later became known as the 1968 generation can be seen as the history of a failure to deidentify with the parental generation. The youngsters born in the late 1930s and 1940s could not free themselves from the feeling, implanted so early in life, of being born guilty.[30] In his diary, Rolf Dieter Brinckmann (born 1940) wrote about the way he and his generation had been conceived:[31]

hastily fucked into being in fear of the coming war, or in the first days of the war. The motive is confused: before the husband goes off to war, he makes his wife pregnant – 'I am only here, because there was a war' and what is then childhood and youth? One long apology because one is there at all 'Sorry, I was born.'

From this perspective, the youth revolts were not so much aimed at their parents, as instead a sort of 'delayed disobedience'.[32] It was

[29] Glen H. Elder and Avsholm Caspi, 'Persönliche Entwicklung und sozialer Wandel. Die Entstehung der Lebensverlaufsforschung', in Karl Ulrich Mayer (ed.), *Lebensverläufe und sozialer Wandel*, Kölner Zeitschrift für Soziologie und Sozialpsychologie Sonderheft, vol. XXXI (Cologne 1990), pp. 22–57.
[30] This is the title of a study of children from Nazi families. See Peter Sichrovsky, *Schuldig geboren. Kinder aus Nazifamilien* (Cologne 1987).
[31] Rolf Dieter Brinckmann, *Rom Blicke* (Reinbek 1979), p. 356.
[32] Odo Marquard, *Abschied vom Prinzipiellen* (Stuttgart 1981), p. 9.

a proxy rebellion, designed in a way to protect and 'clear' a parental generation which could no longer bear its own history.[33]

Surprisingly, many of the 1968 generation do not like the pictures of Georg Baselitz and his friends. Too much deep German soul in heavy oil, they say, and opt instead for uncomplicated pop art from the land of unlimited possibilities. But their rigid fixation on pop art has rendered them blind to the pictures of their own generation, pictures which others have recognised as the first authentic expression of German art since 1945. Perhaps the *Kriegskinder* are afraid of discovering that they are more German than they care to admit.

'If I had had a different birth, had been born elsewhere, born in different circumstances', Georg Baselitz said in a recent interview, 'I would of course have been able to paint happier pictures'.[34]

---

[33] Confirmation for this interpretation can be found in the reconstruction of autobiographical texts and in psychotherapeutic material. The 'damaged lives' of the *Kriegskinder* can be seen as the result of inescapable bonds of subservience. See Wolfgang Türkis, *Beschädigtes Leben. Autobiographische Texte der Gegenwart* (Stuttgart 1990) and Anita Eckstaedt, *Nationalsozialismus in der 'zweiten Generation'. Psychoanalyse von Hörigkeitsverhältnissen* (Frankfurt 1989).

[34] Georg Baselitz, *Baselitz* (Cologne 1990), p. 21.

Index